ALL THE NATIONS

UNDER HEAVEN

ALL THE NATIONS UNDER HEAVEN

Immigrants, Migrants, and the Making of New York

Revised edition

FREDERICK M. BINDER,
DAVID M. REIMERS, AND
ROBERT W. SNYDER

Columbia University Press
New York

Columbia University Press
Publishers Since 1893
New York   Chichester, West Sussex
cup.columbia.edu

Copyright © 2019 Columbia University Press

Library of Congress Cataloging-in-Publication Data
Names: Binder, Frederick M., author. | Reimers, David M., author. | Snyder,
    Robert W., author.
Title: All the nations under heaven : immigrants, migrants, and the making of
    New York / Frederick M. Binder, David M. Reimers, and Robert W. Snyder.
Description: Revised edition. | New York : Columbia University Press, 2020. |
    Includes bibliographical references and index.
Identifiers: LCCN 2018038373 (print) | LCCN 2018039428 (ebook) |
    ISBN 9780231548588 (e-book) | ISBN 9780231189842 (cloth : alk. paper) |
    ISBN 9780231189859 (pbk. : alk. paper)
Subjects: LCSH: Ethnology—New York (State)—New York. | New York (N.Y.)—
    Ethnic relations. | New York (N.Y.)—Race relations.
Classification: LCC F128.9.A1 (ebook) | LCC F128.9.A1 B45 2020 (print) |
    DDC 305.8009747—dc23
LC record available at https://lccn.loc.gov/2018038373

Columbia University Press books are printed
on permanent and durable acid-free paper.
Printed in the United States of America

Cover design: Milenda Nan Ok Lee
Cover photo: © Alamy

CONTENTS

PREFACE

s the 1880s gave way to the 1890s, the reporter and reformer
Jacob Riis trekked through the immigrant streets of lower Manhattan seeking answers to some of the most pressing questions
of his time: What is the relationship of immigration, industry, and poverty?
What kinds of homes will the many ethnic groups and nationalities of New
York find? How should public and private institutions respond to poverty and
bad housing in a growing city? The answers Riis offered in his books, newspaper articles, and photographs are still studied as early examples of muckraking journalism and documentary photography, but his questions endure.
Indeed, they animate the second edition of *All the Nations Under Heaven:
Migrants, Immigrants, and the Making of New York*.[1]

All the Nations Under Heaven is a narrative and analytical history of New
York and its peoples, from the city's beginnings as a Dutch trading post through
its contemporary incarnation as a global metropolis. In an era when immigration, inequality, and globalization are subjects of bitter debate, the history of
New York City offers fertile ground for analyzing the blessings and burdens of
immigration, the volatile history of inequality, and the significance of global
flows of people, goods, and ideas in one great city.

It is common to interpret the twenty-first century as an age of globalization,
but since its founding New York has been shaped by global patterns of trade
and immigration. Indeed, the city's changing position in the world's economy
is central to any understanding of its wealth and human diversity. The most
wrenching changes in New York—and its greatest surges in immigration from
abroad and migration from within the United States—have begun with factors

originating far from the city. In colonial times, New York prospered as an imperial British seaport with strong links to the Caribbean, rising and falling in response to military and mercantile decisions made in London. In the nineteenth century, once the city had become a major presence in the transatlantic shipping economy, starvation in Ireland or economic dislocation in Germany, Russia, and Italy spurred thousands to board ships headed for New York. African Americans chafing at life under Jim Crow or cast adrift economically by the mechanization of agriculture in the American South rode trains or buses to New York. In the years since 1965, when changes in federal immigration law opened New York to a wider range of nationalities, immigrants have again transformed the city's population and contributed mightily to its economy.

0.1 New York City's five boroughs.

Source: Robert W. Snyder collection.

Yet New York's position as a "city of the world," as Walt Whitman called it, has long made it a place with an ambiguous standing.[2] In New York State, since the nineteenth century, the city has been viewed as a wealthy, populous, and suspiciously heterogeneous place that must be kept under state control. To immigrants, New York has long been the first stop in the United States, but to many native-born Americans, the city is an inscrutable outpost of the Old World. Finally, the international factors that have allowed New York to accumulate people and capital are well beyond the city's control. Seen in this light, New York's wealth and power are not signs of permanent preeminence. Instead, they are the gains that came from successfully riding an economic tiger. The panics of the nineteenth century, the Great Depression in the twentieth, the economic slump of the 1970s, and the wrenching economic inequality of the twenty-first century are all reminders that the economic forces that lift up New York can also bring it down.

Indeed, we argue that New York's two fundamental traits—economic dynamism and human diversity—have long made it a city of ceaseless change, one that inspires dreams and sparks conflict but frustrates efforts to establish enduring levels of order and general prosperity.

Immigrant groups have learned to thrive in sectors of the economy—consider Jews in the garment trade and Italians in construction. Yet New York has also been a city of sweatshops and socialists: some of the city's most determined reform efforts have been wrought by newcomers seeking to wrestle their share of prosperity from the capital of capitalism.

The history of women who migrated or immigrated to New York City sharpens the larger questions of liberation, confinement, and change that define the city's ethnic history. Over generations, women have come to New York seeking refuge, new opportunities, and freedom from patriarchal constraints. Sometimes they found new freedom, sometimes they found new forms of exploitation, and sometimes they built lives that their grandmothers would have barely been able to imagine.

The city's ethnic diversity makes New York culturally fertile but never at peace. For our purposes, all New Yorkers are ethnic New Yorkers. The concept of distinct races has no scientific legitimacy. Census categories such as black, white, and Hispanic notwithstanding, it is more useful to think of the city's peoples—such as African Americans, Irish Americans, Jewish Americans, and Dominican Americans—as ethnic groups defined by a shared sense of identity and history.

Immigration changes immigrants, and immigrants change New York. At the same time, New York exerts an incalculable but real cultural force internationally. The city is a floodgate between the United States and the rest of the world, admitting and releasing people, goods, and ideas in transformative quantities. In the middle of the nineteenth century, Irish immigrants found in New York a refuge from famine in Ireland. Within decades, the songs, dance, and comedy of Irish performers had changed American popular culture profoundly. As the nineteenth century gave way to the twentieth, Jewish socialists circulated political tracts in Yiddish on both sides of the Atlantic. In the late twentieth century, rap music from the battered streets of the Bronx and Brooklyn, drawing on African American and West Indian traditions, redefined youth culture worldwide.

Yet the same ethnic diversity that animates the city culturally makes it a politically contentious place. Ethnic mobilizations are an accepted part of politics, and ethnic conflicts sharpen battles over power. New York politics is forever tugged between inclusion and exclusion, between the pursuit of justice and the reality of inequality. Since the days of the New Deal and Fiorello La Guardia in the 1930s, the city has enjoyed a reputation for liberalism sometimes belied by its own history. For all its strengths at absorbing immigrants from Europe, and to a lesser extent Asia and Latin America, New York—like the rest of the United States—has never extended a full measure of justice and prosperity to African Americans. And Puerto Rican New Yorkers, despite being American citizens, suffer disproportionately from poverty.

New York today prides itself on the diversity of its 8.5 million inhabitants—37 percent of them immigrants—and a climate of toleration and accommodation.[3] Yet the establishment of such a climate was not easy and even today is not fully realized. Now, as in the past, conflict is part of New York City life, and racism stubbornly endures in the city. But alignments of conflict do change over time. In the twenty-first century, it is difficult to imagine that in middle of the nineteenth century the streets of New York were once roiled by battles between native-born Protestants and immigrant Irish Catholics. Equally hard to imagine are the years when Jews were barred from universities and professions.

Some of the success that New York has enjoyed at incorporating successive waves of immigrants is attributable to the development, over time, of a political culture that values immigration and accepts diversity (within limits). It is also true, especially for the descendants of European immigrants, that New York and the United States have offered a sustaining degree of security and prosperity that has enabled them to leave their ethnic enclaves. The Huguenots, French-speaking Protestants who were visible during colonial times, began to assimilate and blend into the broader population before the eighteenth century was over. Walking through the East Village in Lower Manhattan, it takes a sharp eye to note the handful of German-language signs that remain from the years in the nineteenth century when the neighborhood, then known as Kleindeutschland, was the largest German community in the United States. At the same time, in the twenty-first century there is a real concern that growing white populations in historically African American communities such as Harlem and

Bedford-Stuyvesant will displace African Americans without fostering either an inclusive integration or an end to the dual real estate market that has long undermined housing opportunities for African Americans.

Although much has been written about the United States being a refuge for millions of people from all corners of the globe, it is in New York City that Americans have grappled longest with what it means to be a nation of immigrants. New York has long stood as a symbol of America's immigrant heritage, and until relatively recently the majority of immigrants entered the United States through New York City's seaports and airports.

In New York, the history of migration and immigration is a chronicle of epic proportions. In this city where many people have their eyes on the future and the past under their feet, it is possible to lose sight of the relationship between yesterday and today. We believe, however, that the story of the city's past and its peoples reveals enduring problems, changes to ponder, and strengths to appreciate.

ALL THE NATIONS
UNDER HEAVEN

CHAPTER 1

A SEAPORT IN THE ATLANTIC WORLD: 1624–1820

In 1613, a Dutch ship bearing a free man of African descent named Juan Rodriguez sailed into the harbor of what would one day become New York City. Others on European vessels had arrived before him, first to explore—as Henry Hudson did in 1609—and later to exchange manufactured goods for furs with the native Lenape. All left except for Rodriguez, who stayed to trade that winter. And so begins the story of immigration in New York City.[1]

Rodriguez, who would today be thought of as either black or biracial, came from Hispaniola, a Spanish colony in the Caribbean. Once he was settled ashore, he seems to have decided to better his situation by switching patrons. By the time Rodriguez's captain returned in 1614, Rodriguez was already working for another ship's master who had arrived earlier. A clash followed. Rodriguez survived. He then vanished from history, but his life speaks volumes about the founding of New York as a colonial seaport in the Atlantic world.

Rodriguez's appearance on the banks of the Hudson is a reminder that New York City, born in an age of ocean exploration and transatlantic trade, was from the start commercial and multiethnic. Its early commercial efforts embedded it in international patterns of trade, empire, and migration that spanned the Atlantic, reached south to the Caribbean, and made the city home to peoples from Western Europe, Africa, Asia, and Latin America.

Nevertheless, in the passage from the seventeenth to the nineteenth century, the city that emerged under Dutch, English, and eventually American rule was not modern-day New York writ small. Commercial purposes and human diversity may be constants in New York, but their influence on each other, their links to global economic patterns, and their impact on the city's political order are difficult to predict. New York is a volatile place, and so was the early Dutch New Amsterdam. When profit-minded Dutch merchants established a settlement at the mouth of the Hudson River in 1624, its economic success, like its ability to include peoples from all around the world, was not guaranteed.[2]

✳ ✳ ✳

In 1624, the Netherlands was the great mercantile center of Europe, a vigorous seafaring power with an abundance of merchant vessels and warships. Amsterdam was a cosmopolitan city with a strong capitalist ethos, known for its stock exchange and banking, and it was headquarters for two great trading companies. The East India Company, chartered by the Estates General in 1602, held a monopoly over lucrative Dutch trade east of the Cape of Good Hope and west of the Strait of Magellan. The West India Company, chartered in 1621, held a twenty-four-year monopoly over Dutch trade with West Africa, the coast of Australia, the West Indies, and North and South America. Its commercial prospects appeared promising: slaves, gold, and ivory from West Africa; sugar from Brazil; salt from Venezuela; a wide variety of products from the West Indies; and furs from North America. Profitable trading ventures and competing English claims ultimately convinced the States General of the necessity of establishing a more secure presence in the land Henry Hudson had claimed for the Dutch nation.[3]

While Dutch commercial interests shaped the founding of New Netherland, the peopling of the colony was shaped by a need for labor and by Dutch notions of religious tolerance. The Netherlands was uniquely tolerant of religious refugees, ethnic and linguistic minorities, and political exiles, who flocked to Amsterdam and other Dutch cities and played significant commercial roles. Protestants fleeing oppressive Spanish rule in the southern Netherlands provinces—Dutch-speaking Flemings and French-speaking Walloons—were the largest group of refugees.[4]

And so, in May 1624, under the command of Cornelius Jacobsz May of Hoorn, thirty families—most of them Walloons from what is today Belgium—reached the Hudson River aboard the *Nieu Nederlandt* and dropped anchor north of Manhattan. The Walloons, who sought freedom in the New World from religious persecution at the hands of Roman Catholic Spain, became the colony's first permanent community of settlers. The next year, a second expedition followed, under the leadership of Willem Verhulst, bringing approximately one hundred additional Walloons with livestock and provisions.[5]

While the Walloons sought security and religious freedom, the Dutch West India Company sought labor and commercial success. The Netherlands was sufficiently prosperous that relatively few Dutch wanted to emigrate to a new colony with uncertain commercial prospects. Indeed, in its early years the settlement at the mouth of the Hudson, New Amsterdam, was dogged by uncertainty: would it be a trading post serving a lucrative trade in furs with the native peoples or a port city with settlers populating its hinterlands?

To attract colonists, the company offered attractive terms. In return for a pledge to remain in New Netherland for six years, a male settler was granted the right to own and sell land, conduct trade within the colony for profit, hunt and fish, and search for precious metals and gems. While public conformity to the Dutch Reformed Church was required, freedom of conscience in private worship was guaranteed. A male settler, in turn, had to assist in the

1.1 The printmaker who created this engraving put stock images of English tobacco planters in the foreground but conveyed realities of New Amsterdam in the background: a seaport city with Dutch gabled roofs and enslaved Africans.

Source: New York Public Library.

construction of military structures and public buildings and serve in the militia in times of war.[6]

Concern about Indian attacks and the need to establish a centrally located headquarters soon convinced the Dutch to consolidate the bulk of New Netherland's population on Manhattan. Under the director-general Peter Minuit, the son of Walloon refugees from Westphalia, Germany, the town of New Amsterdam took shape on the southern tip of Manhattan. Minuit arrived in New Amsterdam in 1626 and soon began negotiations with the native Lenape to secure a claim to Manhattan. The Lenape, also sometimes called the Munsee, lived in small bands such as the Canarsee and the Rockaway in a region that today stretches from Connecticut to New Jersey. They called their territory "Lenapehoking," the land of the people.[7]

Folklore has it that Minuit's purchase of the island for sixty guilders, or roughly twenty-four dollars, has marked him as one of history's shrewdest dealers, but the Lenape did not share European notions of private property. The Lenape used Manhattan as hunting and fishing grounds. In all likelihood, they thought they were accepting trade goods in exchange for allowing the newcomers to use a piece of Lenapehoking temporarily. In later years, as they sought to secure full land rights, the Dutch made additional land purchases from Native Americans living in the upper reaches of the island. Again and again, as the anthropologist Robert Grumet has argued, the Lenape negotiated these agreements "to buy time and protection" in the face of European encroachment. Once the company's dubious title to the land was secured, Minuit gathered settlers onto Manhattan. Construction soon followed, resulting in thirty log houses, Fort New Amsterdam, a stone counting house, and a large mill whose upper loft would be used for church services.[8]

Significant numbers of the original Walloon settlers were ill at ease in the wilder reaches of northern New Netherland, on the site of present-day Albany, and headed south. By 1650, they constituted an estimated 20 percent of New Amsterdam's increasingly heterogeneous population.[9]

* * *

At first, settlers in New Amsterdam traded with Indians. But as the settlement's population grew, settlers encroached on Lenape lands. Dutchmen came to see their Lenape neighbors as little more than a nuisance. Relations between settlers and natives deteriorated, especially under Governor-General Willem Kieft, who arrived in 1638 and displayed a total lack of understanding of Indian culture and sensitivities. A series of provocations beginning in 1639 culminated in the full-scale Kieft's War of 1643–1645, which devastated outlying settlements and took many lives. Kieft's War shook the confidence of settlers in New Amsterdam, but eventually the growth of the settlement resumed. As the historians

Edwin G. Burrows and Mike Wallace observe, "With Europeans at their front door and Iroquois at their back, the Lenapes were doomed." By the end of the seventeenth century, settlers outnumbered the Lenape by about one hundred to one.[10]

The settlers were a heterogeneous lot. In 1643, Father Isaac Jogues, a Jesuit missionary who had escaped from Mohawk captivity and journeyed to New Amsterdam, reported that as many as eighteen languages were spoken in the town of approximately a thousand residents. He was also struck by New Amsterdam's religious diversity: "No religion is publicly exercised but the Calvinist, and orders are to admit none but Calvinists, but this is not observed, for besides the Calvinists there are in the colony Catholics, English Puritans, Lutherans, Anabaptists, here called Ministes [Mennonites], etc." Father Jogues was by no means favorably impressed with what he observed: "The arrogance of Babel has done much harm to all men; the confusion of tongues has deprived them of great benefit."[11]

The Dutch Reformed clergy of New Amsterdam undoubtedly shared Father Jogues's antipathy to ethnic and religious diversity. When Manhattan's first minister, Domine Jonas Michaelius, arrived in 1628, religious toleration was rare in Europe and its colonial outposts. But Michaelius aside, the Dutch nation was unique in these matters. The Dutch in old Amsterdam and New Amsterdam, marked by years of struggle with Catholic Spain, knew the value of religious freedom. Moreover, Dutch merchants recognized that religious bigotry limited one's range of business partners and workers. The company continued policies in America that had proven so successful at home. The West India Company granted the Dutch Reformed Church in New Netherland and New Amsterdam official status and financial support. At the same time, it permitted freedom of conscience and opportunities to worship in private to nonconformists and Jews.[12]

Toleration and conformity were nearly undermined during the director-generalship of Peter Stuyvesant, which lasted from 1645 to 1664. An able administrator, although arrogant and authoritarian, Stuyvesant believed that maintaining the established church was an essential ingredient in creating an orderly community. Significant numbers of Lutherans from Germany and Scandinavia had moved to New Amsterdam, and in 1653 they petitioned Stuyvesant for permission to hold public services. The director-general, apparently fearing discord in the colony and a challenge to his church, passed the petition to the West India Company in Amsterdam. Its response reflected its overriding interest in attracting settlers to New Netherland regardless of their ethnic background or religious affiliation. The West India Company simply told Stuyvesant not to accept any more petitions of that sort but to reject them "in the most civil and least offensive way."[13] But the Lutherans did not leave New Amsterdam.

Three years later, Stuyvesant fined and imprisoned Lutherans on Long Island for holding public services without an approved Reformed minister. The company again ordered him to be less zealous and more flexible in his religious policy. The controversy ultimately ended when the company permitted the Lutherans to worship publicly in Reformed churches after making certain adjustments in their catechism. Neither the pastors in New Amsterdam nor Reformed Church leadership in the Netherlands were pleased with this compromise, but toleration—the company policy—won out in the end.[14]

Despite Stuyvesant's reputation as a religious zealot, Dutch toleration outweighed his pronouncements and attracted settlers to New Netherland. When thirty-one English residents of the outlying hamlet of Flushing signed the Flushing Remonstrance, a document proclaiming their support of religious toleration, Stuyvesant had the leading signatories arrested and tried in New Amsterdam. One of the leaders who refused to recant was banished. When news of the dispute reached West India Company directors in 1663, they told Stuyvesant that while it would indeed be desirable to keep "sectarians" away, such efforts could impede the immigration the company wanted to encourage; therefore, it favored toleration.[15]

Quakers, with their expressive worship and rejection of the Dutch Reformed Church, also tested the boundaries of Dutch toleration. However, in heterogeneous New Amsterdam, Quakers also had friends. As early as 1639, Lady Deborah Moody and a group of dissenters opposed to uncompromising Puritan doctrines left Massachusetts to settle in Brooklyn. As an Anabaptist, she favored toleration of dissenters. In Brooklyn, she became the first woman to obtain a Dutch land grant. She urged cooperation between the Dutch and English and promoted "complete religious freedom." When Quaker missionaries needed a refuge, Moody provided one.[16]

In 1657, several Quakers landed, among them two women who "began to quake and go into frenzy and cry out loudly in the middle of the street, that men should repent for the day of judgment was at hand." Stuyvesant ordered the confiscation of any ship bringing Quakers to the city. He also arrested several Quakers, but when dissenters' protests reached Holland the company again urged toleration.[17]

More significant than the experiences of the Lutherans and Quakers in illustrating the uniqueness of the Dutch in dealing with minority ethnic and religious groups is the story of the establishment of the Jewish community in New Amsterdam.[18] The Netherlands welcomed both Sephardic Jews expelled from Spain and Portugal and Ashkenazi Jews from the east. By the mid–seventeenth century, Amsterdam was a center of Jewish religious and secular scholarship. Jews, as investors and colonizers, figured prominently among those who took advantage of the expanding Dutch commercial empire. When the Dutch captured Recife, Brazil, from the Portuguese in 1630, a sizeable group of Maranos

(Jews who had been forced to convert to Christianity but secretly adhered to Judaism) surfaced and proclaimed their Jewish faith. They were soon joined by hundreds of Jews from the Netherlands and later arrivals from a half-dozen other European lands. During twenty-four years of rule by the Dutch West India Company, the Jewish community of Recife grew to almost five thousand people. Jewish religious life flourished, and Jews prospered as merchants, traders, brokers, planters, and sugar refiners.[19]

All of this was not to last. The Portuguese took advantage of a Dutch war with Britain to recapture their Brazilian colonies. Recife fell in 1654. What had been a haven for Jews now became dangerous, for where the Portuguese were, so, too, were the Inquisition and hostility toward Jews. Under the terms of surrender, the Jews were permitted to leave in peace. Most returned to the Netherlands, but many scattered to the French and British West Indies, to Dutch Surinam and Curacao, and to New Netherland. In September 1654, a group of twenty-three Recife Jews aboard the French ship *St. Charles* arrived in New Amsterdam.[20]

There is ample evidence that Peter Stuyvesant and the Reverend Megapolensis were extremely bigoted toward Jews, perhaps even more so than toward Lutherans and Quakers. Fortunately for New Amsterdam's Jews, their coreligionists in the Netherlands responded to pleas for assistance. Jews in the Netherlands lobbied the directors of the West India Company on their behalf, pointing out the advantages to the colony of additional loyal, productive, tax-paying citizens and reminding them "that many of the Jewish nation are principal shareholders of the Company."[21]

The directors' letter to Stuyvesant on April 25, 1655, was very much in keeping with their handling of the earlier Lutheran issue. It began on a note of understanding and even agreement with Stuyvesant's attitude toward Jews and their presence in New Amsterdam, but once more the directors made it clear that their primary concern was not religious uniformity but turning a profit. The directors reminded Stuyvesant of the financial losses attending the fall of Recife and of "the large amount of capital" Jews had "invested in the shares of this company." He was instructed "that these people may travel and trade in New Netherland and live and remain there, provided the poor among them shall not become a burden to the company or to the community, but be supported by their own nation."[22]

The West India Company guaranteed the Jews' right to remain in New Amsterdam, but it could hardly temper the continued hostility of the town's civil and religious authorities. Numerous municipal impediments—such as discriminatory taxation—prevented Jews from enjoying the full benefits of citizenship. Over the years, as individuals and at times as a community, the Jews petitioned to gain the rights and responsibilities granted to other residents. When Stuyvesant and the New Amsterdam Council rejected their pleas, they turned to the directors of the company, who in most cases offered them at least limited support.

Slowly the Jewish community won privileges previously denied them, chiefly the right to trade with the Indians on the Delaware and Hudson rivers, sell at retail, and become night watchmen. They gained the rights of burghership. They were permitted to become butchers in order to provide kosher meat but were prohibited from engaging in other crafts. And Jews (like Protestant dissenters) were forbidden to hold public religious services.[23]

Jews, as the historian Howard Rock argues, did not really thrive in New Amsterdam. Their connections to the sugar trade, dating to their days in Recife, were not useful in a settlement that made money on furs. A number of the original Jewish refugees from the *St. Charles* left New Amsterdam for the more comfortable and less hostile atmosphere of the Netherlands. Those who remained pursued their rights and in 1656 set down roots in Manhattan when they established New Amsterdam's first Jewish institution, a cemetery on a small plot of land outside the city.[24]

The West India Company, drawing on its desire to transform New Netherland into a profitable venture and Dutch notions of religious tolerance, extended a degree of tolerance to Jews and Protestant religious dissenters. What these broad-minded notions would mean for enslaved Africans was an entirely different matter.

* * *

Settler demands for land in New Amsterdam were met by pushing Native Americans from Manhattan and adjacent areas. The perennial shortage of labor in New Amsterdam was met, with profound long-term and devastating consequences, by importing enslaved Africans. Slavery was present in New Amsterdam as early as 1626. Initially, the men and women held in bondage came in relatively small numbers from the Dutch West Indies. A turning point in the city's traffic in human beings came on September 15, 1655, when the ship *Witte Paert* docked at New Amsterdam with a full cargo of three hundred enslaved Africans. New Amsterdam became a port of destination in the transatlantic slave trade. Many more such voyages followed as the West India Company added slave trading to its list of commercial ventures. "By 1660," notes Leslie M. Harris, "New Amsterdam was the most important slave port in North America." Although many of those in bondage were transshipped and sold in Virginia and Maryland, enough remained that by 1664, 20 to 25 percent of New Amsterdam's population was African.[25]

Neither the Dutch government nor the Dutch West India Company had moral scruples about slavery. And while the Dutch preferred white servants, when they were not readily available they turned to enslaved Africans, who remained in New Amsterdam and labored for the West India Company in agriculture or built fortifications against Indian and foreign attacks. Some individual settlers owned slaves; others leased them from the company. In 1664, on the eve of England's seizure of New Amsterdam, thirty of 254 persons on the city's tax list were slave owners. About half of these thirty were among New Amsterdam's wealthiest individuals, but the remainder were scattered across income levels.[26]

Under the Dutch, slavery was not as tightly defined as it would be under the English, and some enslaved individuals had substantial latitude in their movements. In 1644, when the Dutch were at war with local Indians and eager to preserve the loyalty of Africans if they were needed for combat, the Dutch West India Company granted what became known as "half freedom" to eleven men, enslaved by the company, who petitioned for emancipation. With half freedom, the eleven petitioning men and their wives were granted freedom and land. As a condition of half freedom, they were required to work for the company when asked and pay an annual fee. If they failed to do either, they would be enslaved again. Moreover, even if parents successfully maintained half freedom, their children remained enslaved. The practice endured and despite its obvious limitations helped enslaved Africans in New Amsterdam gain a measure of autonomy.[27]

Alongside those granted half freedom, a few enslaved Africans received land grants on the condition that they settle just outside the colony as a human buffer against the Indians. Still others won outright manumission: thus free blacks existed in the city alongside blacks held in bondage. By the 1640s, the homes of these free black farmers were visible along the Bowery leading north out of the city. By the end of the seventeenth century, Africans had also established their own burial ground outside the city. There, using burial practices from Africa, they interred their dead—many of the skeletons clearly show arthritis from heavy labor.[28]

Africans in New Amsterdam, with names that echoed their origins, like Gracia D'Angola and Simon Congo, struggled to win freedom and maintain an autonomous community. If enslaved, they petitioned for freedom. If half free, they sought freedom for their children. Whenever possible, they sought to own their own land. Africans gathered weekly at a crossroads market, the kind some of them would have remembered from Angola, where the free and enslaved could meet. Also in attendance at the market were Indians and Dutch, who joined in drinking, trading, and games of skill and chance where blacks might best whites.[29]

Unlike the system of slavery beginning to emerge in Virginia, in New Amsterdam enslaved African men had the same standing as white men in the courts. They could even testify in cases involving whites, and they were not subject to special punishments. Moreover, the Dutch armed slaves and allowed them to serve in the militia during emergencies. Indeed, during the crisis year of 1663, when hostilities between the Dutch and English left the colony in an unsettled state, half-free blacks petitioned the company, offering assurances of loyalty in return for the removal of all restrictions on their liberty. The company also recognized long service by those they enslaved and granted them freedom. On the eve of the British takeover of New Amsterdam, some seventy-five half-free blacks, probably including their children, were granted full freedom. Nevertheless, in 1664 nearly seven hundred of their fellow Africans in New Amsterdam were in bondage.[30]

The Dutch system of slavery was relatively loose, but it was also brutal.[31] If religious toleration was one legacy of New Amsterdam, another—manifested in slavery—was a system of white supremacy.

By the 1660s, New Amsterdam was the most ethnically diverse city in North America, but a majority of its citizens were Dutch, and Dutch language, culture, and political and religious institutions dominated. Throughout the period, the Dutch Reformed Church had remained the established church of the colony, but, as the historian Joyce Goodfriend points out, "admission to the Dutch Reformed Church was not confined to persons of Dutch nationality." It played an "integrative role" that "in some respects may have compensated for the divisiveness associated with a heterogeneous population." Ethnic diversity in the city was also complicated by intermarriage. Records indicate that by the 1660s as many as 25 percent of the marriages in the final Dutch years were exogamous.[32]

New Amsterdam was a Dutch port city with step-gabled houses, bowling greens, windmills, and even a canal spanned by bridges. It was a sailor's town with established inns (English, Dutch, and French) where mariners could drink, gamble, and socialize. As the historian Susanah Shaw Romney observes, New Amsterdam was embedded in a network of trade—in which women played important familial and commercial roles—that linked the island of Manhattan with upriver Native Americans, Amsterdam, Brazil, and Africa. Yet the sea lanes that brought sailors and commerce to New Amsterdam could also bring threats.[33]

✳ ✳ ✳

On August 26, 1664, four English frigates appeared in the waters off New Amsterdam. They were undoubtedly an unsettling sight for the town's Dutch burghers, but Peter Stuyvesant found few among them ready to join him in resisting the impending invasion. In fact, New Amsterdam's leading Dutch citizens, including his son, prepared a petition calling for capitulation in order to prevent the "absolute ruin and destruction" of the city. With only four hundred company troops at his disposal, Stuyvesant was forced to accede to the wishes of the citizens. He yielded to the demands of the British commander, Colonel Richard Nicolls, without firing a shot. In the end, the Dutch ceded New Amsterdam to the English largely because, as Thomas Bender notes, it was "on the periphery of the periphery" of the Dutch empire. Possessions in Brazil, Africa, and Asia were far more valuable to the Dutch. By October 20, all the citizens of the city—Dutch and non-Dutch alike—had pledged their allegiance to the English king. Both New Amsterdam and New Netherland were renamed New York.[34]

Under the generous terms of capitulation offered by Colonel Nicolls, all citizens' property and goods would be secure, they would be permitted to continue to follow Dutch practices in matters of inheritance, they would be free to continue worship at the Dutch Reformed Church, and they would not be required to bear arms against any foreign army. Moreover, current Dutch authorities could remain in office for a year, and residents' political liberties would be extended even further. Anxious merchants were told that, in addition to the right to trade with England and her colonies, direct commerce with the Netherlands would be permitted for six months. In fact, it continued uninterrupted for another four years.[35]

A few employees of the Dutch West India Company did leave, and the scarcity and increasing cost of agricultural land on Manhattan encouraged some young men to seek their fortunes in the Hudson Valley. But "out-migration from New York City was not a dominant force in reshaping the city's social structure."[36] Even Peter Stuyvesant, stripped of his office, returned to New York after personally delivering his final report to the directors of the Dutch West India Company in Amsterdam.

Despite their secure position in English New York, the Dutch community welcomed the brief reconquest of the city by Dutch forces in 1673. However, New Orange—as the city was briefly renamed—lasted for less than two years. The Netherlands, defeated in a war with England, in 1674 signed a peace treaty under which the duke of York regained his colony.[37]

The Dutch cultural presence in New York survived under renewed English control. To the chagrin of the English, New York remained a largely Dutch city in its population, language, and architecture. More important, the Dutch held a monopoly over the institutions that define an organized community. The Dutch Reformed Church and its affiliated schools and charitable organizations flourished without the official status they held under West India Company rule.[38]

The English, on the other hand, were slow to develop a cohesive community. Soldiers, government officials, civil servants, and seekers of fortune moved in and out of the city, impairing social stability. There was also a great diversity of religious affiliations among the English. The city consisted of Anglicans, Quakers, Congregationalists, Presbyterians, and even a few Catholics. Most

Protestant dissenters and Jews were tolerated, but it was risky to show one's Catholicism. Except for a small Quaker meetinghouse and the military chapel at Fort George, no English church existed in the city until the Anglican Trinity Church opened for services in 1698. Only then, thirty-four years after the initial English conquest, did Trinity supply "a measure of organizational coherence to the New York City English community."[39]

During the last two decades of the seventeenth century, the arrival of French Huguenots, who were Protestants, along with the migration of increasing numbers of New Englanders, reduced the Dutch majority. By 1698, English and French together accounted for approximately 40 percent of New York City's 4,937 inhabitants. The growing affinity between these groups in matters of marriage, religion, business, and politics did not bode well for continued Dutch dominance.[40]

Under English rule the Dutch church lost its exclusive right of public worship and its near monopoly over charitable and educational activities, and Jews, Quakers, Anglicans, Lutherans, and Huguenots all gained the right to worship in public. The Dutch faltered in the economic sphere as well. While they still predominated in the artisanal occupations and controlled the highly remunerative field of flour processing, the English and French replaced them in the single most lucrative and socially prestigious category: merchant. By 1703, English and French merchants outnumbered their Dutch counterparts by almost two to one.[41]

The frustration of declining Dutch dominance in economic affairs was exacerbated by an act of James II, who tried to strengthen English control of the colonies by merging New York, the Jerseys, and the New England colonies into the Dominion of New England.[42] The capital of the dominion was Boston. Politically, this change transformed New York from a provincial capital to an outlying city. Equally troubling for Protestant New Yorkers was the fact that King James II was a Roman Catholic.

✳ ✳ ✳

When the Glorious Revolution of 1688 brought onto the English throne William, Prince of Orange—a Protestant Dutchman—and his wife, Mary, a disparate group of New Yorkers united by their devotion to the Protestant cause seized power in the city. German-born Jacob Leisler, a wealthy merchant and landowner, emerged as their leader and rose to power. Leisler enjoyed the support of some New Yorkers of Dutch ancestry, along with middling craftsmen, mariners, and shopkeepers of varied ethnic backgrounds.[43]

As self-proclaimed spokesmen of King William and Queen Mary, the Leislerites eagerly declared themselves defenders of the Protestant faith against the Catholicism of James II, whose reign had coincided with a growing Catholic

presence in New York. In proclamations and letters Leisler portrayed his enemies as furthering the "diabolical designs of the wicked and cruel Papists," who
"did threaten to cut the inhabitants' throats" and to burn the city. Leisler's
Rebellion failed, however, and Leisler—brought down by those who had prospered under King James, including a number of wealthy Dutch merchants and
landowners who had accommodated themselves to English rule—was hanged
as a traitor.[44]

For two decades after Leisler's death in 1691, the city's political battles continued to be fought along Leislerian/anti-Leislerian lines. And for even longer, the
anti-Catholicism Leisler articulated was present in the city's political culture. By
the early 1700s, however, an increasing number of New York City's Dutch citizens had become reconciled not only to English rule but also to the increasingly English character of the city.[45] Younger Dutchmen, drawn primarily from
the upper strata of New York society, balanced allegiance to their ethnic culture with mastery of the customs and language of the ruling English.[46]

A pattern was established that would be followed down the centuries by other
white ethnic groups—first biculturalism followed ultimately by acculturation.
Increased contact between youth of the Dutch and English communities led to
increases in exogamous marriages in which English often became the language
of the home. Though elders of the Reformed Church decried such tendencies
and held off demands for English-language services until 1763, they could not
turn back the cultural sea change. Success in business and social life in New
York City required mastery of English.[47]

A study of New York City residential patterns in 1730 reveals how ethnic and
religious factors played a significant role in determining where people lived.
Dutch church members generally resided in the northern part of the city, which
extended not far beyond Wall Street. "Trinity [Church] drew particularly heavily from the East River Wards, and especially, from the southern most tip of
the island." Jews clustered in the South and Dock ward areas, and Presbyterians and Huguenots concentrated in the East Ward. The persistence of Dutch
names said little about allegiances and identities. In a time when English New
York was ascendant, individuals of Dutch origin had reason to shift their loyalties and develop English habits and alliances.[48]

Nevertheless, Dutch elements endured in the culture of New York City.
Numerous Dutch pastimes became part of the New York scene: bowling, sleigh-
ing, Easter eggs, and Saint Nicholas (later Santa Claus) dispensing gifts
at Christmas. Many Dutch words—such as "boss," "cookie," "cruller," and
"stoop"—became part of New York English.[49] Furthermore, the very heterogeneity of the city was in large measure the result of a tradition of broad toleration
instituted by the Dutch and continued by their conquerors. This, more than customs and language, was perhaps the greatest Dutch contribution to the shaping
of New York City.

If New York gradually lost its Dutch character, the heterogeneous ethnic and religious character of the city that dated to New Amsterdam continued to fascinate new arrivals. William Byrd of Virginia, visiting New York in 1685, described the population as "about six eighths Dutch, the remainder French and English."[50] Thomas Dongan, who had arrived as governor in 1683, commented in 1686 on the variety of religious groups he found. Aside from Dutch and French Calvinists, he observed, "Here bee not many of the Church of England; few Roman Catholiks; abundance of Quakers preachers men and Women especially; Singing Quakers; Ranting Quakers; Sabbatarians; Antisabbatarians; Some Anabaptists some Independants; Some Jews; in short of all sorts of opinions there are some and the most part of none at all."[51]

The Anglican Church was the established church, but Anglicans amounted to only 10 percent of the city's church members, and the English tolerated other small groups of Protestants. This was especially important for the Huguenots— French Protestants who fled persecution in the years immediately preceding and following the revocation of the Edict of Nantes, which granted toleration to Protestants in 1685. The Huguenots received a mixed reception in England, where the broad welcome accorded them by the Protestant population as victims of Catholic persecution was tempered by fears of competition among English weavers and Anglican concerns that the Huguenots might ally with native Dissenters. In New York, however, the Huguenots found greater acceptance. They built the core of a distinct French community, with a French-speaking church, and clustered their homes together, most living in the city's East Ward, near Wall Street and west of the East River. By 1682, the refugees had recruited a minister, Pierre Daille, who formed a congregation that worshiped in the Anglican chapel at Fort George. The Huguenot community on Staten Island numbered thirty-six French families by the mid-1690s and existed affably with the island's forty English and forty-four Dutch families.[52]

In their early years in New York, the Huguenots were a refugee community whose numbers included both the affluent and the poor. Indeed, as a percentage of New York's total population, Huguenots were overrepresented on both the highest rungs of the city's economic ladder and the lowest. The richest of the Huguenots competed in business with their English and Dutch counterparts. The poorest, widows among them in particular, survived on charity.[53]

In New York, known for its liberal treatment of refugees, affluent Huguenot newcomers could enter easily into the city's economic and political life. Thanks to familial contacts in England and the Netherlands, some of the men became particularly successful as merchants and in the maritime trades. The wealthy Huguenot merchant Stephen De Lancey was elected assistant alderman in 1691, and by 1700 other Huguenots had been elected constables, tax assessors, and tax collectors.[54]

Over time, however, the Huguenot community vanished because the push to assimilate overwhelmed the bonds of ethnic loyalty. For example, Huguenot parents saw advantages for their sons if they were apprenticed to English masters rather than Huguenot craftsmen. More significant was the rate of exogamous marriages between Huguenots and Dutch and English: the 41 percent rate in the 1690s more than doubled to 87 percent by the decade 1750–1759. By the end of the eighteenth century, between exogamous marriages and mergers between Huguenot and other Protestant congregations, the Huguenot chapter in New York City had all but come to an end.[55]

* * *

In contrast, the Jewish community that dated to Dutch days prospered under English rule. The community remained small, "accounting for slightly less than two percent of the total white population in 1703," but it survived. A continuing trickle of new immigrants, particularly of Ashkenazi origin, offset those lost by assimilation. The Ashkenazi made up roughly half of the Jewish community in 1700, but by 1750 they were the overwhelming majority.[56]

In colonial North America, Jews were not hemmed in by ghetto walls, as they still were in much of Europe, but limitations on their religious life and economic and political practices followed them to the New World. In New York City, guild restrictions excluding Jews from crafts remained officially in effect after the British conquest but were largely ignored in a city where craftsmen were in short supply. Prohibitions against Jews engaging in retail businesses persisted longer.[57]

Throughout the eighteenth century, restraints were officially lightened on individual Jews. The Naturalization Act passed by Parliament in 1740 encouraged a more liberal approach to citizenship rights by providing that a foreigner who became a citizen in one colony automatically became a citizen in all English colonies. Although the applicant was required to have lived in a colony for seven years, the law modified older religious requirements to permit the naturalization of Quakers and Jews. Jewish men could vote, and New Yorkers chose a Jewish constable as early as 1718. Yet in at least one contested election, for Assembly in 1737, Jews were specifically forbidden to cast ballots.[58]

By and large, Jewish men in New York prospered during the eighteenth century as retailers and wholesalers, craftsmen, and importers and exporters. Some, like the merchants Jacob Franks and Lewis Gomez, could be counted among the city's wealthiest inhabitants. By midcentury, Peter Kalm, a Swedish Finnish botanist traveling in the colonies, believed that Jews enjoyed "all the privileges common to the other inhabitants of this town and province."[59]

In realms of religion, Jews persevered against constraints. Under the Dutch, Jews and dissenting Christians were permitted to worship only in private. Jews had some reason to believe that English rule might prove even more liberal in religious matters, but when New York's Jews petitioned Governor Dongan for permission to practice their religion freely and publicly in 1685, the governor referred the petition to the city's Common Council, which ruled "That noe publique Worship is Tolerated by act of assembly, but those that professe faith in Christ, and therefore the Jews Worship not be allowed."[60]

Despite such opposition, by 1695 twenty Jewish families had established a public synagogue in a rented room on Beaver Street, naming their congregation Shearith Israel (Remnant of Israel). In 1730, the congregation dedicated a newly erected synagogue in the center of Jewish settlement on Mill Street, the first to be built in North America.[61]

The situation for Catholics was quite different. Catholics were not welcome in New York or most of the colonies. As a result, few Catholics resided in the city before the American Revolution, and those present could not worship openly. Moreover, as Jill Lepore reminds us, Roman Catholic priests were outlaws, subject to a penalty of death. During the hysteria over a 1741 slave rebellion, one New Yorker expressed the view of most by insisting, "the mother of all this mischief is a priest."[62] Catholics had to wait until the era of the American Revolution to worship openly and to achieve full civil rights.

Women and Africans both found that their lives and legal status declined under the English. While Dutch society was certainly patriarchal, New Amsterdam had not been a male-dominated plantation society of enslaved labor, like the early English colonies to the south. Moreover, the Dutch legal system granted more rights to women than England's. With the change in government, however, Dutch women fell under English law. Their role in the courts and business changed, and their ability to hold property was curtailed.[63]

Africans were not as fortunate as Jews or Huguenots or even Catholics under English rule. Indeed, the transfer from Dutch to British control only increased the importance of slavery on Manhattan. The conquering English confirmed all titles to slaves. Although Africans might resist in cultural realms, such as the holiday of Pinkster, a festival with Dutch and African elements that offered both free and enslaved blacks a day of autonomy and freedom of expression, colonials of African descent were limited by the "tightening vise" of English slavery. Provincial legislation made manumission more difficult to implement, placed restrictions on former slaves who were freed during the Dutch era, and, in 1706, declared that the slave status of blacks would not be affected by their conversion to Christianity. Indeed, the English enacted a number of new restrictions on men and women held in bondage. Most colonists believed that blacks were inferior to whites and that their proper place was in slavery.[64]

Like the Dutch, the English had a labor shortage, especially after 1720, when the city's economy grew rapidly. European immigrants were too few to meet the colony's labor needs until the 1760s, so imported slaves filled the gap. From 1730 to the 1750s, New York's black population grew faster than its white population. The English imported enslaved Africans, but the death rate on the transatlantic passage was so high that most of the city's slaves came from the West Indies, where New York merchants shipped lumber and grain in exchange for sugar and slaves. In some cases, enslaved people imported from the West Indies were Akan-speaking Africans from what is today Ghana; they added a new cultural layer to the city.[65]

By 1746, Africans amounted to one in five New Yorkers. Although the African portion of the population declined in subsequent decades as the city received significant numbers of European immigrants, at the time of the American Revolution blacks still made up about 16 percent of the city's population. In neighboring Kings County (Brooklyn), where slavery was more common than in Manhattan, slaves made up about one-third of the population at midcentury; many white citizens were slave owners. In 1732, of New York's ten thousand people, 1,700 were enslaved. The only colonial city to hold more people in bondage was Charleston, South Carolina, later a hotbed of the Confederacy.[66]

In New York, masters typically owned two or three slaves, who lived and worked in their master's house. One member of the city's elite, William Smith, worked twelve slaves to run his household. Enslaved men also worked as coopers, tailors, bakers, tanners, carpenters, sail makers, masons, and candle makers among other occupations. Some slave owners permitted skilled slaves to hire out their own labor.[67]

As the city became more dependent upon enslaved labor, its white citizens grew fearful of slave uprisings. New York's colonial legislature enacted severe restrictions on slaves, and the courts interpreted these laws in the harshest manner. The English had no system of half freedom as had existed under the Dutch, and English slave owners increasingly defined those they enslaved as property with few or no rights. Yet despite restrictions, enslaved families endured. Slaves who hired out their own labor had possessions and cultivated their own gardens. Elias Neau of the Society for the Propagation of the Gospel in Foreign Parts operated a school for the enslaved. Although he mainly taught religion, contrary to the expectations of most white New Yorkers, he also taught his African students to read and write.[68]

Enslaved New Yorkers did not passively accept their lot. Slave owners chronically complained about runaways and the failure of colonial authorities to exercise strict controls over slavery. According to newspaper ads for runaways, most who made the break for freedom were young males.[69]

Whites' greatest fear in New York was that slaves would rise in rebellion and burn buildings. Wooden structures and an inadequate fire service made arson especially dangerous. In 1712, a slave rebellion began with arson and an ambush of whites who fled the burning building. Governor Robert Hunter swiftly called out the militia and alerted the city's inhabitants. Authorities quickly suppressed the rebellion, captured those suspected of being involved, indicted thirty-nine slaves for murder or as being accessories to murder, and convicted twenty-three of them. All were sentenced, and most were hanged. Three were burned to death, at least one by slow fire.[70]

The 1712 uprising led public officials to impose new restrictions upon all black inhabitants of New York. Even free blacks were seen as a menace, and among the new ordinances were those making manumission more difficult to effect. The city experienced another wave of hysteria over a slave insurrection in 1741. Whether there really was a planned rebellion then is unclear, but many city officials and citizens believed such a plot existed. They retaliated in a panic not only against dozens of enslaved persons but also against several whites suspected of being part of a ring of thieves, arsonists, and potential supporters of the rebels. Before the hysteria subsided, the court, using dubious evidence, convicted dozens of slaves and sentenced them to death.[71]

* * *

In spite of the fear of slave rebellions, real or imagined, the city's merchants pursued economic development during the eighteenth century. New York became ever more integrated into the trade and military enterprises of Britain. Mercantile activity dominated the business life of the town as products from England, the West Indies, and neighboring colonies poured into the port, and New York exported flour, wheat, and meat. The crafts, retail trade, and light manufacturing also flourished. As a result the city's population growth was strong. During England's wars with France, New Yorkers furnished the English army with vitally needed goods. Privateering also increased as individual merchants turned to robbing French vessels, and privateering always had the potential to turn to piracy when there was money to be made. Some New York merchants and sea captains, who had long winked at English prohibitions on trading with Spanish and French islands in the Caribbean, carried out wartime smuggling. To English authorities, this was considered trading with the enemy. To the New Yorkers whose ships sailed south, it was a way to turn a profit.[72]

Because of these activities, the city grew substantially, claiming five thousand residents in 1700 and twenty-five thousand on the eve of the American Revolution. As Alan Taylor notes, the business cycles in New York became more pronounced as the city became a greater part of the Atlantic economy. During the Seven Years' War with France, better known in North America as the French and Indian War, New York privateers and the Royal Navy swept France from the seas.

When the wartime boom ended in 1763, hard times came. One merchant declared in 1764 that "you would imagine the plague had been here, the grass growing in most trading streets."[73] The number of poor rose sharply. Among a post-1763 rush of new immigrants, many could not find employment.[74]

Despite economic ups and downs, of all New Yorkers merchants benefited most from growing Atlantic trade. They lived in substantial houses and ordered fancy clothes and elaborate carriages from England. The more successful merchants had businesses and homes on the southern portion of Manhattan and, for summer retreats, country estates with gardens and pastures less than an hour's carriage ride from town.[75]

Many New Yorkers, however, were simply the "middling sort." Most male New Yorkers labored as mariners, carpenters, cordwainers, joiners, carters, blacksmiths, brick makers, silversmiths, tailors, or coopers. And like other colonial cities, New York had a population of poor people. In 1736, the city opened a poorhouse with rooms for forty. This became the main "central agency of public poor relief" in the eighteenth century. In addition to the public almshouse, churches, ad hoc groups, and individuals aided poor residents. New York's poor included women whose husbands had been killed in England's wars, orphans, men crippled in war, and casual workers (including sailors) who lacked employment during economic downturns. At the bottom of the hierarchy were enslaved and free blacks. As the historian Christine Stansell has written, "As in other eighteenth-century cities, the situation in New York does not bear out the oft-repeated assumption that laboring people profited by some fabled scarcity of labor in America."[76] Substantial inequality began early in New York City's history and has been a defining feature ever since.

Ethnic differences remained in New York, but conflict along ethnic lines declined with time and general well-being. As the historian Patricia U. Bonomi has observed, "As time passed ethnic distinctions were blurred by the familiar agents of intermarriage and acculturation. In times of economic or political stress, ethnic or religious loyalties could still be reinvigorated in the city, but these responses became less automatic with each succeeding generation."[77] Nevertheless, as historians have noted, fears of slave uprisings tended to unite the white population.

For all the growth and change that marked New York City during the eighteenth century, the characteristic that had always been its most distinctive remained constant—the ethnic, racial, and religious heterogeneity of its population. Over the course of the eighteenth century, French and Dutch immigration all but ceased, but English, German, Scottish, and Irish settlers arrived in substantial numbers. In the 1770s, the city held at least twenty-two houses of worship representing at least twelve denominations. When Major Samuel Shaw of Boston visited New York in April 1776 with the newly formed American army, he described the city's people as "a motley collection of all the nations under heaven."[78] That "motley collection" would be tested and transformed in the crucible of the American Revolution.

* * *

New York's location as a seaport midway between the southern colonies and New England at the mouth of the Hudson River assured that it would be a strategic objective in the Revolutionary War. The existence of slavery in a revolutionary republic guaranteed that the conflict would also spawn contending definitions of freedom that embroiled black and white New Yorkers.

The forces of the Crown captured the city handily in 1776, turning it into a British stronghold for the rest of the war. Already Lord Dunmore, the royal governor in Virginia, had offered freedom to any slave who left a rebel master to help put down the rebellion. He repeated his offer on Staten Island in 1776, as did Sir Henry Clinton, who in 1778 became commander of British forces in North America. Not only Loyalists but also African Americans escaping slavery under patriot slaveholders (including George Washington and Patrick Henry) flocked to the city.[79]

The British offer of freedom was limited and opportunistic: Loyalists were allowed to keep their slaves, and slave auctions continued in New York during the war. Nevertheless, African Americans recognized this offer as an opportunity to claim their freedom. Black men served in the Ethiopian Regiment and the Black Pioneers. Others, as scouts and rangers, participated in the irregular warfare that took place on the outskirts of the city throughout the war. Within New York, black men and women who had once been in bondage worked for wages. To be sure, black men also served the patriot cause. But in New York City, the best opportunities for freedom came from serving the king.[80]

Toward the end of the war, as American forces under General Washington advanced on the city, men and women in New York who had escaped from slavery were terrified that they would be returned to bondage. To the shock of General Washington, however, Sir Guy Carlton, the British commander in New York, honored the promise of freedom for black people who had crossed British lines for military service before the end of the war. When the British sailed away from New York in 1783, they took with them twenty thousand soldiers and 29,000 civilians—among them three thousand black Loyalists who took up the king's offer of lands in Nova Scotia. When racism and poverty grew oppressive there, some traveled farther to the British colony of Sierra Leone, which grew to house a substantial settlement of the formerly enslaved. Others went to England: Bill Richmond, born into slavery on Staten Island, became one of the most famous bare-knuckle boxers in the British Isles.[81]

> # For Sale,
> A LIKELY, HEALTHY, YOUNG
> ## NEGRO WENCH,
> BETWEEN fifteen and sixteen Years old :
> She has been used to the Farming Busi-
> nefs. Sold for want of Employ.—Enquire at
> No. 81, William-ftreet,
> New-York, March 30, 1789.

1.2 Slavery was initiated by the Dutch and continued by the British. Because of a gradual emancipation law, it persisted in New York City until 1827.

Source: Schomburg Center for Research in Black Culture.

Washington took over a city already battered by wartime fires and hard use. Loyalist property was auctioned off, the Anglican Church was disestablished, and all creeds, including Roman Catholicism, were accorded full freedom of worship. Contrary to Loyalist fears in the final days of the Revolutionary War, the world was not turned upside down, and so many Loyalists had left with the British that it was easier to integrate those who remained into postrevolutionary New York.[82]

In the immediate aftermath of the Revolution, New York merchants confronted the challenge of making money without the Caribbean trade that had long been vital to the city. Britain forbade its Caribbean colonies to trade with the United States. France and Spain, which had traded with Americans during the Revolution, closed their Caribbean wharves to American goods when peace came. New York, which had found degrees of imperial prosperity under the Dutch and then the British, needed to find a new place in the Atlantic world.[83]

Postwar New York also confronted the problem of assimilating newcomers during the 1790s, when its population nearly doubled, jumping from 33,131 to 60,489. Immigration along with natural population growth and a sizeable influx of people from rural New York and out of state accounted for this spurt. Of the sending nations, the British Isles—especially Ireland—along with France and the German states led the way. Irish immigrants constituted the largest immigrant group during the first ten years of peace. Downtrodden Irish were inspired by the success of the American Revolution and by the potential for economic improvement in New York. The failed Irish rebellion of 1798 sent more boatloads of refugees from Erin to New York.[84]

Other rebellions also contributed to the increase in New York's French population. The vicissitudes of the French Revolution encouraged both republicans and monarchists to seek refuge on Manhattan Island. The slave revolt in France's colony of Santo Domingo, which began in 1793 and sharpened American awareness of slaves' potential for rebellion, added an estimated four thousand refugees to the city's population. Some, like Charles Maurice de Talleyrand, sought temporary refuge, but others established permanent residence. One of their number, John Dubois, would become the city's Catholic bishop in 1826.[85]

Among the newer members of New York's German community were a few veterans of the mercenary force employed by the British during the American Revolution.[86] Immigrants from the Fatherland, several of whom possessed the craft skills for which Germany was recognized, soon joined them. An item in the *New York Gazette* of January 20, 1797, reported that many also arrived carrying a burden of debt. "Forty German Redemptioners Just arrived in the ship Minerva . . . from Hamburg, consisting of carpenters, joiners, blacksmiths, and bricklayers, etc. . . . Their times to be disposed of. For further particulars, enquire of the captain on board."[87]

Religious and political prejudices also affected how New Yorkers responded to immigrants, particularly natives of Ireland and France. During the late 1790s, in the years of an undeclared naval war with revolutionary France, the Federalist-controlled U.S. Congress passed the Alien and Sedition Acts, which limited free speech and gave the president the right to deport "aliens" he disliked. New York Federalists, who valued order and respected British institutions, looked askance at the city's French republicans and Irish political refugees. In 1798, the bookseller and printer Hugh Gaine wrote in his journal, "too many United Irishmen arrived here within a few days," and a letter to the *Commercial Advertiser* warned against "the commodious instrument of the agents of France."[88]

Hostility toward political refugees subsided with the end of the undeclared war with France. Congress allowed the Alien and Sedition Acts to lapse after 1800, and New Yorkers turned their attention to domestic affairs. At the outset of the nineteenth century, there were plenty of indicators of the kind of city New York would be in the years ahead. The multiethnic makeup of its citizenry had been firmly established during the colonial period, and there was no reason to believe that this would be reversed. The city's commitment to commercial enterprise was also unquestioned.[89]

On the other side of the ledger, when the political climate was less hysterical, New Yorkers proved they could be quite charitable toward newcomers in difficulty. City residents raised thousands of dollars to support French refugees fleeing the slave rebellion in Santo Domingo and opened a hospital on Vesey Street to care for their sick. Such was also the case in 1794, when prominent citizens organized the New York Society for the Information and Assistance of Persons Emigrating from Foreign Countries.[90]

New Yorkers also extended benevolence to the native-born poor through the generosity of individuals and churches, charitable organizations, and the city's almshouse. The Society for the Relief of Poor Widows with Small Children, headed by Isabella Graham, herself a widow, was organized in 1797 to help widows with small children who were left without support when their husbands died during the yellow fever epidemic of 1793. While the society outlived its initial purpose, it continued its efforts for over three-quarters of a century. The society was careful about those it aided: only upstanding, virtuous women were its clients. Perhaps more important than the limited number it assisted, the society marked the entrance of women into the public sphere when dealing with New York's unfortunate citizens. Although women had been active in the boycotts of English goods in the run-up to the American Revolution, the society put women into an ongoing group. Many more such charitable organizations and activities were to follow.[91]

In the years after the American Revolution, the number of New Yorkers held in slavery began to fall. Some enslaved families left with the British when they departed from New York in 1783. A year later, the New York legislature granted freedom to slaves abandoned by the departed Loyalists. Even though many American revolutionaries had opposed receiving slaves into the army, about six thousand enslaved African Americans eventually won their freedom by serving the patriot cause. Moreover, some New York slave owners, caught up in the Revolution's rhetoric of freedom, emancipated their slaves. Finally, as white labor became more plentiful and the egalitarian aspects of the Revolution combined with religious doubts about human bondage, slavery came under increasing attack.[92]

In 1785, antislavery advocates organized the New York Manumission Society to work for the gradual abolition of slavery. When the state legislature met that year, those opposed to slavery had a clear majority in both houses, yet they could not agree on the future status of New York's enslaved blacks. While many favored the abolition of slavery, few were willing to grant newly freed black New Yorkers equal civil rights. A handful of radicals argued for complete equality along with emancipation, but when they were unable to convince others of their view and efforts at compromise proved fruitless, abolition failed.[93]

The New York Manumission Society then concentrated on laws to foster individual emancipations and to outlaw the slave trade. But further efforts to enact an abolition bill were unsuccessful. Indeed, when French émigrés fled the slave rebellion in Haiti with their slaves, the number of New Yorkers held in bondage actually increased.[94]

Members of the New York Manumission Society, some of whom were slave owners themselves, achieved a limited victory with the passage of the Gradual Manumission Act of 1799, a law that freed males born after that date at age twenty-eight and females at age twenty-five. A few unscrupulous slave owners subsequently sold their slaves rather than waiting to give them freedom, a practice the Manumission Society successfully fought in the state legislature. In 1820, the census takers found only 518 enslaved black men in the city, and in 1827 legislation emancipating all slaves in the state took final effect. By 1830, there were no slaves owned by New Yorkers living in the city. However, when Southern slaveholders visited the city on business or as tourists, they were free to bring their slaves with them. This practice was not ended by the legislature until 1841.[95]

Emancipation did not bring equality. During legislative debates over the abolition of slavery, white New Yorkers made clear their belief that blacks should not have equal civil rights. A few abolitionists wanted to grant blacks equal suffrage, but even this proposal was omitted from the state's new constitution in 1821. Moreover, on three occasions the state's white voters rejected an equal ballot for black males; not until the nation ratified the Fifteenth Amendment (1870) did black men finally obtain the right to vote.[96]

Voters in New York City were more opposed to black suffrage than those elsewhere in the state, in part because of hostility toward blacks among the Irish and Germans, their chief competitors on the bottom of the economic and social ladder. In an era when most Northern states did not permit African American men to vote, attempts to secure African American voting rights in New York were met with ugly responses. One Democratic paper warned of potential interracial sex and of black arrogance if the proposition passed and asserted that blacks could not be trusted with the ballot.

Because of the virulent racism of the nineteenth century, black New Yorkers were largely limited to low-paying and menial employment. During slavery many enslaved people worked as household servants, and they continued to labor at these jobs after emancipation because few other occupations were open to them. In 1797, the New York Manumission Society found that most African Americans were employed as domestics and laborers; only a few were tradesmen or mechanics. State census takers subsequently reported similar occupational patterns and in 1855 revealed that 75 percent of employed blacks were still common service workers. African American women were even more restricted than men in their opportunities and usually worked as household employees or as laundresses. For those fortunate few who learned a trade, chances to ply them were limited.[97]

Despite all these impediments, a small African American elite, distinguished as much by steady employment as by economic gain, emerged in the nineteenth century. In the 1790s, the most famous black tradesman was Samuel Fraunces, owner of Fraunces Tavern, where George Washington bid farewell to his troops.

Most African Americans working in the food industry, however, did not own taverns but were waiters and porters in hotels and restaurants. Still others worked as barbers; a few even owned their own shops. Lacking capital and clientele to expand, African American tradesmen generally ran small shops and were hindered by city officials' reluctance to grant them licenses.[98]

In maritime work, where such barriers were reduced by a tradition of black seamanship, African Americans in New York and other northeastern ports created an occupational niche for themselves. In 1800, when African Americans made up 10 percent of New York's population, they filled 17 percent of berths on ships that sailed from the city. While they were generally recruited into less-skilled positions that offered few opportunities for promotion, within the positions they filled black and white mariners frequently received the same pay. The work was hard and dangerous—in 1810 the African Marine Fund was organized "For The Relief Of The Distressed Orphans, And Poor Members Of This Fund"—but for black men it offered a rare opportunity for dignity and a chance to explore the world. When they shipped to Southern ports, black seamen helped fugitives from bondage stow away below decks and sail to freedom; at home in New York, they helped them evade "slave catchers." African Americans continued to be overrepresented on ships sailing from New York until the middle of the nineteenth century, when a pattern of recruiting more white mariners, especially immigrants, began the destruction of the African American presence in the merchant marine.[99]

African American New Yorkers also formed organizations to advocate their own goals. Samuel Corning and John Russwurm published *Freedom's Journal*, the first African American newspaper. Some African Americans organized separate black churches that became centers of political and educational life. Others remained in white-dominated churches for a time but eventually left for black churches when they felt unwelcome among white Methodists and Episcopalians. Most African Americans rejected the movement to send them to Africa, popularized by the American Colonization Society, and instead called for the immediate end of slavery in the South. Black abolitionists organized the Committee of Vigilance to assist escaped slaves. David Ruggles became a household name among African Americans for aiding fugitives. Black women also organized to help runaways and promote education.[100]

* * *

New York's harbor, which offered both protection from storms and a route to the American interior via the Hudson River, was an extraordinary asset. But the city's economic takeoff in the nineteenth century was based equally on natural and human factors. The city's first great boost came at the end of the War of 1812, which had disrupted Atlantic commerce and left New York and

Americans starved for goods. With the war's end in 1815, British merchants, taking into account the advantage of New York's location, dumped millions of dollars' worth of manufactured goods in New York at reduced prices, priming the city's economy and giving it an advantage over rival American ports.[101]

In 1818, the Black Ball Line's *James Monroe* sailed eastward in a snowstorm, launching regularly scheduled "packet ship" service between New York and Liverpool. Unlike earlier merchantmen that sailed on irregular schedules dictated by the availability of cargo and the vagaries of the weather, packet ships sailed regularly. Shippers and passengers alike flocked to the new service, driving up both transatlantic trade and immigration. Liverpool, already a major port thanks to American trade, commerce with the Caribbean, and the slave trade, became—after London—the second-largest port in the British Empire.[102]

Equally important changes transformed coastal trade as New York steadily moved to dominate shipping to and from the cotton-producing South. New York merchants made their city the funnel through which Southern cotton passed to the textile mills of England. Supporting industries in finance, banking, and accommodations soon followed. New York became the front office for the slavery-based economy of the Southern states and the destination of planters who headed north for business or pleasure. In the long run, the economic and political ties so fostered would make New York, in effect, the northernmost Southern city.[103]

The most significant factor driving New York to economic preeminence was the opening of the Erie Canal in upstate New York in 1825 after eight years of construction under difficult conditions. The canal created a direct water route between the East Coast and the Great Lakes and Midwest. Before the canal, shipping a ton of wheat worth $40 overland from Buffalo to New York took three weeks and cost $120. With the canal, shipping the same ton of wheat took eight days and cost only a fraction of the original cost. New York's favored geography and the daring of its business leaders extended the city's primacy over Boston, Philadelphia, and Baltimore.[104]

While commerce held sway over the economic life of the city in these years, manufacturing was rapidly rising in significance. During the first quarter of the century, artisans dominated trade from their small shops, yet by the late 1820s shifts from shop to factory and small- to large-scale manufacturing were already in evidence in shipbuilding, sugar refining, and manufacturing musical instruments. The establishment of George Opdyke's ready-to-wear clothing factory in 1832 was an important step in the development of the garment industry that was to become New York's great enterprise, employing nearly thirty thousand people by midcentury. The foundation of New York's garment industry was the production of cheap clothing for slaves, sailors, Southern farmers, western miners, and the urban poor, but by the middle of the nineteenth century manufacturers also produced garments for the middle class.[105]

The spectacular growth of industry and commerce contributed to New York City's emergence as the nation's financial center. Foreign and domestic trade brought a need for banks, insurance companies, auction houses, and a permanent stock exchange. By the century's fourth decade, Wall Street had become the center of the city's financial district, described by an English visitor in 1838 as the most "concentrated focus of commercial transactions in the world. . . . The whole money-dealing of New York is here brought into a very narrow compass of ground, and is consequently transacted with peculiar quickness and facility." From Wall Street, as one historian aptly put it, New York's mercantile leaders with "the backing of British capital . . . were able to provide the credit and loans on which American domestic trade and economic development came increasingly to depend."[106]

New York's success acted as a magnet that drew in people from within and outside of the United States.[107] Until 1820, the leading roles in the city's mercantile affairs had been played primarily by descendants of the original English and Huguenot settlers, while descendants of the Dutch tended to seek their fortunes in real estate. During the 1820s, however, these old "Knickerbocker" families were overwhelmed by an influx of New Englanders from Connecticut, Rhode Island, and Massachusetts. These sons of New England's Puritans altered the tone of New York's business life. Unlike longstanding residents, the newcomers were, as one contemporary described them, "more conservative in character, more grave in temperament, and at the same time, more enterprising, and more insistent in action." Names like Tappan, Macy, Grinnell, Fish, Dodge, Phelps, King, and Whitney would dominate New York's financial and mercantile houses, shipping firms, and shipbuilding industry into the late nineteenth century.[108]

The New England migrants took their place alongside New York's foreign-born merchants from the Netherlands, Switzerland, Spain, France, and France's lost possession of Santo Domingo. Because Liverpool was the city's principal partner in trade and finance, Britons were the largest group of foreign businessmen. Together, they situated New York in the economies of the Caribbean and the Atlantic.

These merchants wrought changes in commerce, finance, and shipping from the top down. Equally transforming, in the near future, would be changes in the city that came from the bottom up. As shipping across the Atlantic quickened, immigrants from Europe—driven by wrenching economic changes, failed revolutions, and flight from hunger—turned their eyes to New York City.

CHAPTER 2

—————

BECOMING A CITY OF THE WORLD: 1820–1860

In 1851, when the immigrant ship *Kossuth* from Liverpool docked at Rutgers Slip on the East River, a sketch artist for an illustrated magazine saw the drama in an everyday event. In the background, mariners clamber in the rigging and reef sails. Immigrant passengers exultantly raise their arms to the heavens (perhaps relieved that they had survived a collision a sea with another ship, the *Henry Clay*) and wave their hats in the air. A man helps a woman ashore. In the foreground, one passenger weeps at bad news, while a reunited husband and wife (she with a baby in her arms) rush to embrace. Amid the bustle of unloading cargo lovers kiss passionately, an aged man is helped away, a pickpocket scores, and a boy with a devilish grin stands on a cart loaded with goods. To the artist, an imperfect draftsman who mangled the spelling of the ship's name, the docking of the *Kossuth*—with all its passion, pain, chaos, hopes, and messiness—was an electric moment. Yet the scene sketched for *Gleason's Pictorial Drawing Room Companion* was but a drop in the flood of migration, principally from Ireland and Germany, that transformed New York.[1]

The passengers and crew on the *Kossuth* were part of a sea change in the Atlantic world. The rise of the packet ships, later to be augmented by fast-sailing clipper ships and steam vessels, quickened maritime commerce and accelerated New York's economic growth. Vessels sailing east from New York above all carried cotton produced by enslaved labor in the South and increasingly the most lucrative product of American agriculture. Coastal shipping strengthened

2.1 "Landing of Emigrants from the Ship *Kossuth*," *Gleason's Pictorial Drawing Room Companion*, 1851.

Source: Robert W. Snyder collection.

the links between Gotham and the South. Vessels sailing west from Europe carried a growing number of immigrants as economic dislocation, famine, and revolution pushed Europeans to seek better lives overseas. New York was the greatest port in the United States, a city with a growing reputation as a center for manufacturing. As people and goods moved across the Atlantic with greater frequency, the city found itself in a maelstrom.[2]

Of the 5,457,914 souls who crossed the Atlantic to the United States between 1820 and 1860, two-thirds disembarked in New York City.[3] Most moved on to other destinations, but enough stayed in the city for their numbers to be transformative. As late as 1835, New York was a city of 207,089 people, only 10.2 percent of whom were foreign born. By 1860, however, New York was a city of 813,669 people, 47 percent of whom had been born abroad.[4]

The most numerous of the new immigrants were Irish Catholics and Germans. In their religion, language, and culture, they brought new ways of life to a city that was, for all its reputation for diversity, strongly British and Protestant. In their numbers, they strained the city's housing, municipal services, and government. As they settled in, they reshaped everything from politics to popular music. The clash between the old city and its newcomers, in an age of mass migration and spectacular economic growth, remade New York.

* * *

The vast majority of immigrants chose a new beginning in America for economic reasons. The process of industrialization, driven by ever more efficient machinery and larger factories, destroyed the livelihoods of many urban craftsmen and rural weavers. Subsistence farmers were driven off the land by landlords seeking more efficient and profitable uses of their holdings or by devastating crop failures. Exacerbating these conditions during the first half of the 1800s was a dramatic rise in population throughout the British Isles and most of continental Europe. The worst spur to immigration was the potato blight of the mid-1840s, which destroyed the crop that fed growing populations. In Germany, the blight affected hundreds of thousands of families. In Ireland, where the blight overlapped with disputes over land ownership, economics, poverty, and British rule, it set in motion a devastating famine. Estimates of the death toll wrought by starvation and disease run as high as more than a million. At the same time, more than a million people emigrated, carrying with them horrible memories of what would come to be called the Great Hunger.[5]

Many of the immigrants were young, single, and of working age. Some hoped to improve their lot. Many Irish simply sought to escape starvation. Yet even when immigrants traveled alone, the decision to emigrate was a family decision rooted in the collective values of an agrarian economy, as the historian Richard Stott points out.[6] Family welfare was the prime consideration, as was proven by the millions of hard-earned dollars that immigrants eventually sent back home to help their families get by and provide passage for others to emigrate.[7]

The establishment of regularly scheduled packet service brought a degree of consistency to transatlantic shipping, and the declining cost of a steerage ticket in the decades before the Civil War put the price of passage within reach of poorer Europeans. Commercial houses on both sides of the Atlantic, recognizing that profits could accrue from human cargo, contracted for ship space and set rates for passage. Some even established their own passenger lines, disseminated propaganda to encourage immigration, and helped immigrants send money home to pay the fares of relatives sailing to America.[8]

Transatlantic voyages in the age of sail took six to eight weeks. Passengers faced seasickness, overcrowding, dirt, hunger, stench, and disease and risked death from shipwreck, typhus, cholera, smallpox, or malnutrition. Death rates among passengers averaged about 2 percent or less, but during epidemics they rose precipitously: about 10 percent in 1817–18 and 1831–34 and about 20 percent in 1847, when the Irish were wracked by both disease and hunger.[9]

Sailing through the Verrazano Narrows and finally into New York's harbor was undoubtedly a relief for the immigrants, but during the first decades of this period the arrival could prove as harrowing as the journey. In the first half of the nineteenth century, processing immigrants through the port of New York fell under the jurisdiction of state and city governments. The earliest arrivals simply walked down a gangplank, where they were met by "runners," agents for boardinghouse operators or companies that transported immigrants to the interior. Runners usually shared the immigrants' nationality and spoke their language. Frequently their goal was to win the new arrivals' trust, then bilk them of as much cash and/or property as possible in return for overpriced travel tickets, exorbitant rates for baggage transport, or highly unfair rents for board-inghouse accommodations.[10]

In 1847, under pressure from immigrant organizations, the state legislature in Albany passed a bill establishing a Board of Commissioners of Emigration, giving it the power and funds to inspect incoming ships and provide aid, infor-mation, and employment assistance to the immigrants. Hospital facilities for newly arrived immigrants were expanded. A state law enacted in 1848 regulated boardinghouse rates and practices. Finally, in an effort to thwart the runners, the Board of Commissioners of Emigration designated the old fort at Castle Garden, located at the foot of Manhattan, as the central landing station for immigrants. Here newcomers received aid, advice, and services from honest brokers and agents, city employees, and representatives of immigrant aid soci-eties. Then the immigrants had to face the human maelstrom that was New York. The encounter would transform all involved.[11]

In 1857, the patrician Protestant lawyer George Templeton Strong noticed a crowd at a construction site on Fourth Avenue, where two Irish laborers crushed to death in a cave-in "lay white and stark on the ground." Irish men and women gathered around them. "The men were listless and inert enough," he wrote in his diary, "but not so the women."

I suppose they were "keening"; all together were raising a wild, unearthly cry, half shriek and half song, wailing as a chorus of daylight Banshees, grasping their hands and gesticulating passionately. Now and then one of them would throw herself down on one of the corpses. Or wipe some defilement from the face of the dead man with her apron, slowly and carefully, then resume her lament. It was an uncanny sound to hear, quite new to me.... Our Celtic fel-low citizens are as remote from us in temperament and constitution as the Chinese.[12]

The sense of distance and disdain in Strong's observation expresses how many native-born New Yorkers viewed the Irish immigrants of the mid–nineteenth century, who were poor, overwhelmingly Catholic in a city dominated by

Protestants, and rural people in a fast-growing metropolis. To be sure, not every Irishman labored with a pick and shovel, and not every Irish woman worked as a scullery maid. As the historian Hasia Diner has noted, "The Irish community in New York always contained several layers."[13] Nevertheless, so many immigrant Irish were funneled into hard physical labor and grinding poverty that as a group they received less of the good and more of the bad that life in New York City offered. In describing his flock, New York's Bishop John Hughes wrote that they were "the poorest and most wretched population that can be found in the world—the scattered debris of the Irish nation."[14]

Even before the famine era, economically wracked Ireland sent more women to America than men. Marriage possibilities for women in Ireland were limited, and America offered them better opportunities. In 1860, 57 percent of New York's Irish born were women, which meant that many would have difficulty finding Irish husbands.[15] Moreover, because of the high rate of industrial accidents among Irish men, who dominated the ranks of laborers employed in dangerous work on the docks and in the construction trades, those Irish women who married in New York faced the possibility of becoming widows. Some women became the heads of families when men deserted (a problem for all immigrant groups).[16] For the widows and children of these victims, starvation and homelessness could be avoided only through income-producing work. Finally, the death of children stole the attraction of motherhood. As Maureen Fitzgerald explains, "With the world's highest known death rate at the time and at least a third of all infants and more than half the children between infancy and age five dying annually, motherhood for the poor in New York City was often a wrenching experience of loss and despair."[17]

A majority of Irish immigrants experienced extreme poverty for at least a portion of their years in New York. Even in the more prosperous male-headed households, industrial accidents, seasonal unemployment, and low salaries dictated that extra income was essential for survival. In these circumstances women made contributions—often by taking in boarders or doing needlework—but family life was still a struggle.

Some young and single women escaped the worst aspects of slum life by becoming nuns and dedicating their lives to helping other poor immigrants. These women served in the diocese's expanding network of charitable agencies, schools, and hospitals and were crucial to developing Catholic institutions to serve the city's unfortunate. Positions were also available in schools run by the church. The premier teaching orders were Sisters of Charity and the Sisters of Charity of the Blessed Virgin Mary. Young women also found positions in the public schools.[18]

Many others, after the 1820s, dominated domestic service in New York City; by 1855, 74 percent of domestic workers were Irish.[19] So common a stereotype was "Bridget," the serving woman, that one guidebook, *Advice to Irish Girls in*

America by the Nun of Kenmare, simply assumed that all Irish women who worked would enter domestic service.[20]

The city's "Bridgets" worked long hours, and a few suffered abuse by their employers. Most lived in middle-class homes, where they at least benefitted from a healthy diet. Because room and board were free, they were able to save part of their wages for their dowries. The historian Christine Stansell writes that between 1819 and 1847 these young women accounted for between one-half and two-thirds of the savings accounts opened by unskilled workers at the New York Bank for Savings. Many Irish men, too, managed to save, as Tyler Anbinder's study of the Emigrant Savings Bank discovered. Together, the savings of Irish women and men supported continued immigration. Prepaid passage tickets, according to estimates, paid for more than 75 percent of all Irish immigration in the fifty years following famine.[21]

Not all single Irish women entered domestic service or the church. One study of the city's prostitutes in 1855 revealed that 35 percent were Irish and 12 percent German. Women of all immigrant groups became prostitutes, which caused alarm for nineteenth-century reformers who wanted to stamp out this immoral trade and the police corruption that went with it. Other women entered the needle trades, where they endured long hours for poor pay. For women with children, labor in the needle trades was impossible to manage, but it attracted about one-third of single Irish working women.[22]

Just as the Irish often were blamed for their poverty, they were also castigated for seeking some measure of relief from its effects. There seemed to be no end of drinking establishments in the immigrant districts. For the first generation of Irish in particular, the saloon was the center of a relatively inexpensive social life, just as the pub had been back home. In 1864, the Sixth Ward had one drinking establishment for every six people. At Peter Sweeney's saloon, for example, one could gain entry for ten cents and quaff whiskey at three cents a glass. The saloonkeeper was a respected figure in his community, a force for sustenance and sociability, and by the Civil War he had become a key figure in local politics. Yet to many a well-meaning reformer the saloon represented both a den of immorality and a prime cause of poverty among the Irish.[23]

The Irish immigrant way of life was indeed different in many respects from that of the native-born, white Protestant American. Politically, economically, and culturally oppressed in their native land, the Irish arrived in New York, competed for menial jobs, and experienced prejudice on all fronts. In this setting, what William Shannon terms the "two-fisted aggressiveness of the Irish" is not difficult to understand.[24] During the mid–nineteenth century, New York City was an arena of ethnic rivalry, competition, and violence. Often unemployed and seeking excitement, young Irish men organized into street gangs whose names reflected a variety of old and new country loyalties. The Dead Rabbits, Kerryonians, and O'Connell Guards provided their members opportunities for raucous sociability and plenty of two-fisted action. So too did the city's many volunteer fire companies, the farm teams for political factions that were more adept at fighting one another than at effectively extinguishing fires.[25]

After 1830, the city witnessed an unusually large number of street riots and brawls. Irishmen were prominently involved in many of them, a circumstance that appeared to confirm that they were indeed a belligerent people with a significant percentage of bully boys. A closer examination of some of those outbreaks, however, reveals more about the Irish condition in New York.

Violence was not the exclusive property of New York's newest and most numerous immigrants. In antebellum New York, Irish Catholics had their own brawlers, like the dockside runner–turned-pugilist John Morrissey, but nativist Protestants had Bill "The Butcher" Poole. Irish gang violence was legendary, but it was often employed for political purposes—to subdue a rival faction, for example—that made head breaking both expressive and purposeful. The Irish often vented their rage and violence against New York's African Americans, who were fellow victims of prejudice but often competitors for jobs as waiters, coachmen, and dockworkers. In their hostility to blacks, however, the Irish adopted racial attitudes that had been expressed by New York working people as early as the colonial period. More recently, such attitudes had manifested in July 1834, when an eight-day antiabolitionist riot ravaged African American homes and churches.[26] Sheer poverty also pushed Irishmen into violence. In 1837, hunger drove Irish workers to loot grain warehouses in what became known as the Flour Riot.[27]

Anti-English sentiments, along with class tensions, help explain the Irish gangs' participation in the famous Astor Place Riot of May 1849, which stemmed from the rivalry between the British actor William Macready and the darling of the American stage Edwin Forrest. Both men were appearing at the same time in rival productions, and ethnic pride and anger were deeply involved as well. The riot involved more than ten thousand workingmen, native and immigrant alike, and led to thirty-one deaths.[28]

***

The sense of difference that animated nativist hostility to the Irish—and which the Irish repaid in kind—was grounded in religion. The two sides did not debate fine points of theology but used religion to express identity and solidarity. The Irish immigrants arriving after 1820 were, with few exceptions, Catholic. The Germans were a religiously heterogeneous lot, with a Catholic majority but many Protestants as well as Jews and freethinkers. By 1860, as Jay Dolan informs us, "for every German Catholic there were six to seven Irishmen." Naturally enough, "the principal authority in the city, the bishop, was an Irishman."[29]

The "Irishman" was John Hughes, who in 1838 succeeded the Frenchman John Dubois as bishop of New York. Hughes became archbishop in 1850, when Pope Pius IX raised the diocese of New York to the position of archdiocese, and continued in office until 1864.[30] Under Hughes's dynamic leadership the Roman Catholic Church in New York moved from weakness to vast power. In 1841, the diocese had but ten churches, one priest for every eight thousand people, and $300,000 in debts. Before fifteen years had passed, Hughes had paid off the diocese's debts, tripled the number of its churches, and established doctrinal unity within his domain. He also created an array of educational, charitable, and social institutions that would form the foundation of Irish Catholic communal life in New York City.[31] Perhaps most symbolic of the changed status of the church was its formal administrative center. When Hughes assumed the bishop's chair, old St. Patrick's Cathedral was located on Mulberry Street on the Lower East Side. At the time of his retirement, and as a result of his efforts, a grand Gothic St. Patrick's was under construction on prestigious Fifth Avenue between Fiftieth and Fifty-First Streets, where it still stands.[32]

No Irishman in politics or business during the antebellum period achieved power comparable to Hughes's dominion within the church. Whether Irish Catholics attended church regularly or not—and many did not—by birth, identity, and heritage they remained Irish and Catholic. This melding of nationality and faith had been forged in Ireland in the face of English Protestant attempts to subvert both. In America, nativist hostility and evangelical Protestant assertiveness posed similar challenges. Hughes's calculating yet forceful responses to these pressures made him popular within the Irish community and warily respected outside it.[33]

Bishop Hughes, in his own way, was as confrontational as any Bowery B'hoy or Dead Rabbit. He was not loved by Protestant America, but he was taken seriously as a spokesman for the city's growing Irish Catholic population—whose votes no political leader could ignore. He demonstrated his political power in a battle over schooling that erupted almost immediately after he took office as archbishop.

In 1840, New York City lacked a public school system. The bulk of the state's school funds earmarked for the city went to the Public School Society, a chartered philanthropic organization founded by Protestant laymen to provide elementary schooling for poor children. The Public School Society was governed by a self-perpetuating board of trustees. Though nondenominational, the climate and orientation of its schools were such that most Catholics could not in good conscience enroll their children. Their objections included the recital of Protestant prayers and hymns, the exclusive use of the King James Bible, and the use of religious, literary, and historical texts displaying anti-Catholic biases, including the frequent use of the derogatory term "popery." With many Catholic parents boycotting the society's schools and a paucity of Catholic schools, large numbers of New York City children did not receive any schooling.[34]

The election of Governor William Henry Seward in 1838 on the Whig ticket had drastic consequences for the city's schools. Sympathetic to the Irish and hopeful of breaking the Democrats' hold on New York City's Irish vote, Seward proposed that public money be used to support Catholic schools. Bishop Hughes responded enthusiastically, worked closely with the governor, and petitioned the city's Common Council for a share of the state school funds. The city council, faced with opposition from the Public School Society, anti-Catholic nativists, and citizens sincerely concerned about church-state separation, twice rejected Hughes's request. Political action then moved to Albany, where the state legislature—having received anti-Catholic petitions, editorials, and tracts—hesitated to support the Hughes-Seward cause.

Bishop Hughes decided to impress legislators with the potential power of the city's Irish voters. Under his leadership, for the first and only time in the city's history, a Catholic political party was established to contest the 1842 state legislative race. Ten assemblymen who supported the Hughes school-aid position ran on both the Catholic and the Democratic slates. All won. Three Democratic candidates who did not support Hughes's school plan were opposed by Catholic party candidates; all three Democrats were defeated. Bishop Hughes had made his point: New York's Irish Catholics had enough influence to tip the balance of power in citywide elections. Bowing to that political reality, the Democratic-controlled legislature prepared to enact a school law for New York City.[35]

The measure that was finally passed did not give Bishop Hughes everything he wanted, but it established in the city a district public school system in which "no religious sectarian doctrine or tenet should be taught, inculcated, or practiced."[36] Public funds would not be forthcoming to support Catholic schools or religious teachings, but Catholic children attending public schools in their neighborhoods would no longer be subjected to teachings explicitly critical of their faith. Nevertheless, the failure to gain governmental funding for the kind of schools he wished moved Hughes in a new direction. He began to build a separate, privately financed parochial school system. During the remainder of his tenure and afterward, the number of parochial schools and the number of children attending them grew considerably. In 1840, almost five thousand children—20 percent of the city's total school population—attended Catholic schools. By 1870, the parochial school population reached 22,215—or 19 percent of the city's total school population.

As population growth outpaced the church's ability to pay for school expansion, many Catholic parents sent their children to public schools, where the reforms established in the state legislature changed the religious climate and made them a viable alternative to parochial schools for most Irish parents. In heavily Catholic districts, Irish Catholics won strong representation on the school boards and among the faculty.[37] Jay Dolan notes that as early as 1843 the elected school board in the Sixth Ward "read like a roll call for the Hibernian society and included two trustees of the parish."[38]

Bishop Hughes's decision to promote the growth of a separate parochial school system became grist for nativist, anti-Catholic propaganda mills. It also was criticized by some who had traditionally been among his friends and supporters, including the reformist Whig newspaper editor Horace Greeley and Orestes A. Brownson, an old-stock American convert to Catholicism. Both objected to what they believed were antiassimilationist tendencies inherent in the move.[39] But if Bishop Hughes displayed a siege mentality and a desire to keep the Irish strong and separate behind the protective barrier of the church, it is perhaps understandable, given Irish history and the intense American nativism during the antebellum years. Foreigners of every nationality felt the sting of nativist barbs, particularly during election campaigns or periods of economic downturn. During the municipal election campaign of 1844, for example, the *Daily Plebian* in a single paragraph spoke of German and Irish "thieves and vagabonds," English and Scotch "pickpockets and burglars," and "wandering Jews" using "their shops as receptacles for stolen goods, encouraging thievery among our citizens." The paper went on to exclaim, "Look at the Irish and Dutch [German] grocers and rum-sellers monopolizing the business which properly belongs to our native and true-born citizens."[40]

The Irish bore the brunt of such nativist attacks. They arrived in the greatest numbers, were the poorest, and were willing to work for the lowest wages. Wages for all laborers dropped during decades of high immigration. Among unskilled laborers, pay dropped from a dollar a day in the early 1830s to seventy-five cents a day in the 1840s. The huge Irish influx of the 1840s helped make "possible the full introduction of factory production" and the consequent lowering of status among workingmen.[41] Mass immigration was not the only cause of the decline in working-class living standards, but as Douglas T. Miller points out, "the immigrant often served as a convenient scapegoat for a variety of frustrations."[42]

The Irish became the primary target of religious bigots because of their near-universal allegiance to the Roman Catholic Church and the growing Irish domination of the priesthood and clerical offices of the church in the United States. The historical enmity toward Catholics was directed more at the church politic and "popery" than at purely religious teachings and practices. Nativists charged that the church politic was the enemy of democracy, social reform, and the broadly Protestant values traditionally promoted in the public schools.[43] In 1850, in response to oft-repeated charges that his church threatened to displace the dominance of Protestantism in American society, Archbishop Hughes declared in a speech entitled "The Decline of Protestantism and Its Causes" that

Protestantism was a sterile religion, in contrast to dynamic Catholicism. As for Catholic intentions: "Everybody should know that we have for our mission to convert the world, including the inhabitants of the United States, the people of the country, the officers of the Navy and Marines, commanders of the Army, the legislatures, the Senate, the Cabinet, the President, and all."[44] As one historian put it, "Rather than pour oil on troubled waters, Hughes preferred to ignite the oil."[45]

While the Democratic Party rewarded Irish Catholic voters with municipal jobs in return for their political loyalty, the Irish association with Tammany Hall's corrupt politics provided further fuel for nativists. While the Democrats found their Irish supporters a highly valuable political asset, their opponents in the city used antiforeign, anti-Catholic sentiment to attract the votes of native-born Americans.

Even given New York's history of racism, the animus of nativists against impoverished Catholic immigrants, particularly the Irish, is striking. From the 1830s to the 1850s, nativist campaigns played upon the electorate's fears and prejudices. Nativists urged that only native-born citizens should be able to run for office, supported a twenty- or twenty-one-year naturalization law, advocated the deportation of foreign-born criminals, sought to exclude Catholics from public life, and supported the reading of the Protestant King James Bible in the public schools.[46] In 1844, the nativist American Republican Party elected its candidate, James Harper, mayor of New York City. In 1855, the Know Nothing movement's candidate for mayor, James Barker, came in second in a four-man race, losing by a mere 1,500 votes.[47]

Some political leaders used nativist rhetoric to gild causes that lacked an obvious immigrant dimension. Nativism was part of a strong anticorruption element in the American Republican movement of the 1840s. The Know Nothing Party of the 1850s, which preserved the proslavery wing of a disintegrating Whig Party, also embraced nativism. But if nativist sentiment was insufficiently potent to inspire by itself an entire political party, it was strong enough to attract politicians periodically.

Alarmed New Yorkers believed that the city was taking in too many destitute Irish men and women. The British government and Irish landlords, many argued, were dumping poverty-stricken Irish on American shores, especially during the Great Hunger. New York State officials, hostile to the immigrant population within their borders, set standards for admission that guaranteed that poor (and Catholic) immigrants would be barred from entry. State opponents of poor Irish Catholics achieved some success in keeping the Irish out of the city and in sending them back to Ireland.

Hidetaka Hirota, who has studied how Massachusetts and New York dealt with immigration before the federal government assumed that role in the 1880s, estimates that tens of thousands of poor immigrants were banned. Indeed, even immigrants who had lived in America successfully for years were deported after they fell on hard times. Although laws prohibited such deportations, nativists succeeded in convincing authorities to deport such persons whether or not they were living in almshouses. Thousands were deported from Massachusetts and New York, returned to Ireland, and simply dumped on Irish soil.[48]

Although some native-born white New Yorkers viewed the new immigrants with sympathy, especially those suffering from poverty, the cultural assumptions of native-born reformers set the stage for conflict. Influenced by the Protestant revivals of the times, these moral reformers combined concern for destitute immigrants and their children with a streak of moralism, especially toward those who seemed to reject Christianity. Protestant Reformers also scorned Roman Catholicism. Building upon the efforts of the Society for the Relief of Poor Widows with Small Children (1797), they founded a number of reform organizations. The most famous were the Association for Improving of the Condition of the Poor (AICP) and the Children's Aid Society, headed by Charles Loring Brace. Disturbed by the number of seemingly destitute children running in the streets and not in school, Brace believed that saving the children demanded radical steps. His solution was to place the children in homes or institutions where they would be removed from degraded conditions. The AICP also called for restrictions to bar paupers from landing and criticized Irish Catholics for sending money home rather than helping poor Irish in New York.[49]

The foot soldiers in this reform effort were often Protestant women who took traditional women's roles as guardians of the home and moral purity in new directions. As religious women and moral reformers, they engaged the sick, abandoned, widows, the destitute, criminals, and prostitutes. Through these efforts, Carroll Smith-Rosenberg points out, middle-class women broadened their roles in the life of the city.[50]

The moral reformers believed initially that poverty was the result of bad character and focused their efforts on the "worthy poor, the sick, the aged, the widowed, and the orphaned who suffered through no fault of their own."[51] Over time, as they studied horrendous living conditions, they concluded that environmental factors also bred poverty. Seeking to ease bad conditions, they turned to the city for funding. Municipal funds were used to help the poor in colonial times, and with large-scale immigration such aid seemed imperative. The practice of providing government aid to private charities became acceptable.

* * *

The experience of Germans in New York shows how the skills, experiences, and culture amassed in the mother country shaped life in America. Compared to the Irish, Germans arrived in America with more money, a wider array of occupational experiences, and a higher rate of literacy. Even though the Germans didn't speak English and stood apart from English-speaking residents socially and culturally, compared to the Irish the Germans adapted to New York City faster and prospered in greater numbers.[52]

To be sure, there were poor German immigrants, such as the German rag pickers and bone gatherers who lived miserably in the Eleventh Ward's "Rag Pickers' Paradise."[53] Nevertheless, after 1845, Germans were increasingly prominent among the city's artisans and skilled tradesmen. "By 1855," Stanley Nadel writes, "Germans were already a majority of tailors, shoemakers, cabinetmakers, and upholsterers, bakers, brewers, cigar makers, locksmiths, paper box makers, potters, textile workers, gilders, turners, and carvers. Over the next two decades they came to dominate most other skilled trades as well."[54]

At the same time, German household organization generally conformed to patterns acceptable to middle-class New Yorkers. German women were expected to stay at home and care for the family. Circumstances forced some of them to search for employment outside their homes, but apparently not in such numbers as Irish women. In the heavily female occupation of domestic service, in 1880 there were only 5,800 Germans so employed, compared with 24,000 Irish. As was the case in so many immigrant families, German women brought in badly needed funds by working at home. "German women tried to avoid wage labor outside home," writes the historian Dorothee Schneider. "Taking in boarders, sewing, taking in wash, or making cigars were the ways of earning additional dollars while officially retaining the status of housewife."[55] Running a boardinghouse brought in badly needed funds, but at the cost of more crowded living quarters and reduced privacy. Nevertheless, the limited presence of German women in the world of paid labor is striking. The skilled employment that German men practiced simply paid better than unskilled work, reducing the pressure on German women and children to enter the workforce and contribute substantially to household income.[56]

Germans also brought a linguistic division to New York. Not since early colonial days, when Dutch vied with English, had a minority tongue been heard in the streets with such frequency. In consequence, Germans experienced the stings of nativism (though not to the same extent as Irish Catholics). Native-born Americans castigated Germans for not speaking English, for being clannish, for loving beer, and for treating the Sabbath as a day of relaxation and recreation. Observers were stunned by not only the German enclave's poverty and crowding but also "by how thoroughly German—and therefore utterly un-American—it appeared." Many New Yorkers accused German workers of driving down the wages of American craftsmen and of contributing to the increase in cheaply made and priced goods, particularly furniture. During the 1850s, their fellow immigrants, the Irish, accused Germans of acting as strikebreakers who threatened their dominant position on the city's docks.[57] Bigots hated German Catholics for being Catholic, and conservatives depicted the small group of intellectual refugees from the revolutions of 1848 as "red republicans," "agnostics," and "freethinkers." Newspapers that were quick to label immigrants as criminals found German names prominent among the safecrackers, counterfeiters, and fences of New York.[58]

Certainly nativism encouraged Germans' separateness and retarded their assimilation. Yet even as victims of nativism the Germans suffered less intense hostility than did the Irish. Germans were not associated with street toughs, gang violence, and the raucous activities of the city's fire companies. Unlike the majority Catholic Irish, only a portion of the German immigrants was Catholic, and few of them held power in a church dominated by Irish clerics. Statistically, German names were less prominent than Irish ones on the city's charity rolls and police blotters.

If Germans faced criticism for their cultural clannishness, their limited participation in the seamier aspects of the city's political life protected them from the kind of nativist criticism directed at Irish-supported Tammany Hall. In the public mind, Germans might be associated with political radicalism, but they were not connected with corrupt city politics. Although most Germans voted Democratic, by the eve of the Civil War a number of those active in abolitionist circles felt more comfortable in the Republican Party. Most important for overcoming all the negative stereotypes directed at them, the Germans received plaudits for being hard workers, skillful in crafts, and shrewd in businesses.[59] They confronted no equivalent of notices reading "No Irish Need Apply."[60]

Heavy German concentrations in the city's Tenth, Eleventh, Thirteenth, and Seventeenth Wards earned the area a number of appellations. Non-Germans most often referred to it as Dutch Town, but to its German residents it was Kleindeutschland (Little Germany). The four wards, occupying what would later be called the Lower East Side, stretched from Division Street north to East Fourteenth Street and from the East River west to Third Avenue and the Bowery. By 1875, the area was more than 64 percent German American, representing approximately half of the city's German population.[61]

Tompkins Square was at the center. Avenue B, occasionally called the German Broadway, was the commercial artery. Each basement was a workshop, every first floor was a store, and the partially roofed sidewalks were markets for goods of all sorts. Avenue A was the street for beer halls, oyster saloons, and groceries. The Bowery was the western border (anything further west was totally foreign), but it was also the amusement and loafing district. There all the artistic treats, from classical drama to puppet comedies, were for sale.[62]

Far more isolated from the general population by virtue of language than the Irish, the Germans also displayed a greater desire to remain apart. Self-segregation warded off nativist hostility, eased the difficulties of coping with a foreign language, and maintained a positive identification with things

German. A resident of Kleindeutschland could make a living without learning English.[63] When allegiance to German wavered, neighbors warned of dangers. "Language saves faith," was an oft-heard slogan in the parish churches of Kleindeutschland.[64]

Yet the great size of New York's German community could obscure its internal diversity. Before the establishment of a unified German nation in 1871, German immigrants rarely identified themselves chiefly as Germans. They were Bavarians, Brandenbergers, Hessians, Swabians, or Prussians. Particularism among Kleindeutschland's population was reflected in speech dialects, loyalties, institutional structures, and residential patterns.

Regional origin played a key role in determining in which neighborhood one lived and, along with religion, was an important factor in the selection of marriage partners. In 1860, 72 percent of Bavarians were married to other Bavarians, and another 18 percent chose spouses from adjoining regions of southwestern Germany.[65]

Among German Catholics and Protestants alike, the linguistic and religious traditions of their homeland fostered a desire for national churches. For Catholics, who constituted the largest group of religiously affiliated Germans, this required the sympathy and cooperation of the Irish-dominated hierarchy, something not always forthcoming. German Catholics resented Irish dominance and believed that Archbishop Hughes was most concerned with the spiritual needs of his fellow Irish. As one Irish priest put it in 1865, referring to German Catholics, "our ordinary authorities almost ignore their existence."[66]

The incentive to establish German national parishes initially came from laymen, who usually led the fundraising, supervised the construction of the church, and only upon completion of the structure applied to the bishop for a German-speaking priest.[67] Hughes had little recourse but to comply with such requests, since the parish had in effect already been established. But he was not always willing to endorse nationalist ventures. In 1850, German parishioners of Most Holy Redeemer Church in Lower Manhattan, angered that Irish onlookers persistently insulted German burial parties at the official Catholic cemetery, founded a cemetery of their own in Williamsburg, Brooklyn. Hughes disapproved. When the Germans continued to use the Williamsburg cemetery after Hughes insisted that there be only "one cemetery for Catholics of all nations," the bishop threatened to close Most Holy Redeemer. Hughes won the battle.[68]

Despite limited support from the city's Irish-led church authorities, German Catholic parishes prospered. The first, St. Nicholas, was established in 1833 on Second Street between Avenue A and First Avenue; the diocese reluctantly accepted it nine years later. By the Civil War, there were seven German parishes, and the number continued to increase during the following decades.[69]

The founder of St. Nicholas and the leading figure in the movement for German national parishes was the Austrian-born Rev. Johann Stephen Raffeiner, who used his considerable personal wealth and fundraising talents to serve the German Catholic communities of Manhattan and Brooklyn. He brought over nuns from Bavaria, encouraged German priests to immigrate to New York, and inspired young German Americans to enter the priesthood.[70]

When Father Raffeiner's later activities centered on Brooklyn, spiritual leadership of Manhattan's German Catholics fell increasingly to German priests led by the Rev. Gabriel Rampler. In 1844, Rampler, with Bishop Hughes's permission, established Most Holy Redeemer Parish on Third Street. The prosperity of the parish was marked seven years later by the erection of an impressive new stone church. The popularity of Most Holy Redeemer stemmed largely from the energy of its Redemptionist priests, who set a pattern for other German Catholic churches by sponsoring a wide variety of social, cultural, and charitable societies, called *vereine*, to meet the competition offered by Protestant churches and secular bodies within the German community. Most Holy Redeemer sponsored mutual-aid societies, youth groups, and singing societies. Physical protection of church property from Know Nothing attacks was provided by a militia company, the Jager-compagnie; a second company, the Henry Henning Guards, was later established. Both military groups were splendidly uniformed, took part in parades, sponsored picnic outings and shooting contests, and generally fostered a strong sense of religious and ethnic pride broader than the narrow regional loyalties many German immigrants brought to New York.[71] Even Archbishop Hughes was impressed. In 1853, he named Father Raffeiner vicar-general for Germans of the archdiocese, an office he held until his death in 1861.

German Protestants also established ethnic churches, but as Protestants in a Protestant nation they felt far more welcome than German Catholics and had no Irish church hierarchy to contend with. Churchgoing German Protestants joined a range of denominations, but most affiliated with one or another form of Lutheranism. As early as 1839, the city had six Protestant German congregations: two Lutheran, one Dutch Reformed, one Evangelical Reformed, one Episcopalian, and one Christian (Algemeine Christliche). As more Germans arrived in New York, the denominations came to include Baptist, Presbyterian, and even Mormon. But the Lutheran growth was most impressive: by 1865, all but two of New York's twenty-four Lutheran congregations were German. Immigrants from German-speaking Swiss areas, Baden, Wurttemburg, Darmstadt, and the Dutch border regions helped establish the German Dutch Reformed Church as the second-largest denomination among New York's German American Protestants.[72]

Church membership tended to be fluid because individual Germans often chose among Protestant denominations or churches on the basis of a minister's dynamism. Whatever their denominational affiliation, German Protestants fostered Germanism and discouraged assimilation by providing ethnic schools, clubs, and cultural and social activities. Unhampered by a non-German hierarchy, the Lutherans in particular achieved great success in assisting newly arrived immigrants.[73]

The general tone of German Protestantism in metropolitan New York was conservative. During the 1840s, German pastors railed against liberal republican movements in their homeland. During the post–Civil War years, most of them would enthusiastically support the Bismarckian drive for German unification. Antiassimilationist laymen and clerics saw the religiously and ethnically diverse population of Manhattan as a constant threat to German identity. Beginning in the 1850s and continuing for the next two decades, German opponents of assimilation pursued cultural autonomy by establishing German communities in Brooklyn and neighboring Long Island.[74]

German immigration also brought German Jews to New York, transforming the profile of the city's Jewish community. The majority of German Jewish immigrants in these years were poor, and their numbers included many unmarried men and women seeking economic opportunities and freedom from anti-Semitism. The earliest arrivals settled in the Five Points, an immigrant neighborhood located in the Sixth Ward close by City Hall, and worked as peddlers, shopkeepers, or in the garment trade. They gave Chatham Square a reputation for the sale of secondhand clothing. Mobility was modest, but by the 1850s a number of the city's immigrant Jews had reached the middle class.[75]

Within the German immigrant community, Jews were not set apart by their faith. As Howard Rock notes, "they maintained their German identity and mixed harmoniously with their fellow Germans, whether in trade-union activity or singing societies or other German cultural events." The German Jews' greatest religious disputes occurred not with Christians but with their fellow Jews. The early German Jewish immigrants brought with them the ideas and worship of Reform Judaism, which originated in Germany in the late eighteenth century and sought to combine Judaism with Enlightenment tenets of reason and science. Reform doctrines and practices clashed with the Orthodoxy that reigned in New York. The city's first Reform synagogue, Temple Emanu-El, founded in 1845, participated in protracted debates about doctrine and worship. Thanks to German Jewish immigrants, by the middle of the nineteenth century New York held a quarter of the Jewish population of the United States, half of the city's Jews were Germans, and New York was the center of the nation's Jewish intellectual life.[76]

Since the 1840s, an alternative to church or synagogue affiliation for Germans, particularly among intellectuals and social reformers, were the Frei Gemeinden, the Freethinkers. Anticlerical and often openly hostile to religion, such groups devoted themselves to promoting ethical principles derived from rational rather than spiritual sources. Despite their nonreligious stance, Freethinkers organized themselves along lines similar to mainline religion, holding "meetings" on Sunday mornings and conducting Sunday and day schools. Their membership never exceeded a few thousand, but the numbers of distinguished German Americans among them heightened their influence, particularly during the 1840s and 1850s. The Frei Gemeinden approach to ethical behavior continues to be espoused today by the Ethical Culture Society, founded in 1876 by Felix Adler, a member of New York City's German Jewish community.[77]

The city's German newspapers and magazines reflected the heterogeneity of New York's German Americans. In one two-year period, 1850–1852, twenty-eight German-language papers could be found in the city.[78] The most influential German-language paper was the secular, pro-Democrat *Staats-Zeitung*, established in 1834, followed the next year by the Whig-leaning *Allgemeine Zeitung*. The emerging Republican party of the 1850s had the support of the *Demokrat* and the *Abendzeitung*.[79] The market for German-language publications was fluid, varied, and competitive.[80]

Lodges, mutual-aid societies, militia companies, and ethnically oriented bars were common among immigrant groups, but Germans stood out for the scope and variety of their communal activities—from local bars to the Stadttheater (opened on the Bowery in 1854) to mammoth beer gardens where whole families gathered. In 1848, Ferdinand Maximilian Schaefer introduced New York to lager beer, with its special fermentation process and distinctly crisp flavor. Its popularity soon spread beyond German neighborhoods, pushing aside the British ales that had been part of the city's diet since the colonial period.[81]

At the very heart of German social life in New York City were the vast numbers of fraternal lodges and *vereine*, or associations, sponsored by occupational groups, German regional organizations, and churches. The variety of *vereine* was staggering. Most common were the sickness and benefit societies, but there were also *vereine* dedicated to singing, literature, amateur dramatics, and shooting (*schutzenvereine*). Political refugees of the 1848 revolutions sponsored gymnastic societies, the *Turnvereine*, which combined physical fitness with active support of the free-soil and abolitionist movements. Socialists among the Forty-Eighters established the New Yorker Socialistischer Turnverein, which added to the agenda the promotion of Marxism and trade unionism.[82]

The public events of German associations became a distinct part of the city's festival life. The Scots, the Welsh, and the Irish also had their field days, but these German *volksfests* were truly special. Sunday performances of singing and dramatic groups attracted hundreds. In their leisure time and performances, German immigrants brought to New York new forms of pleasure and expressiveness that included both men and women. Exuberant yet orderly, their mixing of men, women, and alcohol contrasted sharply with native-born middle-class standards of propriety. The *Tribune* covered with fascination and approval a *Turnverein* festival that drew 12,000 to the Harlem Pleasure Gardens in the spring of 1856.

The pleasures of the festival consisted in an enormous straining of enormous muscles on the part of the Turners, who had gymnastic apparatus erected for their accommodation; in listening to very tolerable music from a number of German bands, and to an intermittent thunder-storm of singing from a dozen German song-societies; in irregular waltzing on rather rough grass-plots; in watching eighty starred policemen and a number of shadows eagerly initiating themselves into all German customs, as they had little else to do; in sitting on the grass and talking to one's friends—German women are not afraid to sit on the grass . . . and last and greatest in drinking lager beer. . . . The amber nectar flowed in a thousand streams.[83]

New York Germans also transformed the city's commercial life. Opportunities provided by an expanding economy enabled a number of German Americans from rather humble backgrounds to make spectacular advances. "Brewer princes" like Jacob Ruppert and Max Schaefer, the piano manufacturer Henry Steinway and his sons, and the rubber magnate Conrad Poppenhusen all became prominent before 1860. Many German Jewish financiers, with names such as Straus, Guggenheim, Kuhn, Loeb, and Lehman, started out as peddlers and merchants. Some enterprising dry-goods peddlers invested their earnings in retail clothing stores and later turned to manufacturing inexpensive, ready-to-wear clothing.[84]

The economic dynamism that encouraged peddlers to become retail store-owners had different consequences for workers. Early in the 1850s, while New York's economy was booming, there was considerable cooperation among the immigrant workers as they struck for higher wages and shorter hours. During the massive tailors' strike of 1850, for example, there was class unity between German and Irish workers. However, a downturn in the economy beginning in 1854 and culminating in the Panic of 1857 proved disastrous to organized labor and exacerbated ethnic and racial tensions. Language difficulties and the hostility of native-born and Irish workers toward Germans in the 1850s prompted German workers to form separate German trade unions.[85]

Conflicts between labor and capital within the German community during the antebellum period attracted the attention of radical and utopian thinkers. Among the more prominent was Wilhelm Weitling, who arrived in New York in 1847. Two years later his Arbeitbund (Workers' League) was organized to promote a brand of communism strongly influenced by Charles Fourier, the French utopian socialist. Weitling envisioned a system of producer and consumer cooperative schemes, advocated public education, and critiqued nationalism. By 1852, New York's German artisans had grown weary of Weitling's notions, which seemed far removed from their immediate interests in higher wages and improved working conditions. The idea of producer cooperatives did, however, have considerable appeal in Kleindeutschland, and some were actually launched. They were doomed, however, by weak support for such projects among non-German trade unionists and the founders' lack of capital and managerial training.[86]

More lasting in its impact on New York's German workers was the Marxian socialism introduced into the city by Forty-Eighter refugees, most notably Joseph Weydemeyer. After arriving from Germany in 1851, Weydemeyer worked closely with German trade union leaders to establish the *Allgemeiner Arbeitbund* (later *Amerikanisher Arbeitbund*), a party whose platform combined the goals of socialism and trade unionism. Wisely, he added objectives particularly dear to German sensibilities, such as resistance to "Sunday" laws and temperance legislation. When Weydemeyer left the city to settle in the Midwest in 1856, the movement was salvaged by Frederick Sorge, a refugee who had fought in the 1849 uprising in Baden. Sorge formed a Communist Club in Manhattan and shortly thereafter brought the organization into Marx's International Workingmen's Association.[87]

Many German radicals did not necessarily recognize women as their equals. Like other American men of their time, they believed that "the family was sacred," thought that the task of women in the movement was to be men's helpmates, and consigned women to the domestic sphere. Nevertheless, German women established a separate group within the socialist camp and tried to place their issues on the movement's agenda.[88]

✳ ✳ ✳

The presence of the Irish and Germans was complemented by the presence of other immigrant groups from Britain and Europe. Scots frequented taverns like the Burns House, read the *Scottish Patriot*, and attended Presbyterian churches.[89] Welsh New Yorkers, eager to preserve their language and customs, published the first Welsh newspaper in the United States, the *Cymro American*, in New York in 1832. The elite among New York's English immigrants celebrated Queen Victoria's birthday and organized several London-style social clubs, the most esteemed being the St. George's Society. Those less high up in the social order found conviviality at one of the handful of English-style pubs.[90]

Irish Protestants, called Orangemen for their allegiance to the Protestantism of William of Orange, who had assumed the English throne in 1689, saw themselves as a people apart from the city's growing number of Irish Catholics. These Protestant Irish, mostly from Ulster, brought their Orange Order to the city as early as the 1820s.[91] Orangemen celebrated Boyne Day on July 12, marking the anniversary of William of Orange's victory over King James II at the Battle of the Boyne in 1690, which ensured Protestant ascendancy in Great Britain and Ireland. To flaunt their feelings of triumph over Irish Catholics, on Boyne Day in 1824 Orangemen marched in a predominantly Irish Catholic neighborhood with banners waving. A street brawl broke out between the two factions of Irishmen.[92]

By 1860, the 8,074 French, who constituted the city's fourth-largest immigrant group and who had few laborers or destitute among them, were found in greatest numbers along the Hudson River wards, Washington Square, near Fifth Avenue in the fifties, and on the East Side above Tenth Street. In the years after 1830, small numbers of immigrants arrived from Switzerland, the Netherlands, Bohemia, and the Scandinavian countries. These immigrants tended to locate in the East Side wards, some of them in areas dominated by other national groups with similar linguistic roots: French-speaking Swiss among the French, German-speaking Swiss and Dutch among the Germans.[93]

The city's immigrants even included a few from those ethnic groups who would dominate migration patterns by the early twentieth century. The first Greeks, for example, arrived as refugees from the turmoil of the Greek War for Independence in the 1820s and were followed by merchants who settled in Lower Manhattan after 1870. Poles also numbered among the early arrivals. By 1852, there were enough to create a Polish Democratic Club with two hundred members. The first arrivals from Italy, mainly from northern Italy, found housing in and around the Five Points. The city's first Chinese immigrants also appeared during this era, but their numbers were small. A census taken in 1855 recorded thirty-eight Chinese men living in Lower Manhattan. Some were sailors, others, operators of boardinghouses, proprietors of small businesses, peddlers, or cigar makers. Some of these male settlers married Irish women, and a few even became American citizens. By 1873, the *New York Times* reported some five hundred Chinese were living in New York, about half of them in the emerging Chinatown of Lower Manhattan.[94]

✳ ✳ ✳

Rapid population growth, sharpened by immigration, pushed the boundary of the city's settled area ever northward. By 1865, paved and graded streets reached to Forty-Second Street, while housing was already available in sections of the east fifties. Beyond that frontier were the suburban Manhattan villages of Harlem, Bloomingdale (now the Upper West Side), and Yorkville (now the east eighties). So was born the commute to work, a journey made possible by advances in mass transportation: first twelve-passenger omnibuses, then horse-drawn railways, and finally the 1832 opening of the New York and Harlem Railroad. During the 1830s and 1840s, more and more of the buildings in Lower Manhattan were converted to commercial use as residents who could afford to moved uptown or to Brooklyn.[95]

Lower Manhattan as an area of residence was left to the thousands of immigrants pouring into the city. Lacking the funds to pay for uptown housing and the costs of daily transportation to work, they had to live within walking distance of their jobs at the East River docks, shipyards, and warehouses or the inland shops, factories, and commercial houses.

At first, most working-class immigrants lived on the East Side. During the 1820s, a core of Irish settlement developed in the Sixth Ward, roughly the area from City Hall north to Canal Street between Broadway and the Bowery. During this time, the Tenth and Eleventh Wards to the north and east of the Sixth had heavy enough concentrations of Germans to be called Kleindeutschland. With the huge influx of immigrants after 1840, however, neither the Irish nor the German neighborhoods were able to absorb all their recently arrived countrymen.

Irish or German residents might dominate particular buildings or streets, but overall there was no ethnic homogeneity in New York's wards. The Sixth Ward was strongly associated with the Irish, but in 1855 it held "approximately fourteen thousand Irish, fifty-two hundred Germans, twelve hundred English and Scotch, one thousand Italians and Polish, and fifteen hundred persons of other nationalities." The New York State Census of 1855 demonstrates that the largest percentage of foreign-born residents resided in the Sixth Ward and the adjacent Fourth Ward on the East River, yet even there 30 percent of the population was native born.[96]

Nonetheless, the presence of German and Irish immigrants was strongly felt in certain wards. In 1855, the Irish constituted 46 percent of the population of the First Ward, 45.6 percent of the Fourth Ward, and 42.4 percent of the Sixth Ward, while the Germans dominated the Tenth, Eleventh, and Seventeenth Wards with 30.3 percent, 33.6 percent, and 27.3 percent respectively.[97]

To house these immigrants and to reap the huge profits from ever-rising land values and skyrocketing rents, landlords converted single-family homes into dwellings for multiple families. A small brick row house that might have once held one middle-class family, spread out over three rooms, now held three immigrant families—one in each room.[98] A city inspector's report in 1834 found "many mercenary landlords who only contrive in what manner they can stow the greatest number of human beings in the smallest space."[99]

By the mid-1840s a more "efficient" style of multifamily dwelling, the tenement, appeared in the city and spread. A report by the Council on Hygiene described a typical midcentury tenement as "a structure of rough brick, standing on a lot twenty five by one hundred feet; it is from four to six stories high, and is so divided internally as to contain four families on each floor—each family eating, drinking, sleeping, cooking, washing and fighting in a room eight feet by ten, and a bedroom six feet by ten."[100] Tenements, most of which were dreadfully cramped,[101] came to house most immigrants. By 1864, the Council on Hygiene reported that there were already 495,592 people living in 15,309 tenements in New York City. Their numbers continued to grow.[102]

Although indoor plumbing, central heating, and gaslight had begun to appear in better housing as early as the 1840s, not until the 1860s could tenement dwellers expect the luxury of one water spigot per floor, and that was only in the newest structures. Before the 1860s—and long after for most tenement dwellers—water had to be carried up from street pumps or wells located in the yards close by the outdoor privies. Beginning in 1852, a popular philanthropic endeavor was to establish public bathhouses in the congested immigrant districts of the city. The first of these was the People's Washing and Bathing Establishment on Mott Street.[103]

Rents in tenements depended on the amount of light and ventilation in an apartment. While single rooms in the dark interior of the building could be had for as little as seventy-five cents a week, apartments with windows could rent for as much as thirteen dollars a month. Most primitive of all tenement accommodations were cellar apartments, where more than 29,000 newcomers to America dwelt in 1850.[104]

To help make ends meet, immigrant families took in paying boarders, usually unattached young men and women. Boarders brought income to a family, but they often made cramped dwellings even more crowded. More popular, particularly for single men, were boardinghouses.[105] Though hardly luxurious, boardinghouses were generally clean and offered decent food, the companionship of fellow boarders, and a degree of privacy. Rent in better boardinghouses was usually higher than that charged by families who took in boarders. An 1857 description of one such establishment for eighty male boarders indicates that the living quarters were cramped but clean and that the food was plain but abundant. A Sunday dinner there included meat, potatoes, cabbage, and squash eaten in an atmosphere of joviality. Saturday evenings were given over to cards, board games, and dominoes, and once a year the lodgers held a dance, complete with orchestra.[106]

As a general rule, boardinghouse residents shared a common language: there were German boardinghouses, French boardinghouses, and those where Irish, Scots, and other English-speaking immigrant workers lodged.[107] As might be expected in this diverse city, in 1855 one Sixth Ward house owned by a German couple housed twenty-one male lodgers, including fourteen Germans, three Irishmen, two Dutchmen, one Frenchman, and one Hungarian.[108]

✳✳

New York's leap from small town to major metropolis in just a few decades overwhelmed the city's municipal services. Prior to 1866, roaming hogs served as the city's principal garbage collectors, but the pigs brought health problems. Those who operated "piggeries" fought against any legislation to remove the foul-smelling pigs from the streets or to curtail operations of their businesses.

The reformers were not immediately successful. The battle to rid New York of swine lasted for years.[109]

Immigrant residents of tenement districts were at higher risk of sickness and subject to periodic outbreaks of diseases brought on by filth and impure water: typhoid, dysentery, and typhus. From 1849 to 1859, when the Irish constituted 53.9 percent of the city's foreign-born population, 85 percent of the foreign-born patients admitted to Bellevue Hospital were Irish.[110]

Cholera, which the historian Charles Rosenberg calls "the classic epidemic disease of the nineteenth century," struck the city in 1832, 1849, and 1866.[111] Immigrants, living in crowded and unsanitary conditions where the waterborne disease spread easily, bore the brunt of the outbreaks. They were also blamed for their own vulnerability to the illness. During the first cholera outbreak in 1832, before the scientific bases of diseases were discovered and made known, it was widely assumed that cholera victims were the recipients of God's punishment for their intemperate ways. A Board of Health report on the epidemic stated that "the low Irish suffered the most, being exceedingly dirty in their habits, much addicted to intemperance, and crowded together into the worst portions of the city."[112] Indeed, among the immigrants the Irish—being the most numerous, weakest upon arrival in the city, and comparatively poorer—suffered the most. In 1849, Irish-born residents (about one-quarter of the city's population) represented more than 40 percent of the city's death toll from cholera.[113]

Not until the completion of the Croton Aqueduct in 1842 did clean water begin to flow into the city, and not until 1849 did the government begin to build a municipal sewer system. Yet even after municipal services were instituted, it often took years before the improvements were felt in the poorer districts. For example, in 1857 the sewer system served but 138 miles of the city's nearly five hundred miles of streets.[114] In 1865, when forty-five of ninety tenants in a building on First Avenue contracted typhoid fever, which spread through contaminated food and water or close physical contact, the investigating police surgeon found that the tenement's outdoor privies were in dilapidated condition, "less than six feet from the house," and "not connected with a sewer."[115]

Investigations of tenement houses by city and state bodies, the private Citizens' Association of New York, and the Association for Improving the Condition of the Poor (AICP) documented appalling conditions and called for reform legislation. Such crowding, declared the AICP, "breaks down the barriers of self-respect, and prepares the way for direct profligacy." Their efforts to aid the poor immigrants led to the enactment of the Tenement House Law of 1867, a measure with low standards that nonetheless was a first step toward housing reform.[116]

Manhattan had no distinct racial ghetto before the Civil War, but the limited incomes of African Americans pushed them into some of the city's worst housing. Among the city's poor, blacks and whites frequently resided in the

2.2 The Five Points, 1827: rough, rowdy, and interracial.

Source: Museum of the City of New York.

same blocks and sometimes occupied apartments in the same tenements. On occasion, black families took in white boarders.[117]

The best-known slum in New York City was the Five Points—so named because it was at the juncture of Anthony, Orange, Cross, Mulberry, and Little Water streets, at the edge of the Lower East Side and a short distance from City Hall. The land was rural in the early eighteenth century, and the bucolic Collect Pond was the area's scenic attraction. By the 1790s, however, the area had become a center for slaughterhouses and tanneries. The Collect Pond grew so polluted that it was drained and covered over. By the 1830s, the Five Points was well known for economic inequality, crowding, and prostitution. The Old Brewery captured in one building the poverty and congestion of the district: converted into a tenement in 1837, it housed as many as a thousand residents before it was torn down in 1852.[118]

Charles Dickens confirmed the neighborhood's fame when he described his visit to the Five Points in 1842: "This is the place, these narrow ways, diverging to the right and left, and reeking everywhere with filth. . . . Here too, are lanes and alleys, paved with mud knee-deep . . . ruined houses, open to the street, whence, through wide gaps in the walls, other ruins loom upon the eye . . . hideous tenements . . . all that is loathsome, drooping, and decayed is here."[119]

Within the Five Points, a section known as Cow Bay was famous for being the home of both the Irish and African American poor. Typhus fever, small-pox, tuberculosis, pneumonia, and bronchitis were all too common among the city poor, black and white. Cholera devastated the Five Points in 1832.[120]

* * *

The poverty Dickens found in the Five Points was real, but it was only one aspect of that complex and culturally fertile neighborhood. In the Five Points, the social mixing of Irish and African Americans led to racist charges of amalga-mation and the swapping of dance steps and musical styles that produced extraordinary hybrids. At a hall under African American management called Almack's, Dickens witnessed the performance of William Henry Lane, also known as "Master Juba." Dickens was mesmerized: "Single shuffle, double shuf-fle, cut and cross-cut; snapping his fingers, rolling his eyes, turning in his knees, presenting the backs of his legs in front, spinning about on his toes and heels like nothing but the man's fingers on the tambourine; dancing with two left legs, two right legs, two wooden legs, two wire legs, two spring legs-all sorts of legs and no legs—what is this to him?"[121]

Master Juba's kind of footwork would evolve into what is today known as tap dancing. An equally important form of performance, blackface minstrelsy, emerged in the 1840s in the theaters near the Five Points. In minstrelsy, white men put on blackface makeup to sing, dance, joke, and present short plays. Min-strelsy was indelibly shaped by white supremacy, but its instrumental music, using fiddles and banjos, and its dance steps were powerfully influenced by Afri-can American styles. Blackface was a mask that white men put on to comment on the issues of their day and to express both their feelings of racial superiority and their fascination with aspects of African American culture. It was, in the words of Eric Lott, a case of "love and theft." Minstrelsy never transcended its origins in a racist culture, but in specific minstrel performances it was possible to glimpse a melding of black and white rhythms and sounds, raucous expres-sions of plebeian experiences, and a recognition of African American human-ity that would eventually characterize the best in American popular culture. Minstrelsy, like the Five Points, absorbed and expressed the best and worst to be found in Lower Manhattan.[122]

* * *

For African Americans, the cultural dynamism of the Five Points did not trans-late into political power. Despite the hardships that Irish and German immi-grants found at home and at work, they were white in a city and state where white men, even poor and working-class men, had the vote by the 1820s. Black men could vote only if they met a severe property requirement that effectively disenfranchised them. For both Irish and Germans, however, the route to electoral politics and power was comparatively open.

The loyalty of the Irish to the Democratic Party and Tammany Hall evolved over time. In Tammany's early days, as it evolved from a fraternal lodge to a political machine, it claimed to represent the interests of the city's workingmen against both aristocratic privilege and foreign competition. Such competition included immigrant laborers as well as imported goods. By the 1820s, however, politics were changing in a more democratic direction. When New York's constitutional convention of 1821 did away with the property requirement for white male voters, it enabled increasing numbers of poor Irishmen to become voters capable of swinging municipal elections. The rising tide of immigration, along with the Jacksonian democratization of politics (illustrated by the election of a mayor by popular vote beginning in 1834), led Tammany to jettison its nativist stance. The Democratic Party shifted from tolerating immigrants to wooing them.[123] At the same time, as shops gave way to factories and as unskilled and semiskilled laborers replaced craftsmen as the numerically dominant representatives of the working class, urban politics also changed. Richard Stott describes how

> a new and distinctively working-class style of politics began to emerge in the 1840s and 1850s. Related to change taking place in working-class life, it paid attention less to ideology than to the personal qualities of political leaders. Pugilists came to dominate working-class politics in the city, and elections themselves became stormy, brawling affairs. At the same time, also, the saloon emerged as central to the city's political life.[124]

The stage was set for the Irish arrival in New York City politics.

The Irish, with their history of opposition to oppressive landlords and British rule, came to America with a tradition of political involvement. Experiences with popular demonstrations, mass meetings, and other forms of political action on behalf of Irish Catholic causes were readily applied in New York City politics.[125] The Irish in New York knew well how to use their saloons and street gangs for Tammany. In return, Tammany expedited naturalization; protected saloon keepers from overzealous enforcers of closing laws; opposed nativism and prohibition; hosted picnics, balls, river excursions, and other social events; and, most importantly, provided jobs for Tammany supporters. A legion of lamplighters, fire wardens, meat inspectors, policemen, laborers, and contractors all knew that their livelihoods depended on Tammany victories at the polls.[126]

In time, politically minded Irish demanded more substantial rewards, including public office or a place in the Democratic leadership. The most

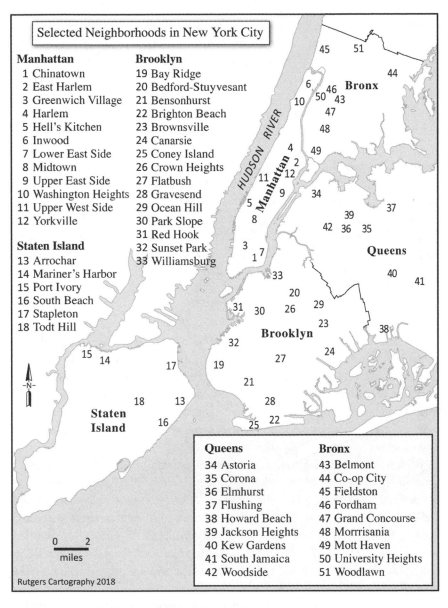

Selected Neighborhoods in New York City

Manhattan
1 Chinatown
2 East Harlem
3 Greenwich Village
4 Harlem
5 Hell's Kitchen
6 Inwood
7 Lower East Side
8 Midtown
9 Upper East Side
10 Washington Heights
11 Upper West Side
12 Yorkville

Staten Island
13 Arrochar
14 Mariner's Harbor
15 Port Ivory
16 South Beach
17 Stapleton
18 Todt Hill

Brooklyn
19 Bay Ridge
20 Bedford-Stuyvesant
21 Bensonhurst
22 Brighton Beach
23 Brownsville
24 Canarsie
25 Coney Island
26 Crown Heights
27 Flatbush
28 Gravesend
29 Ocean Hill
30 Park Slope
31 Red Hook
32 Sunset Park
33 Williamsburg

Queens
34 Astoria
35 Corona
36 Elmhurst
37 Flushing
38 Howard Beach
39 Jackson Heights
40 Kew Gardens
41 South Jamaica
42 Woodside

Bronx
43 Belmont
44 Co-op City
45 Fieldston
46 Fordham
47 Grand Concourse
48 Morrrisania
49 Mott Haven
50 University Heights
51 Woodlawn

Rutgers Cartography 2018

2.3 Selected neighborhoods in New York City.

Source: Robert W. Snyder collection.

successful of these was Mike Walsh, an Ireland-born journalist who in 1840 formed his partisans into "the Spartan Band" and three years later established a weekly newspaper, *The Subterranean*. Walsh, a talented public speaker, called for more attention to workers' rights and wider participation for workingmen within the Democratic Party. He acted the gadfly at political meetings, virtually forcing himself on Tammany's leaders, who finally nominated and helped elect him to the state assembly in 1846. In 1850, Walsh won election to the U.S. House of Representatives, where he remained until his death in 1859.[127]

Germans, with their wide religious, regional, and class differences, found their own pathways into the electoral system. Unlike the Irish, who became a strong presence within the Democratic Party, Germans were spread across parties. Within individual political organizations, Germans might act as an ethnic bloc and thereby gain leverage. In the grand strategy of New York politics, however, Tammany could never count on the Germans in the way it counted on the Irish. As a consequence, German New Yorkers never received the political rewards that strict party loyalty earned for the Irish.

* * *

To African American New Yorkers, the waves of immigrants who arrived after 1830 brought unwelcome labor competition. Immigrants desperate for work took whatever jobs were available, often at the expense of blacks. Though the numbers of African Americans were too small to offer much competition to immigrants, in some occupations the two groups clashed. Conflict occurred over securing positions as house servants, barbers, stevedores, brick makers, and coachmen.[128]

Both African Americans and immigrants, especially the Irish, believed that each stood in the way of the other's opportunities, and the occasional use of black strikebreakers aggravated a tense situation. In 1854, employers replaced striking white longshoremen with blacks, only to discharge them when the strike failed.[129] A few years later, economic conflicts with racial overtones led to violence in Brooklyn. One tobacco factory there employed a mixed labor force, but when another hired only African Americans, a mob of angry whites burned it.[130]

African American men usually held laboring or service jobs, which paid little. By the Civil War, a few had achieved middle-class levels, typically as small businessmen, teachers, ministers, or in food service. But contrary to the fear that blacks would drive whites out of jobs, large-scale immigration meant that blacks in New York lost some of their better-paying positions. Discrimination was too great in the city for blacks to achieve better employment.

For black women, the situation was even worse. Although some white women were employed in manufacturing, black women were shut out of these jobs. In

1860, the largest job category for black women was servant, but with the immigration of Irish women such positions became harder to find. Black women could easily find employment, however, doing others' laundry—and poverty pushed them to seize the job. Over one half of black women, compared to only 10 percent of white women, were in the paid labor force. African American women had virtually no choice about working.[131]

Neither the state nor the city of New York passed codes segregating their black citizens, but African Americans still found themselves barred from public facilities. Blacks did use the city's horse-drawn streetcars at times, but treatment varied. Some companies refused African Americans permission to ride, while others allowed them to travel on a separate outside platform, regardless of the weather. Angered by their treatment, individual African Americans organized a Legal Rights Association and took transit companies to court. After Elizabeth Jennings, a black woman on her way to church, was injured when she was forcibly ejected from the Third Avenue omnibus in 1854, she sued and won damages. Her counsel was Chester A. Arthur, future president of the United States. Similar suits against the Sixth and Eighth Avenue lines won changes in transit policy; by the time of the Civil War, most of these public conveyances admitted African Americans.[132]

During the antebellum period, blacks were regularly ejected from the ferry connecting Manhattan and Brooklyn and kept out of most theaters, restaurants, and places of public amusement. Frederick Douglass said that on the Hudson River steamers blacks were "compelled sometimes to stroll the deck nearly all night, before they can get a place to lie down, and that place frequently unfit for a dog's accommodation."[133]

Although a few black children did attend white schools, New Yorkers largely segregated their public and private schools. The Manumission Society founded the first African Free School in 1787 and organized several others for newly freed blacks before transferring their control and management to the privately operated New York Public School Society in 1834. During the 1850s, these "colored schools" became part of the city's newly created public school system. Through these years, the schools taught basic elementary education, stressed moral uplift, and operated on a racially segregated basis. African Americans also operated several schools of their own from time to time, but these ventures lacked adequate financing to survive.[134]

The situation across the river in Brooklyn was similar. African Americans apparently attended some mixed schools until the 1820s, when segregation became more rigid and black Brooklynites established their own schools. When a public school system was created, black schools were placed under white control but continued to employ black teachers.[135] In both New York and Brooklyn, black public schools were underfunded and black teachers paid lower salaries than their white colleagues. Prejudice dictated that black education, no matter how thorough, did not lead to good jobs. Most African American students left at an early age to seek employment. An African American New Yorker commented in 1859, "It is a common complaint of colored teachers that their pupils are taken from school at the very time when their studies become most useful and attractive."[136]

New York's African Americans fought back against racial injustice, developing their own organizations in the struggle. In the words of Manisha Sinha, "New York's African American fraternal organizations, benevolent societies and churches, like those elsewhere in the North, were preeminent sites not only of black leadership but also of mass participation." The most important African American organization was the church. There, ministers could speak openly about discrimination in the city and about the millions of enslaved African Americans in the South. Black churches were active in the abolitionist movement and ran charities for orphans. The Rev. Samuel Cornish served for twenty years on the executive committee of the American Anti-Slavery Society, while other ministers joined similar antislavery groups. Cornish, along with John Russwurm, also founded the nation's first black newspaper, *Freedom's Journal*. Black church women organized, raised money for the cause of freedom, and sued the Third Avenue omnibus for discrimination. By the 1850s, African American women had formed over a dozen organizations to address their concerns.[137]

On the streets, free blacks claimed a presence in everything from individual displays of style to grand celebrations of emancipation. As the historian Shane White writes:

> The pageantry of a black procession, over a thousand strong, striding out down Broadway, flourishing banners and slogans; the style of a black dandy, immaculately turned out, leaning against a post on the Battery and checking the time on his fob watch with a nonchalant flick of the wrist; the spectacle of strikingly dressed black men and women alighting from their carriages on Orange Street as they arrived for the African Ball for the benefit of Greek freedom; the theater of an insouciant black defendant ragging a pompous magistrate in the police station; the panache of a rollicking crowd of black men and women moving to the relentless beat in a sweaty, smoky dance cellar—all of these and more bold public displays helped define the meaning of African American freedom in New York.[138]

Black New Yorkers were beset by both local inequalities and the massive reality of New York City's links to the South and its economy of enslaved labor. As the biggest city in the United States and its premier port, New York was the site of the North's largest free black community and a place of business for Southern planters. Fugitives from slavery and slave catchers, abolitionists and their opponents all made their way to New York City. Their different imperatives made the city volatile and dangerous for African Americans.

In 1838, when Frederick Douglass arrived in New York fleeing slavery in a Baltimore shipyard, another fugitive warned him of the city's "slave catchers," who kidnapped blacks off the streets regardless of their legal status and sold them into bondage. In turn, a black seaman directed Douglass to David Ruggles, who assisted fugitives from slavery and worked to thwart slave catchers. Ruggles helped Douglass get married, gave him some money, and directed him to New Bedford, Massachusetts—a seaport with many free blacks and a strong abolitionist movement where a man fleeing from slavery would be safer. Douglass moved on to New Bedford and eventually became one of the foremost journalists and abolitionists in American history.[139]

Douglass's arrival in New York as part of his own exodus was logical; so was his departure. New York was a prime destination for fugitives who had fled slavery by stowing away on a coastal vessel or bribing a captain to take them north: the city's transportation links made it a good jumping-off point for safer places farther north. At the same time, the city's slave catchers, its history of riots against abolitionists, and the presence of enslaved men accompanying visiting Southern slave owners limited New York's appeal.

New York had its own abolitionist movement, led by African Americans like Ruggles, a secretary and an energetic presence in the New York Committee of Vigilance, and also by whites. White abolitionists tended to be either Quakers or evangelical Protestants of a reformist bent, like the Tappan brothers, Arthur and Lewis, who were wealthy merchants. The affluence of some white abolitionists did not endear them to white workers with little money. And in a city with many Catholic immigrants, the Protestant aura of abolition limited the movement's appeal. Catholics also saw in abolition the threat of revolution and a challenge to property rights. Despite these tensions between the movement and the city, abolitionists offered quiet aid to fugitives, launched legal proceedings against slavery, and organized large demonstrations against returning people to bondage. New York was also a significant stop on the Underground Railroad, the network of antislavery activists that helped people escape to freedom.[140]

While African American New Yorkers benefited from having white abolitionists as allies, the 1850s marked a turning point. The Fugitive Slave Act of 1850 strengthened the hand of slave catchers and stoked fears that free blacks would be captured, enslaved, and sent to the cotton kingdom. Free African Americans in New York and other northern cities knew "they were in constant danger of enslavement."[141] A second blow for free blacks was the 1857 Dred Scot decision of the U.S. Supreme Court, which held that blacks had no rights that white people had to acknowledge.

New York had long been embedded in the political economy of slavery. As late as 1860, ships sailing from New York transported enslaved Africans from

Africa to slaveholding Cuba. But as debates over human bondage heated up in the 1850s, the prospect of a national conflict over slavery threatened to destroy customary patterns of commerce and politics in New York City.[142]

* * *

The Democratic Party, whose strong Southern wing upheld slavery, enjoyed two bases of support in New York City: immigrants who appreciated Democratic opposition to nativism and elite businessmen who wanted to preserve the city's links to the slavery-driven cotton economy of the South. New York City was less than congenial, however, to the new and growing Republican Party, which was committed to limiting the spread of slavery. The Republicans were officially antinativist, as the historian James M. McPherson has observed, but they "took on some of the cultural baggage of nativism" as they became "the party of reformist, anti-slavery Protestantism" and "dynamic, innovative capitalism." To many Republicans, slavery and Roman Catholicism both stemmed from ways of life that were backward, ignorant, and repressive. Although the Republican Party was strong in upstate New York, it was weak in New York City, where its guiding ideas were especially unattractive to many Irish Catholics.[143]

During the 1850s, opposition to slavery—or at least the spread of slavery—among German Forty-Eighters gave Republicans hope of making significant inroads in New York's German community. Although notable members of the city's Forty-Eighter population became Republicans, in the presidential election of 1856 the majority of German Americans voted for the victorious Democrat James Buchanan. The Democratic Party's traditional proimmigrant, antinativist stance and the association of some city Republicans with temperance, Sunday observance, and nativism dictated the outcome.[144] Buchanan turned out to be a weak president who was overwhelmed by the looming prospect of civil war. At the same time, New Yorkers were little inclined toward anything like racial equality. In 1860, a statewide bid to eliminate the property qualification for black males and place them on the same footing as white males for voting was rejected in New York City, 37,471 to 1,640.[145]

The turbulent year of 1857 revealed deep political and cultural fault lines in New York. A recession hit the city and then spread to the rest of the nation and Europe. Banks and other financial businesses collapsed. When unemployment rose in New York City and construction nearly stopped, workers claimed a right to work and demanded that the municipal government provide jobs. The unemployed mounted large demonstrations. The economy eventually improved, but rioting in the same year suggested that political and ethnic differences were reaching a boiling point. In 1856, Republicans had gained control of the state legislature and passed laws that required costly licensing fees and Sunday closings for New York's beer gardens and saloons, mainstays of life in immigrant

New York City. Fearful that the city's own police would not enforce such laws, the legislature established a new force composed of few immigrants and many nativists. When the new liquor laws went into effect in July 1857, attacks on policemen and fighting between rival gangs led to the "Bowery Boy Riot," which took twelve lives. German resistance to Sunday closings led to the loss of one life.[146]

* * *

Ethnic and political divisions within the city overlapped with national divisions over slavery. In the pivotal presidential election of 1860, waged over slavery and the threat of disunion, the Republican Abraham Lincoln faced three other candidates in a race fragmented along party and regional lines. Lincoln won the presidency; he carried New York State but lost New York City.[147] After Lincoln's victory, six states in the Deep South called conventions to discuss secession. In New York, Mayor Fernando Wood, mindful of his city's strong economic and political links to the South, proposed that New York secede from the Union. The idea failed in part because the provisional Confederate government seized the opportunity to establish lower tariffs and trade directly with Britain and Europe. Southern merchants also repudiated their debts to the North, in effect casting off their economic subordination to New York City.[148]

Once Lincoln entered the White House, tensions came to focus on the control of Fort Sumter, a federal installation in the harbor of Charleston, South Carolina, a secessionist hotbed. In the early hours of April 12, 1861, Confederate artillery began a bombardment that would end with the fort's surrender. The day after the firing started, an article in the *New York Herald* opened with the words "Civil war has begun!"[149]

CHAPTER 3

PROGRESS AND POVERTY: 1861–1900

P resident Abraham Lincoln's call for volunteers to put down the insurrection in the South sparked a massive rally in Union Square to support the war effort. As officers raised regiments and businessmen organized federal efforts to purchase arms and supplies, Emile Dupré, an immigrant German merchant, wrote to his parents in Braunschweig. "New York looks like an armed camp," he observed. "There are armed men everywhere, everyone carries a revolver, and we're living in an absolute torrent of commotion. Heaven knows how it will turn out. Both sides are deadly serious and will probably have to wear each other out before they can even think of settling their differences or making peace."[1]

Dupré considered enlisting, then backed off and established a successful career supplying the Union Army. Skeptical about the war but quick to see the business opportunities it offered, he moved between New York; Washington, DC; and Alexandria, Virginia, all the while noting the performance of German soldiers in the field and the promotions of German officers. Meanwhile, his brother enlisted and died of typhus. When the federal government instituted a draft, Dupré paid an African American man to serve in his place. As the war drew to a close, he wrote his parents from Brooklyn to say that he did not anticipate a permanent return to Germany: "In the 10 years I've been here I've made a lot of dear friends, in other words I have found a second homeland. After a hard struggle I am finally able to see a quieter future up ahead, and perhaps more than that; who knows? I don't know if I could be happy over there in all that peace and quietude after living in such exciting times over here." In 1866, with peace restored, Dupré capped his career by joining the Open Board of Stock Brokers, a rival to the New York Stock Exchange. Before the year was over he died, like his brother, from typhus.[2]

Dupré's success as a merchant was notable in the New York of German immigrants during the Civil War, but his experiences with quickened events, ethnic loyalties, and family tragedy were common. Although he suffered the loss of a brother, in business terms he had a good war. The same cannot be said of other immigrant New Yorkers, who experienced the wartime city as a place of hard times and bitter conflicts.

New York entered the Civil War a divided city in a divided state. The nativism, condescension, and anti-Catholicism of many New York Protestants infuriated Irish Catholics. Republicans (who were antislavery, expansive in their vision of federal power, and often native born and Protestant) confronted Democrats (who sought to limit federal power, were politically aligned with the slave-holding South, and were friendlier to immigrant Irish Catholics). The Democrats were strong in New York City, but Republicans held power upstate. In the state capital of Albany, Republicans used the state government to limit the city's powers.

The political mismatch between the city and state was complicated by the gulf between the city's rich and poor and the city's close economic ties to the slave-labor economy of the cotton-producing South. By 1860, the three previous decades in New York City had seen extraordinary economic and demographic growth that set off booms, busts, and rioting. What would the war bring to this city?

* * *

In the early days of the conflict, immigrant New York caught the city's martial spirit. Recruiting stations were set up throughout Kleindeutschland, and men enlisted in the Steuben Guard and the German Rifles. Members of the New York Socialistischen Turnverein so dominated the Twentieth Regiment New York State Volunteers that it was known as the Turner Regiment. The Garibaldi Guard and the Polish Legion also marched off to war.[3]

The Irish were conspicuous in their enthusiasm for military service. The Sixty-Ninth Regiment, blessed by Archbishop Hughes at St. Patrick's Cathedral, was only the most famous of the Irish units soon organized into the Irish Brigade commanded by Thomas Francis Meagher, an exiled Irish rebel. Irishmen enlisted for reasons beyond rations and pay. By donning uniforms they hoped to silence nativist charges of disloyalty, strike a blow against the English cotton lords allied with the South, and gain military experience that they might use one day in the cause of Irish freedom.[4]

African American men also sought to join the Union cause, but with different results. In May 1861, soon after Lincoln's call for troops, black New Yorkers

3.1 Irish New York at war: the 69th Regiment celebrates mass in Virginia, 1861.

Source: Library of Congress.

were drilling in a private hall. The city's police commissioner, who feared that their actions would spark "popular indignation and assault," ordered them to stop. In July of the same year, black New Yorkers offered the governor three regiments, with all necessary supplies and pay, for as long as the war lasted. He rejected them.[5] Overall, New York City would contribute one hundred thousand men to the Union army.[6] Equally important to the Union was New York's economic contribution to the war effort.

Secession severed New York's business ties with the South, but the city's merchants and bankers refocused their efforts and played a pivotal role in financing the war. Throughout the conflict, as Sven Beckert points out, the federal government worked with New York financiers to sell bonds and negotiate loans. The U.S. secretary of the treasury even traveled to New York City to meet the bankers and negotiate loans as the national debt grew fortyfold.[7]

Most New York industries prospered in the war, and both craftsmen and laborers found work. Shipyards built vessels for the Union Navy, manufacturers geared up to provide uniforms and supplies, and exports of wheat and beef surged through the harbor. Although Confederate raiders decimated the American merchant marine, leading shippers to use vessels of other nations, overall the war strengthened New York's position as the nation's premier port.[8]

Patriotism and profits could collide, however. When Brooks Brothers found itself short of cloth for making uniforms, it used shredded rags to create a substitute called "shoddy." Tailors complained that the firm was sending soldiers "suits of clothing that disgrace the State" and paying low wages. Brooks Brothers replaced the ersatz uniforms, but other contractors continued the practice. When soldiers wore the uniforms in the rain, they fell apart.[9]

During the war, New York's rich became richer and more numerous. Burrows and Wallace calculate that in 1863, the city's upper 1 percent of income earners (1,600 families) held 61 percent of New York's wealth. Over the course of the conflict, the number of millionaires in the city grew from "a few dozen" to "several hundred." Some were worth more than $20 million. Department stores, opera houses, theaters, restaurants, and bawdy houses competed for their dollars.[10]

The situation was different for working-class New York. As immigration declined and young men left the city for military service, there was a shortage of labor. Normally this would be expected to produce a rise in wages, but the war caused substantial inflation, and working-class families were unable to earn enough to compensate for rising prices for food and other necessities. By 1863, food prices had doubled and even tripled.[11]

Worst of all, casualties mounted. On the battlefields of Shiloh and Antietam, the carnage wrought by advances in weaponry surpassed anything seen in previous wars. At Fredericksburg, in December 1862, the Irish Brigade launched repeated attacks against Confederate troops stationed behind a stone wall at Marye's Heights. Of the 1,400 men who charged, 545 were killed or wounded. Observers recognized their courage, but the brigade's historian wrote, "It was not a battle, it was a wholesale slaughter of human beings."[12]

* * *

On January 1, 1863, Lincoln issued the Emancipation Proclamation, which freed all slaves in portions of the Confederacy that were not occupied by Union forces. The war to preserve the Union had become a fight to end slavery, a move that would prove controversial in New York City.[13]

In March 1863, the Lincoln administration, faced with growing war-weariness and declining enlistments for military service, enacted a draft. Under the law, a man faced with conscription could hire a substitute or buy his way out of service with the payment of a $300 bounty—as J. P. Morgan did. The blatant inequality of the draft prompted much anger among poor and working-class New Yorkers.[14]

To many Irish workingmen, it seemed that the war to preserve the Union had become a crusade to uplift African Americans at their expense. Antiwar politicians and newspapers fed this resentment. Benjamin Wood of the *Daily*

News (the brother of former mayor Fernando Wood and a sharp critic of the Lincoln administration) argued that the draft "would compel the white laborer to leave his family destitute and unprotected while he goes forth to free the negro, who, being free, will compete with him in labor." Irish laborers in particular feared the possibility of freed slaves flocking northward to threaten their livelihoods. During the war, Archbishop Hughes warned Secretary of War Cameron that Catholics would fight for the nation and the Constitution but not to free the slaves: "Indeed they will turn away in disgust from the discharge of what would otherwise be a patriotic duty." As one African American New Yorker put it, it is "well known by both white and black that the Most Rev. Archbishop do hate the black race so much that he cannot bear them to come near him."[15]

On Saturday July 11, 1863, when authorities began the draft lottery in a building at Third Avenue and Forty-Sixth Street, responses were muted. When the call-up resumed on Monday, July 13, violence erupted. Firefighters and workers wrecked the draft office and set it aflame. Rioters cut down telegraph poles to disrupt communication and swarmed across the city, overwhelming the police. Some of their targets suggested the rioters' antipathy to the rich and Republicans, whom they blamed for the war and the draft. Rioters chased rich men on the streets and vowed to burn the home of the president of Columbia College, a notable Republican. Mobs threatened the offices of newspapers associated with Republicans, like the *New York Times* and Horace Greeley's *Tribune*. The *Times* armed its staff with rifles and Gatling guns. The *Tribune* was saved by policemen, who charged with nightsticks to drive off successive attacks. An angry crowd attacked Brooks Brothers for being an unfair employer. Several other Republican businesses came under assault. Expressing a wartime surge in anti-Semitism, crowds attacked Jewish-owned stores on Grand Street.[16]

Before the riot was one day old, the rioters identified their ultimate prey: black New Yorkers. A mob pillaged and burned the Colored Orphan Asylum at Fifth Avenue and Forty-Third Street, forcing aside firefighters who tried to quell the blaze. The children at the orphanage narrowly escaped to a police station, with the older children carrying the younger ones. Rioters beat and lynched African American men. Boardinghouses where black men lived and the homes of African American families were sacked and torched. Crowds attacked African American prostitutes and assaulted black men married to white women.[17]

African Americans lived in enclaves scattered around the city: in the Five Points, in southern Greenwich Village, and along Sixth Avenue in the west twenties and thirties. Their numbers were large enough to make them conspicuous but generally too few to mount an effective defense. Blacks fled to police stations, to Long Island or New Jersey, to Upper Manhattan, or to the African

3.2 William Jones, an African American, was lynched on Clarkson Street in Greenwich Village during the 1863 Draft Riots.

Source: New York Public Library.

American settlement at Weeksville in Brooklyn. Where circumstances allowed, they banded together to defend themselves. In Minetta Lane, in Greenwich Village, blacks kept watch from rooftops and sang psalms to maintain morale.[18]

The fighting ripped through immigrant New York. The rioters were overwhelmingly Irish, but Irishmen could be found on both sides of the battle lines. Archbishop John Hughes, aging and infirm, issued a statement imploring "all persons who love God and revere the holy Catholic religion" to "dissolve their bad associations with reckless men." Priests persuaded rioters not to burn the home of the president of Columbia College. One Paddy McCafferty led to safety children fleeing the destruction of the Colored Orphan Asylum. Militiamen of the Eleventh New York Volunteers under the command of Colonel Henry O'Brien used rifle fire to clear a mob from Second Avenue near East Thirty-Fourth Street. When O'Brien returned to the neighborhood to check the condition of his home there, he was beaten and tortured to death. In Kleindeutschland, the *Turnverein* and *schutzenverein* patrolled streets to quell disorder. Irish Catholic officers in the ranks of the metropolitan police held firm,[19] but in the end New York City's own forces of order were inadequate against the mobs. It took the arrival of Union troops to rout the rioters with rifle fire and bayonets. By Friday, the upheaval that began on Monday was over. The viciousness of the episode led to initial exaggerations of the death toll, but the best estimates calculate that some 119 people died. African Americans, shaken by the violence, left the city; their percentage of New York's population dropped by 20 percent.[20]

Tammany Hall worked to limit the impact of the draft on New York's restive white workers. Under the leadership of William M. Tweed, a Protestant of Scottish ancestry who had entered politics as a firefighter, Tammany aligned itself with prowar Democrats who wanted to preserve the Union but did not share the emancipatory vision of radical Republicans, abolitionists, and African Americans. Tammany condemned the rioting and supported the Union war effort; the district attorney who prosecuted rioters was a Tammany man. At the same time, Tammany sought to protect New York's working class from the blatant economic discrimination of the draft. Tweed had learned the importance of law and governmental structures as a municipal alderman and member of the House of Representatives. When New York established a fund to hire substitutes for poor men or municipal workers who were drafted—effectively removing the threat of conscription from working-class men who did not want to serve—Tweed sat on the board that dispensed the money.[21]

African American New Yorkers, on the other hand, received little in the way of justice. A Merchants Relief Committee raised money to help blacks who fled during the rioting, but no public funds were used to provide aid; a New York County plan to compensate victims for their lost property proved to be of little value. Upper-class New Yorkers, to show solidarity with African Americans, for a time made a point of hiring black servants instead of Irish ones. More substantially, after the Lincoln administration began to admit black men into the Union Army, Republicans in the Union League Club worked to establish the Twentieth Regiment United States Colored Troops. The African American regiment was cheered in March 1864 when it marched to war through the streets of Lower Manhattan. A year later, however, when New York marked the assassination of Abraham Lincoln, the city council barred blacks from the official mourning procession. African Americans lobbied with the Union League Club and eventually were permitted to bring up the rear. More than two hundred African American men, protected by troops and police, marched with a banner that read "Abraham Lincoln Our Emancipator, To Millions of Bondsmen He Liberty Gave."[22]

* * *

In New York, the Civil War had spawned both bitter conflict and staggering wealth. As Kenneth T. Jackson notes, at the war's end "New York City was thriving as never before and poised to join London and Paris as one of the great urban agglomerations in the world."[23] The potential for moneymaking in New York was extraordinary, but hanging over the city like smoke was a large question: how would it be possible to govern a city so riven by racial, ethnic, and social conflict? Into the breach stepped Tammany Hall.

Tammany, under Tweed, recognized that there were political and financial benefits to taking up the cause of immigrants, especially Irish Catholics, who were scorned by the strongly Protestant and native-born Republican Party. After the war, Tammany wrapped itself in the American flag to establish its loyalty to the reunited nation. Tammany also pushed an expansive program of public works, endearing itself to real estate developers, contractors, and immigrant workers. Equally important, in the name of the Democratic Party, white supremacy, and states' rights, Tammany announced its strong opposition to federal efforts to promote racial equality—including black suffrage in New York State. In 1868, Tammany organized the Democrats' national nominating convention in New York City.[24]

The new Democratic order ushered in by Tammany, linking Jim Crow Southerners and Northern urban political machines, would endure for many decades at the national level. In *Harper's Weekly*, Thomas Nast attacked the alliance in a searing cartoon depicting a prostrate black man in a Union Army uniform. Above him, with their feet planted firmly on his back, are the Confederate veteran and Ku Klux Klan founder Nathan Bedford Forrest, the Wall Street financier August Belmont, and a Five Points Irishman with apelike features (a staple of nativist iconography since before the Civil War) brandishing a club labeled "a vote." In the background, the Colored Orphan's Asylum burns.[25]

The federal government took steps to curb the postwar political order represented in Nast's cartoon. In New York City, federal laws and polices widely associated with Reconstruction in the South were also used to curb Tammany. The Fifteenth Amendment gave black men the right to vote despite the hall's opposition. To secure African American voting rights, federal marshals supervised elections in New York City from 1870 to 1892.[26]

Despite these efforts, within the city and state of New York Tammany was a rising force. In 1870, Tweed, who then held a seat in the New York State Senate, worked in the legislature to pass a new municipal charter that strengthened home rule in New York City and delivered it to elected officials who were part of Tammany Hall. With Tweed as head of Tammany, the Irish came close to the apex of power. Tweed's closest political associates were Irishmen—Peter "Brains" Sweeney, the city chamberlain, or treasurer, and Richard "Slippery Dick" Connolly, the city's comptroller.[27]

The chicanery of the Tweed Ring—its ties to a plasterer, for example, who charged the city $500,000 for plastering a county courthouse and $1 million for repairing the same work—could obscure its strengths. Tweed was intelligent, affable, opportunistic, and blessed with organizational skills. He grasped that the city' charter, which was set by the state legislature, could strengthen or weaken both home rule and his own powers. Equally important, he knew how to sell his vision of New York, which embraced growth and development, to everyone from the "best men" to hustling contractors to working-class immigrants. His kickbacks, double billing, and creative budgeting may have stolen from the rich and cheated the poor, as the historian Thomas Kessner argues, but while his reign lasted Tweed had a knack for appearing to serve the interests of a broad range of New Yorkers. In a city where the Draft Riots and ethnic conflict were searing memories, Tweed's largesse seemed to offer a kind of social peace.[28]

In 1871, the limits of Tweed's peacekeeping became apparent when New York City's old hostility between Protestant and Catholic Irish erupted at the annual parade of the Orange Order, a Protestant fraternal organization that celebrated the defeat of Catholic forces at the Battle of the Boyne in 1690. Tensions had been rising for years: many Orangemen, along with other New York Protestants, claimed that Catholics threatened American values and were undesirable citizens. At the same time, Irish Catholics were growing in number, and the service of Irish Catholics in the recent war had deflated nativist charges; the predominantly Irish Sixty-Ninth was renowned for bravery and sacrifice.

Nevertheless, in 1871 Orangemen insisted on holding their annual parade on July 12. Rumors of violence and threats by both Irish Protestants and Catholics prompted the city and state to provide police and military protection for the marchers. When the parade and its military accompaniment reached the west twenties along Eighth Avenue, shots were fired and rocks thrown. Panic ensued. The militia lost control and fired indiscriminately; the death total was sixty-two, mostly Irish Catholics killed by militia bullets.[29]

In the long run, the Orange riot did not turn out to be a harbinger of further violence. New York's ethnic order was changing, and Orange processions soon petered out.[30] In the near term, however, the bloodshed on Eighth Avenue threw into question Tammany's ability to keep the peace.[31]

Even more damaging were articles in the *New York Times*, published that summer, documenting the vast corruption of the Tweed Ring, amounting to as much as $20 million.[32] Urgent meetings and calls for reform followed, especially from New York's financiers and merchants, who feared that the Tweed Ring's spending would destroy the city's credit rating and wreck its standing in the international bond market.[33]

The ring, for all its associations with immigrants, had significant Irish and German opponents. Their motives ranged from outrage at Tammany's corrupt expenditures to disappointment at not receiving enough of the spoils. Thomas Nast, the cartoonist whose caricatures of Tweed and Tammany in *Harper's* pilloried the boss and his organization, was a German immigrant. So was Oswald Ottendorfer, editor of the *New Yorker Staats-Zeitung*, who used his organizational skills and the power of the press against Tweed. Irish immigrants Mathew O'Rourke, who had worked for the county auditor, and Sheriff James O'Brien,

3.3 In *Harper's Weekly*, the cartoonist Thomas Nast, a German immigrant, mocked "Boss" Tweed and the Tweed Ring (1871).

Source: Thomas Nast, Library of Congress.

who felt ill-treated by Tammany, both provided vital information on the Tweed Ring's operations. Charles O'Connor, the chief prosecutor in the Tweed trials, was an Irishman. In alliance with native-born reformers and with the power of the *Staats-Zeitung* and *New York Times* behind them, they played significant parts in breaking the Tweed Ring's stranglehold over Tammany Hall. A German Reform Party, led by Ottendorfer and his colleagues August Belmont and William Steinway, endorsed the Republican William Havemeyer for mayor in 1872. With broad support from reform elements throughout the city, Havemeyer achieved victory. Tweed was tried, convicted, and jailed, but he escaped to Florida. He was caught trying to flee to Spain. Jailed again, he died a broken man in 1878.[34]

The animus against Tweed, and a belief that the majority of ordinary New Yorkers could not be trusted to elect "the best men" to office, prompted Ottendorfer—along with some of the richest men in the city—to support a constitutional amendment. Under it, the expenditures of city governments in New York State would be placed under the control of boards elected by taxpayers who either owned property assessed at more than $500 in value or paid annual rents of more than $250. In effect, to prevent the rise of another Tweed Ring a property qualification would disenfranchise and disempower New York State's urban poor and working class. The measure, which was required to pass twice in the state legislature before being put before the state's voters as an amendment to the state constitution, passed once in the state legislature in 1877. It failed in 1878, thanks to opposition by the rural and urban poor and Tammany Hall. Left hanging in the defeat of the plan was the question of how to govern a city that was as economically dynamic and ethnically diverse as New York.[35]

＊＊＊

Even as New York City's economy moved forward in booms and busts, its immigrant groups continued to evolve. Germans, like other immigrants, constructed new identities as what would later be called ethnic Americans.[36] German immigrants increasingly participated in religious, political, economic, and charitable life as German Americans rather than as Bavarians, Prussians, or Hessians. Bismarck's successful campaign between 1864 and 1871 to forge a unified German Empire fostered such a great a sense of nationalism among New York's German residents that many Forty-Eighter republicans overcame their hostility to the Prussian monarchy. The Franco-Prussian War, which broke out on July 19th, 1870, found the vast majority of New York German Americans enthusiastically supporting the Fatherland.[37]

Yet the shift from German particularism to ethnic unity as German Americans took time. As memberships in regional associations, choices of marriage partners, and the persistence of regionally based German neighborhoods testify, localism remained a potent force. Continuing immigration from the German Empire, which peaked in 1882, was one factor. Despite unification, imperial Germany was only loosely held together in terms of culture, religion, and dialects. German newcomers in these years brought with them strong feelings about their areas of origin. Regional loyalties were also passed on to American-born children who joined and participated in the activities of *landsmannschaft* associations and subscribed to German-dialect newspapers like the *Plattdeutsche Post* and the *Schwabbisches Wochenblatt*.[38]

German American politics in New York was also diverse. Some Germans found a political home as Democrats, but German political tendencies were too varied to fit into the Democratic Party alone. Germans also became a significant presence in New York's Republican Party and could also be found in socialist and anarchist groups.[39]

During the 1870s and 1880s, antisocialist laws in Germany prompted the immigration of a new generation of German radicals. For a few Germans, anarchism had an appeal. In New York, German radicals created a culture spread across many clubs, complete with newspapers, theaters, social gatherings, music events, and meetings devoted to political discussions.[40] Anarchists, socialists, and more moderate immigrants all grappled in the 1870s with a nationwide depression that started with railroad failures, surged through supporting industries and finance, and brought economic hardship to the nation and New York City. Lasting until the 1890s, this long depression was accompanied by business and government hostility to labor radicalism. In 1874, when New York workers speaking English and German rallied in Tompkins Square Park in the heart of Kleindeutschland to support a railroad strike, the police charged with clubs. Samuel Gompers, then a young Jewish immigrant cigar maker from England, recalled, "It was an orgy of brutality. I was caught in the crowd on the street and barely saved my head from being cracked by jumping down a cellarway. . . . A reign of terror gripped that section of the city."[41]

German New Yorkers lived in either of two "politically separate worlds," one defined by socialism and the other by the mainstream American parties. Radical German workers read the *Volks-Zeitung* and supported the United German Trades or Socialist Labor Party. More numerous were the German Americans who were, like the Irish, increasingly aligned with the Democratic Party and remained so as Tammany enacted tenement legislation and served other immigrant causes. Middle-class Germans read the *Staats-Zeitung*, which Ottendorfer edited, and were either fiscally conservative Democrats or, even more numerous, Republicans. The growing German American population—from 15 percent to 28 percent of the city's total between 1860 and 1890—assured

3.4 German Americans at the Atlantic Garden celebrate the French defeat at Sedan during the Franco-Prussian War (1870).

Source: New York Public Library.

greater political influence and patronage for the community. The number of customhouse jobs held by German Americans, for example, rose from twenty-three in 1861 to fifty-four in 1884.[42]

Kleindeutschland in the 1870s was a vital neighborhood. Although more affluent residents were by then departing for uptown neighborhoods like Yorkville, a dense array of German cultural and political institutions thrived downtown, ranging from local bars to theaters to halls dedicated to particular *vereine* to large beer gardens on the Bowery and Avenue A. Just as German socialists and anarchists broadened New York's political culture, German beer gardens offered forms of sociability that challenged Victorian Americans. Although native-born middle-class Americans feared that mixed-sex leisure and public drinking would lead to moral ruin, Germans happily mixed men, women, and alcohol without problems. In the early 1870s, the writer James McCabe Jr. described the Atlantic Beer Garden, at 50 Bowery, where up to four thousand people, largely Germans, enjoyed music, wine, and, most of all, beer.

> The consumption of the article here nightly is tremendous, but there is no drunkenness. The audience is well behaved, and the noise is simply the hearty merriment of a large crowd. There is no disorder, no indecency. The place is thoroughly respectable, and the audience are interested in keeping it so. They come here with their families, spend a social, pleasant evening, meet their friends, hear the news, enjoy the music and the beer, and go home refreshed and happy. The Germans are very proud of this resort, and would not tolerate the introduction of any feature that would make it an unfit place for their wives and daughters.[43]

✳ ✳ ✳

If the Germans had special places in New York's popular culture and radical politics, the Irish loomed large in both the Democratic Party and the Roman Catholic Church. Ironically, Tweed's downfall permitted Irish Catholics finally to attain the highest seats of political power in the city. Writing of the urban Irish in America in 1870, Lawrence H. Fuchs states that the "most important communal organization . . . next to the church itself, was the Democratic Party, and for Irish men, the party probably was more important than the church. In and through the party they found sociability, jobs, and a way to claim American identity."[44]

In 1871, John Kelly became the first Irishman to lead Tammany Hall. He entered the political world as a volunteer firefighter (just like Tweed) and went on to serve as an alderman and a member of Congress. In the House of Representatives, he gained a reputation as the only Catholic and as a vigorous foe of nativists. Fortunately for this reputation, Kelly was in Europe during the Tweed Ring scandals.[45]

A well-known comparison between Kelly and Tweed has it that Kelly found Tammany a horde but left it an army. The gibe suggests that Tammany under Kelly ran a powerful machine devoted to municipal plunder. It is more accurate to view Tammany and its leadership under Kelly and his successors in light of its adversaries and imperatives. Tammany, as Tweed's downfall confirmed, had real enemies in the Republican Party, in the state legislature, in the press, and even among fellow Democrats. The hall was not omnipotent, but it was pragmatic. Kelly and his successors were professional politicians dedicated to winning elections in order to stay in power. They understood the importance of political structures that connected leaders and constituents, grasped the real needs of the urban poor, and faced the city without the condescending moralism that could afflict reformers. Sometimes victory required bribes, kickbacks, stuffed ballot boxes, and men to strong-arm opponents. Sometimes it meant naturalizing large numbers of immigrants as quickly as possible to turn them into Tammany voters. Sometimes winning required fiscal cutbacks, and sometimes it demanded that Tammany provide jobs or charity for constituents in need.[46]

The rivalry between Kelly and John Morrissey speaks volumes about Tammany's roots and its post-Tweed direction under Kelly. Morrissey was a prominent Irish Catholic street tough in the antebellum years, when fights between Protestant and Irish Catholic gangs were common in New York. He arrived from Ireland as a child and grew up working in factories and running with a gang in Troy, New York. He made his way to New York City as a young man, where he worked as a runner unloading immigrants' baggage and leading them to lodgings—a job that required a blend of strength and connections. His skill with his fists led him to a career as a bare-knuckle prizefighter, then as a Tammany strong-arm man. After making substantial money in gambling, saloons, and horse racing (he established thoroughbred racing at Saratoga), he successfully ran for Congress with Tammany support.[47]

Temperamentally pugnacious, Morrissey clashed with Tweed and then with Kelly, whom he accused of being out of touch with the interests of ordinary Irish Americans. An often-told story has it that Mayor William Wickham, a businessman supported by Kelly, once declined to meet with Morrissey. The former prizefighter returned to City Hall in a swallowtail coat. Along the way he told a friend, "I'm going in full dress to make a call, for that is now the style at the Hotel Wickham. No Irish need apply now." In 1877, Morrissey made his last electoral bid, a successful run for a seat in the New York State Senate against a corporate lawyer from Tammany. He died a year later and was buried in Troy, New York. More than a century later, ballads sung in Ireland and the United States celebrated his exploits as a bare-knuckle boxer.[48]

Kelly, unlike Morrissey, was more interested in attracting wealthy businessmen and professionals to Tammany than in serving the city's hard-pressed working-class communities. To court middle-class voters, Kelly endorsed low taxes and spending cuts on public works and poverty relief but maintained the allegiance of working-class Irish by loudly defending them against anti-Catholics and nativists. Under Kelly, New York City in 1880 gained its first Irish mayor: the shipping magnate William R. Grace. Grace made his fortune in the shipping business while a resident of Peru; he continued to be interested in that country's affairs when he moved to New York after the Civil War.[49]

Even then, the Irish did not have absolute control over Tammany or the Democratic Party. When Grace was serving his second term as mayor in 1884, Irish and Germans constituted more than three-quarters of the city's population. One estimate found 58 percent of the positions of power within the Democratic Party were still held by "old-stock" Americans, compared to 29 percent by Irish and 10 percent by Germans.[50]

If the Irish failed to control the Democratic Party fully, they did dominate what Fuchs calls their most important communal organization: the Roman Catholic Archdiocese of New York. The growth of the church in New York City had been phenomenal since 1820, when there were but two churches to serve the city's Catholic population of approximately 30,000. By 1840, the church had established eight new parishes as the Catholic population reached close to 90,000, and in 1865 somewhere between 300,000 and 400,000 Catholics attended thirty-two churches. In the United States, Catholic parishes were generally organized along ethnic-language lines. Thus, of the thirty-two New York churches, eight were German speaking, one was French speaking, and twenty-three were English speaking, which in effect meant their parishioners were overwhelmingly Irish.[51]

Just as the Protestant moral reformers had formed organizations in the antebellum era to deal with rising immigration, so too did Catholics. Before the great famine in Ireland, Archbishop Hughes had traveled to Ireland to recruit women for the Mercy Sisters to found a House of Mercy to aid poor immigrants. By the late 1860s, the House of Mercy had found shelter for ten thousand, some of whom received training for domestic service.[52]

Crucial to the growth of the Catholic Church and especially its many hospitals, welfare organizations, and religious schools was the role of Irish women. As Maureen Fitzgerald notes, "The great majority of Catholic [welfare] institutions were managed almost exclusively by women religious."[53] In 1885, the Catholic Church reported it had 285 diocesan priests, eight orphanages, three homes for the aged, and six hospitals, among other institutions.[54] By the 1890s, over three thousand nuns lived in New York City; they were mostly the children of the famine Irish.

In the 1890s, Catholic schools were no more successful in winning governmental funding than they had been under Cardinal Hughes. However, in a compromise for giving up the fight for state aid to religious schools, Catholic religious hospitals and welfare organizations (like their Protestant counterparts) did receive money from the state.[55]

Disputes between Catholics and Protestants persisted over a program of the Children's Aid Society, led by Charles Loring Brace, which placed destitute Catholic children in Protestant institutions. Catholics considered it an attempt to impose Protestant religious views on Catholic children. To combat the Protestant agencies and aid the poor and unfortunate, Sister Irene Fitzgibbon founded the Foundling Asylum in 1869. It served thousands of women and infants of different faiths and provided daycare for working women in an age when daycare was unavailable. An estimated twenty thousand people attended her funeral.[56]

The most extreme form of placing out was the "orphan trains" that that sent children west to mostly rural (and Protestant) homes, a program some Catholics considered tantamount to kidnapping.[57] To combat the Protestant placing-out system, Catholics needed funding for charities that took care of their children. They convinced the city, with help from Tammany Irish Catholics, to pass an 1875 law requiring destitute children to be placed in institutions of their own background.[58]

* * *

In post–Civil War New York ethnic power—built on political organization, religious institutions, and associational life—was matched by the economic power of the city's elite, who were overwhelmingly native born and Protestant. The depression of the 1870s did hurt some of those who made their fortunes during the Civil War, but the richest New Yorkers still had awesome power and capital. As the number of merchants among them declined, the number of manufacturers rose. In the 1880s and 1890s, they expanded into national industries such as railroads, oil, steel, and minerals. J. P. Morgan operated in an international world of finance. The New York rich built mansions along Fifth Avenue, purchased art from Europe, ate at fancy restaurants, joined private clubs, and supported the Metropolitan Museum of Art, the New York Philharmonic Orchestra, and the Metropolitan Opera. Elite private schools taught Protestant values and prepared their students for not only higher education but for commanding roles in society and business; they were thus called prep schools. They began to send their sons to Harvard and Yale and not simply local Columbia University.[59]

Some Jews mixed with the predominantly Protestant elite. Germans made their own entry into the city's elite and even appeared in the *Social Register*. A few organizations included Jews and Catholics, but these were exceptions to the general trend. Affluent Jews and Irish Catholics stuck to their own clubs and causes. Wealthy Irish Catholics could join the Catholic Club or the Gaelic Society, send their daughters to the Academy of the Sacred Heart, and send their sons to St. John's College, which eventually became Fordham University.[60]

Amid the tension between old and new money, New York saw a rise in anti-Semitism. By the end of the nineteenth century, the German Jews who had arrived in the middle of the century were rising to the new heights of affluence, even as Southern and Eastern European Jews—poorer and unassimilated—were immigrating in growing numbers. In response, anti-Semitism in New York's elite grew sharp. A new strain of nativism, a successor to the older bigotry aimed at Irish Catholics, questioned whether newly arrived Jews (and Italians) could ever become Americans. Jewish New Yorkers who had risen since the middle of the nineteenth century were excluded—not entirely, but in significant ways— from the institutions that had once accepted them. "By the 1890s," Sven Beckert explains, "upper-class anti-Semites had driven Jewish members out of the Union Club, closed Saratoga hotels to Jews, and banned the mentioning of Jewish organizations in the Social Register."[61]

German Jews, who had by this time risen into the middle class and even the city's elite, had resources of their own. Grand synagogues, designed in a Moorish Revival style that suggested both the pride and antiquity of Judaism, could be found in Midtown. The Lehman, Seligman, and Schiff families built mansions on Fifth Avenue. In 1896, the Straus family—descended from a general store owner who had immigrated to Georgia in 1852—bought Macy's department store.[62]

Despite these signs of German Jews' entry into the elite, their interactions with the native-born Protestants who comprised the rest of the city's upper crust had limits. German Jews socialized in their own circles and sustained a different network of charitable institutions, but when they stepped outside this network they could be stigmatized as objectionable social climbers. Gender played a complex role in these matters. Sexism left women with limited social roles in the world of elite New York, but one arena open to them was organizing the social events that defined who was in the elite and who was out. The novels of Edith Wharton, with their acute observations of these matters, also had their own exclusionary tones. Wharton was herself a product of an older New York that was beginning to falter before new money and new arrivals. In her novel *The House of Mirth*, Lily Bart's response to Simon Rosedale—she sees him as pushy, scheming, and vulgar—reflects ideas about Jews that were widespread in the Gilded Age and present in Wharton's own thinking.[63]

Private clubs, dinner parties, balls, and other social events might have kept the public from seeing the elite, but some aspects of their lives were for display. The fabulous mansions along Fifth Avenue and other select addresses allowed public viewing in addition to providing places for the elaborate social affairs of the "Four Hundred." So too were the elite's "cottages" in Newport, Rhode Island. Carolina Astor, the social leader of the New York City's rich, may have wanted privacy at times, but attendance at the opera was another matter. To be noticed, Mrs. Astor arrived at the opera in the middle of the first act and sat in her box, where she received others in attendance. She rarely stayed for the whole opera, but during the "second act she would quietly slip out of her box, on her way to some dinner party or ball." After that, others slipped away too.[64]

There were occasions, however, when class counted for more than prejudice. For all these efforts at social exclusion, in politics the city's elite could unite across ethnic boundaries, as Beckert points out, "when it came to the defense of their common interests." So the elite did in 1877 and 1878, when they attempted to amend the state constitution to restrict the franchise and thwart elected officials who might spend on the scale of Boss Tweed. That effort failed, but with the rise of labor unions, strikes, social unrest, and unemployment in the 1870s, New York's elite would have more than one chance at defending capital against labor.[65]

✳ ✳ ✳

Entry into the ranks of the super-rich was a rarity in Gilded Age New York, especially for immigrants. Far more common was the modest but significant movement of immigrants and their children into marginally better lives: from bottle washer to barman, from construction laborer to foreman. Most Irish were still working class during the Gilded Age, but politics offered the chance to become middle class. In 1888, Irish control of the city's politics meant access to 12,000 jobs as firemen, policemen, and teachers. The Irish held about one-third of these positions. The municipal work force grew to thirty thousand with the consolidation of New York City in 1898, when the city assumed its modern five-borough form.[66]

When adaptations to American life were accompanied by economic mobility, immigrants and their children experienced the awkward confusion that can accompany the transition from working- to middle-class status. The topic became a staple of variety shows in the last quarter of the nineteenth century.[67]

On stage, the immigrant neighborhoods of Lower Manhattan were deftly depicted by Ned Harrigan, an American-born Protestant songwriter, playwright, and actor raised among Irish immigrants in the Corlear's Hook section of the Lower East Side. During the last quarter of the nineteenth century, Harrigan's performances with Tony Hart (the Massachusetts-born son of Irish immigrants) and his compositions with David Braham (a Jewish immigrant from London) illuminated and lampooned the lives of a wide range of immigrants and African Americans who lived crowded into Lower East Side tenements. Harrigan's songs, plays, and sketches drew immigrant, working-class, and middle-class audiences. Their turns in variety shows and their fully developed productions at the Theater Comique paved the way for vaudeville and musical theater.[68]

Harrigan and Hart both started out in minstrelsy, and their songs and productions never escaped the stereotyping and racial hierarchies of such shows. "McNally's Row of Flats," a song of 1882, celebrates life in a drafty, rat-infested tenement owned by Timothy McNally, "a wealthy politician and a gentleman at that." The building contains a "great conglomeration of men from every nation": "Ireland and Italy, Jerusalem and Germany / Chinese, Nagers and a paradise for cats / All jumbled up together in the snow or rainy weather / They represent the tenants in McNally's row of flats."[69]

Harrigan employed the ethnic stereotypes that were common in his time, but he also had a uniquely acute grasp of the tensions, changes, and exchanges that defined life on the Lower East Side. His plots and lyrics, as the historian James R. Barrett argues, "captured *both* the casual ethnic prejudice *and* the unmistakable fascination with urban diversity that characterized much of American culture." In one play, Dan Mulligan and his wife Cordelia worry that their son Tommy will marry Katrina Lochmuller, the daughter of their German neighbors. *The Mulligan Guard*, their signature play, poked fun at the target companies that were a part of immigrant life. The Mulligan Guard's rivalry with an all-black outfit, the Skidmore Guards, expressed ongoing conflicts between Irish and African American New Yorkers. In one play, the two units book their dress balls in the same hall on the same day. Predictably, they are unable to share the same space. The conflict appears to be settled when the Skidmore Guards take an upstairs room while the Mulligans remain downstairs. The Skidmore Guards dance so vigorously, however, that they crash through the floor and land on the heads of the Mulligan Guard.[70]

Harrigan depicted the give and take of life in immigrant communities, where street life and human connections mattered. Nowhere was this more important than in politics, where the combination of structure and a human touch for constituents extended Tammany's reach from City Hall to city sidewalks. Harrigan's song "Muldoon, the Solid Man" recounts how Muldoon emigrated from Ireland, settled into a tenement, and persevered at politics until he was a "solid man" who could be counted on to do the machine's work. Muldoon, as the lyrics explain, is invited to every party and raffle and eloquently addresses public meetings. He controls the Tombs—the jail where many of his constituents spend the summer—and marches in the St. Patrick's Day Parade. The song's chorus gets at his supporters' small pleasures: "Go with me and I'll treat you dacent; / I'll set you down and I'll fill your can / As I walk the street each friend I meet / Says: There goes Muldoon, he's a solid man."[71]

For people who had known poverty and indecent treatment on the job or in an overcrowded tenement, Muldoon's offer of a full lunch pail or a bucket of beer was something to be appreciated. But such benefits could not overcome the debased working-class standards of living, characterized by low wages, overcrowded housing, and high death rates among infants. Honest John Kelly's Tammany could not overturn the inequalities of Gilded Age New York. Indeed, Kelly's courtship of middle-class voters demanded low levels of taxation and public spending, which left few funds for consistent help to the poor.[72]

* * *

The leadership of the Catholic Church remained hostile to anything that smacked of socialism, and Tammany stood for self-preservation leavened by pragmatism. The richest New Yorkers justified their accumulations with claims that the market was simply rewarding the survival of the fittest. As industry grew and inequality deepened, old ideas about America being a democratic republic that rewarded individual producers seemed increasingly anachronistic.[73]

3.5 Conspicuous consumption in the Gilded Age: the Vanderbilt Mansion on Fifth Avenue, built in 1882 and expanded in 1893.

Against all odds, however, in 1886 the city witnessed a mayoral election that brought out immigrant voters in support of an insurgent candidate—Henry George. American born in a city of immigrants and Protestant in a city of Roman Catholics, George had worked as a journalist in California. Encounters with business monopolies in the form of the Associated Press and Western Union, which colluded to limit the number of newspapers with access to their news-distribution system, and his shock at the rampant inequality in New York City motivated him to inquire deeply into the origins of wealth and poverty. Over a decade, his reading, writing, and research took form in a massive book: *Progress and Poverty: An Inquiry Into the Cause of Industrial Depressions and of Increase of Want with Increase of Wealth*, published in 1879. In it George challenged the conventional economic thinking of his time and asked why economic progress in the United States was accompanied by so much poverty. In his book, he argued that both workers and investors suffered at the hands of landowners, who did no work and invested no money but grew rich on rents and the rising value of their lands. His solution was to eliminate all taxes save one: a levy on landowners based on the increasing value of their land. To promote the book more effectively, in 1880 George went to the nation's communications capital, New York City. There he pushed his book to a higher profile (it appeared in thirteen languages by 1886) and found New Yorkers who were receptive to his message—socialists, reformers, trade unionists, and Irish nationalists.[74]

In New York, the political concerns of immigrants have long had a global dimension. George arrived in the city at a time when growing numbers of Irish New Yorkers embraced the Land League, a movement to break the power of the landlords who dominated Ireland's exploitative peasant agriculture. George's ideas meshed with the Land League's. He not only covered it as a journalist but joined in its cause, endearing him to the Irish and strengthening the radical critiques that the movement injected into Irish American political life. To leftists, as the editor of *Der Socialist* argued, George's vision was not socialistic but still "would be an advantage for the workers and a heavy blow for capitalism." To reformers and to members of the recently formed Central Labor Union (CLU) grappling with growing corporate power yet wary of socialism, George seemed to steer between laissez-faire capitalism and outright revolution.[75]

In 1886, the newly formed United Labor Party, an offshoot of the CLU, persuaded George to run for mayor. One of his strongest supporters was Father Edward McGlynn, a fiery priest at St. Stephen's in Manhattan and the son of Irish immigrants. McGlynn supported the Land League and preached a Catholic version of the social gospel. George's candidacy, with its support from Irish, working-class, and Catholic voters, frightened both Democrats and Republicans. Tammany Hall and its critics within the Democratic Party cooperated to nominate for mayor Abraham Hewitt, an industrialist of modest origins with a prolabor reputation and who had served in the House of Representatives. The Republicans nominated a young upstart from an old and wealthy family with a reputation as a reformer: Theodore Roosevelt.[76]

The George campaign set up storefront offices throughout the city, established a labor-organized effort to recruit volunteers and solicit small donations, and started its own newspaper to bypass criticism in the mainstream press. George crisscrossed the city, giving stump speeches from the back of a wagon. Hewitt, the Democratic candidate, called George a dangerous radical. Roosevelt accused him of stirring up class conflict. The leadership of the Roman Catholic Church also took aim at George and silenced Father McGlynn. Tammany distributed a statement from the vicar-general of the archdiocese calling George's ideas not only ruinous to workers but also "unsound and unsafe, and contrary to the teachings of the church."[77]

George received 68,110 votes but was defeated. He outpolled Roosevelt, who received 60,435, but still finished behind Hewitt, who got 90,552 votes. The claim that George was "counted out" or defrauded by Tammany cannot be proven or disproven. However, a study of election returns suggests that George won strong support in working-class Irish, German, and Jewish neighborhoods. The poorest and newest immigrants seem to have voted for Hewitt, however—perhaps to protect whatever benefits Tammany sent their way and perhaps in deference to the Catholic Church.[78]

The coalition that supported George broke up, foundering over differences within the Irish and union segments. The United Labor Party dissolved. Father McGlynn's activism led to his temporary excommunication. In the short run, Tammany learned from George the value of community organization. Under Richard Croker, Kelly's successor, Tammany created a citywide network of clubs that inserted the hall's presence into neighborhood life. Croker also centralized contributions to Tammany from businesses and decentralized patronage, firming up the hall's financial support while ensuring the loyalty of Tammany men who owed their prosperity to Boss Croker.[79]

Tammany faced another crisis in 1892, when the Rev. Charles Parkhurst preached a sermon decrying the city as a hotbed of sin supported by Tammany and police corruption. When the city's district attorney challenged him, he visited brothels and saloons that operated after hours and backed his words with facts. Then he led a crusade against the city's vice business and the police, who were accused of harboring prostitutes and saloons that stayed open when the law decreed that they should be closed.[80] Many of Parkhurst's charges were true. As the historian Timothy J. Gilfoyle concludes, the police may not have controlled every prostitution operation in the city, but they kept their fingers in the most gainful ones.[81]

Parkhurst's charges led to the formation of the Lexow Committee in the New York State Senate, named for its chair, Clarence Lexow—an upstate

Republican of German ancestry who saw city life as a sinkhole of corruption. The investigation by the Lexow Committee led to the prosecution of several policemen and the resignation of others. The committee and the vice reformers also produced a movement to defeat Tammany with a reform candidacy headed by William L. Strong, a Republican who won the mayoralty decisively in 1894 in an election that saw significant working-class defections from Tammany.[82]

Tammany was only temporarily out of power; it would return during the Progressive Era. And the charges of police corruption leveled in the Parkhurst affair, Daniel Czitrom observes, led officers to found the Patrolmen's Benevolent Association, which "gave beat cops a new voice and in effect institutionalized the insular job culture that put loyalty to fellow cops above all else."[83]

In the years after his unsuccessful mayoral bid, George moved to the political center. Nevertheless, for decades his broad critique of inequality, along with his affirmation of the role of government and taxation in creating a more just economic order, animated populists, progressives, and an eclectic collection of reformers.[84] When he died while making a second mayoral bid in 1897, New York was in the midst of a new surge in immigration. The newest arrivals were

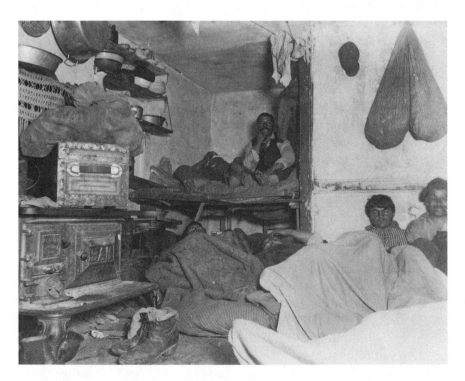

3.6 How the other half lived: Lodgers in a tenement on Bayard Street, 1889.

Source: Jacob A. Riis, Museum of the City of New York.

primarily from Southern and Eastern Europe, foremost among them Jews and Italians. Their response to the city, and the city's response to them, would profoundly shape New York in the twentieth century.

✳ ✳ ✳

For the city's African Americans during the Gilded Age, neither major political party nor Tammany offered significant support. Republicans had at times defended black New Yorkers, but their enthusiasm for a crusade for racial equality dimmed after the 1870s, just as the national Republican Party turned away from the plight of African Americans in the South. The Democrats had never been supportive of African Americans and were a racist party. In the South, blacks were subjected to lynching, disfranchisement, segregation, sharecropping, and poverty. Jim Crow's stranglehold was complete.

The state did pass civil rights laws that barred discrimination in public accommodations, but these laws were not always enforced. The state also outlawed segregated schools in 1900, but since housing was becoming increasingly segregated and schools served neighborhoods, the city's schools became or remained racially segregated. Nor did legislation touch employment and housing, which were discriminatory throughout the city.[85]

The worst episode of violence against African Americans since the Draft Riots occurred in 1900. The city's African American population had increased substantially during the 1890s, from 23,000 to 60,000, as Southern blacks migrated to New York and settled in the Tenderloin, in the western part of Midtown. Tensions over housing and jobs were high, particularly with Irish New Yorkers living in that area. Then, on a hot night in August 1900, a black man, Arthur Harris, killed a white police officer. Harris's girlfriend, May Enoch, was waiting for him when she was approached by a plainclothes policeman and charged with "soliciting." Unaware that the white man was a policeman, Harris believed that his girlfriend was being harassed, and he intervened. The two men started to fight. In the scuffle Harris stabbed the officer, who died the next day. Not only had a white officer died at the hands of a black man, but also he was the son-in-law to-be of an acting police captain. The racially tense area was poised to explode.[86]

Rumors of violence abounded, and several days later another fight between blacks and whites set off a full-scale riot. For two days the white residents of the neighborhood ranged the streets, beating African Americans. Streetcars were also unsafe. One observer recalled, "Every car passing up or down Eighth Avenue . . . was stopped by the crowd and every negro on board dragged out . . . the police made little or no attempt to arrest any assailants."[87]

The police joined the assaults on African Americans, both on the streets and in the jails. Most of those arrested were black, including some who had purchased revolvers. African American leaders were outraged and demanded that white rioters and policemen be brought to justice. A group of prominent African Americans organized the Citizen's Protective League, which gathered statements from victims about their experiences at the hands of the predominantly Irish New York police. Because many whites were shocked at the violence and disturbed by the role of the police, hopes were high for some form of disciplinary action. However, the grand jury refused to indict a single officer, and eight cases brought to court against individual policemen were dismissed. The police department set up its own investigating board, whose rules restricted the right of lawyers to cross-examine members of the force. The board concluded, "There is nothing in the evidence taken by your committee which will justify preferment of charges against any officer."[88]

Tammany Hall Democrats would not move against the police, and the department fended off criticism of officers' actions in the riot. Departmental corruption had been little reformed by the Parkhurst crusade, and there were no African Americans on the force. (There would be none until 1910, when Samuel Battle joined the force.) Blacks had no influence in Democratic Party politics. Racial hatred ran deep, and African Americans, constituting less than 2 percent of the city's population, could find few politicians willing to offer their support.[89]

While some white newspaper criticized police brutality and some sympathetic white citizens tried to bring offending officers to justice, they could do little other than urge police reform or suggest that black voters cast their ballots for Republicans. Frank Moss, a well-known reformer, compiled mountains of evidence to no avail.[90] The entire episode was a forerunner of things to come.

CHAPTER 4

SLUMS, SWEATSHOPS, AND REFORM: 1880–1917

S adie Frowne, a Jewish girl raised in Poland, immigrated in steerage class with her widowed mother to New York City to join relatives. Shortly after they arrived, her mother died of consumption. Frowne made her way to Brownsville, Brooklyn, where she found a room in the house of friends and a job in a garment factory. At work, she learned to handle unwanted attention from men, joined a union, and found a boyfriend. She described her life in an interview with *The Independent* magazine in 1902, when she was sixteen years old:

> The machines go like mad all day because the faster you work the more money you get. Sometimes in my haste I get my finger caught and the needle goes right through it. It goes so quick, though, that it does not hurt much. I bind the finger up with a piece of cotton and go on working. We all have accidents like that. When the needle goes through the nail it makes a sore finger, or where it splinters a bone it does much harm. Sometimes a finger has to come off. Generally, though, one can be cured by a salve.[1]

Work in the factory left her exhausted, but she insisted on going out for fresh air at Coney Island with her boyfriend, Henry. She was fond of dancing and the stage. "I go to the theater quite often," she said, "and like those plays that make you cry a great deal. 'The Two Orphans' is good. Last time I saw it I cried all night because of the hard times that the children had in the play. I am going to see it again when it comes here."[2]

Sadie Frowne was one of several million immigrants who came to New York between 1880 and World War I. Although young women had been working in garment factories before the Civil War, in the early twentieth century the scale of the industry expanded dramatically. Like many other Jewish and Italian women, she found work in the garment industry; their struggles to define their own lives in a new city shaped everything from family life to labor politics to popular culture.

Global processes and events framed the dramas of their lives. Owing to the unprecedented scale of movement of people, goods, ideas, and images around the world, the decades stretching from the 1870s to World War I have been called "the first age of globalization." Of course, world trade had a much longer history, and New York had been part of it since the seventeenth century. But by the late nineteenth century, the scale of international trade and communication was unprecedented. Moreover, Frowne and millions of other immigrants around the world were on the move. The economic and political processes that inspired and responded to their immigration would end the long depression of the late nineteenth century, inspire movements for change, and end in a world war.

4.1   Mulberry Street on the Lower East Side, 1900.

Source: Detroit Publishing Co., Library of Congress.

Just as the Irish and Germans had redefined themselves and New York City in the middle of the nineteenth century, Jews and Italians were about to do the same in the early years of the twentieth.

As the nineteenth century gave way to the twentieth, economic upheaval was shaking Southern and Eastern Europe. In the Austro-Hungarian Empire, commercial agriculture consolidated estates and forced thousands of peasants to leave. In Eastern Europe, imported American grain from the Midwest undercut local production, a damaging blow to farmers and grain merchants that set both on the road to the United States. In southern Italy and Sicily, where conditions had been bleak for generations, landlords began squeezing peasants off the land. To make matters worse, taxes were unbearable, population growth high, and prospects for alternative employment poor. Worldwide competition for wheat and grapes after 1870 drove prices for these products down. Tariff wars a few years later only added to the peasants' woes. European workers who labored in small handcraft industries, sometimes operating out of their homes, experienced growing competition from factory production. Everywhere rising population created additional pressures for immigration.[3]

Railroads and steamship lines printed thousands of pamphlets in dozens of languages explaining the wonders of the New World. Letters from those who had gone before urged their relatives and countrymen to join them. Mary Antin, a Russian Jewish immigrant, recalled that "America was in everybody's mouth ... people who had relatives in the famous land went around reading their letters for the enlightenment of less fortunate folk. . . . All talked of it."[4] Some letters contained prepaid tickets, which made the voyage possible for many of Europe's poor, but thousands came on their own.[5]

Eastern Europeans like Antin lived far from the Western European ports such as Bremen, Liverpool, and Rotterdam, from where ships sailed for America. Italian immigrants embarked from Naples, Palermo, or Mediterranean ports. In both regions, improved railroad systems eased the journey. Nevertheless, some emigrants, eager to leave but too poor to afford train fare, made their way to the ports on foot or by horse- or donkey-drawn carts.

Improvements in oceangoing steamships cut the cost and the time required for the American journey to a matter of days. Steerage, in which most immigrants traveled, was hardly luxurious. Edward Steiner described his voyage in 1906: "Crowds everywhere, ill smelling bunks, uninviting washrooms—this is steerage. The food, which is miserable, is dealt out of huge kettles into the dinner pails provided by the steamship company. . . . On many ships, even drinking water is grudgingly given, and on the steamship *Staatendam* . . . we had literally to steal water for the steerage from the second cabin."[6] As the ship steamed up into the harbor, exhilaration mixed with fear. The Statue of Liberty, a gift from France in honor of liberty and Franco-American friendship dedicated in 1886, suggested a welcome, especially with the inscription in 1903

TABLE 4.1 Changing profile of immigrant New York City, 1880–1920

Country of Origin	1880*	1900**	1920
Austria	5,371	71,427	126,739
Germany	218,821	322,343	194,154
Ireland	277,409	275,102	203,450
Italy	13,411	145,433	390,832
Poland	9,521	32,873	145,679
Russia/Soviet Union	4,760	155,201	479,797

* Before 1900 numbers are for New York City and Brooklyn.
** After 1900 numbers are for New York City.

Source: Kenneth T. Jackson, ed., *Encyclopedia of New York City*, 2nd ed. (New Haven, CT: Yale University Press, 2010), 640–41.

of Emma Lazarus's poem "The New Colossus"—"Give me your tired, your poor . . ."—on a bronze tablet placed on the statue's pedestal. But Ellis Island, just past the statue, raised the prospect of rejection.

The federal government had assumed total control of immigration during the 1880s and in 1892 opened a reception center for newcomers on Ellis Island. Federal procedures buffered immigrants from the abuses of the runners and con men who had once preyed on immigrants landing on the wharves of Lower Manhattan or outside Castle Garden. The average immigrant passed through Ellis Island in a few hours, and 98 percent gained entry.[7] But passage through the island always carried a risk of being sent back for medical or political reasons. The Immigration Act of 1903, reflecting concerns aroused after an anarchist assassinated President William McKinley in 1901, banned anyone with a "loathsome" disease as well as "polygamists, anarchists, or persons who believe in or advocate the overthrow by force or violence of the Government of the United States."[8]

Immigrants who passed inspection boarded ferryboats for a short trip to New Jersey or Manhattan. Unscrupulous agents who sought to exploit innocent newcomers still awaited them on shore, but such predatory efforts were reduced by efficient immigrant-aid societies. Most new arrivals traveled farther, seeking friends and families ready to receive them in other cities. Hundreds of thousands, however, remained in New York City. The choice had merits.

As the twentieth century approached, New York maintained its position as the nation's largest city. For a brief period, Chicago seemed a viable challenger, but with the merger of Manhattan, Brooklyn, Queens, the Bronx, and Staten Island to form the five-borough New York City in 1898, the city easily outdistanced its Midwestern rival. Consolidated New York contained more than three million inhabitants and on the eve of World War I housed a population twice as large as Chicago's.

New York remained America's leading port. While the city slipped from its commercial high point of 1850, when 70 percent of America's exports and imports went through its harbor, at the turn of the twentieth century nearly half of the nation's shipping came through New York. Approximately two of every three immigrants to the United States entered through Ellis Island.

World commerce gave the city financial supremacy as well. New York was home to the nation's leading banks. The New York Stock Exchange anchored Wall Street, and giant law firms emerged after the Civil War to serve the needs of the metropolis and the nation.[9] These enterprises required the employment of large numbers of professional and other white-collar workers who, in turn, contributed to the city's growth.

While shipping, commerce, and finance gave New York preeminence among American cities, laboring jobs and manufacturing lured most immigrants, as such jobs usually did not require knowledge of English or high levels of training. Rapid industrial growth characterized New York from 1815 to 1880, after which crowded streets and high rents hindered the development of most space-demanding enterprises. New York was a city of light manufacturing, a hive of industries such as publishing, metalworking, food processing, and the manufacture of clothing and luxury items. These industries, especially garment manufacturing, required a large-scale labor force. Immigrants met the demand. Of all the city's industries that attracted immigrants, the garment trade was by far the leader.[10]

A trickle of immigrants became a tidal wave after 1880. After 1880, for example, many more Greeks from the rural provinces of Greece and the territories of the Ottoman Empire followed the first Greeks, who had arrived in modest numbers as refugees from the turmoil of their war for independence in the 1820s. Poles joined their countrymen in the Williamsburg-Greenpoint section of Brooklyn. The city's Scandinavian population soared by 50 percent between 1900 and 1920. The city's Arabs, who did not arrive until the 1870s, grew to several thousand by 1920. Most of them lived on the Lower West Side of Manhattan and in Brooklyn. By 1900, half the Syrians in the United States, who were overwhelmingly Christians, resided in New York City.[11]

Not all immigrants were as welcome, however. In 1882, Congress passed the Chinese Exclusion Act, which banned most Chinese immigration. It became virtually impossible for Chinese, including the wives of immigrants already in the United States, to come to New York.[12] The city's Chinatown developed as a bachelor society where men outnumbered women by a ratio of more than six to one.[13]

The arrival of more numerous Italian and Jewish immigrants also aroused hostile reactions. Nativists saw the newest immigrants, coming from Southern and Eastern Europe, as ineligible for admission to American society. New York had a strong strain of pluralism, but it was also the home of Madison Grant, a patrician lawyer and founder of the New York Zoological Society, who spoke loudly:

> The man of old stock is being crowded out of many country districts by these foreigners, just as he is to-day being literally driven off the streets of New York City by the swarms of Polish Jews. These immigrants adopt the language of native Americans, they wear his clothes; they steal his name; and they are beginning to take his women, but they seldom adopt his religion or understand his ideals.

Pluralism, even in a city of immigrants, had its limits.[14]

✳ ✳ ✳

The two largest groups settling in New York City were Italians and Jews; their arrival would change New York as much as the Irish and Germans had before then. Old Protestant New York was shaken by the arrival of Irish and German Catholics in the mid–nineteenth century. The arrival of Jews and Italian Catholics at the turn of the twentieth century pushed white Protestants even further to the margins.

Two million Jews left Europe for the United States between 1881 and 1914, 75 percent of them from the Russian Empire and the rest primarily from Hungary, Romania, and Austrian-ruled Galicia. Nearly three-quarters of them settled in New York City. By 1910, Jews from Russia and Poland constituted the city's largest immigrant group. The *Jewish Communal Register* of 1917–1918 required more than 1,500 pages to catalog the organizations and institutions established by and serving the city's approximately 1.4 million Jews.[15]

The Jewish immigrants had faced bigotry, violence, and economic dislocation in their native lands. Russian Jews were required, with few exceptions, to remain in a limited area called the Pale of Settlement. The czar's May Laws of 1882 forced a half-million Jews to relocate from rural villages to cities and towns. Other decrees subjected Jews to long-term military service, banned them from certain professions, and severely restricted their access to universities. Slavic anti-Semitism exploded in pogroms, government-sanctioned riots, and bloodbaths against Jews; these gathered force in the early 1880s.

The infamous Kishinev pogrom of 1903 cast a shadow that endured into the twenty-first century. After 1905, intense oppression by the czarist government swept well-educated, politically active, cultured Jews into the immigrant stream. As Jews watched or read about homes and business burned and fellow Jews murdered, they concluded that immigration to America was their only salvation.[16]

Leading rabbis and their followers never joined the mass migration, but as persecution intensified and economic conditions worsened, Jews representing every other walk of life became part of the flow. For all that Jews suffered in Eastern Europe, they had acquired urban experiences and work skills that would serve them well in New York. By 1900, well over half of the Eastern European Jews arriving in New York came from urban centers and could be categorized as skilled or semiskilled workers.[17] Official immigration figures for the period 1899–1914 reveal that 40 percent of all Jewish arrivals had been employed in the clothing industry, others in building and furnishing, machine and metal, and the food industry—all trades that were good preparation for urban life.[18]

With few exceptions, Jews came to America to stay. The demography of Jewish immigration suggested its transforming dimensions. Forty-three percent of the Jewish immigrants were female; 25 percent were children. For other nationalities, the percentages were 30.5 females and 12.3 children. Jews, compared to other immigrants, had a low rate of return. For non-Jewish immigrants, the rate of return was approximately 30 percent. For Jews, from 1905 to 1920, it never rose over 8 percent. Jews might maintain familial and cultural ties with Eastern Europe, but they meant to start new lives in America.[19]

As Jewish immigrants moved into New York City, they occupied Lower East Side streets that had been the domain of the Irish and Germans. Yiddish became the dominant language in a twenty-square-block area from the Bowery to the East River and from Market Street to Fourteenth Street. However, within this district of Jewish settlers and the Yiddish they spoke could be found variety aplenty. The historian Moses Rischin detailed the district's geography:

Hungarians were settled in the northern portion above Houston Street, along the numbered streets between Avenue B and the East River, once indisputably *Kleindeutschland*. Galicians lived to the south, between Houston and Broome, east of Attorney, Ridge, Pitt, Willett, and the cross streets. To the west lay the most congested Rumanian quarter . . . on Chrystie, Forsyth, Eldridge, and Allen streets, flanked by Houston Street to the north and Grand Street to the south, with the Bowery gridironed by the overhead elevated to the west. . . . From Grand Street reaching south to Monroe, was the preserve of the Russians—those from Russia, Poland, Lithuania, Byelorussia, and the Ukraine—the most numerous of the Jewries of Eastern Europe.[20]

As the Jewish population of New York City grew, the Lower East Side became by far the most congested district in the five boroughs. The area's Tenth Ward, embracing about one half a square mile of Manhattan defined by the Bowery and Rivington, Norfolk, and Division Streets, was by the turn of the century reputed to be more densely populated than the worst districts of Bombay. By 1900, the Jewish population had risen to 330,000, and the Irish and Germans had virtually abandoned the area. However, Jewish immigration was so large that even as the Lower East Side grew to a peak of 542,061 in 1910, it held a decreasing portion of the city's growing Jewish population. Though 75 percent of New York City's Jews lived there in 1875, the percentage dropped to 50 within a little more than ten years and fell to 28 percent by 1915 as real estate and transit development opened up new neighborhoods to Jews in Brooklyn and the Bronx.[21]

Poverty, despair, and dislocation breed crime, and they did so on the Jewish Lower East Side. Violent crimes were rare, but arson, gambling, fencing stolen goods, picking pockets, and juvenile hooliganism victimized the neighborhoods and attracted wide attention. Prostitution was rampant on Allen, Chrystie, and Forsyth Streets.[22] In 1909, an article in the muckraking magazine *McClure's* referred to the Lower East Side as "the world's brothel," and a federal study reported that three-quarters of the more than two thousand prostitutes brought before the New York City Magistrate's Court between November 1908 and March 1909 were Jewish.[23]

As books and articles called attention to crime among Eastern European Jewish immigrants, an anti-Semitic piece in the September 1908 issue of the *North American Review* by New York City's police commissioner Theodore Bingham galvanized the Jewish community to action, particularly the uptown German branch. Bingham exaggerated the extent and variety of crimes committed by immigrant Jews and Italians and argued that Jews had a particular "propensity" for crime. Under pressure, Bingham apologized and retracted some of his more outlandish claims, including the charge that Jews, who made up 25 percent of the city's population, constituted 50 percent of its criminal element.[24]

The stir caused by the Bingham incident, the reality of criminal activity, and a sense that Jewish immigrants were generally unruly convinced German-Jewish leaders of the need to bring a semblance of order and unity to the community. Led by Rabbi Judah Magnes, they created the New York City Kehillah, a confederation of Jewish organizations in 1908. The Kehillah never succeeded in unifying the community, however, because socialists and labor unions refused to enroll, and many Orthodox Jews mistrusted the organization's secular thrust and its Reform Jewish leadership; it disbanded officially in 1925.[25]

More enduring as a source of both assistance and interethnic unease were the encounters between German and Eastern European Jews in educational institutions and settlement houses. Between 1846 and 1886, the German-Jewish population of New York City grew from approximately seven thousand to 85,000. By the time Eastern European Jews immigrated in large numbers, German Jews had left behind Lower Manhattan and moved to more comfortable, even affluent, neighborhoods to the north. They had become, in a phrase that has lingered, "uptown Jews." The newest Jewish immigrants, Eastern Europeans, populated the Lower East Side.[26]

German Jews viewed Eastern European Jewish culture with distaste and worried that the new arrivals would jeopardize German Jews' standing in the city. Ultimately, however, New York's German Jews had to acknowledge that they would have to share the city with their East European brethren. The uptowners concluded the newcomers would have to be Americanized—which meant they would have to become as much like German Jews as possible. The leaders of the German Jewish community set out to accomplish this goal with boundless energy, through the establishment of associations and agencies designed to provide both vocational and citizenship training, the largest of which was the Educational Alliance.[27]

Immigrant Jews resented the hostility toward all things Yiddish, which was quite pronounced in some German-dominated organizations. Nevertheless, Lower East Siders were drawn to the five-story Educational Alliance building on East Broadway, with its reading room, stage, gymnasium, and showers. And directors of the Educational Alliance, while upset by stiff-necked resistance to aspects of their Americanization programs, learned to be less heavy-handed in their approach. By the turn of the century, they had become more responsive to the interests of their constituents, even to the point of offering classes in Yiddish language and culture.[28]

The result was enthusiastic participation in numerous programs. From nine in the morning to ten in the evening, the Educational Alliance conducted classes in literature, history, philosophy, art, music, vocational subjects, and more. English-language classes, offered throughout the day and evening, were popular among all ages. In addition, the library, numerous clubs, a gymnasium, lecture series, a day-care center, and other facilities and programs drew approximately 37,000 people each week.[29]

Anywhere German Jews perceived potentially embarrassing problems among the new immigrants, they countered with organized remedies. New York's German Jewish community established the Hebrew Orphan Asylum, Clara de Hirsch Home for Working Girls, and Jewish Big Brothers and Sisters, all designed to keep the young from straying from the straight and narrow. The Jewish Prisoners Aid Society and the Lakeview Home for Jewish Unwed Mothers directed their efforts at those already in trouble, and the National Desertion Bureau addressed the serious problem of Jewish husbands who out of poverty and despair had abandoned their families.[30]

Eastern European Jews, who had a long tradition of communal organization and philanthropic activities, also worked to help themselves. Building on
shared connections to their hometowns and cities in Eastern Europe, towns-
people, or *landslayt*, formed *landsmanshaft* organizations. The *landsmanshaft*
provided its members sociability and a sense of cultural continuity. Perhaps
most important, it offered social services that reduced their dependency upon
outside charities for obtaining a job, housing, life insurance, sickness and death
benefits, and burial plots.[31] While these were male organizations, several had
women's auxiliaries. Early in the new century some loose, nationality-based fed-
erations of *landsmanshaftn* were formed: a Galician one in 1904, Polish in
1908, and Romanian in 1909.[32] Some of the larger *landsmanshaftn* eventually
established vocational or business subgroups.[33]

Most Eastern European Jewish immigrants at one time or another belonged
to a *landsmanshaft*. And there were other sources of aid and comfort in the
community. Synagogues, trade unions, and fraternal organizations like the
Independent Order B'rith Abraham (1887), the Workmen's Circle (1900), and
the Jewish National Workers' Alliance (1912) engaged in benevolent-society
activities.[34] Increasingly they were formed along national lines, and some
even transcended nationality to embrace all immigrant Jews. With greater
resources to draw on, they launched more ambitious projects than those of
the *landsmanshaftn*.[35]

✳ ✳ ✳

When Eastern European Jews arrived in New York, the city's dynamic economy offered multiple outlets for the labor skills and commercial energies the
immigrants had accumulated in Europe. The volatility of the city's economy
was equally important as an incentive to work. Booms and busts, especially in
the garment industry, sharpened the need to make money in anticipation of
hard times. In 1900, approximately one-third of the Jewish immigrants were
engaged in commercial enterprises such as peddling, selling from a pushcart,
or running a retail shop. An overwhelming majority of the 25,000 pushcart vendors in the city were Jews.[36]

Religion and gastronomic preferences also drove commerce. In 1910, five factories specialized in the manufacture of Passover matzos. Jews so loved seltzer
that the number of firms producing soda water grew from two in 1880 to more
than one hundred in 1907. Tending a pushcart or trudging up and down tenement staircases as a peddler were not easy ways to make a living, but the swell-
ing numbers of potential customers in Jewish immigrant neighborhoods offered
opportunities to work one's way up to storekeeper. As Selma Berrol has argued,
many Eastern European Jews were "willing to endure self-exploitation and

privation to amass the reserve that would enable them to become bosses and landlords themselves."[37]

For those arriving in the city prior to 1905, the best available opportunity to earn a livelihood lay in manufacturing, particularly in the garment industry, which had grown to some ten thousand firms employing 236,000 workers by 1890. By the end of the century, Jews constituted three-quarters of the labor force in this industry, and six of every ten Jewish workers were engaged in the production of clothing.[38]

Jewish dominance in the garment industry was the product of skills acquired in Europe. As many as 10 percent of the Eastern European Jewish immigrants were skilled tailors, and many more of the semiskilled and unskilled had some experience in European garment factories. It was easy to learn to press a garment or run a sewing machine. Eighty percent of the garment factories were located below Fourteenth Street and thus within walking distance of most Lower East Side tenements. German Jews owned some 90 percent of garment-manufacturing businesses during the 1880s. In the 1890s, when German Jewish proprietors began to abandon the garment industry for other branches of commerce and Russian Jews took their places, workers and employers could converse in the common language of Yiddish.[39]

The worst conditions for garment workers were in tenement workshops, where garment manufacturers cut overhead costs by farming out jobs to workers who toiled in their own tenement apartments. Workers labored up to fourteen hours in busy seasons. In addition to dim light and stale air, the heat was oppressive because stoves were kept lit to heat clothes irons. It was not the temperature of sweatshops that earned them their name, however, but the process of subcontracting. The manufacturers "sweated" profits from contractors, and the contractors in turn "sweated" profits from laborers. Hard times came with seasonal layoffs and, even worse, with economic depressions like that of 1893. In September of that year, one-third of the city's 100,000 unemployed were garment workers.[40]

The worst abuses began to decline only as a result of legal restrictions, starting with the 1892 Tenement House Act. Increased mechanization of production also contributed to moving more of the work into factory lofts. Between 1900 and 1915, the number of workers employed in licensed tenement shops dropped from 21,000 to 5,700. Workers in the factories of major manufacturers generally endured a sixty-hour week and had to pay for their own needles, thread, knives, and even, until 1907 for most workers, sewing machines. During the height of the season, both the pace of production and hours were increased to sixty-five and even seventy per week.[41] Many of the factory workers were young women, who found factories a relative improvement over working in a cramped tenement but suffered sexual harassment on the job.[42]

4.2 Jennie Rizzandi, nine, and her parents sewing garments in their home, 1913.

Source: Lewis Hine, Library of Congress.

The Lower East Side was a neighborhood of sweatshops and socialists, and each contributed to the district's energy. Garment workers protested when conditions became unbearable and at times called strikes. A surge of strikes and boycotts in 1886 established Jewish workers' anger and capacity for action. Two years later, Jewish socialists, with financial assistance from New York unions formed by German workers, established an umbrella labor organization in 1888—the United Hebrew Trades—which published the socialist Yiddish weekly *Arbeiter Zeitung*. (The episode was one of many examples of German radicals preparing the way for Jews who would follow them in New York's fertile blend of ethnic and political culture.) But a sustained, mass-supported Jewish labor movement did not arise until the second decade of the twentieth century. Striking cloak makers might accept union leadership or assistance but failed to join or build sustainable working-class institutions.[43]

The socialists who sponsored the early unions tended to be Russian Jews, intellectuals, and radicals who believed that Jewish religion and culture hindered the promotion of universalistic ideals. The union cause gained better leaders after 1905, when the failure of a Russian revolution in that year resulted in the emigration of large numbers of Bundists, Jewish socialists who worked to reconcile international radicalism and Jewish cultural autonomy. Bundists not only proved to be more able organizers than the earlier socialists but were also, as Irving Howe writes, "more Jewish" radicals. Among them were Sidney Hillman and David Dubinsky, who would gain fame as union leaders in New York and nationwide. Anarchists also established themselves in the world of Jewish radicalism in New York. Emma Goldman, an immigrant from Russia, made her way to New York in 1889 and found the city to be "a new world, strange and terrifying." Soon she was a regular in the cafes of the Lower East Side, an anarchist activist, and eventually an orator of national renown for her speeches on behalf of anarchism, free speech, women's rights, and free love. The differences among Jewish radicals were significant, and there was always a tension between addressing Jewish concerns and humanity at large. What the radicals of the Lower East Side held in common was not a single doctrine but a belief that it was possible to create a better world, one without hatred and inequality.[44]

Immigrant Jewish workers admired socialists who effectively organized and led unions and used traditional Jewish concepts and biblical references to press for social justice. Jewish working people enthusiastically joined the socialist-sponsored Workmen's Circle, enjoying its social and cultural activities as well as its excellent program of life and medical insurance. But while nearly one-third of the members of the Socialist Party in Manhattan and the Bronx in 1908 were Jewish, the vast majority of Jewish unionists and Workmen's Circle members were not enrolled in the party. Furthermore, in pre–World War I New York City immigrant Jews did not gravitate by experience to ballot-box party politics. Working-class electoral politics was the arena of the Irish. In 1912, the New York State Assembly district with the lowest percentage of registered voters was the predominantly Eastern European Jewish Eighth District.[45]

Until the era of World War I, Lower East Siders who did go to the polls in national elections generally followed their German brethren and cast their votes for the party of Lincoln. The Republicans' progressive wing had proven responsive to Jewish concerns about immigration policy and was vocally critical of Russia's anti-Semitic policies. At the local level, things were different. Two political strains competed for the East Side vote—the Democrats of Tammany Hall and the socialists. Tammany Hall expertly played the ethnic card. In 1900, the hall's Henry Goldfogle won election to the first of several terms in Congress. The next year, Tammany maneuvered Jacob Cantor into the Manhattan borough presidency, and he was followed by a string of Lower East Side Jews who held that office.[46]

Yet there was a considerable segment of the Jewish population for whom Tammany was anathema and who voted for candidates—regardless of party— who offered clean government, legislation to improve living and working conditions, opposition to immigration restriction, and criticism of czarist Russia.

In 1886, they had supported Henry George's candidacy for mayor; in 1901, they helped elect the Fusionist Party's Seth Low mayor. Theodore Roosevelt's progressivism and defense of Russian Jewry gained considerable Lower East Side support for Jewish Republicans running for state and local offices. William Randolph Hearst, a non-Tammany Democrat who was considered an advocate of Jewish interests in the United States and abroad, carried the Lower East Side in his unsuccessful bids for mayor in 1905 and governor in 1906. In the 1912 three-way race for governor, the Lower East Side gave the majority of its votes to the Progressive Party's candidate, Oscar Straus. He was irresistible: a Jew; a Democrat who served as Secretary of Commerce and Labor in Theodore Roosevelt's Republican administration; and, in 1905, following the second Kishinev pogrom, chairman of the National Committee for the Relief of Sufferers by Russian Massacres.[47]

Democrats, Republicans, and Socialists, as Hasia Diner points out, all vied for the Jewish vote. The real beginning of Jewish socialist electoral politics on the Lower East Side came in 1906, when Morris Hillquit ran for Congress on the Socialist ticket. He ran and lost five times. For all their enthusiasm, his supporters were unable to overcome Tammany's vote buying and the cooperative efforts of local Democrats, Republicans, and Hearst's Independent League to ensure his defeat.

Meyer London, another Socialist Party candidate running from the Lower East Side's Twelfth District, finally won a seat in 1914 on his third attempt. London, a Ukrainian-born labor lawyer, received broad community support in this campaign, including that of the Orthodox religious community and the Zionists, both traditionally hostile to the Socialist Party. Perhaps this backing was thanks to a growing realization that socialism was, as Moses Rischin characterized it, "Judaism secularized." Equally important in explaining Meyer London's appeal is the climate of American politics during what is now called the Progressive Era. In this period, the Socialist Party was a "big tent" bringing together reformers, radicals, and a host of dissenters ranging from Midwestern farmers to urban industrial laborers, including Jewish sweatshop workers. Within New York, Jewish socialists were part of an "urban progressive stream" that challenged entrenched inequalities, poor living conditions, and Tammany politics at its most expedient. Jews in the Socialist Party were one voice among many in a call for change.[48]

"Nationally," as Diner points out, "New York City provided Socialist candidates with almost half their votes, and most of these votes came from Jews." Yet the most enduring strength of Jewish socialism in New York was not its electoral power but its direct link to the Jewish labor movement that had been growing in New York since the 1880s. Socialists were common among the leaders and members of the International Ladies Garment Workers Union, the Amalgamated Clothing Workers, the Cap and Hat Workers, and the United

Hebrew Trades—an umbrella organization with a membership of more than 250,000 in 1917. When the Jewish labor movement spoke in New York City, on matters as mundane as institution building or as grand as forging a better future, socialist ideas were present.[49]

London's vision—deeply humane and rooted in the immigrant community—appealed to many who did not go so far as to join his party.[50] His election suggested that immigrant Jews were willing to work within the American electoral system and eager to transform the tenements and sweatshops. Jewish socialism in these years expressed both unhappiness with the present and hope for the future.[51]

The ebb and flow of political ideologies among Jewish immigrants was matched by changes in their religious observance. A minority of New York's East European Jews remained truly Orthodox. Most fashioned a religious identity out of a range of practices, such as joining a synagogue, attending High Holy Day services, or conforming to dietary laws.[52] In 1887, the city's Orthodox leaders attempted to bring some semblance of order and prestige to their community by bringing Rabbi Jacob Joseph of Vilna to assume the title of Chief Rabbi. The attempt to duplicate in New York City the authority such a title bore back in the Pale failed. Simple indifference on the part of many immigrant Jews, a lack of unity within the religious community, and the jealousy and resentment of many leaders made his job impossible.[53]

Despite the multitude of synagogues, the future of Jewish religious observance was uncertain in the Jewish immigrant community at the turn of the century. In addition to the secular outlook of the majority, trained rabbis were in short supply, and religious education suffered from inadequate facilities, poor teaching, and, in many cases, parental indifference. In 1914, when nearly all of the 275,000 Jewish children between the ages of six and fourteen were attending public school, under a quarter of them were receiving religious instruction.[54]

Jews responded to the pressures of American culture, as Annie Polland and Daniel Soyer note, by developing new forms of worship. Religion ceased to be a unifying element among Jews, but that did mean that Jews abandoned religion. "The synagogue," they write, "could not contain all of religious life. Home life, directed by immigrant women, became another site for religious expression and adaptation."[55]

Adaptations in traditional Judaism initiated in New York City led to what the historian Jeffrey S. Gurock terms "the emergence of the Americanized synagogue."[56] Though the effects of this effort would not be felt to any extent before World War I, efforts to revitalize Orthodox Judaism significantly culminated in 1912 with the formation of the Young Israel movement. Young Israel synagogues would come to offer decorous services led by broadly educated rabbis able to deliver sermons in English and to converse on matters secular as well as religious. In 1913, the organization of the United Synagogue of America by theologians based in New York's Jewish Theological Seminary marked the formal beginning of a third stream of Judaism in America, the Conservative movement. In their efforts to maintain the essentials of tradition while recognizing and adapting to change, in seeking to achieve "a synthesis of the old and the new, the rational and the spiritual" Conservative synagogues ultimately attracted many of the children and grandchildren of the immigrant generation.[57]

＊＊＊

If Eastern European Jews were divided about religious observances, they shared a passion for education. No immigrant group matched the Jews in enthusiasm for schooling. Jewish parents valued education for more than its cultural contributions: they knew that schooling could lead to jobs. Even their daughters, whose participation in traditional religious schooling had been historically limited at best, were encouraged to attend public school. Learning to read and write could be a step toward becoming a bookkeeper or typist. Vocational courses in the needle trades were also popular among Jewish girls.[58]

Jewish immigrants strongly desired that their children enter the professions or become manufacturing or retail entrepreneurs, but during the years of mass immigration educational attainment eluded all but a few. For one thing, facilities were limited. In 1914, Bronx and Manhattan combined had only five high schools, and even though by 1910 80 percent of CCNY's graduates were Jews, mostly of Eastern European origin, the total class consisted of only 112 students.[59] Even if more facilities had been available, necessity required many children to leave school to work at an early age.[60]

Progressive reformers and German Jews believed the city's schools provided the best hope for Americanizing immigrant children by eliminating perceived cultural traits and introducing new values. As Superintendent of Schools William H. Maxwell put it, the school "is the melting pot which converts the children of the immigrants . . . into sturdy, independent American citizens."[61] Children would learn English, proper manners, and hygiene and would receive a solid grounding in the essentials of democracy. Improving economic and social conditions was viewed at best as a possible "by-product of their efforts to achieve a productive citizenry."[62]

School authorities could be overbearing in their passion to help their pupils. In the schools of District Superintendent Julia Richman, a German American Jew, students who spoke Yiddish received demerits. A trace of an accent could bring down a teacher's wrath. A young Jewish woman recalled an English teacher's response to her reading of a passage from Shakespeare: "I must have had an accent, because she said, 'You people come here and don't want to learn English!' And she really made me feel like dirt."[63]

Overbearing educators collided with the community they served when teachers at PS 2 on Henry Street attempted to have students' adenoids removed. It was commonly believed that enlarged adenoids inhibited learning. Mothers of the intended victims rushed to the school denouncing the "pogrom." Plans for the surgery were quickly abandoned.[64] There were also examples of sensitive, dedicated teachers like the one a former Lower East Side student remembered as "an absolutely beautiful person. She changed the course of my life. She gave us everything she had and more. . . . And I was introduced to everything that was cultural and good in the United States."[65]

The belief that education provided the ladder of success for immigrant Jewish children has attained mythical proportions, but it *is* largely myth. The relatively rapid mobility of immigrant Jews and their children was attained largely through the crafts and commerce, endeavors that did not require diplomas.[66] The desire to learn, however, was real. For thousands of immigrants who were forced to leave school for work, the night became prime education time. In 1906, the majority of the one hundred thousand students enrolled in the Board of Education's evening classes were Jewish immigrants; 40 percent of the students were women.[67] Classes ranged from elementary school to high school to Americanization, but probably two-thirds of those enrolled were there to learn English.

For immigrants who aspired to higher levels of learning, a variety of institutions offered classes and lectures on all matter of subjects drawn from the

4.3 Library at the Henry Street Settlement House, 1910.

Source: Lewis Hine, Library of Congress.

fine and practical arts, humanities, social sciences, biblical and classical literature, and contemporary politics. Among the lecture topics offered at forums
aimed at immigrants were "The Times of the Roman Emperors," "Pictures from
Hindu Life," and "Practical Electricity." Lecture series in Yiddish offered by the
Board of Education drew 75,000 people a year by 1915. The sponsors of evening
enlightenment, like the topics, were numerous and included the Educational
Alliance, the People's Institute at Cooper Union, unions, Zionists, and socialists.[68] Enthusiasm for libraries was no less. A *New York Evening Post* reporter
commented in 1903, "The Jewish child has more than an eagerness for mental
food: it is an intellectual mania. He wants to learn everything in the library and
everything the libraries know. He is interested not only in knowledge that will
be of practical benefit, but in knowledge for its own sake."[69]

✳ ✳ ✳

A hunger for learning, along with a desire for entertainment and a sense of community, inspired a flowering of Yiddish newspapers. Between 1885 and 1914,
twenty Yiddish dailies were established, representing every shade of belief
and opinion within the immigrant community from Orthodox Judaism to
anarchism.

The *Forverts* (Forward) was founded in 1897. Within a decade of its founding, it had become the largest Yiddish newspaper in the world. By 1912, its ten-
story plant on lower Broadway was producing a paper reaching 140,000 readers.[70]
The success of the *Forverts* was thanks to its brilliant editor, Abraham Cahan. His
paper took much of its inspiration from the newspapers of the German socialists that preceded him, but under his direction it espoused a Lower East Side
brand of socialism, promoting the cause of organized labor and taking stands
on bread-and-butter issues. The socialism of the *Forverts* was never that of
narrow, partisan politics or ideology but rather, in Cahan's words, that of "justice, humanity, fraternity—in brief, honest common sense and horse sense."[71]

As committed as he was to the humane ideals of socialism and to the pragmatic goals of trade unionism, Cahan was also determined to lead his readers
into full participation in American life. He spoke out on behalf of public schooling and particularly supported education for girls and women.[72] He explained
to his readers the intricacies of baseball and urged parents to allow their sons
to "play baseball and become excellent at the game." On no account must they
"raise the children to grow up foreign in their own birthplace."[73]

His most successful vehicle for communicating, teaching, and helping was
the "Bintel Brief" (Bundle of letters), a column introduced in 1906. Readers
wrote for advice on the problems of living in a new land, asking questions about
everything from labor exploitation to the duties of children toward their parents to marital infidelity.[74] For thousands of immigrants, Abraham Cahan and
the *Forverts* were teacher and textbook.

On the Lower East Side, civil society was manifested in print, in lecture halls, and in coffee shops and cafes that served as gathering spots for Jewish intellectuals. Many of these eateries had their own special clientele representing a particular political philosophy. Although the atmosphere tended to be uniform—with smoke from Russian cigarettes and the aroma of hot tea emanating from glasses—the arguments varied with the patrons.[75] Among them were the "sweatshop poets" like Morris Winchevsky, David Edelstadt, Morris Rosenfeld, and Yosef Bovshover, who had experienced factory labor and wrote against life in the shops. "Don't look for me where myrtles grow!" wrote Rosenfeld. "You will not find me there, my love; where lives wither at the machines, there is my resting place." Such writers were heroes to the Jews who attended their lectures and read their work in the Yiddish press.[76]

While thousands sought sociability and enlightenment in cafes and lecture halls, others gravitated to more relaxed venues. Young and old alike spent their leisure hours hanging out in the candy stores that proliferated in the neighborhood. Street games and street gangs also abounded on the Jewish Lower East Side, as they did in Italian and Irish neighborhoods. Dancing was a rage among young adults. In 1907, thirty-one dance halls dotted a ninety-block area between Houston and Grand streets, east of Broadway.[77] Movie theaters were also popular. In 1908, the *Forverts* reported, "There are now about a hundred movie houses in New York, many of them in the Jewish quarter. Hundreds of people wait in line."[78]

Young Jewish women in particular found in popular culture and entertainment multiple opportunities to break free from the authority figures of their work, families, and neighborhoods. In dance halls, nickelodeons, vaudeville shows, and trips to Coney Island, daughters of the Lower East Side experimented with style and self-expression and mingled with potential romantic partners without adult supervision. Parents might fear the loss of control over their children, and reformers might fear that young women could be corrupted. Italian families, with their notions of family-centered leisure, seemed to have been particularly concerned about losing their daughters to the lures of bright lights. Nevertheless, as Kathy Peiss has pointed out, young women embraced the new world of leisure because it offered autonomy denied them elsewhere.[79]

Jews of all ages could embrace the popular culture of turn-of-the-century New York in part because other Jews, immigrant and native-born, had such a big role in shaping it. As performers and showmen, Jewish influence made popular entertainment a two-way bridge between immigrant communities and the mainstream, with influences flowing both to the audience and back to the performers.[80]

Of all the vehicles of Jewish immigrant culture, none matched the popularity of the Yiddish theater. The first Yiddish play produced in New York appeared in 1882; by 1918, twenty Yiddish theaters were attracting an audience of two million people to one thousand performances annually.[81] Initially the theaters offered broad comedies, romantic musicals, melodramas on biblical and historical themes, and plays dealing, sometimes seriously and sometimes comically, with immigrant experiences. These theaters also produced corrupt Yiddish versions of European dramas.[82]

Popular with the masses, the productions were dismissed as *shund* (trash) by the intellectuals, who called for serious theater. Their fondest hopes came to fruition beginning in 1891, with the arrival of a talented playwright from Russia, Jacob Gordin, and the establishment soon afterward of the Independent Yiddish Artists Company by the actor-director Jacob Adler. Adler declared that he would offer "only beautiful musical operas and dramas giving truthful and serious portrayals of life" and would reject "all that is crude, unclean, immoral."[83] *Siberia*, the first collaboration of Adler and Gordin, was an instant success. Gordin's *Jewish King Lear* followed three months later. It was a sensation. Gordin went on to write more than seventy plays, championing the cause of realism in the Yiddish theater and earning for himself the title "the Yiddish Ibsen." He inspired a whole generation of Yiddish dramatists.[84]

* * *

Lower Manhattan, including the Lower East Side, was sufficiently dense and sprawling that it could accommodate a variety of immigrant groups. Among them was the second-largest immigrant group to reach New York in these years, the Italians. Even though the offices of the *Forverts* were barely a fifteen-minute walk from the Italian enclave on Mulberry Street, Old World experiences and New World realities gave Jews and Italians contrasting experiences. The newcomers from Italy were usually *contadini*, Sicilian and South Italian peasants or laborers, most of whom were illiterate. They left behind much suffering and destitution and arrived in New York to grapple with poverty, low-paid laborers' jobs, inadequate housing, and prejudice.

Italian immigrants, as Thomas J. Ferraro points out, brought with them long-established customs for dealing with landowners, the church, and governments. They would put these to use in New York City in settings as varied as tenements, construction sites, and religious shrines. They held to a "mother-centered order of the family" that resonated with the prominence of the Virgin Mary in Roman Catholicism as an "expression of hope and the renewal of courage" and embraced "the cult of Honor for communal intrigue and masculine self-esteem." They were also proud. "They were ferocious realists," Ferraro argues, "who understood where power lay and why it was wielded, but they would have hated—*hated*—to be considered anyone's victim."[85]

In 1850, Italian New Yorkers numbered only 853 in the city's official count. The pace of emigration picked up after that and grew rapidly from 1880 to 1914.

Italian newcomers were at first mostly young men who had emigrated with the intention of making enough money to return home and purchase land. In some years, more than 50 percent did so. Those who intended to establish permanent homes in America usually lodged as boarders and saved as much as they could to bring their kin over. Many married men returned to Italy to bring back their wives and children. Bachelors often went home to find spouses and then return to America with them. With such marriages, the early pattern of male migration gave way to a family immigration that became crucial to Italian life in New York City.

By 1900, New York City counted nearly 250,000 Italians, and numbers continued to grow during the years of peak immigration between 1900 and 1914. Little Italy in Lower Manhattan's Fourteenth Ward rapidly became the city's most famous Italian colony, but even before 1900 Italians were settling uptown. Northern Italians from Genoa, Piedmont, and Tuscany located in Greenwich Village as early as 1890. After 1900, southern Italian immigrants sought housing in Greenwich Village and began to move to other parts of Manhattan and to settle in Brooklyn and the Bronx. By 1913, Brooklyn claimed 235,000 Italians to Manhattan's 310,000. In 1913, New York's five boroughs had more than twenty-five individual Italian districts, ranging in size from 2,000 to 100,000, and smaller groups of Italians were scattered throughout the city.[86]

Building projects like the construction of reservoirs, bridges, and especially subways after 1900 influenced patterns of Italian settlement. Like Irish men before them, Italian males provided the manual labor required in a growing city. They preferred to live near their places of work, such as the subway routes under construction in the Bronx, Brooklyn, and Queens. As the historian George Pozzetta points out, "settlement patterns of Italians were often exclusively determined by local employment opportunities."[87]

Italian Harlem, above Ninety-Sixth Street on the eastern side of Manhattan, is a case in point. The first Italians to live there, workers brought in by an Irish American contractor as strikebreakers to build the First Avenue trolley tracks, lived in a shantytown along 106th Street. Others followed, and Italian Harlem claimed four thousand residents by 1880. It reached its peak as an Italian neighborhood in the 1920s. Initially, Italians shared the neighborhood with Irish and Jews, but the latter gradually moved out as the Italians moved in. In the Bronx, a small colony of Calabrians, Campanians, and Sicilians developed when Italian workers built streets and railways in that borough and helped construct the Croton Reservoir in neighboring Westchester County. As was often the case elsewhere, they moved into frame houses vacated by the Irish. In Brooklyn, the first Italian enclave was at Hamilton Ferry, where laborers found homes near the waterfront where they worked.[88]

Labor contractors—called *padroni*—shaped patterns of settlement when they took a share of the newcomers' wages in exchange for finding jobs and housing. (Some also wrote letters home for the illiterate immigrants and helped them find their way during the early days of settlement.) Native-born Americans looked down on *padroni* and disapproved of their promotion of contract labor, which appeared to many as scarcely different from slavery. The federal government in the 1880s and later New York State outlawed such activities. After 1900, they became less important in the Italian migration process and by 1910 were virtually out of the immigrant trade.[89]

Among Italians, regional loyalties were as important as jobs in determining residence. Many—who thought of themselves as Genoese, Calabrian, Neapolitan, or Sicilian rather than as Italian—preferred to live among family members and people from their own regions and villages. Some had traveled on prepaid tickets provided by the relatives or neighbors who were on hand to greet them at Castle Garden and later Ellis Island. The *New York Times* reported in 1897 that when the SS *Trojan Senator* arrived, the 1,100 Italians on board were welcomed at the dock by over five thousand friends and relatives.[90] Other immigrants came on their own but with knowledge of where friends and family were located in New York City. The historian Donna Gabaccia has traced the pattern of Sicilian immigration (especially the village of Sambuca) to Elizabeth Street in Manhattan.[91] A federal government report in 1908 noted the clustering of Italian immigrants:

> In the Mulberry Bend district are to be found Neapolitans and Calabrians mostly; in Baxter Street, near the Five Points is a colony of Genoese; in Elizabeth Street, between Houston and Spring, a colony of Sicilians. The quarter west of Broadway in the Eighth and Fifteenth wards is made up mainly of North Italians who have been longer in New York and are rather more prosperous than the others, although some Neapolitans have come into Sullivan and Thompson streets to work in the flower and feather trades.[92]

No matter where the immigrants settled, their housing was often overcrowded and unhealthy. Arriving with few, if any, economic resources and not knowing English, Italian immigrants could not earn enough money to afford decent quarters. They moved into tenements vacated by Irish, Germans, and others who were improving their lot. Italian residences were described in 1884 as "old and long ago worn out. They are packed with tenants, rotten with age and decay, and so constructed to have made them very undesirable for dwelling purposes in their earliest infancy."[93] Even new housing was of poor quality. Robert Orsi notes, "Housing stock in Italian Harlem was deteriorating from the moment it was built. Unlike West Harlem, which was constructed with the care lavished on luxury neighborhoods, East Harlem was always a working class community and the immigrants inhabited substandard buildings from the first days of the community."[94]

The Danish-born journalist and reformer Jacob Riis brought the city's slum conditions to public view in his book *How the Other Half Lives*, published in 1889. Riis, whose writings combined ethnic stereotypes with outrage at bad housing, painted a grim picture of neighborhoods such as Mulberry Bend. "Under the pressure of the Italian influx the standard of breathing space required for an adult by the health offices has been cut down from six to four hundred cubic feet."[95] Housing built before the enactment of the Tenement Act of 1901 was too small to house extended families. To make ends meet, families took in boarders or lodgers whose presence aggravated overcrowding. Immigrants and their families sometimes found themselves living in dark and damp cellars.

Sensational press reporting stereotyped Italians as criminals. Especially prominent were the charges that Sicilian immigration had brought with it members of the Mafia and that Sicilian criminals resorted to written threats— "Black Hand" letters—demanding money in return for protection of businesses. Black Hand threats and violence were certainly common in the city's Italian districts, but little evidence existed of large-scale Mafia migration to the United States. Nevertheless, charges about the Mafia prompted the New York City police to establish a separate Italian division in 1904 to investigate crime and extortion threats in Italian neighborhoods and possible ties to criminals in Sicily.[96]

When Lieutenant Joseph Petrosino of the New York City Police Department was murdered in Palermo in 1909 while investigating possible Mafia connections to New York City, public opinion was inflamed.[97] Images of dangerous and violent Mafia and Black Hand criminals helped feed anti-immigrant and anti-Italian sentiment.

Italians also had their defenders, who insisted with reason that they were no more likely to be criminals than other immigrants or native-born Americans and that the vast majority of Italian immigrants struggled to make a living at physically demanding, low-paying jobs. Kate Claghorn in her 1908 report for the U.S. Industrial Commission wrote, "All classes [of Italians] are highly industrious, thrifty, and saving. They are strict in keeping to their agreements; always pay their rent, doctor's bills and lawyer's fees. They are considered very desirable tenants."[98] Moreover, Black Hand activities ceased around the time of World War I.[99]

✳ ✳ ✳

The vast majority of Italian men toiled as laborers. Life in rural Italy taught them how to use a shovel, and jobs demanding muscle power were plentiful in the expanding city. However, as important as common labor was to Italian males, they found jobs in other occupations as well. Among the most fortunate immigrants were those who found employment on the municipal payroll; the sanitation department claimed the greatest number. Many observers noted the Italian organ grinders and rag pickers who rummaged "the garbage cans, gleaning paper, rags, bones, [and] broken glass." Italians also became barbers—providing half of New York's supply—shoemakers, masons, waiters, teamsters, and bartenders. The historian Thomas Kessner observes that musicians were about the only Italians categorized as professionals in the 1880 census. A few Italian immigrants opened small shops; others attained the position of *padrone*. But the most noticeable entrepreneurs were the street merchants who sold their wares on New York City's streets. Kessner found a few who began as peddlers and acquired dozens of pushcarts and control of vending stands.[100]

Increasingly Italians gained entry into the city's rapidly expanding garment business. Some shop owners turned to them to counter the union-organizing efforts of Jewish needle-trade workers. Italians also found work on the waterfront. In 1880, just when Italians began to arrive in large numbers, practically all of Manhattan's longshoremen were Irish. When a strike led by the Knights of Labor temporarily crippled the shipping industry, employers looked to Italian laborers when they wanted to hire strikebreakers. Employment on the docks was riddled with corruption and payoffs, but once Italians gained a foothold

4.4 Demonstration against child labor, 1909.

Source: Bain Collection, Library of Congress.

their numbers increased rapidly. One scholar observed that bosses loved Italians because of their "eagerness . . . for the work, their willingness to submit to deductions from the wages, leaving a neat little commission to be divided between foreman, saloon keepers, and native bosses."[101]

Because some Italian workers were used as strikebreakers, they earned reputations as scabs. The accusation has some accuracy but fails to grasp the conditions that led some Italian workers to become strikebreakers. Most of them had no contact with trade unions before emigrating to America, and for those who intended only to stay in America for a few years before returning home, unions appeared to offer few benefits. Thus, employers were quick to use Italian immigrants to break strikes or as a source of potential replacement workers with which to threaten employees contemplating union organization.[102]

Among Italian men, agricultural work in Italy had prepared them for little more than poorly paid laborer's jobs. In addition, many of them were illiterate. High-paid work in the New York City economy was beyond their reach. Like the Irish before them, they took what jobs were available. The dilemma pushed Italian women into the labor force. While Italian women were less likely to do wage work than their Jewish counterparts, economic necessity frequently made their employment necessary.

As the rapidly expanding New York economy at the turn of the century provided numerous jobs for women workers, the garment industry became a particularly rich source of employment for young Italian women. In 1905, some 85 percent of young, single Italian women were working in garment and garment-related jobs.[103] While single women accounted for the largest number of Italian women workers, married but childless women also headed for the garment shops. When children came, it was nearly impossible for married women to work for wages outside of the home. And Italian families tended to be large. The shops that employed Italian women, like those that employed Jewish women, were unsanitary, unsafe, dirty, poorly lit places that paid low wages. In the infamous Triangle Fire of 1911, Italians as well as Jews died.

Economic and demographic factors compelled Italian parents to see their children not as students but as wage earners. Although New York had compulsory school laws, they were not always enforced. Working at home was a practice that Italians brought with them from southern Italy. Work began at very young age, and children dropped out of school as soon as it was permitted by law or even before. New York law permitted boys of ten to sell papers, which they did until they were strong enough to do hard physical labor on the docks or construction sites. "Girls never went to school," Miriam Cohen reports, "but were made to work."[104] Young girls made garments and artificial flowers. Just how much authority Italian women had in their communities is debatable, but in the home they prevailed. Mothers instructed the young girls in garment homework and taught them how cook, clean, keep a home, and prepare to marry an Italian man.[105]

Married Italian women also earned money by taking in boarders, a common immigrant practice. A federal commission reported that nearly one-fourth of southern Italian families took in boarders.[106] Since Italian families were a part of an extended clan—aunts, uncles, and cousins—and because more single men than women immigrated, there was usually a supply of potential boarders. When they were taken in, women's work cooking, cleaning, and performing family tasks only grew more onerous.

Because few Italian women immigrated to New York City by themselves, Italian women's labor was embedded largely in a family context. Most women came as wives, daughters, or sisters and lived within kinship networks. Rarely did the census takers find unmarried Italian women living alone. Ellis Island officials looked upon all single women as possible prostitutes; it was risky for young women to travel alone. Once here, women, if single, were expected to marry, raise children, care for the home, and in general not participate in the larger society as paid workers. While most did conform to the greater part of this formula, the reality of paid work was quite different from cultural expectations. Even with the whole family working, the family incomes of Italian immigrants were among the lowest in the city, often below the "essentials of a normal standard of living in New York City."[107]

Economic mobility through education, often exaggerated in retrospect as an avenue for the earliest Jewish immigrants, was even less plausible for Italians. Unlike Jewish parents, Italian mothers and fathers generally were distrustful of the city's public schools, which they saw as, among other things, competitors for control of their children. Southern Italians, Miriam Cohen writes, "came from a society in which, given the social, demographic, and political conditions, schooling had little place." She notes further, "if Italian families invested in advanced schooling for their offspring at all, they were more likely to invest in the boys than the girls." Family life was extremely important to Italian immigrants, who arrived in America with strong family structures in which outsiders were viewed with distrust. As strangers in a new world, many continued to view nonfamily institutions such as public schools with suspicion.[108]

For many, especially Italians, the public schools were part of American society's attempt to force its culture on the newcomers and their children. This perspective clashed with the ideals of the Americanization movement in the early twentieth century, which found expression in settlement houses, government agencies, YMCAs, and schools. Some of the Americanizers were settlement workers or other reformers who sought to improve immigrants' lives with English classes for adults, a little American history, and civics. Other Americanizers were later criticized for forcing the values of patriotism and employer-based capitalism on the immigrants. The response of immigrants was mixed.

Some hailed the various programs; others believed "Americanization" was simply an attempt to stamp out immigrant cultures.[109]

Immigrants were more enthusiastic about efforts to enter American society that grew from the bottom up, from the initiative of immigrants themselves. New York unions and labor struggles were on the rise during the first two decades of the twentieth century, and, despite an early association with strike-breaking, many Italian workers were drawn into union activity. Jews may have formed the backbone of the emerging garment unions, the International Ladies' Garment Workers' Union and the Amalgamated Clothing Workers of America, but Italian men and women were involved too. The great clothing industry walkout of 1909 found Italian working people divided. Most opposed the strike, and some took jobs as scabs, but newspapers such as the *Corriere della Sera* backed the strikers. Salvatore Ninfo, the chief organizer among Italians, said that more than one thousand Italian workers had joined the strike. Subsequent strikes in the garment trades won increasing Italian support. Skilled Italians, such as bricklayers, were more successful in their union-recruitment efforts. Italians replacing Irish at the docks were initially slow to organize or join unions, and unskilled construction workers were rarely touched by unions.[110]

* * *

Italian Americans found their own unique routes into American politics. Tammany Hall ignored Italians during the last decades of the nineteenth century. Despite their growing numbers, Italians were unfamiliar with electoral politics and had a very low naturalization rate because so many intended to return to Italy. In 1902, Rocco Corresca, an Italian bootblack, recalled his formative contact with the Irish-run Democrats: "There are some good Irishmen, but many of them insult Italians. They call us Dagoes. So I will be a Republican."[111]

After 1900, however, Tammany showed greater interest and began competing with the Republicans in forming political clubs in Italian districts. Even then, few from those communities ran for office, and only a handful were elected; most Italian officeholders gained their positions by appointment. Fiorello La Guardia, the most successful Italian American politician to emerge in New York City, faced an uphill battle to win a seat in Congress. In 1914, seeking election in a solidly Tammany district, he ran as a Republican and lost. Yet in the next contest, by marshaling Italian and anti-Tammany voters, he narrowly won election to the House of Representatives, the first New York Italian American to do so.[112]

Some Italians found both the Republicans and Democrats unresponsive to the problems of poverty and working-class life and joined the Socialist Party, even though Jews dominated it in New York City. A few had experience with both socialism and anarchism in Sicily and formed Italian American socialist clubs, such as Brooklyn's Club Avanti. Socialists drew their Italian members from among shoemakers, garment workers, and even barbers, but even at their peak they attracted few from this immigrant community. Anarchism, while it never represented a majority of Italian immigrants, was nevertheless a strong presence in Italian neighborhoods. As Jennifer Guglielmo argues, the *sovversivi* (subversives) had an impact "much larger than their numbers because they established quite visible alternative cultural and political spaces in their neighborhoods, which became popular centers for immigrant education, political discussion, labor organizing, and recreation."[113] The most well-known Italian radical was Carlo Tresca, who founded and edited a series of radical newspapers. In 1914, he was editing *L'Avvenire* (The future) from Harlem. The most prominent newspaper to emerge from the Italian immigrant world, however, was the more conservative *Il Progresso*, which began in 1880 with a small budget and a staff of three and by 1915 had a circulation of 82,000.[114]

Progressive reform movements that drew some Jewish immigrants into politics were less compelling to Italians. Settlement houses succeeded in serving the Jewish community, but Italians saw settlement-house workers as outsiders competing for control of the family. If political parties and settlements made only limited headway in the city's Italian neighborhoods, Italians' own associations were more successful. Some, in typical immigrant fashion, sought to help people adjust to their new environment and protect them from unscrupulous persons who preyed upon the innocent. Most notable was the Society for the Protection of Italian Immigrants, formed in 1901. Like other ethnic groups, Italians organized dozens of mutual-aid societies to provide death benefits, sickness insurance, funds for emergencies, and serve as social centers. Mostly with small memberships, they were usually organized around men from particular villages in Italy. Many locals finally banded together to form the Sons of Italy, a national organization that became influential within the Italian communities of New York City.[115] The professional elite within the immigrants became members of the *prominenti*, "a loose confraternity of successful wealthy (by immigrant standards) Italians."[116] Northern Italians also had similar associations, whose members remained aloof from their southern countrymen.

＊ ＊ ＊

The Catholic Church, a stronghold of Irish power in New York City since the middle of the nineteenth century, did not provide a substantial base for Italians. Although Italian immigrants came from a country where practically everyone was at least nominally Catholic, in New York City the church was Irish-run.[117] Irish clergy could be harsh in their views of other ethnic Catholics, particularly Poles and Italians. Cardinal McCloskey refused a request from Polish Catholics for their own church, remarking that "what they needed was not their own church but a pig shanty."[118] An Italian priest had been appointed to serve northern Italians in New York as early as 1859, but his efforts were not successful. Nor was the church prepared for the great influx after 1880.[119]

To meet the needs of newly arrived Italian Catholics, Italian priests were appointed to serve in "annexes" of parishes, usually a basement room provided for services. This accommodation permitted an Irish-run parish to offer its Italian members a separate service. The Irish hierarchy was critical of Italian parishioners, who they thought were lax in observance, anticlerical, and ignorant of doctrine. The Irish believed that Italian priests were poorly trained and represented the "dregs of Italy."[120] One priest wrote: "The Italians are not a sensitive people like our own. When they are told that they are about the worst Catholics that ever came to this country, they don't resent it, or deny it. If they were a little more sensitive to such remarks they would improve faster. The Italians are callous as regards religion."[121]

Irish priests saw Italian shrines and beliefs about the evil eye as little more than paganism, but these were elements of the folklore and deeply localized religious practices that Italian peasants had brought to New York from Italy. Jacob Riis observed how Italian immigrants erected shrines and altars and concluded that they had a "strange artistic genius." Italian immigrants erected shrines in their homes, carried statues of saints through the streets, and set up illuminated arches to celebrate Christmas and *feste* dedicated to the patron saints of their hometowns in Italy. Despite the fretting of the Irish church hierarchy in New York, Italians carried on enthusiastically with processions and practices that took religion out of the confines of the home and into the streets, bridging faith and home, family life and public life. All of these would become part of the folklore of Italian neighborhoods in New York.[122]

Italian Catholics in turn distrusted the church they found in their new country. In Italy, they had viewed the church with suspicion as a hierarchical organization unresponsive to their needs. The men, especially, scorned church-going as "women's work." The Irish-dominated church here seemed ill-suited to their concerns. Moreover, in Italy Catholicism was the established religion and individual churches often the only social organization in a village. In America, however, Catholicism was a minority religion that competed with other faiths and social organizations. As a result many immigrants, particularly the men, did not attend church and had little to do with it.[123] Richard Gambino, a sociologist raised in Brooklyn, recalled of his father, "Typical of males of contadino origins, my father had been an infrequent churchgoer, attending Mass only on major holidays like Christmas and on those traditional occasions when family loyalty made presence compulsory—weddings and funerals."[124] As a result, the Irish-dominated church was slow to work with Italian Americans and to recruit them as priests and nuns. In light of such ambivalence, Protestants believed that Italian immigrants represented a fertile field for evangelism and sent missionaries into Italian neighborhoods. While the Protestants did achieve some conversions, few Italians joined their churches.[125]

In the long run, the Irish-run Catholic Church and Italian immigrants achieved a modus vivendi. The church hierarchy, beginning with Archbishop Michael A. Corrigan and followed by John Cardinal Farley, neither of whom displayed the anti-Italian prejudices common to the Irish, requested more Italian priests and expanded parish activities in Italian neighborhoods. To counter Protestant missions and settlement houses, Catholic charities were established to serve Italian immigrants. By 1911, the city had fifty Italian Catholic churches served by more than eighty Italian priests. Church leaders also encouraged Italian parishes to build parochial schools. While the new parishes enjoyed some limited success in this endeavor, Italians—poor to begin with—were reluctant to raise funds to pay for Catholic schools when public schools were free. Besides, the parochial schools were inevitably staffed by Irish nuns who appeared indifferent to Italian pupils. Early efforts to recruit Italian girls as nuns were not successful.[126]

* * *

More secular in their orientation were the settlement houses launched in the late nineteenth century, when a new generation of reformers settled into urban neighborhoods to live alongside the poor and immigrants and provide them with education and social services. The settlement-house movement, launched in 1884 at Toynbee Hall in London, soon spread to New York and other American cities. Most settlement-house workers were old-stock Americans, but their numbers also included German Jews. Most settlement workers were middle class and took up their vocation knowing little about the immigrants, but the most dedicated among them made a fervent commitment to the settlements and to urban reform. Prominent among them were women, who as settlement-house workers drew on older ideas of women's reform networks, the social gospel, new notions of social welfare, and growing efforts by college-educated women to find fulfilling careers. Many women who built lives as social reformers could trace the beginnings of their careers to work in a settlement house. Equally significant, before World War I the meetings of native-born settlement workers and immigrants in New York would ignite some of the strongest reform impulses to emerge in fields such as public health and education.[127]

New York's most famous settlement was Lillian Wald's Henry Street Settlement House, funded by the Jewish financier Jacob Schiff. The settlement ran a variety of programs to improve the lives of the newcomers and attracted more Jews than Italians. Henry Street's impact on African Americans was limited, but white women in its orbit, such as Wald and Mary Ovington, were involved with the founding of the National Association for the Advancement of Colored People and the National Urban League. Both became major organizations for African Americans.[128]

One of the most important programs launched at Henry Street was the Visiting Nurse Service, which sent nurses into the homes and neighborhoods of the poor. In 1917, one hundred nurses made almost a quarter of million home visits, providing medical care that recognized the dignity and independence of the patient.[129] Working and living in immigrant neighborhoods, settlement-house leaders concluded that the urban environment needed substantial improvement and became involved in efforts to improve tenements, working conditions, public health, schools, and support for mothers. Their work became central to the social policies and legislative successes of the Progressive Era.[130]

Wald, founder of the Henry Street Settlement, drew strength from varied sources that suggest the centrality of ethnicity and women's concerns in urban reform. Born into a German Jewish family, Wald moved in Jewish circles but embraced a secular universalism. Her work in public nursing was animated by both enduring ideas of women as natural healers and new practices in public health. She lived in "a homosocial world that was also homoerotic," as Blanche Weisen Cook puts it, but lobbied effectively in wider worlds dominated by men. Wald was middle class in her origins but devoted herself to the cause of New York's garment workers. In 1909, when New York's garment industry was rocked by a great strike, strikers met in the backyard of the Henry Street Settlement.[131]

In the years between 1909 and 1914, Italian and Jewish workers grew in numbers and power in the needle trades, which characteristically had German Jewish owners and more recently arrived Eastern European Jewish immigrants as workers. From this surge of strikes and union organizing emerged the International Ladies' Garment Workers' Union and the Amalgamated Clothing Workers' Union.[132] Italian women participated in garment-industry strikes, but, as Jennifer Guglielmo points out, ethnic and workplace divisions and the Italians' wariness of garment unions that had limited interest in recruiting them delayed their entry into industrial unionism. A few Italians joined the Industrial Workers of the World; others engaged in wildcat strikes.[133]

Twenty thousand workers from the shirtwaist shops, mostly young Jewish women but also Italians and others, initiated the most angry and dramatic strike—a walkout begun on November 22, 1909. Never before had there been a massive strike of women in the United States. Young Jewish women such as Rose Schneiderman and Clara Lemlich, both of them socialists, became leaders. During the meeting to consider a strike, Lemlich leapt to her feet and shouted in Yiddish, "I am a working girl, one of those striking against intolerable conditions. . . . I offer a resolution that a general strike be declared—now."[134] The crowd shouted agreement.

The justice of the strikers' cause and their courage and their commitment won broad public sympathy and support from the college-educated reformers of the Women's Trade Union League (WTUL) and members of the German Jewish establishment led by Rabbi Stephen Wise. The strike and subsequent walkouts led to improved labor conditions, but the 1911 Triangle Fire revealed the limits of the unions' influence.

The Triangle Waist Company was one of the few firms that had not settled with the ILGWU after the 1909 uprising; it remained a nonunion shop, and its employees were largely young women.[135] On March 25, 1911, a fire broke out in the Triangle building. Panic, coupled with exits locked by management and with flammable cloth and debris lying around, led to a disaster. A majority of the workers escaped, but 146 lost their lives. Many jumped to their deaths; others were burned alive. The city was stunned.[136]

In a meeting at the Metropolitan Opera House, Rose Schneiderman, a socialist, union activist, and a leader in the WTUL's New York chapter condemned a system in which "The life of men and women is so cheap and property is so sacred!" Schneiderman's career was grounded in building alliances between labor and middle-class reformers, but she said bitterly that she could not "talk fellowship" in the aftermath of the Triangle Fire. "It is up to the working people to save themselves."[137]

Despite such class-conscious anger, the reforms enacted in response to the Triangle Fire were the product of a broad coalition. Middle-class reformers, workers and their unions, the WTUL, and key politicians pushed for reforms including state inspection of the factories. Traditionally, Tammany Hall was not enthusiastic about reform. In the nineteenth century, most urban-reform movements in New York City were either strongly Protestant and moralistic or were aimed at curbing the power of city government—and with that the power of Tammany. However, Al Smith and Robert Wagner, who were rising Tammany men under its leader Charles Murphy, reinvented themselves as urban reformers. Mixing principles and pragmatism—both lives and votes were at stake—they pushed for strong state action for better conditions for factory workers. Now Tammany was ready to reach out to immigrant workers and use the power of government to improve industrial conditions.[138]

In the aftermath of the Triangle Fire, an alliance of Tammany men and Progressive reformers in New York achieved victories that became part of the emerging welfare state. Progressives' moralism and technical expertise, combined with immigrants' passion for justice and Tammany's understanding of practical politics, produced an effective alliance. Tenement-house reform, improved health departments, and factory legislation established the idea of a robust public sector that would distinguish politics in New York City and New York State for decades and culminate in the New Deal in the 1930s.

* * *

To a notable degree, most of the defining issues of this time involved gender. Immigrant women seeking better working conditions, Greenwich Village bohemians embracing free love and the formation of an urban gay community, and socialists aiming to overthrow capitalism all wrestled with what it meant to be a man or a woman. Debates over these issues animated places as different as settlement-house meeting rooms and tenement kitchens, but they inevitably bumped up against one point: women could not vote. As the socialist firebrand Clara Lemlich put it: "The manufacturer has the vote; the bosses have votes, the foremen have votes, the inspectors have votes. The working girl has no vote," she concluded.[139]

Politically active women grasped that they needed the vote to achieve social reform and control their own lives. To gain the vote, however, they had to win a succession of state-level votes on suffrage. And by the early twentieth century, only a few Western states had granted the vote to women. Then the National

4.5 New York City suffrage parade, 1915. Votes from immigrant Jewish men helped women win the right to vote in New York State in 1917.

Source: Bain Collection, Library of Congress.

American Woman Suffrage Association (NAWSA) relocated to New York City, a metropolis of millions with a politically potent mix of rich, poor, native-born, and immigrant, with excellent communications connections. The membership of the NAWSA grew from 13,150 in 1893 to 100,000 in 1915.[140]

The NAWSA was the largest prosuffrage organization. Although it was less than militant, it represented groups that ranged from the Woman's Christian Temperance Union to the National Women's Trade Union League to the National Council of Jewish women. Upper- and middle-class women did not always see eye to eye with immigrant and working-class women.[141] Crucial for the movement's success were the settlement-house women, who brought cohesion and energy to the coalition.

Women's organizations printed thousands of leaflets, held parades and rallies, and demonstrated to pressure men into voting for suffrage.[142] In 1915, 25,000 suffragists, clad in white and led by women on horseback, marched up Fifth Avenue. It was the largest such demonstration up to that time in New York City, but a statewide vote on suffrage during the same year was defeated.

Suffragists knew that a victory for suffrage in New York State required votes from populous New York City. But the movement, led by white, Protestant, Angle-Saxon, upper- and middle-class women, clearly needed more support to win in New York City. As another vote on suffrage in New York State loomed in 1917, suffragist leaders reached out to Jewish, Catholic, and working-class men in immigrant communities. Their actions proved decisive. At the last minute, Tammany Hall, sensing a shift in the political winds, abstained from opposing women's suffrage. In the 1917 referendum, New York City reversed its vote of 1915, and 59 percent of male voters favored the ballot for women, enough to offset antisuffrage votes elsewhere in the state. Despite Tammany's turnaround, Irish Catholic men—Tammany's mainstay—were the voting bloc least favorably disposed toward votes for women. The support of Jewish male voters in particular helps explain the suffragist victory.[143]

In the 1917 suffrage vote, immigrants and old-stock Americans combined their efforts to win votes for women. Prospects for further reform were fading, though: in the same year that New York women won the right to vote, the United States entered World War I.

CHAPTER 5

NEW TIMES AND NEW
NEIGHBORHOODS: 1917–1928

For Helen Wagner, the daughter of an immigrant German cigar maker growing up in the Yorkville section of Manhattan before World War I, the German language was as much a part of her life as the constant aroma of beer from the nearby Ruppert brewery. Most of her neighbors were German, and nearby Eighty-Sixth Street was thick with German restaurants. She spoke German at home and heard it on the streets. All of that changed when the United States entered the Great War against Germany. "The war years were really pathetic," she recalled.

> You couldn't walk the street with a German paper under your arm. You'd be abused from one end of the block to the other. They went so far they abused the poor little German dogs that walked the street. That's the hatred that was. We kept speaking German at home, but we avoided it on the street. We had cousins and uncles over there. Lord knows how many of them were nearly killed by my brothers.[1]

New York on the eve of World War I was a metropolis at the intersection of international currents of migration, ideas, trade, and culture, but it was also a city in a specific nation, the United States, whose government could powerfully shape and even override local opposition to the war—which was considerable. The Great War cut immigration to the United States and, particularly, to New York.

World War I, as the scholars Timothy J. Hatton and Jeffrey G. Williamson put it, "brought an end to mass migration and closed the door on the first global century."[2] Europeans spent their resources making war, not searching for new colonies and trade routes. As U.S. banks loaned money to the British war effort, London declined as a world financial center, and New York rose. Wartime press censorship, surveillance, and prosecutions for disloyalty ended the reforming years of the Progressive Era. Indeed, the conservative wartime mood continued after the war as authorities cracked down on radicals and cut immigration from Southern and Eastern Europe. At the same time, African American migration to the city increased as blacks sought wartime jobs.

After the war, African American Harlem replaced the immigrant Lower East Side as the city's center for both slumming and cultural and political ferment. Immigrants settled into the postwar city, riding new subway lines out of the crowded Lower East Side to neighborhoods of new homes built by developers. In the postwar decades, both immigrants and African Americans wrestled with what it meant to be an American and a New Yorker.

✳ ✳ ✳

When the European powers blundered into war during the summer of 1914, New Yorkers were initially divided. Individuals were tugged by competing loyalties. One young German, educated at Harvard and Gottingen, declared in 1914, "Soberly gratified though I might be at every German setback, every German victory set my Teutonic heart beating faster."[3] In other cases, divisions ran within ethnic groups. As late as 1917, when the United States declared war on the Central Powers, the *Staats-Zeitung*, the voice of German New York's middle class, insisted that German Americans were loyal citizens and blamed "the German military party" for the debacle.[4] As war loomed ever closer, the paper emphasized the conflict's significance for German Americans and lamented the threat it posed to *Deutschtum*, or Germanness, in the United States. In contrast, the socialist *Volkszeitung* openly opposed the conflict and stressed the broader theme of socialist opposition to the war. It prominently and enthusiastically covered Meyer London, the antiwar Jewish Socialist congressman from the Lower East Side.[5]

The split within the German press in New York City occurred in the context of larger pressures on German Americans. Given their traditions of achievements in science, higher education, art, literature, and music, Germans had generally been highly esteemed in the United States. In 1917, however, many Americans defined German culture in light of militarism and imperialism. Politicians like Theodore Roosevelt insisted that the nation could not tolerate disloyalty and demanded that "hyphenated" Americans must commit themselves to the American cause without reservation. To Roosevelt, once the nation declared war, a socialist critic of American involvement was nothing more than a "Hun . . . inside our gates."[6] In the election for mayor in the fall of 1917, Mayor John Mitchell played the patriot and denounced the Socialist candidate, Morris Hillquit, as a virtual traitor for his criticism of the war.[7] The most extreme statement from a New Yorker came from the Rev. Newell Dwight Hillis of the Plymouth Congregational Church in Brooklyn, who announced from the pulpit his belief "that Germans were genetically defective" and advocated the sterilization of millions of German American men.[8]

Even loyal Germans found themselves under suspicion, and some took steps to prove their support for the war effort. One association of New York German societies offered its shooting range to the War Department. Old German American institutions in New York changed their names. The German Hospital and Dispensary became Lenox Hill Hospital, and the German Polyclinic became Stuyvesant Polyclinic. The Germania Life Insurance Company insisted that it was an American company, loyal to the United States; it was the first insurance company to purchase Liberty bonds. When that gesture proved inadequate, the managers changed the Germania's name to the Guardian Life Insurance Company and began to withdraw from European operations. German-speaking churches switched to the English language or became bilingual, schools stopped teaching German, and the German-language press saw a sharp decline in readership. Even the Metropolitan Opera Company echoed the spirit of hysterical patriotism and refused to perform the works of German composers like Richard Wagner.[9]

Although no ethnic group experienced the emotionalism of the war more deeply than German Americans, other ethnic groups also found their lives disrupted. Jewish New Yorkers who had fled Russian pogroms were understandably opposed to an American alliance with czarist Russia. Thus the Yiddish-language socialist *Forverts* at first opposed American involvement in the war. When the czarist regime was overthrown, the *Forverts* reconsidered its opposition to American participation in the conflict and concluded "it is no longer a capitalistic war. Neither is it imperialistic or nationalistic. It is a war for humanity."[10]

The war split the Progressives, who had made New York an international center of reform, along intimate lines. John Dewey, a philosophy professor at Columbia University, supported U.S. entry into the conflict; Randolph Bourne, a writer and one of Dewey's students, opposed it. Ultimately, most progressives came to support the war. To many, it was a chance to defend civilization overseas, strengthen the nation-state, and invigorate American democracy. A strong majority of socialists, however, opposed American participation in the war and subsequent U.S. participation in the Allied intervention against the Bolsheviks in Russia. Government repression fell heavily on antiwar socialists and all the war's opponents. When a handful of Jewish anarchists living in East Harlem printed circulars denouncing U.S. intervention against the Bolsheviks, the government arrested, tried, and convicted them for violations of the Sedition Act. Although debates about their case eventually led to greater freedom of speech, they did little for these anarchists, who were deported to Russia along with other victims of government repression.[11]

At the war's outset, the city's Irish Americans had little reason to support the British. Irish nationalism had been a transatlantic movement since the days of the United Irishmen in the 1790s, and by the early twentieth century, writes the historian Kevin Kenny, "some of the leading proponents of Irish physical force nationalism anyplace in the world were to be found in New York City." Not only did Irish operatives in New York develop German support for a rebellion against British rule in 1916, but one of the leaders of the Dublin forces in what became known as the Easter Uprising was James Connolly, a socialist who had lived in the Bronx and worked as an organizer for the Industrial Workers of the World before World War I. His execution, along with other leaders of the rebellion, provoked outrage among Irish on both sides of the Atlantic.[12]

Shortly after the Easter Uprising, a gathering of three thousand New York Irish hailed the rebellion and thanked Germany for supporting the cause of Irish freedom. John Devoy's *Gaelic American*, Judge Daniel E. Cohalan, and the *Irish World* all severely attacked America's pro-British foreign policy. Nevertheless, the bulk of the city's Irish eventually supported the American war effort, as did Irish leadership of the Catholic Church.[13] They were, after all, Americans of Irish descent and no longer living in Ireland. The "Fighting 69th" regiment, recruited mainly from the city's West Side Irish, won great praise for its military action against Germany.

African American New Yorkers were divided on the war. Although they faced segregation and discrimination throughout the city, some African American men believed that if they fought or died for democracy in the fields of France, they would win their rights in America. W. E. B. Du Bois, the most prominent spokesman for black equality, at first opposed the war but finally endorsed African American participation. However, other African American leaders, such as the socialists A. Philip Randolph and Chandler Owen, urged blacks not to participate.[14]

Two New York regiments in the American Expeditionary Force sent to France, one African American and the other made up of immigrants, embodied the hopes and contradictions of the U.S. war effort. The 369th Infantry, a regiment of African Americans, served within the French army. They fought heroically and won praise in the press as the Harlem Hellfighters. Ultimately,

5.1 Decorated soldiers of the 369th U.S. Infantry, nicknamed the Harlem Hellfighters, after World War I. Because of segregation in the U.S. Army, the unit served under a French command. Harlem gave them a jubilant homecoming.

Source: National Archives.

the French government awarded the entire regiment the Croix de Guerre. But the Harlem Hellfighters served in segregated units largely commanded by white officers, and they endured racist taunts and worse at the hands of white Americans. The 308th Infantry, with many Yiddish-speaking Jews, was part of the 77th Division, which was known as the "Melting Pot" Division because it contained so many immigrants. In France, soldiers from the 308th Infantry, many of them immigrants who hoped to disprove charges that they were weak and disloyal, were part of what journalists dubbed the "Lost Battalion": an American formation that endured 72 percent casualties fighting off repeated German attacks.[15]

If the Harlem Hellfighters had hoped their fighting in France would bring changes in New York, they were rudely mistaken. After a victory parade up Fifth Avenue, they discovered that for African American men in New York, just as before the war, good jobs and adequate housing were hard to find. The men of the Lost Battalion, who were all white, fared slightly better. But even they had to endure the bigotry that was hurled at Jews and immigrants in the postwar years.[16]

***

The hostility to radicals and suspicion of disloyalty among ethnic groups continued after the end of the war in November 1918. Within the Left, the Bolshevik Revolution provoked a split in the Socialist Party over whether the United States too was ripe for revolution; those who thought it was left the party eventually to form the Communist Party. Among Americans made fearful and conservative by the war, the Bolshevik seizure of power heightened the general mood of intolerance and conformity and raised heated but implausible fears of revolution in the United States. In 1919, New York's state legislature launched an expansive investigation of radicalism in the Empire State. Prominent in its efforts were probes of immigrant communities, especially in

5.2 Aftermath of a terrorist bombing on Wall Street in 1920 that killed thirty-eight and contributed to antiradicalism and nativism.

Source: *New York World-Telegram and the Sun* Newspaper Photograph Collection, Library of Congress.

New York City. Its dragnet eventually prompted sharp criticisms, but not before its findings led to the expulsion of five socialists from the State Assembly. At the same time, the Justice Department conducted raids and deported 249 radicals to the Soviet Union on the SS *Buford*. Among the deportees was Emma Goldman, the immigrant anarchist, who would be disappointed by the lack of freedom she found in the Soviet Union. Fears of radicalism were heightened in 1920s, when a bomb exploded on Wall Street, killing thirty-eight and wounding hundreds.[17]

The antiradicalism of the postwar years was matched by a strong streak of hostility toward immigrants, especially those from Southern and Eastern Europe. Nativists such as the lawyer Madison Grant attacked not only the religious and ethnic origins of immigrants but their mental capacities and their politics. While there were plenty of anarchists, socialists, syndicalists, and communists in the Jewish and Italian neighborhoods of New York City, nativists exaggerated their numbers and disregarded constitutional rights in their efforts to subdue them. Equally important, the eugenics movement, popular by the 1920s, held that immigrants from Southern and Eastern Europe were inferior to the people of Northern and Western Europe, the so-called Anglo-Saxons, Teutons, and Nordics.

The decline in European immigration that distinguished the 1920s had its roots in the years before the United States entered the Great War. In 1914, more than 1.2 million newcomers arrived on American shores, but during the next three years, under wartime pressures, the combined total was under one million. A literacy test established in 1917 failed to halt immigration—only 2 percent of Europeans were barred from entry at Ellis Island—but the turmoil of war did reduce the number of Europeans who sought entry.

In 1918, while the United States was at war, only 110,330 persons arrived. After hostilities ended, immigration began again. In 1921, 800,000 people were admitted; many settled in New York City. In the 1920s, Congress passed new laws that severely reduced European immigration. The first quota law of 1921 cut European immigration substantially, but it did not satisfy those who feared that America was being overrun by a horde of inferior immigrants. As a result, Congress passed a more restrictive law in 1924, grounded in national-origins statistics; it took effect in 1929. The law permitted about 150,000 Europeans to enter the United States annually but tried to skew the flow of immigrants to exclude Southern and Eastern Europeans and admit instead immigrants from Great Britain, Germany, and Ireland. Asian immigration had been effectively halted long before the 1920s.[18]

Opposition to the anti-immigrant impulse was strong in New York City. At Columbia University, the anthropologist Franz Boas attacked the intellectual foundations of racist eugenics and immigration restrictions. In Congress, representatives from New York City, including Emanuel Celler and Fiorello La

Guardia, strongly opposed immigration restrictions. Indeed, in the vote on the 1924 bill, twenty out of twenty-two Democratic members of the New York State delegation in the House of Representatives voted against the act. But their efforts were overwhelmed in a country gripped by nativism.[19]

Overall immigration during the 1920s was roughly half what it had been in the decades since 1900. During the 1920s, before the national-origins system became effective, about six hundred thousand new immigrants settled in New York. This new national-origins system, however, was set to cut immigration further after 1929; it established a quota of less than six thousand for Italy, about three hundred for Greece, and a few thousand for Russia and Poland.[20] The major sources of immigration for New York City for the previous thirty years were virtually shut off. Increases of newcomers from Canada and Mexico (which had no quotas) were recorded during the decade, but these nationals did not generally settle in New York City. Without new immigrants, and with the children of European immigrants coming of age during the 1920s and 1930s, the second generation would be setting the agenda for New York City's ethnic groups.

✳ ✳ ✳

As immigration slowed, the movement of people within New York City accelerated. In the 1920s, Manhattan's population fell while Queens, the Bronx, and Brooklyn grew—a change made possible by the expanding city subway system and new housing construction. From the time Mayor George McClellan threw the switch on the first subway in October 1904 until 1940, the city built more than eight hundred miles of underground track. Over two hundred miles of rapid transit were built between 1914 and 1921 alone, helping stimulate postwar urban decentralization. In spite of the decline in immigration, the city had a plentiful supply of construction workers and real estate entrepreneurs on hand to create housing in new neighborhoods. One historian has noted that the prosperity of the 1920s produced 658,789 new one- and two-family houses and apartments, "a volume of new housing which has never again been equaled, quantitatively or qualitatively." About one-third of the new buildings were one- or two-family units; most were multifamily dwellings. New laws enabled buildings with self-operated elevators to replace the old walk-up tenement, and a surge of construction in the outer boroughs produced tens of thousands of four- and especially six-story apartment buildings.[21] The building boom was set off by a combination of factors: available land, tax abatements, amortized mortgages, modest construction costs, and robust demand for new housing. Changes in tax laws and the easy availability of loans completed the requirements for the 1920s expansion.[22]

As mass transportation made getting to work anywhere in the city much easier, farmland in Queens and the Bronx gave way to apartment buildings. Amenities like sewers and libraries followed as the mayoral administration of John Hylan (1918–1925) embarked on major public improvements vital for neighborhood expansion. The construction of dozens of new public schools, many of them built in the outer boroughs, relieved overcrowding in the city's classrooms.

Private entrepreneurs built stores, recreational amenities, and hotels. When the New York Giants refused to permit the Yankees to play in their park because the Yankees drew larger crowds, their owner Jacob Ruppert built Yankee Stadium directly across the Harlem River in the Bronx. Opening day of the 1923 season drew a large crowd and many celebrities to the stadium, including baseball commissioner Judge Kenesaw Mountain Landis and New York's governor, Alfred E. Smith. Babe Ruth completed the festivities by hitting the first of his many home runs at the ballpark, soon dubbed the "House That Ruth Built." That same year, only a few blocks away, the luxurious Concourse Plaza Hotel had its grand opening, during which Governor Smith told an avid audience that the "Bronx is a great city. . . . After seeing this new structure, I am convinced that anything will go in the Bronx."[23]

The population of the Bronx nearly doubled from 1920 to 1940. Queens went from 469,000 to 1,297,129, and some of its neighborhoods, such as Jackson Heights, more than tripled. Brooklyn's rate of growth, which had been substantial before 1920, was considerably lower between World War I and World War II, but that borough's population nonetheless increased. Coney Island, in Brooklyn, exploded from a seaside resort of 33,000 in 1910 to a community of 280,000 residents by 1930. Manhattan's population reached its peak about the time of World War I and then began to decline; Brooklyn replaced it as the most populous of New York City's boroughs after 1920.[24]

Who moved to the new neighborhoods? The Irish, for one. Even though the number of Irish immigrants to the United States declined, a rising proportion of those who did immigrate settled in New York City. During the 1920s, 40 percent of immigrants from the Emerald Isle settled in New York City, helping revitalize old Irish neighborhoods. The new immigrants joined an Irish community that was increasingly on the move to more desirable neighborhoods. Before the turn of the twentieth century, middle-class Irish had begun to leave Manhattan's slum districts and migrate across the Harlem River and East River into the West Bronx and Brooklyn. During the early years of the twentieth century, some Irish neighborhoods in the outer boroughs were established by laborers who settled where they worked. Both working- and middle-class Irish developed ethnic enclaves in the Inwood section of northern Manhattan, Woodlawn in the Bronx, and Woodside in Queens.[25]

Marion Casey has traced the movement of Irish workers into Mott Haven and other sections of the Bronx once they discovered that they could afford the new apartments. As she put it, the "most striking conclusions about the Bronx Irish community in the period 1920–1930 is its relative youth, and the shift to working-class apartment dwellers from the middle-class home owners typical of the [borough's] nineteenth-century Irish." The Bronx was available because the major change in "the Bronx of the twenties and thirties was the rise of new neighborhoods . . . due to the opening of new transit lines and to state efforts to spur residential construction." Frank Hanrahan was typical of these movers. He was born in 1915 to Irish parents in a cold-water tenement on 101st Street in Manhattan, an overwhelmingly Irish neighborhood. A few years later, the family relocated to West 147th Street, another mostly Irish neighborhood. In 1921, Hanrahan and his family moved to the Bronx. They were buoyed by his father's good credit rating (established when he joined the city fire department in 1917) and enticed by the new homes built on the former grounds of estates and summer retreats. The IRT subway cemented the arrangement, linking new Bronx housing to the rest of the city via mass transit. After World War II, Hanrahan moved again, as did many white New Yorkers, to Queens.[26]

During the 1920s, some new Irish immigrants made the Bronx their first stop. Immigrant William O'Dwyer, later mayor of New York from 1946 to 1951, went directly from the boat by subway to an Irish saloon in the Bronx, where he made arrangements to find a room and job. His contact told him, "There are several Irish men who have been successful in the grocery business. I talked to a manager of one of them. If you mind your business and work hard, there is no reason why you should not succeed."[27]

Many Irish found housing in the older neighborhoods, such as Mott Haven, but for the more affluent, new apartments in University Heights and Fordham were readily available. Only 5 percent of New York's Irish-born population lived the Bronx in 1900, but by 1920 the figure was 9 percent, and by end of the Great Depression it was 24 percent.[28]

A point made by the historian Deborah Dash Moore, who has chronicled the changing lives of New York Jews during this era, is relevant to other ethnic groups as well: as they moved to emerging neighborhoods in the Bronx, Brooklyn, and Upper Manhattan, they established enclaves that enabled them to become Americans in an ethnic context. Geographic and economic mobility did not mean an end to ethnic identity. At the turn of the century, the majority of the city's Eastern European Jews lived in the Lower East Side and in other crowded tenement districts. With jobs and education, they began to move, and in the 1920s alone 160,000 abandoned their old neighborhoods. In the mid-1920s, statisticians announced the "startling fact" that Brooklyn had about as many Jews as Manhattan and the Bronx together and that the movement of the

5.3 Housing construction followed new subway lines into vacant land, creating homes for immigrants and their children. Inwood, pictured here around 1915, became the home of Irish and Jews.

Source: Don Rice Collection.

Jewish population was toward Brooklyn and the Bronx and away from Manhattan.[29]

These upwardly mobile Jews followed the paths of Germans and Irish before them. A prime destination was the great Bronx thoroughfare opened as the Grand Boulevard and Concourse—four-and-a-half miles long, 182 feet wide, and completed in 1909. For the immigrants and their children who flocked to it, Constance Rosenblum notes, the Grand Concourse "represented the ultimate in upward mobility." In its new apartments, families were transformed "from greenhorns into solid middle-class Americans." For Jews, the Concourse was a destination so attractive that it drew residents not only from the Lower East Side but also from Harlem and from Williamsburg and Brownsville in Brooklyn.[30] Brownsville, Brooklyn, which before World War I was considered a slightly better neighborhood than the Lower East Side, began to lose whatever attraction it had. Its population peaked in the mid-1920s as residents began to seek better housing. The exodus slowed during the Great Depression but rose rapidly after World War II.[31]

Neighborhood growth also transformed both the neighborhoods people left and the neighborhoods they moved to. In Brooklyn, Boro Park grew with the construction of rows upon rows of modest semiattached single-family homes and multifamily apartments built in the 1920s. The novelist Michael Gold told of his visit to the "suburb" of Boro Park: "Real estate signs were stuck everywhere. In the midst of some rusty cans and muck would be a sign, 'Why Pay Rent? Build your House in God's Country.'"[32] While Jews had moved to Boro Park before World I, their numbers greatly increased during the postwar years; by 1930 they accounted for half of the neighborhood.[33]

Anti-Semitic restrictions closed some neighborhoods to Jews, among them Fieldston in the Bronx and Brooklyn's Park Slope, but Jewish builders and real estate entrepreneurs filled the residential gap by providing housing and new opportunities for Jewish tenants. Changes in taxes, the easy availability of loans, modest construction costs, available land, and high demand for homes all fueled the housing expansion of the 1920s. An attractive neighborhood for rising Jews was the Upper West Side along Central Park West, Riverside Drive, and West End Avenue. A surge in apartment construction there faltered during the depression of the 1890s, but beginning after 1901 a second boom saw the erection of many large apartment structures on West End Avenue. Some Jews moved there before World War I, but the big surge came during the 1920s. As Harlem became increasingly African American, thousands of Jewish families moved to Brooklyn or the Bronx; the most affluent among them went to Manhattan's West Side.[34]

Studies of New York's Jewish population during the interwar years describe a changing but persistent Jewish culture. The city's Orthodox represented only a minority of its Jews, but the 1920s and 1930s marked the "heyday of New York's Orthodox," according to Jenna Weissman Joselit.[35] As the more prosperous Orthodox Jews left the Lower East Side after 1900 and settled in middle-class neighborhoods, they established new Orthodox enclaves. In the Upper West Side of Manhattan, in Boro Park and Williamsburg in Brooklyn, and in the Bronx, the more affluent Orthodox combined ancient ritual with modern middle-class trappings; synagogues grew larger and more elaborate, as did *mikvahs*, or ritual baths.[36]

English-language sermons became standard after World War I, and English prayers often supplemented Hebrew in Orthodox as well as in Conservative and Reform synagogues. Since organizational life was built around men's and women's clubs, rabbis encouraged women to participate more actively in the life of the community as well as make a proper Orthodox home. Finally, Orthodox communities began to emphasize Jewish day schools that stressed secular as much as religious education.[37]

As Deborah Dash Moore notes, in the Bronx the Grand Concourse "did not forget its Jewishness in the pursuit of middle class security."[38] Intense synagogue building among all the major branches of Judaism occurred during the 1920s, along with the expansion of other Jewish organizations, such as the Jewish community centers and YMHAs. But the new synagogue centers became the main expression of the second generation. They contained athletic facilities and schools as well as sanctuaries for prayer. Jewish philanthropy, which had been the preserve of the wealthy German Jews, was reconstructed after the war into a modern community-wide endeavor.[39]

New York City's Italian inhabitants, although not as upwardly mobile as Jews or as politically successful as the Irish, also began to move from slums in the early twentieth century. The first Italians to settle in Upper Manhattan in the 1870s were construction workers seeking housing away from the congested Mulberry Bend. By the end of the century, East Harlem contained an established Italian community, which grew substantially during the 1920s and 1930s as Jews and Irish left for greener pastures. Although less crowded than Mulberry Bend, East Harlem was still a working-class community with dirty and congested streets and inadequate housing. Many Italian dockworkers located along the Brooklyn waterfront, close to their jobs. Indeed, Brooklyn became so attractive for Italians that by 1930 it claimed nearly half of the city's Italian stock.[40]

Italian life centered on work, family, and the home. As the folklorist Joseph Sciorra notes, the idea of *lavorro bon fatto*, or work well done, sustained a man building a brick wall or a woman preparing a meal. Memories of peasant hardships made home ownership a goal of many Italian immigrants and their children, but the communal dimensions of Italian life blurred the boundaries between domestic life and the neighborhood. The boundaries of Italian homes stretched out into the streets, where sidewalk shrines and religious processions marked the communities of Italian New Yorkers.[41]

Robert Orsi has described the *festa* of the Madonna of 115th Street in Italian East Harlem during these years as an intense expression of popular religion, a "sacred theater" for the community. After weeks of preparation, each July 16 the *festa* began in front of the Church of Our Lady of Mount Carmel. Thousands jammed the streets of the already overcrowded neighborhood to find security and meaning in the immigrant drama.[42]

While differences between Irish and Italian versions of Roman Catholicism appeared in such celebrations, Italians gained some ground in the church. In the years following World War I, the Catholic Church, though still dominated by Irish clergy under the leadership of Patrick Cardinal Hayes, had some success recruiting Italian women as nuns and employing them as teachers in Italian parish schools. It also recruited more Italian priests both from Italy and New York and built a number of churches and schools in Italian neighborhoods.[43]

✳ ✳ ✳

Along with expanding transportation networks and new housing construction, rising incomes made possible the movement of European immigrants and their children to better neighborhoods. By the time of World War I, most Germans had moved into skilled laboring positions or middle-class occupations, and the Irish were not far behind. Politics had given the Irish jobs on the city payroll, especially as policemen and firemen. For Irish women, school teaching had beckoned. In 1910, three-quarters of public school pupils were foreign-born, but the majority of teachers had been born in New York City. Among these pedagogues the Irish predominated, constituting 20 percent of the total. As Deborah Dash Moore notes, immigrants before World War I learned from "teachers named Jones, O'Reilly, Smith and Kennedy." Irish women still entered public school teaching in the 1920s, but Jewish women were rapidly overtaking them.[44]

Many Irish employed in the private sector held working-class jobs. For example, so many Irish labored in the transit system of the 1930s that the Interborough Rapid Transit was sometimes referred to as the Irish Rapid Transit. Because many transit positions required dealing with the public, command of English gave them an advantage in getting jobs as guards, conductors, and motormen. Though second- or third-generation Germans usually held a majority of the skilled craft positions on the lines, Irish men also could be found in skilled jobs, and a few held managerial and supervisory positions.[45] The Irish domination of transit jobs before 1940 was the product of political connections: Tammany clubs took care of their own.[46]

A few Irish women found jobs as domestic servants, as they had in the nineteenth century, but this low-paid occupation was increasingly being taken over by African Americans. Irish accents could also be heard in the Schrafft's and Stouffer's restaurant chains, where many Irish women found jobs. Still other Irish women went into nursing, a field they ultimately dominated. In addition, they found white-collar jobs in the phone company, so much so that one woman recalled those positions as "part of the Catholic Church."[47]

Of all immigrant groups, New York's Jews made the most rapid economic progress. Most German Jews who immigrated in the latter part of the nineteenth century had attained middle-class status or higher before World War I. Some Eastern European Jews, who began their New World careers in the city's garment industry, owned their own shops within a short period of time. Others, who had begun as peddlers, gradually opened more stable retail businesses and prospered modestly, as did real estate entrepreneurs during the building boom of the 1920s.

* * *

The stage and entertainment industry offered another avenue for "making it" in New York City. The immigration of the 1920s that invigorated New York's Irish community also shaped Irish contributions to popular culture and commercial leisure. Newcomers with musical talent found jobs in flourishing Irish bars, restaurants, and clubs. The development of radio gave them opportunities to perform before even larger Irish American audiences. Irish sports were also popular: in 1928, the Gaelic Athletic Association began to build a stadium in the Bronx for Irish football and hurling.[48]

Vaudeville launched the careers of Jewish performers such as George Burns, Al Jolson, the Marx Brothers, and Eddie Cantor.[49] Athletics also opened doors for a few young men. Before World War I, practically no Jewish or Italian immigrants were professional baseball players, but during the interwar years a handful of Jews and Italians played in the big leagues. Jewish and Italian youths of New York City lacked access to facilities necessary to develop baseball skills. The comedian George Burns recalled that

> our playground was the middle of Rivington Street. We played games that needed very little equipment. . . . When we played baseball we used a broom handle and a rubber ball. A manhole cover was home plate, a fire hydrant was first base, second base was a lamp post, and Mr. Gitletz, who used to bring a kitchen chair down to sit and watch us play, was third base. One time I slid into Mr. Gitletz; he caught the ball and tagged me out.[50]

Among Jewish second-generation boys, another barrier existed: opposition from parents. To serious-minded Jewish immigrants, baseball players were little more than layabouts. Irving Howe remembered his father's opposition to his playing baseball was so intense that his "mother would sneak out my baseball gear and put it in the candy store downstairs."[51] However, not all Jewish parents objected to their sons' ball playing. Some enjoyed sports themselves, while others realized that their children might achieve American-style success through sports. Of the few Jewish athletes who would emerge from the city streets and make it to the major leagues, the most famous was Hank Greenberg who signed with Detroit in 1930. Here was a son of the Bronx who was idolized by millions.[52]

Jewish youngsters loved basketball even more than baseball. Basketball could be played year-round in gyms, while baseball required outdoor fields. Although few could make a living playing professional basketball before World War II, New York's Jewish youth played in recreational centers, boys clubs, YMHAs, public schools, and colleges. City College of New York won a national championship during the 1949–1950 season with a predominantly Jewish team.[53]

Although Italian and Jewish boys played baseball, basketball, and street games, they achieved their greatest fame in boxing. Like poor Irish immigrants before them, Jewish and Italian youth facing hostile neighborhood toughs quickly learned to defend themselves. For the best, the next move was the ring. Professional victories and paychecks brought prestige and even parental acceptance for Jewish boxers. One historian has observed: "They were regarded as race heroes who defended the honor of the Jewish people and proved to the world that the Jewish man had athletic ability and was not meek and cowardly but rugged, brave and courageous."[54] The most famous Jewish boxer was Benny Leonard, a fast but powerful lightweight acclaimed as pound for pound one of the best fighters of all time. In the 1920s, Jeff Sammons notes, Irish, Italian, and Jewish fighters topped the boxing championship lists; during the 1930s,

Italians were first and Jews second in producing winners. As Jews eventually moved out of boxing, the pattern of succession that went from Irish to Jewish passed to Italians and then to African Americans and Latinos.[55]

In sports, only a few stars earned high salaries. For many Jewish parents, education was the path to professional success. Jewish graduates of Hunter College and the City College of New York, especially women from Hunter, made their appearance as teachers as early as 1910, and after World War I they rapidly moved into positions as public school faculty.[56] Others who received professional educations opened offices as physicians, dentists, and lawyers. However, the growing number of applications from Jews during the 1920s prompted Columbia, the only Ivy League university in the city, to restrict Jewish enrollment. New York University's Bronx campus thought of itself as "a preserve on University Heights set apart from the larger city," and it too restricted Jewish enrollment, but the downtown campus was open to Jewish students. Jewish educational quotas, including in medical schools, were part of the growing anti-Semitism of post–World War I America. New York City was not exempt from this ugly trend.[57]

Business was more important than the professions for Jewish mobility. While most Jews remained employees, a growing number were owners and operators of small establishments. By 1937, reports Henry Feingold, Jews owned two-thirds of the city's 34,000 factories and 104,000 wholesale and retail enterprises.[58]

Men managed most Jewish-run enterprises, but within them Jewish women found employment. While larger white Protestant–dominated firms refused to hire Jews (or other ethnic Americans, for that matter) before World War II, Jewish-run businesses needed clerks to keep their books, manage their records, work as secretaries, and wait on customers. Here was an opportunity for Jewish women, who in increasing numbers were earning high school diplomas required for such jobs. As early as 1914, one commentator compared Italian and Jewish women: "It is interesting to note that the Jewish girl is to be found in office work and stenography while the Italian girl is found in factories."[59] Around the time of World War I, the same observer summarized data about young Jewish women age fourteen to sixteen: 5 percent were working in factories, 10 percent in office work, and 75 percent still in public and trade schools. Those still pursuing their educations represented the highest percentage of any ethnic group.[60] Jewish women also found jobs in the city's department stores. By 1932, Jewish women reportedly represented about half of their employees. One journal commented that department stores had to hire many gentile young women to fill in during the Jewish holidays.[61]

For many aging first-generation Jews, opportunities for upward mobility were limited. They remained toilers in the garment trade and other working-class occupations. Irving Howe, recalling his boyhood in the 1920s, wrote that the streets of the East Bronx were "crammed with Jewish immigrants from Eastern Europe, almost all of them poor. We lived in narrow five-story tenements, wall flush against wall." If they were not as bad as tenements on the Lower East Side or in Brownsville, "they were bad enough."[62]

As a group, the upward mobility of Italians was less rapid than it was for Jews. Italian men and women had begun work at the lower levels of manual labor, and while many improved their lot, they remained a predominantly working-class population. A 1916 survey of Italian-born men revealed that half were laborers; by 1931, in another survey, laborers constituted only 31 percent. This was a sign of some mobility, but laborers were still the largest single occupational group for Italian men.[63] Some of the better jobs were on the docks, but dockworkers faced a harsh world of corrupt labor practices.

Italian women in the labor force were also working class. Around World War I, while 43 percent of Italian girls age fourteen to sixteen were still in school, 40 percent worked in factories, and only 1 percent found jobs as white-collar workers. By age eighteen most had dropped out of school and gone to work in manufacturing.[64]

After World War I, more Italians stayed in school longer, and a growing number of both men and women found white-collar employment.[65] Yet the situation did not change significantly until the end of the 1930s. Vito Marcantonio, a congressman from East Harlem in the 1930s and 1940s, grew up in that Italian neighborhood at a time when practically no child continued beyond elementary school. East Harlem did not even have a high school before 1934. Marcantonio and one other neighborhood youngster attended De Witt Clinton High School, four miles away in the Bronx. When Marcantonio returned home at night, other youth taunted him with the nickname "The Professor." While Marcantonio was not deterred, his companion dropped out of high school after one year.[66]

For working-class Italians, competition for jobs could breed both ethnic animosities and ethnic niches. Italians and Irish found themselves in conflict along the Brooklyn waterfront.[67] At the same time, in city agencies Italians dominated the sanitation department.[68]

One way to avoid conflict was to own and operate a small business. A Works Progress Administration (WPA) survey of New York's Italians during the 1930s found that Italians owned and operated ten thousand grocery stores, 673 drug stores, and 757 restaurants.[69] Italians initially dominated as importers of Italian food products, but World War I virtually destroyed the industry, and the Smoot-Hawley Tariff of 1930 made things even worse for importers.[70]

Italian Americans working with American produce nevertheless created a rich culinary tradition for themselves. In Italy, rich food was reserved for the affluent. In America, Italian immigrants and their children created a cuisine grounded in abundance. "Pasta and olive oil," Hasia Diner writes, "along with meat and cheese, defined a good life, a life of choice." Truck farms and fruit and vegetable vendors served growing Italian demands for food. Within Italian families, women gained prominence and central household roles as cooks and homemakers. In family feasts and restaurant meals, the regional cuisines of Italy were refashioned into pillars of Italian American identity.[71]

* * *

Of course, some immigrants and their American-born offspring engaged in illegal activities to make money. The enactment of Prohibition, the product of a national crusade against alcohol that was aimed in large measure against immigrants, ironically opened the door for ethnic bootleggers.[72] It was big business, conducted on a national scale. One such entrepreneur bragged, "we had a bigger company than Henry Ford . . . and we had lawyers by the carload, and they was on call twenty-four hours a day."[73] New York City was never congenial territory for prohibitionists, because most immigrants and their descendants—be they Irish, German, Italian, or Jewish—did not consider drinking alcohol a crime or a sign of moral laxity. Jewish gangsters like Waxy Gordon and Dopey Benny were two of the many city bootleggers providing thirsty New Yorkers with their booze. Benny also branched out into labor racketeering and became involved with the garment unions. His thugs became adept at shooting scabs for a reported $60 cost and wrecking nonunion shops for up to $500.[74]

From Brownsville emerged Murder Inc., a combination of criminals—mostly Jewish but some Italians—who specialized in killing of rival gang members.[75] Though not a member of Murder Inc., the most notorious Jewish criminal was the gambler Arnold Rothstein, who was best known as the likely fixer of 1919 World Series. He lived comfortably on the West Side of Manhattan and bankrolled so many illegal activities that one wag called him the "Morgan of the underworld, its banker and master of economic strategy."[76] Rothstein was murdered in 1928, but authorities were unable—or unwilling—to solve the crime. His reputation lives in the character inspired by his reputation, the gangster Meyer Wolfsheim in F. Scott Fitzgerald's novel *The Great Gatsby.*[77]

Italian mobsters also flourished during Prohibition. According to the historian Mark Haller, New York City bootlegging was dominated by Jews, Italians, and to lesser extent Irish and Poles. As did Jewish criminals, Italians became involved in labor racketeering, especially along the Brooklyn waterfront, which had turned from being heavily Irish to Italian after 1910. Like Murder Inc., these gangsters engaged in a variety of criminal activities and were known to kill criminal rivals and others who would not do their bidding. In return for favors, Italian criminals also worked with Tammany leaders to win elections.[78]

* * *

New York's Asian population remained largely insulated from the city's other ethnic groups and scarcely felt the prosperity of the 1920s. Chinatown had been shaped by racist immigration laws, and only a few merchants could bring their wives or "paper sons" to America. Chinatown remained a lonely and isolated bachelor society, with six men for every woman. By 1900, the area was attracting tourists, whose guides told lurid tales of opium dens, prostitutes, and "tong wars," the disputes been rival protective associations fought out by hired gangs. Chinatown, dominated by the Chinese Consolidated Benevolent Association, did have tong wars, prostitution, gambling, and gang fighting, but their prevalence was overdramatized, and the violence generally ended by the 1930s. Most Chinese men in New York were not involved in tong wars but in a struggle to make a living running shops, restaurants, and hand laundries.[79]

Because of immigration laws, the city's Chinese population numbered only 12,000 in 1940, although a WPA survey insisted its true size was several times the official figure.[80] About half of the Chinese lived and worked in Chinatown, with the others scattered throughout the city. The latter mostly ran the ubiquitous Chinese hand laundries, estimated to number from seven to eight thousand by 1930. The hand laundry was one of the few occupations open to Chinese workers, but it required long, lonely hours to eke out a living.[81]

Other Asians were present in minuscule numbers. Japanese immigration was unrestricted until the Gentlemen's Agreement of 1907, and the National Origins Act of 1924 contained a provision totally barring further Asian immigration. But most Japanese immigrants had settled in the West or in Hawaii, and New York claimed only a few thousand, mostly males, by the eve of the Great Depression. In the 1890s, Japanese New Yorkers had generally settled in Brooklyn near the Navy Yard where they found employment as kitchen workers, stewards, mess boys, or cooks in the yard or on battleships. A number of Manhattan's Japanese were also in food service, but a few others worked for the Japanese government or businesses or ran their own independent small enterprises. Among the latter were operators of amusement concessions at Brooklyn's Coney Island. On the whole, these jobs did not pay high wages, and thus the Japanese community lived a marginal existence. Although the city contained no Japantown, it did support several Japanese churches, and many Japanese workers congregated in boardinghouses.[82]

Korea, as a possession of Japan, was also affected by the immigration restrictions imposed on the latter. A WPA study found about two hundred Koreans in the city during the 1930s, most of whom were domestic or restaurant workers. A small number of Filipinos and Asian Indians had also settled in New York, either in Manhattan or Brooklyn. Indian immigrants formed a Pan Aryan Association and an Indo-American Association, both of which focused on ending British rule in the homeland. Filipinos apparently worked as sailors or laborers and lived by the docks of South Brooklyn. The WPA study even located a colony of Indonesians in Brooklyn, commenting that other Brooklynites did not "even know of their existence." Like many other Asians they worked at domestic service jobs, washing dishes in restaurants, or as pin boys in local bowling alleys.[83]

From Bengal came another group. Bengalis had been trading and peddling goods in American ports since the 1880s, when a number jumped ship in New York and other ports around the time of World War I. By the 1930s these ex-seamen, who lived scattered throughout Manhattan, formed a community in Harlem. Most were single Muslim men who lived as boarders and worked at semiskilled jobs. Like other Asian immigrant groups their numbers were not large, but they added to New York's tradition of diversity. Bengali women were so few in number that Bengali men married Puerto Ricans, African Americans, and West Indians, adding new threads to the city's ethnic tapestry.[84]

＊＊＊

Among smaller groups, ethnic culture also remained strong. The Norwegians of Brooklyn, originally part of a seamen's community, had declined in numbers, but during the 1920s substantial Norwegian immigration provided reinforcements. Most Brooklyn Norwegians remained employed in the shipping and building trades. Their tie to maritime industry held the community together, as did Lutheran churches and *Nordisk Tidende* (Norse news), the leading Norwegian newspaper on the East Coast.[85] Finns, who had followed Norwegians to Brooklyn and congregated in the Sunset Park section, also published a newspaper: *New York Utiset* (New York news). The small Finnish community maintained several women's organizations, a Finnish Aid Society, and several co-ops.[86]

New York City also contained the nation's largest number of Greeks, who lived in three different Manhattan neighborhoods. The city's Greeks operated a day school and supported several Greek Orthodox churches. Greeks, like Jews and Italians, maintained theater troupes and a variety of fraternal organizations.[87]

Among the other Eastern Europeans were Romanians, Hungarians, Czechoslovaks, Slavs from Yugoslavia, Estonians, Lithuanians, and Latvians.

These groups supported restaurants, churches, day schools, bookstores, importing shops, and newspapers. Some newspapers, such as the Hungarian *Amerikai Magyar Nepszava*, were published daily; others appeared weekly. The Elore Hungarian Players provided a taste of Budapest theater in New York City.[88]

* * *

In politics, international events reshaped the Left in New York City. Socialists and anarchists debated whether to emulate Bolshevik tactics in the United States. Ultimately, socialists split over the issue; supporters of the Soviet Union became communists. Within mainstream electoral politics, the latest immigrants posed little threat to the Irish and Tammany's domination of the city's politics. Indeed, New York's Irish and the Tammany Hall machine reached the peak of their power in politics during the 1920s. The eight-year mayoralty of John Hylan (1918–1925) was followed by Jimmy Walker's mayoralty of nearly six years (1927–1932); both were Tammany stalwarts. In 1926, at the beginning of Walker's administration, the Board of Estimate—then a powerful branch of city government—consisted of six Irish Catholics, a German, and a Jew. Nor did it hurt that Al Smith, a Tammany politician from the streets of New York City, was governor of the state.[89]

Nevertheless, the political dominance of the Irish and Tammany was shaky. Although changes in naturalization procedures after 1900 made it more difficult to obtain citizenship, in the 1920s Jews and Italians were voting in growing numbers. In Brooklyn, where the number of Jewish and Italian citizens increased as immigrants naturalized and their children came of age, Irish politicians saw power beginning to slip from their hands. In 1919, Hyman Schorenstein became the first Democratic Jewish district leader in Brownsville. And in that borough's Crown Heights section, Irwin Steingut became a Democratic Party leader in the early 1930s.[90]

Still, Italian and Jewish attempts at either significantly influencing or controlling City Hall or the Democratic Party were frustrated. Jews and Italians did not fare well in the Walker administration when it came to appointments. Jews, with one-quarter of the city's population, won only 9 percent of Walker's cabinet appointments. Italians, with 17 percent of the population, received only 1 percent.[91]

If Jews and Italians were junior partners in Tammany, immigrant New York as a whole was viewed with suspicion in the rest of the United States. In 1928, Al Smith—a Tammany man, friend of workers and immigrants, a Catholic, and a reforming governor of New York State—ran for president. He was soundly defeated by the Republican candidate, Herbert Hoover, in part because of anti-Catholicism.

* * *

Jews and Italians may have been frustrated politically, but their plight was small compared to the struggles of African Americans. Black New Yorkers, who faced racism and lacking a strongly defined political turf of their own, had little hope of influencing white politicians. For many years after the Civil War, African Americans had remained faithful to the Republican Party but received few rewards for their loyalty. In the twentieth century, however, the growth of African American communities in Harlem (and later Bedford-Stuyvesant) offered the potential for greater political empowerment and the possibility of electing black officeholders.

In 1913, Harlem African Americans, frustrated with both political parties, organized the independent United Civic League to pressure white politicians and eventually elect black office holders. In 1917, the league succeeded when Edward Johnson became the first African American elected to the New York State Assembly.[92] In the 1920s, several other African Americans won election. In addition, black Harlemites took over the Republican Party in their district. The victory proved to be pyrrhic, however, as blacks began moving into the Democratic Party during the 1920s and as Tammany only reluctantly gave black Harlemites much say in party affairs.[93]

African Americans also tried to use their votes to influence white politicians to improve conditions in Harlem. John Hylan, mayor from 1918 to 1925, was the first New York chief executive to hold conferences with blacks. He responded with political appointments, although African Americans remained underrepresented on the public payroll. As in the past, the jobs granted to African Americans were at a low level. As late as 1930, the city employed only five black firefighters, and only ninety of the city's 17,700 police officers were black. David Goldberg notes that when one of the first African American firemen retired in 1936, "only six of the 6,717 members of the FDNY were black." The situation was only slightly better in the police and sanitation departments.[94]

Mayor Hylan made a few governmental improvements in Harlem but failed to resolve one of the city's most vexing municipal racial problems: segregation and discrimination at Harlem Hospital. In the early 1920s, this hospital served a predominantly African American clientele, yet its medical staff remained nearly all white. Nor could African American nurses and doctors find employment in the city's other hospitals. In 1925, Mayor Hylan made modest changes to address this pattern of exclusion and agreed to appoint several African American doctors to the Harlem Hospital staff. His actions did not fully meet African American demands for robust inclusion. In 1929, under Mayor Jimmy Walker, the city brought Harlem Hospital under closer supervision as part of the newly established Department of Hospitals and sought to expand black medical participation in the hospital.[95] Little progress was made in achieving the latter goal until after Walker's departure from City Hall. To his credit, the flamboyant mayor did increase the number of African Americans on the city payroll overall to a high of 2,275.[96]

In Brooklyn, some African Americans won political appointments late in the nineteenth century, but they were too few to leave a strong legacy.[97] As a black community, Bedford-Stuyvesant developed more slowly than Harlem. Consequently, Brooklyn's African Americans lacked a geographic base from which to influence politics. Both parties in Brooklyn gave African Americans a few patronage jobs but little else.[98]

* * *

With immigration dramatically reduced, the American South and the Caribbean—especially Puerto Rico—became prime sources of new migrants to New York. By the late nineteenth century, only a few Puerto Ricans had arrived in the city; prominent among them were political exiles who formed the first Puerto Rican organizations dedicated to overthrowing Spanish rule. Also prominent among the first Puerto Rican migrants were cigar makers, most of whom were literate and attracted to left-wing politics. After the United States defeated Spain in the Spanish-American War and annexed Puerto Rico, Puerto Rican migration increased. In 1917, the Jones-Shafroth Act granted Puerto Ricans American citizenship and the right of unrestricted migration to the United States. While new migrants lived throughout the city, a Puerto Rican *barrio* emerged in East Harlem, which had listed its first Puerto Rican residents as early as 1890. The 1920 census counted 7,364 persons of Puerto Rican birth in the city. During the 1920s, thousands of other islanders left for New York, primarily skilled or semiskilled urban workers who took the often run-down apartments in East Harlem, replacing Jews and later Italians who were leaving for newer housing. Puerto Ricans found employment in the Brooklyn Navy Yard and moved into nearby Fort Greene. In 1930, the New York Health Department reported nearly 45,000 Puerto Ricans in the city. *El Barrio* in East Harlem soon contained Puerto Rican theaters, fraternal orders, political clubs, and churches. Holy Agony, the first Roman Catholic Church catering to Puerto Ricans, opened in 1930. While struggling to make ends meet, Puerto Ricans (and a smaller number of other Latinos) created a cultural renaissance. Dance halls, Spanish-language dramas, vaudeville, and films became part of life in East Harlem. The musician Julio Roué used his office as a booking agent for other Latinos and began New York's first Spanish-language radio station. Migration slowed during the Great Depression, and it practically stopped during World War II, but the foundation for the large post–World War II Puerto Rican migration had been laid.[99]

As for African Americans, conditions in the South—lynching, segregation, poverty, and the boll weevil—propelled many to leave; frequent train service from Maryland, Virginia, and the Carolinas made the city a destination. New York City, despite its tradition of discrimination, seemed to offer African Americans better opportunities. New York and Brooklyn combined had fewer than twenty thousand blacks in 1860, but the figure reached 33,888 in 1890 and 60,666 ten years later.[100]

While European migration to New York City declined following the outbreak of World War I, that of African Americans from southern states continued to increase. During the "Great Migration" of 1910–1920, about five hundred thousand African Americans headed to northern cities, including New York. In 1910, the city claimed more than ninety thousand black residents; by 1920, the total nearly doubled to 152,407. In 1930, it reached 327,706, about 4.7 percent of the city's total population.[101] The focal point of this new migration was a neighborhood in northern Manhattan: Harlem.

At the turn of the century, Harlem was a practically all-white residential community with a rural quality. Annexed to the city in 1873, Harlem experienced a building boom tied to improved transportation. Many German and Jewish middle- and upper-middle-class families sought its genteel quality.[102] Harlem's fringes contained some Italians in the east and a handful of Irish and African American families. A number of African Americans worked as domestics in the homes of the affluent white residents, but few expected their numbers to increase.[103]

A Harlem building boom in the first years of the new century suddenly collapsed in 1904–1905, leaving many houses vacant and builders and landlords eager to find tenants. When the Lenox Avenue subway line was completed, connecting Harlem to Lower Manhattan, the stage was set for Harlem's metamorphosis. A black realtor, Philip Payton Jr., organized the Afro-American Realty Company to serve African Americans interested in renting or buying in Harlem. Many African Americans, jammed into overcrowded housing in San Juan Hill in Manhattan's west sixties and other run-down neighborhoods, welcomed the opportunity to move.[104] Because of housing discrimination black New Yorkers, unlike second-generation whites, usually could not obtain housing in the rapidly expanding boroughs, even if they had the money.

Although whites continued to move to Harlem between 1910 and 1920, many of them became anxious as African Americans entered "their" neighborhood. John Taylor, the founder of the Harlem Property Owners' Improvement Corporation, shouted, "Drive them [the blacks] out, and send them to the slums where they belong."[105] But landlords could not prevent whites from moving out, and rather than face vacant buildings and financial ruin, they rented to black newcomers. By 1914, fifty thousand African Americans called Harlem home. Black churches and YMCAs quickly opened to serve them.[106]

The African American cultural and business elite bought homes along 139th Street, called "Strivers' Row," in buildings designed by the acclaimed

architect Stanford White. A few blocks away was Sugar Hill, which had the reputation of being the center of Harlem's cafe society. Harlem, holding two-
thirds of New York's 300,000 African American residents in 1930, became a
must on the itineraries of foreign visitors. James Weldon Johnson, the African
American author, journalist, and activist, called Harlem "the recognized Negro
capital of the world" in the 1920s. During that decade, Harlem's writers, musicians, actors, artists, and journalists produced an astounding artistic output
stressing racial consciousness and African American culture. The writers and
artists of what became known as the Harlem Renaissance, Cheryl A. Wall
argues, sought "to achieve through art the equality that black Americans had
been denied in the social, political and economic realms." The result was "a
combustible mix of the serious the ephemeral the aesthetic the political and
the risqué." In Harlem, black Americans redefined themselves as city people
and became, despite all inequalities, an important force in American culture.
Harlem's nightclubs attracted whites eager to hear the nation's most famous
black jazz bands and blues singers. Among the most famous performers was
Paul Robeson, who was so popular that it took him an entire "afternoon to walk
down Seventh Ave from West 143rd Street to West 133rd Street."[107]

African American writers produced books emphasizing themes of the black
poor as well as the successful. A major refrain was black pride. Writers such as
Langston Hughes, Claude McKay, and James Weldon Johnson published during the era, as did Walter White, a leader in the National Association for the
Advancement of Colored People. Jessie Fauset scoured the regional black press
to discover new talent. A key person in obtaining publishers for these new black
writers was the white writer and publisher Carl Van Vechten, who became controversial when he published *Nigger Heaven*, a sympathetic portrait of black
life. The title referred to the segregated seating for blacks in theaters, but it
offended many African Americans.[108]

Black nationalists thrived in Harlem. One of the most popular of the period
was Marcus Garvey, founder of the Universal Negro Improvement Association.
A native of Jamaica, Garvey had lived in Harlem since 1916. His message of racial
pride, freedom for African colonies, and black economic development found a
ready audience among many poor and working-class black New Yorkers.
Although Garvey's economic schemes failed and he was eventually convicted
of mail fraud and deported, he left his mark on black consciousness. Later black
leaders echoed his emphasis on black pride and the need for African Americans to build and control their own institutions.[109] Garvey's popularity was sign
of both the transnational dimensions of his movement and Harlem's status as
global center for black culture.

Garvey's reputation was large, but he was not the only West Indian leader
in Harlem. Since 1900, West Indians had been immigrating to New York City.
A number of them had lived and worked in the Panama Canal Zone before

immigrating to the United States.[110] Like other immigrants, the West Indians formed their own community and fraternal organizations. For the religious there were Anglican (Episcopal) churches. Out of this community emerged a generation of activists.[111]

Among West Indians, Hubert Harrison, Richard B. Moore, and Frank Crosswaith became active in politics. The socialist Helen Holman became well known for her support of women's suffrage.[112] Few blacks won elected office, but the street life of Harlem was alive with political speakers. The neighborhood's open-air meetings, Irma Watkins-Owens writes, were "Harlem's first adult education centers." Audley Moore, one of the outspoken street-corner speakers, said she got her PhD by listening to street preaching. Also prominent among Harlem's activists was A. Philip Randolph, who became head of the Brotherhood of Sleeping Car Porters and Maids.[113]

The vitality of Harlem in the 1920s was matched by its poverty. Harlem's housing stock certainly contained large and solid homes, but because of high prices it became necessary for families to double up or take in boarders to make ends meet. The historian Gilbert Osofsky compared the rents paid by whites and blacks for a three-room apartment in New York City and concluded that blacks paid $8 more per month. In 1927, the National Urban League found that the typical New York white family paid $6.67 per month per room, while Harlem blacks were charged $9.50. Landlords rarely exhibited much interest in maintaining buildings where African Americans lived.[114]

High rents pushed some African Americans to throw rent parties, in which tenants laid out food and music for guests who paid admission to join in the fun. Frank Byrd recalled them in an interview archived with the Library of Congress:

> The party hostess, eager and glowing with freshly straightened hair, would roll back the living room carpets, dim the lights, seat the musicians, (usually drummer, piano and saxophone player) and, with the appearance of the first cash customer, give the signal that would officially get the "rug-cutting" under way. Soon afterwards she would disappear into the kitchen in order to give a final, last minute inspection to the refreshment counter: a table piled high with pig-feet, fried chicken, fish and potato salad.

The proceeds from such parties helped people cover the rent, but their gaiety was the product of an unfair housing market that extracted money from African Americans.[115]

The employment situation was no better. There were few chances to become professionals or even skilled workers. One of the best obtainable jobs for black men was working as a redcap carrying luggage in the train stations. Cheryl Greenberg's study of Harlem depicts a community that was in a depression amid a nation and city in an Age of Prosperity.[116] "Most Harlem families," she concludes, "remained poor in the 1920s." The cultural impact of the Harlem Renaissance was enduring, but even the greatest literature, painting, sculpture, music, and dance could not overcome political and economic inequality.[117]

* * *

By the late 1920s in New York, immigrants, the children of immigrants, and African American migrants were having a noticeable effect on American popular culture. Jews and African Americans were particularly prominent—although from unequal positions—in new forms of music and theater, nurtured in New York City, that redefined American culture. The medium of radio strengthened the city's status as a communications capitol, and radio shows brought to national audiences performers such as Eddie Cantor, a Lower East Side boy who started out in vaudeville. Jews, foremost among them Irving Berlin, became ever more prominent in the city's song publishing industry, Tin Pan Alley. Berlin rose to fame with "Alexander's Ragtime Band," which capitalized on the popularity of the ragtime music pioneered by African Americans. As the Broadway musical emerged as a distinct form of theater, Jewish performers, songwriters, and composers made significant contributions.[118] In Harlem, African American musicians were participating in a growing jazz scene by the late 1920s. Segregation cast a shadow over their performances, however. Small's Paradise and the Savoy Ballroom were integrated, but the Cotton Cub was segregated.[119]

In 1927, the film *The Jazz Singer* dramatized the tugs between heritage and stardom in immigrant families when it chronicled Jakie Rabvinovitz's struggles with his family's desire to see him become a cantor and his own desire to become a "jazz singer." The film, with its street scenes set on the Lower East Side and its soundtrack of Jolson singing, looked at the present but perpetuated one of the oldest of American theatrical conventions: blacking up. For African Americans, putting on blackface was a straitjacket that denied their individuality and confined their performances to a narrow range of expression. For Jolson, like other white artists of his generation, putting on blackface was a way of becoming fully American (at the expense of another ethnic group) and performing in a passionate style associated with African Americans. *The Jazz Singer*, which shows Rabinowitz taking his dying father's place in the synagogue yet going on to become a successful jazz singer, suggests that an American son can have both the blessings of a distinct heritage and stardom. Even if that was possible for Jews, any realization of that ideal was still in the future for African Americans.

The Jazz Singer looked back to the Lower East Side, and implicitly the Old World, as its starting point. Yet in the 1920s an Italian immigrant painter in

New York City, Joseph Stella, presented a vision of New York that recognized the past but looked passionately to the future. Stella, the son of a government functionary in Italy, immigrated to New York City and began medical school in 1896. He quickly entered art school, however, and in 1913–1914 produced *Battle of Lights, Coney Island, Mardi Gras*, a swirling, abstract painting that reveled in the lights and energy of the amusement park. In 1920–1922, he produced *New York Interpreted (The Voice of the City)*, which depicted iconic images of New York City—the port, skyscrapers, the bright lights of Broadway, the subway, and the Brooklyn Bridge—in new ways. Stella recognized New York's roots in the past—there are classical religious references in the painting—but he reveled in the city's sensations. He pushed his artwork in the direction of the Futurists, his contemporaries, who sought new ways make art dynamic. New York, for Stella, was a city where the future was vividly on display, a place where "Steel and electricity had created a new world."[120]

Stella's painting was a unique record of an immigrant's encounter with New York. Most New York families with immigrant roots took satisfaction in simpler achievements: a new apartment in the Bronx, a modest level of prosperity, and larger hopes for their American-born children. Dreams and ambitions varied with individuals and ethnic groups, but the contrary tugs of the past, the present, and the possible animated many New York neighborhoods where European immigrants raised American-born children. In his novel *The Fortunate Pilgrim*, Mario Puzo reconstructed the world of his immigrant Italian mother in Hell's Kitchen on the West Side of Manhattan in 1928.[121] The conversations there were in Italian, but they had their counterparts in other neighborhoods and other languages all around the city. "Each tenement was a village square; each had its group of women, all in black," wrote Puzo, "sitting on stools and boxes and doing more than gossip. They recalled ancient history, argued morals and social law, always taking their precedents from the mountain village in southern Italy they had escaped, fled from many years ago."[122]

Even as they faced great hardships, the women loved the city that had made possible their liberation. They felt a guilty loyalty to "customs they had trampled into the dust," but they had hopes they had never entertained in Italy. Through it all, they wrestled stoically with the fact that their children, raised in New York, were becoming strangers to them.

> Each in turn told a story of insolence and defiance, themselves heroic, long-suffering, the children spitting Lucifers saved by an application of Italian discipline. . . . And at the end of each story each woman recited her requiem—*Mannaggia America*—Damn America.
>
> But in the hot summer night their voices were filled with hope, with a vigor never sounded in their homeland. Here now was money in the bank, children who could read and write, grandchildren who would be professors if all went well.[123]

Such hopes—whether expressed in Italian or Yiddish or the other languages of immigrant New York—were extracted from lives of labor and sacrifice. They were also testaments to how immigrants had made homes for themselves in the city. In 1928, however, these hopes were on the verge of being tested in an economic disaster and a new world war. Out of these trials would emerge new ideas about government and politics, what it meant to be an American, and what it meant to be a New Yorker.

CHAPTER 6

TIMES OF TRIAL: 1929–1945

I n her work at the Henry Street Settlement House on the Lower East Side, Lillian Wald watched economic troubles arrive with an unsettling murmur of hard times. "Increasingly," wrote Wald, "in the winter of 1928–1929, months before the stock market crash, we were made aware of the foreboding of our neighbors." As with other downturns, there was "no sudden avalanche, but a creeping daily change—shortening hours of work, an increasing number of dismissals, wage cuts, and the uneasiness which none can comprehend unless they have learned to recognize and share it. It permeates a neighborhood like a thickening fog of anxiety and fear."[1]

Compared to the rural areas and inland factory cities that were the first to suffer economic distress in the 1920s, the Great Depression came slowly to economically dynamic New York. Even the stock market crash of October 1929, which looms large in retrospect, was not immediately a cataclysmic event. By the start of 1931, however, New Yorkers had seen layoffs, bank runs, men selling apples on street corners, and people sleeping in Central Park. By the end of the year, New York City hospitals reported that ninety-five people had starved to death.[2]

The Great Depression was a global disaster, and New York was not spared its effects. Immigration declined as few Europeans saw opportunities for prosperity in the United States. Equally important, the Depression set off a period of economic upheaval and political experimentation that changed what people expected from government and politics in New York and the nation. When the Depression was succeeded by World War II, New York would be challenged and mobilized as never before. The polyglot metropolis was at once the destination of refugees, the target of enemies, and a city tugged between the ideals of democracy and the realities of bigotry and exclusion. Puerto Ricans and African Americans from the South increasingly moved to New York seeking the freedom and prosperity that European immigrants had found before them.

In 1931, in a city of breadlines, most of these changes lay in the future. What was palpable to people in all walks of life was that they lived in a frightening time. Carl Van Doren, a literary scholar and historian, noticed that he kept having the same dream. "It was," he wrote, "a dream of fear."[3]

* * *

The Great Depression battered nearly all New Yorkers, especially in its early years. Lines of unemployed men and women patiently waited for handouts at soup kitchens while apple sellers stood nearby. In Central Park, Riverside Park, and vacant city lots, the homeless and unemployed lived in settlements of shacks called Hoovervilles. One historian reported that on a single day in January 1931, 85,000 people "waited for free meals at eighty-one locations in front of churches, the Salvation Army, and other charitable institutions."[4] In 1930, the Municipal Lodging House in the city provided more than four hundred thousand lodgings and one million meals for homeless men and women; the next year, both figures doubled.[5] About one-fourth of New York's workers were unemployed by 1933. Mary Agnes Hamilton, a British author, journalist, and member of the Labour Party researching a book on conditions in the United States, visited Manhattan and wrote: "One only has to pass outside the central island bounded by Lexington and Sixth Avenues to see hardship, misery and degradation, accentuated by the shoddy grimness of the shabby houses and broken pavements. Look down from the Elevated, and there are long queues of dreary-looking men and women standing in 'breadlines.'"[6]

Manufacturing and mechanical industries were especially devastated. By 1934, more than one-third of workers in those occupations were on relief. The building industry was also hard hit. The construction of offices, homes, and apartments was curtailed, and the middle-class dreams of many New Yorkers were put on hold. Despite Depression-era projects connecting the city and the suburbs (the George Washington Bridge in 1931, the Lincoln Tunnel in 1937), the pace of suburban growth declined. The completion of the Triborough Bridge in 1936 and the Queens-Midtown Tunnel in 1940 augured increased development of the outer boroughs, but many Manhattan residents simply could not afford to move.

Manual laborers in manufacturing and construction—mainly Italians and Poles and to a lesser extent Irish, Germans, and Jews—suffered. In

6.1 Breadline beneath the Brooklyn Bridge during the Great Depression.

Source: FSA/OWI Collection, Library of Congress.

Lower Manhattan's Little Italy, 16.5 percent of the families had no adult wage earner in 1930. Two years later, the figure was 47.6 percent. Uptown, Robert Orsi notes, "The residents of Italian Harlem did not need outside researchers and statisticians to inform them about the plight of their community. They could see Italian Harlem crumbling around them; they inhabited its primitive housing and walked its dangerous streets." One social worker said, "Evictions were going on right and left. Landlords not being able to collect their rent were putting people on the streets." As Simone Cinotto points out, "Italians were disproportionately represented among the recipients of city and federal subsidies, particularly in Harlem, where the poorest among them lived."[7]

New York's Jewish industrial workers also experienced difficulties. A 1930 study by the Federation of Jewish Philanthropies concluded that "the normal absorption of Jews within the American economic structure is now practically impossible."[8] Alfred Kazin, who grew up in Brownsville during the 1930s, recalled, "From the early thirties on, my father [a painter] could never be sure in advance of a week's work. . . . It puzzled me greatly when I came to read in books that Jews are a shrewd people particularly given to commerce and banking, for all the Jews I knew had managed to be an exception to the rule." He concluded, "I grew up with the belief that the natural condition of a Jew was to be a propertyless worker like my painter father and my dressmaker mother and my dressmaker uncles and cousins in Brownsville—workers, kin to all the workers of the world, dependent entirely on the work of their hand. All happiness in our house was measured by the length of a job."[9]

Hardest hit were New York's African Americans. The *Herald Tribune* reported that Harlem was "the poorest, the unhealthiest, the unhappiest and the most crowded single large section of New York City."[10] Deteriorating social and economic conditions in the city's African American neighborhoods took a further tumble during the Great Depression. Median black income in Harlem fell 44 percent between 1929 and 1933; in the worst years of the Depression, more than 40 percent of blacks were out of work, nearly twice the proportion of whites.[11]

The city's economy remained about as closed to African Americans as it had been for the three previous decades. Construction crews hired only a few African Americans, and those employed on the subways served as porters, not as higher-paid motormen. Department stores and other large employers of white-collar workers generally refused to hire black workers. Some of Harlem's larger stores made token gestures by taking on a few black clerks in the 1920s. In 1934, L. M. Blumstein, the owner of a large department store on 125th Street, said that he had given a donation to the National Urban League and had hired a few African Americans as porters, maids, and elevator operators over the previous five years. Blumstein admitted that 75 percent of his customers were black but that he did not see the need to employ black sales clerks.[12]

African American women found jobs at the demeaning "slave markets," which were certain street corners of the Bronx where they congregated, carrying signs advertising themselves as available for housework. Housewives went from woman to woman, "shopping" for the lowest-priced workers. A state committee reported it was "not surprising that householders find it very easy to secure day-work help for 15 and 20 cents an hour."[13] Cheryl Greenberg reports, "Some women who applied for home relief after trying their luck in these slave markets were actually rejected by relief officials because the wages they reported were so low the case workers suspected they had lied about their pay or they had been supplementing it with profits from illegal activities. It was impossible, relief officials concluded, for these women to have been able to survive on so little."[14]

Given the deplorable conditions, it is easily understood why more than 40 percent of black families in 1933 were on relief. Public support funds were woefully inadequate, paying only $2.39 per week in 1932, and many individuals who were out of work were unable to receive any help at all.[15] Inevitably housing and health conditions for African Americans deteriorated further during the 1930s, yet rents remained higher in Harlem than elsewhere. Modest slum clearance and public housing projects inaugurated under the New Deal late in the 1930s had a minimal effect upon either Harlem or Bedford-Stuyvesant.[16]

Rising relief rolls were a sign of hard times, but they alone do not tell the extent of suffering because not all sought government aid. New York Chinese experienced an estimated unemployment rate of 30 percent in the early years of the Depression as falling incomes led to slumps in business at hand laundries and restaurants, the mainstays of the city's Chinese population. One estimate claimed that 150 Chinese restaurants failed in 1930 alone.[17] To make ends meet, Chinese turned to job sharing and aid from communal associations. When a relief office opened in Chinatown, African Americans and white New Yorkers appeared—but no Chinese.[18]

Even white-collar workers and city employees suffered. One white-collar worker reportedly told persons handing out food in a soup kitchen, "I wouldn't do this, but if I eat here it makes what little there is at home last longer for my wife while I am walking the streets." Yet white-collar workers on the whole did get by better than blue-collar ones, which meant that Jewish New Yorkers fared better. Beth Wenger notes, "The employment patterns of New York Jews helped them survive the economic crisis in a comparatively fortunate position. Jewish concentration in white-collar and skilled occupations resulted in less severe economic dislocation relative to groups that predominated in manual unskilled positions." Conditions among Italians who were white-collar workers were better than among the less skilled; a Depression-era survey in Italian East Harlem revealed that the overwhelming majority of parents thought that office work was the most desirable employment for their children.[19]

Facing limited job prospects for their children and realizing that white-collar work offered a likelier path to economic stability and mobility, many New Yorkers kept their children in school longer. The number of students attending high school increased 45 percent between 1930 and 1935.[20] While Italians and others increasingly stayed in school longer, Jews continued to lead in seeking educational opportunities. High school enrollment became the norm for both Jewish men and women. Although Jewish men were more apt to attend college than Jewish women, Jewish women were more likely to avail themselves of higher education than females from other ethnic groups. In 1934, Jewish women represented more than one-half of female students attending New York's public colleges.[21] Besides keeping their children in school, families coped in other ways. Young couples postponed marriage or married and moved in with their parents until they could earn enough to afford their own housing. Couples also had fewer children during the Great Depression.[22]

The growing economic and psychological pain of New Yorkers echoed overseas. With so many people out of work during the early 1930s, fewer Europeans looked to America as the land of opportunity. In the early 1930s, more people returned home than arrived. After 1935, the spread of fascism made many Europeans desperate to seek a haven despite economic conditions in the city, but America's restrictive immigration policies remained tightly enforced. As a result, only approximately one hundred thousand immigrants settled in New York during the 1930s. Caribbean immigration virtually stopped during that decade, and some West Indian New Yorkers returned to their home islands.

Within the United States, Puerto Ricans and African Americans migrated north in smaller numbers.

* * *

Unemployed New Yorkers, both working class and middle class, turned to traditional sources of aid. Protestant, Roman Catholic, and Jewish religious agencies and charities all expanded their activities in response to the emergency. Jewish philanthropies, as did others, reported a drop in income and an increase in applications for aid. Many New Yorkers feared that their mobility was blocked and that they would never find jobs commensurate with their educations.[23]

During the 1920s, Archbishop Patrick Cardinal Hayes coordinated Catholic welfare efforts through Catholic Charities, whose annual parish appeals soon grossed one million dollars. In the 1930s, however, Catholic Charities soon found itself unable to meet all requests for aid. By the time Francis Cardinal Spellman assumed the leadership of the Diocese of New York in 1939, it had a $28 million debt and was struggling to make ends meet.[24]

Harlem's churches, which had traditionally helped the poor, expanded their efforts to aid unemployed residents.[25] The largest and most prestigious church, Adam Clayton Powell Sr.'s Abyssinian Baptist, provided food, clothing, coal, and kerosene to those in need. A cooperative effort of Harlem churches led by the Rev. Shelton Hale Bishop of St. Philips Protestant Episcopal Church also gave away food, clothing, and carfare and searched for jobs for the unemployed.[26]

Because African Americans were segregated and had little political power, during the Depression black churches, which already were the most important social institutions for African Americans, became even more crucial. Moreover, Harlem was saturated with churches, ranging from storefronts, such as depicted in James Baldwin's first novel *Go Tell It on the Mountain*, to large congregations such as Abyssinian Baptist.

African American churchwomen played vital roles in these institutions, in part because they were the congregations' majority of members. For every sixty-four male members there were one hundred women in the congregation—a much larger ratio for women than was usual in Protestant churches.[27] Churchwomen served in the soup kitchens, provided day care, helped young mothers, and strove to improve conditions for working women. They also worked outside of the church in secular organizations involved in racial and community politics. Nevertheless, the growing activism of black women did not propel them into leadership positions. "Generally, the top positions in church efforts were reserved for ministers, and many women still viewed themselves in some sense as religious followers."[28]

The most colorful figure in Depression-era Harlem was George Baker, known as Father Divine. Claiming to be God, he attracted many followers, both white and black, and raised funds to run fifteen "heavens" in Harlem, which served daily banquets for all visitors. Whether all participants really believed Father Divine was God is not known, but allegedly three thousand people a day willingly accepted his meals.[29]

More significant in political realms was Adam Clayton Powell Jr., the most charismatic preacher to emerge in the 1930s. Powell succeeded his father as pastor at Abyssinian Baptist Church in 1938, organized the Equal Employment Coordinating Committee, and initiated boycotts of companies that would not hire black workers. Politically agile, Powell cultivated support from both communists and black nationalists. In 1941, he became the first African American elected to the city council. In 1945, he was elected to Congress.[30]

* * *

The policies and politicians that had seemed adequate in the 1920s became far less so during the crisis of the Depression. Welfare associations like the Charity Organization Society, the Children's Aid Society, the Urban League, and the New York Association for Improving the Condition of the Poor all expanded their efforts to meet Depression needs. In the end, however, private charities were overwhelmed by the magnitude of the crisis. New Yorkers, like Americans elsewhere, turned to government, first to municipal and state agencies and eventually to Washington.[31]

In November 1929, before the full weight of the Depression came to bear on New York City, Fiorello La Guardia—a liberal Republican who represented predominantly Italian East Harlem in Congress—made his first run for mayor. His opponent was the incumbent mayor, Jimmy Walker, "Beau James," a Tammany man buoyed by the fact that Democrats outnumbered Republicans in New York City. Walker, the historian Thomas Kessner argues, was most at home in the glittering world of the 1920s, with its high spending, titillating nightlife, and wild speculation. His city was "the sparkling mecca of the polished rich." A stylish dresser with a showgirl mistress, the mayor was the writer of the popular song "Will You Love Me in September as You Do in May?" In the eyes of many, he symbolized the times.[32]

La Guardia charged that the mayor was a front man for Tammany Hall who did not represent the will of New Yorkers. He attacked Walker when the mayor managed to have his salary raised to $40,000 annually from $25,000. Walker retorted, "Why that's cheap! Think what it would cost if I worked full time!"[33] La Guardia nonetheless suffered a crushing defeat at the hands of Walker.

Under the Depression's pressures, however, dapper Mayor Walker quickly proved unable to cope with a deteriorating economy and large-scale political corruption. New York City's government, overwhelmed by demands for assistance, could not balance its budget without curtailing municipal services and laying off employees. A desperate Mayor Walker dismissed several thousand schoolteachers in 1930–1931, and more city cutbacks followed.[34] Social workers reported that they "saw much more distress last winter [1930–1931] than they had ever seen before."[35]

Even though municipal funds were increasingly limited, New Yorkers nonetheless recognized that government continued to represent a source of possible employment. The sociologist Roger Waldinger observes:

> In 1933, under Tammany, 6,327 individuals applied for government jobs; six years later, 250,000 job seekers knocked at the municipal service's door. Openings in just one city agency, the newly competitive welfare department, attracted 100,000 test takers in 1939. The search for upward mobility through civil service also accelerated, as applications for promotional exams climbed from 6,270 in 1935 to 26,847 in 1939.[36]

Yet it was not relief or jobs alone that caused New Yorkers to focus on their municipal government. In the face of economic hardship, the all-too-traditional graft and poor quality of municipal services became more glaring and, for many, unacceptable. As stories surfaced and rumors circulated about corruption in city government, including the office of the mayor, Governor Franklin Roosevelt appointed a commission headed by Judge Samuel Seabury to investigate.

Seabury's investigations in 1930 revealed payoffs to the police, clerks, and bondsmen. Then the commission turned to magistrates and labor racketeering. Among a growing list of public officials taking graft, the investigators uncovered the county registrar of Brooklyn, the Hon. James A. McQuade, who had managed to accumulate more than $500,000 in five years on an annual salary of $12,000. He claimed he had friends who had loaned him large sums. When asked if he could remember who had trusted him with hundreds of thousands of dollars, he replied, "Oh Judge, offhand I could not." The trail of corruption pointed to City Hall, and Mayor Walker faced the possibility of prosecution. Confronted with the challenges that faced the city in the Depression, Walker's charm was inadequate. In 1932, he resigned and sailed off to Europe.[37]

The stage was set for Fiorello La Guardia. When Walker quit, Joseph V. McKee, an Irish Tammany politician and president of the Board of Aldermen, became acting mayor until the 1933 election. In that year, La Guardia appealed to discontented voters and ran as a Republican-fusion candidate supported by

6.2 Mayor Fiorello La Guardia, who led New York City through the Great Depression and World War II, speaks over the municipal radio station in 1940.

Source: Fred Palumbo, *New York World-Telegram and Sun* Newspaper Photograph Collection, Library of Congress.

good government clubs. The "Little Flower," as La Guardia was called, won a plurality of votes in a three-way race.[38] He would be reelected in 1937 and 1941, an extraordinary feat for a fusion reform candidate. Indeed, many consider La Guardia to have been New York's greatest mayor.

The feisty mayor was perfect for polyglot New York and its immigrant population. His father was an Italian Protestant and his mother Jewish; he was Episcopalian. La Guardia had served as an interpreter at Ellis Island and represented the Lower East Side and East Harlem in Congress.[39] The languages he spoke included Yiddish, Italian, German, and Croatian. Once, when charged with being anti-Semitic, he challenged to his accuser to debate the campaign's issues "ENTIRELY IN THE YIDDISH LANGUAGE."[40]

La Guardia also benefited from having spent the decade before his mayoralty sharpening his own critique of economic inequality and affirming the contributions of immigrants to American society. He was, as his biographer Howard Zinn put it, a "radical in Congress" who opposed Prohibition and immigration restrictions. Both positions won him support in New York. He also developed a critique of the free market, a stance that left him more ready than most to move decisively when the American economy collapsed.[41]

Yet the new mayor could not and did not appease all groups. In 1933, Italians supported him overwhelmingly. Jews also favored La Guardia, though not as strongly as Italians. Jews became increasingly supportive of the mayor as he raised the number of city positions available to them through civil service. He also appointed a number of Jews and Italians to high municipal jobs and chose a Jew and an Irishman as his running mates for the president of the board of alderman and comptroller, respectively.[42] Jewish voters also generally approved of the social programs of the La Guardia years and applauded his attacks on Nazism (he was more cautious in criticizing Mussolini). La Guardia also did well among New York's growing number of African American voters. At the same time, La Guardia's hostility to Tammany made him unpopular with the many Irish voters loyal to the hall.[43]

Many of La Guardia's supporters were drawn to him because of his crusade against political corruption and gambling. Moreover, he was a most conspicuous mayor. He rushed to the scenes of fires and took to the airwaves to read the funnies to children over the radio during a newspaper strike. "I felt," said the mayor, "that the children should not be deprived of them due to a squabble among the adults." At times the mayor pushed projects that seemed to be highly personal or ethnically motivated. One of the mayor's first acts was to refuse to grant permits for organ grinders, insisting that they were nothing more than beggars. La Guardia knew that most organ grinders with their monkeys were Italians, and he felt humiliated by their presence on the streets. When the mayor was petitioned to reverse his decision, he stood firm.[44]

As Jews and, to a lesser extent, Italians gained politically during the Great Depression, African American political leaders also sought more influence. They won control of the Democratic Party in Harlem and elected a few more African Americans to city and state offices. In 1941, the voters sent Adam Clayton Powell Jr. to the city council.[45] The hiring of more African American police officers and firefighters and the increased number of African Americans holding municipal jobs represented progress, but African Americans remained underrepresented in governmental employment. In 1940, when African Americans made up about 6 percent of the city's population, they were only 1.7 percent of municipal workers.[46]

In the Depression, African Americans banded together to boycott stores that would not hire black clerks. The coalition that fought for fair employment included ministers such as Adam Clayton Powell Jr., the colorful nationalist and anti-Semite Sufi Abdul Hamid, black and white communists, and working-class blacks. The New York NACCP, which also joined the protests, had been working to end discrimination in New York City since the 1920s. Under the banner "Don't Buy Where You Can't Work," Powell built a coalition to end discrimination at businesses in Harlem that refused to employ African Americans or employ them in only menial positions. An initial target was Blumstein's on 125th Street, which refused to employ African Americans as saleswomen even though the vast majority of its customers were African American. The management at first refused to yield to the threats of a boycott. The initial campaign against Blumstein's relied heavily upon churchwomen who organized as the "Harlem Housewives League." "Don't Buy Where You Can't Work" eventually won an agreement to hire black women as sales clerks. It did not go unnoticed, however, that the store hired light-skinned women as the first black women salespersons.[47]

Despite internal divisions, redbaiting, and a court injunction banning picketing, the coalition won its share of fights, and eventually all the stores on 125th Street, Harlem's main shopping street, hired black employees.[48] The coalition eventually fell apart after achieving modest success, but African Americans continued protesting and won limited gains at Harlem Hospital, including the appointment of more black medical and administrative personnel.[49]

* * *

As New Yorkers struggled to make ends meet, they realized that municipal and state governments, along with private philanthropy, were inadequate for meeting the needs of the city and its people. Fortunately for them, similar ideas were percolating in Washington, DC. President Franklin D. Roosevelt, the former governor of New York State, drew into his administration many New Yorkers who had cut their political teeth in the Progressive Era. Together, in complex and sometimes contradictory ways, they advanced the idea that government had a responsibility to support a common standard of living and protect individuals from social and economic hardships that they could not overcome alone. Roosevelt's wife, Eleanor, the conscience of the White House, had been a settlement-house worker on the Lower East Side. Frances Perkins, Roosevelt's secretary of labor and the first woman cabinet member, had witnessed the Triangle Shirtwaist Factory fire. Harry Hopkins, who also started out as a New York settlement-house worker, became a driving force behind the New Deal's relief and employment programs. In early days of the New Deal, Roosevelt agreed to provide jobs under the Civil Works

Administration. Roosevelt and La Guardia had a close relationship even though the mayor was a Republican. New York was quick to apply for and receive funds.[50]

Municipal funds were inadequate to meet the costs of battling the Depression, but federal and state monies were forthcoming. Mayor La Guardia turned to Robert Moses, the "master builder" and "power broker," to use them in a vast series of city projects. Moses, who already had considerable experience in state and regional government, quickly used Civil Works Administration funds to hire 68,000 men to refurbish city parks and beaches.[51] Later, using Works Project Administration (WPA) money, he built more parks and repaired others. The *New York Times* claimed the work of the Parks Department was "little short of miraculous."[52]

Although Moses's early achievements won support from La Guardia, critics—most significantly Robert Caro—have argued that Moses was high-handed to the point of being undemocratic and did not serve the interests of African Americans fairly. His grand state park, Jones Beach, which opened in 1929 on Long Island, was beyond the reach of most Harlem residents. In the summer of 1936, New York City opened ten new municipal pools and another renovated facility. Moses supervised the project, which was supported with federal funds. One of the pools was built in an African American section of Harlem and another in East Harlem, where the population was more strongly Italian. New York's pools were officially integrated, but in some areas—among them East Harlem and Washington Heights—whites harassed African American and Puerto Rican youths on the way to public pools to discourage them from swimming. The bigots' assaults were not always effective, but they certainly tarnished the democratic ideal of integrated public recreation. Moses, a conservative on racial matters, lived comfortably with the idea of "separate but equal" and did not press for police action to reduce the harassment of African Americans and Puerto Ricans who sought to swim in city pools. Moses's public works may have been extraordinary, but he held the common racial prejudices of his time.[53]

Federal funding was also available for road repair, sewer lines, and other repairs that had been delayed. Under Moses, the city added networks of roads and undertook major construction projects. The mayor believed New York City should have its own airport instead of using Newark's. To dramatize the point in 1934, he refused to disembark from his flight when the plane landed in Newark, saying that the ticket said "New York," not "Newark." In 1939, with the aid of the federal government, the city opened an airport in northwestern Queens that was eventually named LaGuardia Airport.[54]

Federal funding also provided workers to build health centers, several new college campuses, and dozens of similar facilities. La Guardia had proposed to abolish the city's municipal radio station, claiming lack of funding and a weak signal. Then the chair of CBS proposed that a larger appropriation be given the station, and the funds came from the WPA to build new facilities.[55]

Construction of public housing, curtailed by the Depression, resumed with New Deal funds. Utilizing federal money, 17,000 family units were completed, a step forward but hardly adequate to meet the city's housing needs.[56] This modest beginning was eventually followed by more elaborate public housing.[57]

The limitations of Moses's projects for African Americans were not enough to turn black New Yorkers against La Guardia and the New Deal. Mason Williams points out that the New Deal brought to Harlem and other black neighborhoods many benefits: new school buildings, the Colonial Park swimming pool, health centers, a new theater, and improved conditions at Harlem Hospital. These new public works were one incentive among many for African Americans to vote for Franklin Roosevelt as president and La Guardia as mayor. Even if the projects did not overcome the inequalities that dogged African Americans, they were far more generous than what typical Republicans were offering. Indeed, since the turn of the century, the Republican Party had offered little for African Americans in New York City or elsewhere in the nation.[58]

The construction of new public facilities helped reshape the city, but perhaps just as important in defining the New Deal in New York was its human element. Harry Hopkins, especially, thought that people needed to have self-respect and meaningful work. The New Deal in New York City reached out to a broad section of the labor force, including people in the arts. Hopkins said, "Hell, they've got to eat just like other people."[59]

A major success of the federal government's WPA was its arts project, which employed artists, musicians, actors, and writers who gave performances, published a guide to the city, and created murals in public places such as post offices. These projects have been criticized from the left for offering an idealized vision of America and from the right as leftist propaganda. Nevertheless, they offered an inclusive vision of American culture, established the idea that the arts were a part of public life, and nurtured the early careers of writers and artists who went on to acclaimed careers.[60]

WPA projects in New York City conveyed the significance of ethnicity in the city's past and present. The Federal Writers' Project *New York City Guide* described Manhattan as an international seaport, animated twenty-four hours a day by a "moving mass" of commuters, children playing in the streets, protest marches, late-night jazz clubs, and the sound of ships bearing "German, Austrian, Polish, Italian refugees." Manhattan was also, according to the guide, "the greatest city of the Jews," "The world's Negro metropolis," "The world's most populous Italian city outside of Italy," and "the world's third Irish city."[61]

WPA projects amplified the experiences of immigrants and migrants who might otherwise have been ignored. The African American writer Ralph Ellison, who did interviews for the WPA, heard a railroad porter say "I'm in New

York, but New York ain't in me" and worked the line into his novel *Invisible Man*. Ben Shahn, a Jewish immigrant from Russia, painted a mural for the Bronx Central Post Office titled *Resources of America*, which depicted rural and industrial workers.[62]

The WPA made possible one of the greatest depictions of African Americans' movement to northern cities by supporting the work of Jacob Lawrence, who worked for Harlem's Art Center, which ran programs for all age groups in painting, drawing, and other arts. Lawrence rendered the story of the Great Migration in sixty small tempera paintings, each with a caption, that depicted sharecropping and lynchings in the South, families boarding northbound trains, and the injustices that migrants experienced in northern cities. Lawrence's depiction of the migration, released in 1941 when the artist was only twenty-three, quickly entered the collections of the Phillips Gallery in Washington, DC, and New York City's Museum of Modern Art; it has been acclaimed "a landmark in the history of modern art." Lawrence went on to have a long career as an artist and professor.[63]

The WPA came to an end in 1943, but in New York its presence had strengthened the idea that government had a role to play in supporting the arts. When the city came in possession of the neo-Moorish Mecca Temple, it turned the building into the City Center for the Arts. Because WPA funds were no longer available, private donations provided the foundation for the new center, which offered dance, plays, and operas.[64]

✳ ✳ ✳

For all the excitement of La Guardia's tenure and all the benefits of government programs, for some New Yorkers more fundamental changes felt necessary. Labor organizers sought to revive the city's unions from their sluggishness of the 1920s. The Amalgamated Clothing Workers' Union, centered in New York, had fallen from 177,000 dues-paying members in 1920 to only seven thousand in 1932.[65] On the eve of the New Deal, the ILGWU had lost 60 percent of its hundred thousand members and suspended publication of its newspaper. At the ILGWU's headquarters, the elevator no longer ran because the union did not have enough money to pay its electricity bill.[66] But with a prolabor mood in both Albany and Washington, unions like Amalgamated and the ILGWU experienced a new militancy and made substantial gains during the New Deal years. By 1934, the ILGWU claimed a membership of more than two hundred thousand, the largest in its history, and it looked to political action to win further benefits.[67]

Struggling municipal unions, like that of the badly divided teachers, faced a city short of funds. In response to the Depression, the Board of Education hired low-paid substitutes and cut salaries and other services. Federal funds eventually led to new classroom construction and an expansion of educational programs, but the teachers' union would have to wait until after World War II for official recognition.[68]

The experience of the predominantly Irish transit workers was somewhat different. Before the 1930s, workers on the city's subways and buses were so poorly organized and paid that if alternative employment became available, transit workers would leave the system. When the Depression hit, alternative employment dried up, and wage cuts set the stage for considerable prounion sentiment. Transit workers—led by Irish-born Mike Quill, communist activists, and Irish Republicans—established the Transport Workers Union (TWU) in the early 1930s. The union's first success was organizing workers on the Interborough Rapid Transit line (IRT). The strong Irish connection was obvious when TWU members, celebrating their victory in Madison Square Garden, marched into the arena while a band played "The Wearing of the Green."[69] The first TWU contracts signed in 1937 brought important benefits to its members.[70] After the city consolidated the subway lines and assumed their direction, the TWU generally maintained its bargaining position in spite of La Guardia's opposition to the closed shop and municipal workers' right to strike.[71]

The city's Chinese laundrymen also organized during the Depression. Not only did technological changes threaten their small-scale enterprises, but large-scale laundries persuaded the Board of Aldermen to pass a laundry ordinance that established a $25 annual registration fee and required laundries run by one person to post a $1,000 bond upon applying for a license. Both of these measures imposed hardships on Chinese laundrymen and had the potential to force them out of business. When Chinatown's most powerful organization, the Chinese Consolidated Benevolent Association, offered virtually no assistance, the laundrymen organized the Chinese Hand Laundry Alliance, hired a lawyer, and successfully pressured the Board of Aldermen to reduce the registration fee and bond price. Bolstered by this achievement, the Chinese Hand Laundry Alliance became a leading organization in Chinatown; it spoke out for laundry workers and opposed discrimination against Chinese Americans. As the 1930s progressed and the Japanese invasion of China gained strength, the alliance mobilized opposition to Japan in the United States.[72]

∗ ∗ ∗

The suffering of the Great Depression in New York City also generated renewed radicalism, which took the form of both socialism and communism. The male students of the City College of New York were well known for the communists among them, and the Young Communist League (YCL) also had a presence among the women of Hunter College. The YCL had a small membership at Hunter, and the faithful sometimes grew frustrated that other Hunter students did not share their views. Yet these women distributed party literature, "solicited names on petitions and sold the communist *Daily Worker* on Manhattan street corners."[73] As Lucy Dawidowicz recalled, "the YCL took precedence over our classes, especially required courses, which we cut a lot."[74]

Although the Communist Party never claimed more than a few thousand members in the city, it had many sympathizers and influenced both the trade unions and the newly formed American Labor Party. Mike Quill, for example, was closely associated with the Communist Party for many years, as were some Jews, in particular some teachers, social workers, and white-collar employees.[75] Italians tended to be more conservative than Jews, but the notable Italian radicals Vito Marcantonio, who served in Congress, and Peter V. Cacchione, a communist member of the city council, attracted Italian votes during the depths of the Depression. Communists also made special efforts to win over African Americans. Many blacks appreciated the party's protests against racial injustice. Communists also won much praise when they took up the cause of the Scottsboro Boys, nine African American youths in Alabama who were falsely accused of raping two white women.[76]

A major problem for the Communist Party's attempt to recruit African Americans was the African American church. Harlem's churches, which were already assisting needy African Americans in the grim days of the Depression, did not share the party's atheism. Moreover, communist support for the creation of an all-black state in the South alienated African Americans who thought the proposal would leave them isolated. Harlem communists also had to contend with lingering competition from Garveyism and socialist critiques of communism from Frank Crosswaith and A. Philip Randoph.[77]

Despite these obstacles, in the years of the Depression Harlem communists—black and white—gained a deserved reputation for bravely defending the rights of African Americans when few others would. In pursuit of a united front against fascism, Harlem communists—responding to both Soviet urgings and grassroots conditions—reached out beyond their own confines and sought a wider array of allies. Relatively few African Americans followed the path of Benjamin Davis or Bonita Williams to become a prominent communist; more common were African American activists who worked with communists on selected issues where they shared a common cause, as did the politically adroit minister and politician Adam Clayton Powell Jr.[78]

Not content with New Deal policies, radicals came together in 1936 to form the American Labor Party. The party's base was in the world of left-leaning Jewish garment workers, immigrants, and their children, who belonged to the Amalgamated Clothing Workers' Union and the ILGWU of David Dubinsky. Specifically, the ALP drew support from left-leaning Jews who wanted to vote for Franklin Roosevelt without being associated with the Democratic Party and its New York bosses. The ALP also provided a place on the ballot for Mayor

La Guardia, who won nearly half a million votes on the ALP ballot line in his 1937 reelection campaign. Communists and their sympathizers, such as Mike Quill of the Transport Workers Union, also became active in the ALP, making the party an arena for conflict between communists and anticommunists on the Left. Eventually, during World War II, the anticommunists in the ALP would leave to form the Liberal Party.[79]

For a brief period in the 1930s and 1940s, however, communists—working on their own initiative and on the instructions of the Comintern in the Soviet Union—worked with other radicals and liberals to support the New Deal and oppose the rise of fascism in Europe.[80] Communists, once dismissive of American culture as backward or insufficiently radical, now celebrated the culture and history of the United States. Praise for the "common man," workers, and farmers animated both political actions and the projects of the Federal Arts program. Paul Robeson, already a renowned African American actor and polymath, performed "Old Man River" from the Broadway musical *Showboat*, turning it into a song of protest. In Greenwich Village, already a center for the arts and dissent, the Almanac Singers (who included Pete Seeger and Woody Guthrie) used topical folk songs to voice a left-of-center politics that adhered to the Communist Party line but tried to attract supporters from beyond the party. For New York Jews who were the children of immigrants, this Popular Front ideology, and the New Deal's emphasis on celebrating the strength of an inclusive vision for the United States, provided a way of being both Jewish and American.

* * *

New Dealers and communists spoke of democracy and justice in a spirit of universalism, but in New York City they had to develop appeals to specific ethnic groups and confront varied forms of bigotry. Unions and political parties made direct ethnic appeals and built bases of support in ethnic neighborhoods, even as economic despair and keen competition for jobs fostered intergroup tensions. A 1938 study by the American Jewish Congress claimed that anti-Jewish specifications in help-wanted ads were at an all-time high. Medical and law schools also tightened their restrictions against Jewish applicants.[81] The percentage of Jews in Columbia University's College of Physicians and Surgeons fell from 46.94 in 1920 to 6.45 in 1940.[82]

Jewish women encountered gender bias in addition to anti-Semitism when they attempted to become doctors or lawyers. Quotas and other restrictions were common against women in those years. Moreover, Jewish parents, like nearly all immigrant parents, were more apt to support their sons' career aspirations than their daughters. Hence, many Jewish women chose to become teachers, a profession that required fewer years of formal education. Jewish women had begun to enter the teaching ranks as early as World War I, but these were mostly German Jews. In the 1920s and 1930s, the daughters of Eastern European immigrants entered the profession in growing numbers. For Jews, teaching had relatively high status compared to other feminized professions, such as nursing, which was considered menial and "the bastion of Irish-American women, who controlled entrance into both nursing schools and hospitals." Most young women received their teacher training at Hunter College (limited to women) and coeducational Brooklyn College, founded in 1930.[83]

To many Irish New Yorkers, the increase of Jewish women in the teaching ranks and Mayor La Guardia's extension of the civil service to include a growing number of municipal jobs seemed to represent a loss of opportunity. Appointments of Jews and Italians to non–civil service jobs in city agencies and the election of others to municipal offices appeared to be further signs of declining Irish influence in governing New York City.[84] Some Catholics, among them Irish Catholics, believed that anti-Catholicism was a bigger problem than anti-Semitism. Ronald Bayor reports that the often anti-Semitic *Brooklyn Tablet*, the official paper of the Roman Catholic Diocese of Brooklyn, declared that Jews were overrepresented in the professions and had nothing to complain about.[85]

* * *

The most violent outburst of the 1930s in New York City took place over home-grown racism in Harlem. The trouble began on March 19, 1935, when an African American youth was caught trying to steal a knife from the S. H. Kress and Company store on 125th Street. When police arrived, the manager decided not to press charges, but rumors quickly spread that the youngster had been beaten and killed. When the police attempted to break up a protest, crowds gathered and began smashing store windows and looting shops. A night of looting and clashes between Harlemites and the police followed. By the time calm was restored, three African Americans were dead, and more than two hundred people were injured, eight of them police officers.[86]

A commission established by Mayor La Guardia concluded that the explosion on March 19 would "never have been set off by the trifling incident described above had not existing economic and social forces created a state of emotional tension which sought release upon the slightest provocation." If the conditions responsible for the episode continued, the report argued, "a state of tension will exist in Harlem and recurrent outbursts may occur."[87]

Some authorities blamed the communists, who were very active in Harlem in the 1930s, for inflaming the crowd, but the mayor's commission rejected this idea. Instead, after holding hearings and investigating the riot and Harlem, the commissioners specifically cited poor housing, health, and public facilities, as well as unemployment, inadequate relief, run-down schools, and Harlem's antagonism toward the police as the underlying causes of the riot. So dismal was the picture the commission painted that Mayor La Guardia did not release the final report.[88]

The commission made recommendations to improve social and economic conditions in Harlem. The city instituted a few improvements, and the mayor promised better social services for the community, including more places in public housing. Increased numbers of African American nurses and doctors won positions at Harlem Hospital and in municipal offices. The mayor also made symbolic gestures, such as inviting the heavyweight boxer Joe Louis to City Hall before a title bout.

* * *

Events overseas also aggravated conflict among New York's ethnic groups. The rise of Nazism in Germany and the triumph of Mussolini's Italian fascism triggered strong responses among many of the city's Jews, Italians, and Germans. Nazism even came to America.

Among Jews and other victims of Nazi persecution who succeeded in gaining entry visas to the United States were distinguished artists, musicians, scholars, and intellectuals. The New School for Social Research, originally founded as a university for adult education, responded by creating a "university for exiles." Under the leadership of Alvin Johnson, the New School hired dozens of refugee scholars, chiefly Germans, and helped find places for others.[89]

Of the German Jewish refugees who escaped to America from 1938 to 1940, several thousand settled in Upper Manhattan's Washington Heights. Many of them were people from country towns or provincial cities in Germany, where they were often shopkeepers, cattle dealers, or business people. In contrast to the nineteenth-century German Jewish immigrants, many of these newcomers were Orthodox. Their adjustment to New York was not easy, and some professionals had to change careers to survive.[90]

Such was the fate of the Kissingers, an Orthodox family with a strong German identity that immigrated in 1938 and settled into Washington Heights. The father in the family found little demand for his occupation as a teacher, grew depressed, and eventually found sporadic work as a bookkeeper. The mother was the main source of income, working as a servant and then as a caterer. Their two sons juggled work and high school. Heinz, the older of the two boys, eventually changed his name to Henry in hopes of fitting in better at school. Henry Kissinger served in the U.S. Army from 1943 to 1946, studied at Harvard after World War II, and eventually served as secretary of state.[91]

Immigrants fleeing European fascism found that New York, even though it was a city of refuge, had its own fascist element. A few local Nazi units had been organized in the 1920s. The Depression years' major pro-Nazi group was Fritz Kuhn's German American Bund. Claiming only a few thousand members, many of whom were recent German immigrants, and centered in Manhattan's Yorkville, the Bund made strenuous efforts to win the support of German American New Yorkers.[92] It had little success in that endeavor, yet with its Nazi-style uniforms and salutes, the Bund was an ugly, frightening organization. It supported Hitler, verbally attacked Jews in America, assailed a Jewish boycott of German goods, and held political rallies complete with Nazi banners and music. In 1939, it conducted a massive rally at Madison Square Garden, during which an audience of twenty thousand heard speeches in praise of Hitler. When a reporter on the scene laughed at their carryings on, she was beaten.[93]

While not necessarily endorsing fascism, many of the city's Italian Americans admired Mussolini's accomplishments. The historian Nancy Carnevale points to one Mussolini supporter who insisted that Italian Americans should appreciate Mussolini for "having raised Italians from despised 'barbers or fruit vendors' to 'a people respected all over the world.' "[94] Among Mussolini's more prominent supporters was Generoso Pope, editor of the city's major Italian-language newspaper, *Il Progresso*. Pope was connected to Tammany and had contacts in Washington, DC. Until 1940, his newspaper was friendly to the Italian leader, as were other Italian-language newspapers and organizations, such as the Sons of Italy.[95]

The rise of anti-Semitism in Italy, which accompanied the growing ties between that nation and Nazi Germany, had no significant effect on relations between the city's Italian and Jewish communities—in part because the worst actions in Italy took place under German direction in the latter years of World War II.[96] However, conflict did erupt between Italian New Yorkers and African Americans. Many Italian Americans defended Mussolini's invasion of Ethiopia, while African American leaders supported Ethiopia's pleas to the League of Nations for assistance and condemned Italy for its aggression. After Italy attacked Ethiopia, African American religious leaders helped organize the Committee for Ethiopia, which was chaired by the Adam Clayton Powell Jr.[97]

When the African American boxer Joe Louis, who was idolized in Harlem, fought a heavyweight title bout against the Italian Primo Carnera in July 1935, Mayor La Guardia posted 1,500 police officers to keep the peace, the "largest detachment ever assigned to a prize fight." While the crowd was not unruly that night, street fighting between Italian American and African American New Yorkers occurred throughout the summer. In Harlem, African Americans on one occasion smashed the windows of Italian-owned stores, and the number of Italian-owned bars in the area declined. Black nationalists urged a boycott of Harlem stores owned by Italians.[98]

Another contributor to the climate of racial and ethnic tension was Father Charles E. Coughlin, the Detroit radio priest. Originally Coughlin had been supportive of Roosevelt and the New Deal, but in the mid-1930s he began to attack FDR and his policies, praise Nazism, and characterize Jews as dangerous radicals or plutocrats who had too much power in the United States. His journal *Social Justice* and his organization, the Christian Front, held some appeal to Catholics, particularly among the Irish. Coughlin's vehement attacks on Jews aggravated Irish-Jewish tensions and stirred up anti-Semitism in New York. To make matters worse, the Catholic Church did not condemn either the radio priest or the Christian Front.[99]

Christian Front activities in the city led to several street brawls in the Bronx and Upper Manhattan. The organization encouraged gangs of youth in those neighborhoods to break the windows of Jewish merchants and to beat up Jewish children. Jewish leaders accused the heavily Irish police force of doing little or nothing to stop anti-Semitic violence. Evelyn Gonzalez reports that in the lower Bronx, where Irish and Jews lived near each other and some Irish resented the slightly better housing and economic status of some Jews, "Irish youths roamed the streets during the late 1930s and early 1940s, vandalizing Jewish businesses and physically attacking Jewish-looking people."[100]

Although the Great Depression concentrated most people's attention on domestic economic issues, the prospect of war in Europe loomed large. Rising tensions in Europe and ethnic politics in New York overlapped from 1936 to 1939 during the Spanish Civil War, when rightist military forces under Francisco Franco tried to overthrow the moderately leftist and democratically elected government of Spain. Nazi Germany and Fascist Italy supported Franco, while the Soviet Union and Mexico supported the Spanish Republic. Debates over the war echoed in New York neighborhoods. Italians split over the war along pro- and anti-Mussolini lines, while leftist and liberal Jews were prominent among supporters of the Spanish Republic. Jews were disproportionately represented in the Abraham Lincoln Brigade, one of the military units organized by the international communist movement to fight Franco.[101]

In the view of Father Coughlin, the radio priest, however, Franco was the protector of the Catholic Church, so Jews—many of whom strongly supported the Spanish Republic—became the target of his wrath. In Washington, the New Deal regime was aware that Italy and Nazi Germany were aiding Franco with troops, planes, equipment, and supplies, but the president adopted a policy of aiding neither side. For FDR, the critical factor was his concern that aiding the Spanish Republic would cost him Catholic votes. The Roosevelt administration discouraged (but did not halt) Americans who fought for the Spanish Republic as members of the Abraham Lincoln Brigade and resisted calls for direct aid to the hard-pressed Republic. Only later did FDR concede that nonintervention had been a mistake.[102]

As war in Europe threatened, lines of conflict sharpened. German Americans increasingly attacked the Bund and Hitler's Germany, and some reached out to improve German-Jewish relations in the city. In 1933, a self-proclaimed leader of Nazism, Heinz Spanknobel, tried to order Victor Ridder, one of the publishers of the *Staats-Zeitung und Herold*, to support the Nazi cause, but Ridder threw him out of his office, and his paper subsequently became increasingly anti-Hitler.[103] Yorkville was also the center of anti-Nazi organizations like the German Workers Club and the German Central Book Store, which sold the very books that Hitler had banned. The anti-Nazi newspaper *Deutsches Volksecho* also had many readers in Yorkville.[104]

While most New Yorkers focused on Europe, the Second World War actually began when Japan attached China in 1931. After the initial assault, which left Manchuria under Japanese possession, the two nations maintained peace for several years. Then in 1937, the Japanese military used a fake incident to renew its war against China, a war that lasted until 1945. The fighting in China, which set Mao Tse-tung's Communists and Chiang Kai-shek's Nationalists against the Japanese—and sometimes against each other—echoed into Chinatown. Although affluent business owners in Chinatown who tended to support the Nationalists were influential in the neighborhood, over time the Chinese Hand Laundry Association emerged as the focal point of Chinese resistance to Japan. Despite Chinatown's small population, residents held rallies, raised money to assist China, wrote members of Congress, and passed out flyers calling for aid to China. After the Japanese attack on Pearl Harbor in December 1941, the United States entered the war and became an ally of China. Two years later, Congress repealed the Chinese Exclusion Acts.[105]

As Hitler's armies overran Poland in September 1939, New York's Polish community joined the growing chorus against the spread of fascism. On October 15, 1939, an estimated hundred thousand Polish Americans marched up Fifth Avenue in their third annual General Pulaski Day Parade. Beyond celebrating their Polish heritage, the marchers protested against the Nazi and Russian conquest of Poland.[106] Other ethnic groups reacted in similar fashion as Hitler's armies engulfed their homelands.

* * *

When the United States entered World War II, the Bund was generally discredited and subjected to investigation by the federal government; the FBI rounded up and interned a small number of German and Italian aliens. Ethnic groups like the Poles and Czechs wanted their nations liberated from Nazism and enthusiastically supported the war effort. The city did not experience the kind of ethnic persecution that occurred on the West Coast, where Japanese Americans were interned in prison camps.[107]

Jews, of course, had special reason to support a war against Nazi Germany, and they too participated in the various civilian war drives with enthusiasm. Jewish students at the City College of New York complained that they were not asked to do enough to support the war effort.[108] Jewish leaders called for efforts to assist their coreligionists in escaping European death camps. Several rallies were held at Madison Square Garden, but these had little effect on federal government policies.[109]

For German American and Italian American New Yorkers, the war appeared in a different light. The United States was, after all, at war with their homelands. Yet both of these groups vigorously backed America's war goals. Italian newspapers that had supported Mussolini and Italian organizations that had praised him reversed policy after Pearl Harbor, denouncing the dictator and fascism and calling for all-out support of the American military. The *New York Times* reported, "The American flag was hung up and pictures of Mussolini were taken from store windows or turned to the wall in Little Italy on the lower East Side and Harlem."[110] The first Columbus Day Rally held after American entry into the war featured professions of Italian American loyalty to the United States and wild cheers for President Franklin Roosevelt. That demonstration of patriotism, held at Columbus Circle in Manhattan, was sponsored by Generoso Pope, publisher of *Il Progresso*, who only two years before had been an ardent supporter of Mussolini.[111]

The federal government prosecuted the most dedicated German Bundist friends of Hitler for sedition, and several of the organization's leaders were imprisoned. But by 1941, Bund followers were few even in Yorkville, the center of German American New York. When *New York Times* reporters visited that district right after Germany's declaration of war against the United States, they found a hushed, tense, and anxious neighborhood where the majority of residents appeared to be loyal to the United States and opposed to Hitler and Nazism. German-language signs were removed from a theater at 158 East Eighty-Sixth Street, and German-language films were stopped.[112] During the nation's first scrap-metal drive, Yorkville, a neighborhood of Czechs and Hungarians as well as Germans, participated eagerly. After collecting piles of metal, Yorkville youths hung effigies of Hitler above their heaps of scrap.[113]

German military intelligence did have an established spy ring in New York, but the effectiveness of the plot was compromised even before the war began when a German-born American who had been coerced into spying by the Gestapo became a double agent and went to work for the FBI. Working from an office on West Forty-Second Street, William Sebold helped the FBI identify and arrest thirty-three German agents in June 1941. All were tried in Brooklyn, convicted, and imprisoned. A subsequent effort to insert German saboteurs into New York City by landing them on Long Island by submarine in 1942 also failed when one of the German spies, who had worked in Manhattan as a waiter before the war, had a change of heart and divulged the plot to the FBI. All eight members of the team were tried by a military commission and found guilty. Six were executed; the two who informed on the operation were imprisoned.[114]

6.3 During World War II, African American workers battled discrimination to find employment. Here, a welder is trained in Brooklyn, 1942.

Source: Marjory Collins, FSA/OWI, Library of Congress.

Contrary to fears that New York's German, Italian, or Japanese residents would become enemy agents, wartime New York was a city with a sense of unity. As the historian Steven H. Jaffe points out, the city witnessed war-bond rallies in Italian neighborhoods and parties for German American GIs headed for basic training. Japanese Americans suffered from acts of discrimination, but in New York they weathered the war much better than their counterparts on the West Coast. Small groups of Japanese Americans demonstrated against Japanese imperialism. The anti-Semitism of the prewar years persisted, but it was countered by an inclusive wartime spirit.[115]

Ideals and patriotism are part of the explanation for the city's mood, but economics mattered as well. The city's economy boomed during the war. Nearly nine hundred thousand New Yorkers entered the armed forces, and workers were needed to fill jobs in war-related businesses. The city's garment factories produced clothing for the armed forces, and shipbuilding and waterfront work expanded. The Brooklyn Navy Yard employed an all-time high of 75,000 persons during the war. Although popular memory exaggerates the number of women who worked at the yard, it nevertheless employed significant numbers of women, including from immigrant and African American families. Hundreds of thousands of soldiers and countless tons of military hardware sailed

6.4 Mott Street, 1942: Italian Americans parade in honor of neighborhood men in the armed forces.

Source: Fritz Henle, FSA/OWI, Library of Congress.

for Europe from New York Harbor. Massive government spending brought the Depression to an end.[116]

The government and private groups insisted that all racial and ethnic groups should support the war, and all groups benefitted from the expanding wartime economy. Even African Americans, backed by a presidential order banning discrimination and a similar New York State action, found new opportunities. African Americans won places as nurses at municipal hospitals and as transit workers in the city's bus and subway systems. Some unions that had traditionally barred black members changed their policies.

These gains did not come without a struggle. In 1941, African American groups organized a boycott against two privately owned transit firms, the Fifth Avenue Bus Company and the New York Omnibus Company, to protest their discriminatory hiring policies and their refusal to employ black drivers. A hesitant TWU finally worked with African American organizations to effect changes. The Citywide Citizens' Committee, an interracial group, pressured New York Telephone to hire African American operators. Six African American operators were hired in 1944; two years later, the phone company employed some two hundred. The historian Cheryl Greenberg tells us that before this breakthrough there were only 230 black operators in the entire nation. Other protests led to changes in city and private welfare agencies' discriminatory policies.[117]

During the war, the department store Gimbel's changed its hiring policies and hired 750 African Americans.[118] A few other retail stores, large and small, began to employ African Americans as stock and sales persons. But not all followed suit. A study a year after the war revealed that only about one-half of these enterprises employed African Americans in sales.[119]

War propaganda hailed Roosevelt's four freedoms—freedom of speech, freedom from fear, freedom of religion, and freedom from want—but there remained a gap between the nation's highest ideals and the realities of New York City streets.

* * *

"Dimouts" reduced the lights of Broadway and the rest of the city in the early years of the war to eliminate the glow on the horizon that helped U-boat commanders target Allied shipping. Nevertheless, Times Square was alive with soldiers, sailors, and aviators from across the United States and Allied nations. Men and women found plenty of places to gather because movie theaters, playhouses, bars, and nightclubs were open throughout the war. Gay and lesbian New Yorkers carved out enclaves of their own in places like the bar at the Hotel Astor and the Oak Room at the Plaza Hotel. Men and women discovered a greater degree of independence and sexual freedom, even as they lived under the shadow of early death and loss.[120] The 1944 musical *On the*

Town, based on Jerome Robbins's ballet *Fancy Free*, brought together the talents of Leonard Bernstein, Betty Comden, and Adolph Green to convey the urgency of three sailors on leave and the women they meet "trying eagerly to cram a whole lifetime into a day." They part at the end with the promise to meet "some other time."[121]

A year later, an Academy Award–winning short film, *The House I Live In*, featured Frank Sinatra singing the song of the same name to attack the anti-Semitism that surfaced in New York City before and during the war. The film begins with Sinatra protecting a young boy from a gang that attacks him because of his religion. Condemning bigotry in a spirit of humanism and wartime unity, Sinatra then sings of the United States as a country of community, freedom, and democracy. Even in its idealism, however, the song bumped up against another form of bigotry that scarred New York City. The original lyric had spoken of "neighbors white and black," but the film softened the line to "all races and religions" in deference to widespread white opposition to integrated housing.[122]

In New York, housing was widely in demand, and the wartime shortage of housing prompted the imposition of rent control. Yet here again African Americans were the most deprived. Poor housing, inflation, low incomes, and tensions between black New Yorkers and white police led to frustration that exploded into yet another Harlem riot in 1943. An incident during a hot August weekend involving two white policemen and several blacks triggered rumors that a black soldier had been shot. The resultant riot left five blacks dead and many others injured. Little city action followed.[123]

African Americans in New York City, as elsewhere, experienced the economic recovery at a slower rate than did whites. The Fair Employment Practices Committee, established to fight job discrimination, lacked teeth, and New York City's black citizens continued to face widespread discrimination and segregation. Indeed, the WPA rolls became increasingly black because so many African Americans could still not obtain other jobs.[124] Overall, Cheryl Greenberg argues, "Unquestionably, Harlem blacks were better off in 1943 than they had been before the Depression." There is no question, however, that blacks still faced segregation and discrimination in jobs, health, housing, and general well-being in 1945. Some gains occurred thanks to the wartime economy and not necessarily because of policies implemented by the municipal administration and the New Deal.[125]

Even Mayor La Guardia, popular among black voters for his criticism of firms that would not employ African Americans, in effect accepted public racial segregation when he allowed the Navy, then a highly segregated institution, to train white but not black women in a municipal college and a high school. In addition, on the eve of the 1943 riot, the mayor agreed to permit the Metropolitan Life Insurance Company—a firm with a history of racial discrimination—to build Stuyvesant Town, a large Manhattan housing project, which would be available to whites only.[126]

Metropolitan Life, although it had thousands of policyholders in Harlem, had "refused to hire one black agent in or out of that community."[127] The company had already constructed the all-white Parkchester housing project in the Bronx, but that had been on vacant land. Building Stuyvesant Town required the city to acquire and clear existing housing and make tax concessions. Stuyvesant Town was, in effect, a quasi-public project.[128]

But when civil rights advocates pressed Metropolitan Life to open Stuyvesant Town to African Americans, the company refused. Metropolitan Life had the active aid of the powerful Robert Moses, who insisted that charges of racial discrimination were irrelevant because the project was a private development. Winning the mayor's approval was another matter. La Guardia wanted to improve the city's housing stock, and the project was an attractive way of doing that. At the same time, he could not ignore the fact that the development was quasi-public, and he certainly had no wish to appear to condone racial discrimination. In the end, however, the mayor agreed to the contract, expressing the hope that the courts would address the issue and open the housing to all.[129]

The triumph of discrimination at Stuyvesant Town triggered a movement for city enactment of a fair housing law. In the city council, three members— Republican Stanley Isaacs, Democrat Adam Clayton Powell Jr., and Communist Benjamin Davis—eventually won passage of such a bill in 1944. The law did not cover Stuyvesant Town retroactively, as had been originally suggested, but only future housing projects. The gap between the law's principles and implementation set the stage for conflicts to come not only in the racially charged arena of housing but in other areas of public life where the aspirations of African American New Yorkers collided with the city's embedded patterns of racism.[130]

Tens of thousands of New Yorkers joyfully poured into the streets upon hearing of Japan's surrender on August 14, 1945. People were eager to celebrate the war's conclusion and anticipated the end of rationing, dimmed lights on Broadway, and the acute housing shortage. For them victory meant the speedy return of servicemen and -women and a chance to live in a peaceful world.

Yet New Yorkers, like other Americans, could not be certain of what lay ahead in either the nation or the world. Anti-Semitism persisted during the war, but by its end—and the revelations of Nazi death camps—there was a growing consensus that it was discredited as the shameful ideology of the Third Reich. As Deborah Dash Moore has argued, military service in the war changed the image of Jews as weak victims and affirmed both the Jewish and American identities of Jewish GIs. Italian Americans, serving under a shadow of suspicion for sympathy with Mussolini's Italy, nevertheless distinguished themselves in wartime. Jewish and Italian GIs returned to New York with a stronger foothold in the American mainstream. The situation of African American New Yorkers was more problematic. For African Americans, wartime had not brought an end to discrimination—after all, the United States had fought the war with a segregated military. But in wartime and postwar activism, African Americans forced a recognition of the gulf between American ideals of democracy and the reality of racism. The effects of their efforts on New York would be profound.[131]

Pessimists feared a postwar economic slump and racial and ethnic conflict, but La Guardia anticipated a bright future if the city and nation continued the New Deal model of cooperation between the city and federal government. Yet even as New York City appeared to be at the summit of its powers, the wartime mobilization that boosted the city's economy was creating new factories and new jobs in the country's southern and southwestern states. Before long, sunbelt manufacturing would challenge the economic supremacy of New York. And even as the New Deal appeared to be triumphant in the city and state of New York, others imagined a different future, one in which the federal government's role would not be expanded but reduced.

CHAPTER 7

CITY OF HOPE, CITY OF FEAR: 1945–1997

A ndrea Ramsey, born in Harlem, grew up in the Morrisania section of the Bronx in the 1950s. As she told the Bronx African American History Project,

The community itself was very vibrant, with a mixture of immigrants from the Caribbean and migrants from the South. People didn't visit each others' houses, but we knew each other from being on the street. In those days there were no play dates or anything like that. You just went out and played, and you knew all kids in the neighborhood, and all the kids and all the families knew you.

There wasn't a lot of adult supervision. It was mostly from the window where my grandmother would look out at us. When the sun went down, we came upstairs, where we'd sit on the fire escape and watch other kids outside.[1]

Ramsey's Morrisania emerged during the 1930s. In the hard times of the Depression, white landlords—who had previously barred blacks from the neighborhood—feared losing tenants. To maintain their rent rolls, they opened their doors to black families. In turn, economically secure African American families in Harlem migrated to Morrisania to obtain bigger apartments at a lower cost. In contrast to other white New York neighborhoods, the historian Mark Naison reports, there was little opposition to blacks' arrival in Morrisania because it was a working-class neighborhood dominated by Jews, including an influential number of communists, trade unionists, and tenant activists who did not hold the racist views common in other neighborhoods. Jews eventually left the neighborhood (a reminder that in New York an integrated neighborhood often appears in the interval between one majority and another). By the late 1940s, Morrisania—with nearby industrial jobs, good transit connections, and ample shopping—was the largest African American neighborhood in the Bronx. Its theaters and clubs housed a lively music scene, featuring Afro-Cuban music, jazz, rhythm and blues, and calypso. Morrisania was a source and magnet for musical talent and the home of artists such as the singer Maxine Sullivan, the trumpet player Henry "Red" Allen, and, in the 1960s, Thelonious Monk.[2]

For Ramsey, whose father managed a vegetable stand in Harlem and whose mother was an office assistant, life in Morrisania was an intense blend of packed services at St. Augustine's Presbyterian Church, a grandmother who read to her often, and school at PS 23 (attended by "mostly black" students, with a few whites and Latinos, and taught by teachers who were mostly Jewish and Irish, with a few African Americans). Girls and guys sang on street corners. In the summers, she stayed with her grandmother at Rockaway Beach. She has only a "vague" memory of racial tension in the neighborhood. And while Morrisania had its gangs, and the Fordham Baldies (an Italian gang) terrified Ramsey at Evander Childs High School, her good memories from the neighborhood far outnumber the bad. "Most people were generous. They really had to help each other to survive. There were people who were on home relief, but they were never made to feel bad about it. It wasn't a perfect world, far from it, but it left me with a feeling that was good."[3]

Ramsey's memories of her Morrisania childhood reflect the belief—not rare among African American New Yorkers in the early 1950s—that New York was a city of opportunity where African American migrants from the South and immigrants from the Caribbean would find good lives. The African American magazine *One World* concluded in 1951: "Right now, most of the Bronx's 75,000 Negroes live between 160th Street and Crotona Park South. To them, the Bronx is a borough of hope, a place of unlimited possibilities."[4]

In the three decades after World War II, this optimism would be tested by demographic changes, economic upheavals, and political struggles. Although New York in 1945 was dominated by European immigrants and their children, its population would be transformed in the decades that followed. In 1940, New York was 93 percent white, and 69 percent of these whites were immigrants or people with at least one immigrant parent. White New Yorkers, many of them of immigrant stock, left the city for the suburbs. At the same time, Puerto Ricans and Cubans, alongside African Americans from the South, took their place. By 1980, New York was 60 percent white, 25 percent black, and 19 percent Hispanic. At the same time, industry left the city, and shipping moved to the New Jersey side of the harbor, undermining economic opportunities for newcomers.[5]

The economic transformation of the city was matched by a hardening of its ethnic and political culture. New York has always been tugged between the particular and the universal, the selfish and the generous. By the 1960s, newly arrived African Americans and Puerto Ricans could see the emerging outlines of a narrower, meaner city. By the 1970s, when New Yorkers like Andrea Ramsey were grown adults, the structures, certainties, and hopes of postwar New York had been severely shaken.

* * *

Living standards improved for most New Yorkers in the quarter-century after World War II, thanks to a strong economy. The Great Depression and the war had curtailed new housing starts, and many potential homeowners had accumulated savings during the high-employment war years. Pent-up demand for housing kindled a boom in construction. The port of New York was vigorous in the early postwar years, and the city remained America's leading financial and banking center. New York maintained a solid base in manufacturing, with one million New Yorkers employed in that sector through the 1950s. New York, like the rest of the United States, had little competition from Europe and Japan, whose economies were rebuilding after the war.[6]

Immigrants from Europe, the Caribbean, and Asia looked to New York for new opportunities. Puerto Ricans, who were American citizens and exempt from immigration restrictions, poured into the city. So, too, did African Americans from the South. New York, despite its own homegrown racism, offered possibilities absent in the Jim Crow southern states.

Both racial and religious discrimination came under attack in the early postwar years. In 1945, ethnic organizations prodded New York's state legislature to pass the nation's first law banning employment discrimination on the grounds of race, religion, or national origin.[7] The city also established the New York City Commission on Human Rights (CCHR) to deal with discrimination in housing, employment, public accommodations, and education. The CCHR initially focused on incidents of religious prejudice, but after the 1960s racial matters received more attention.[8]

The American Jewish Congress joined with other organizations to press the state and city to outlaw discrimination at nonsectarian colleges and universities. After a city council investigation revealed widespread bias, Mayor William O'Dwyer announced that public funds and tax breaks would be withheld from nonsectarian institutions that employed racial or religious criteria in admitting students. Columbia University and New York University, including their professional schools, dropped their quotas on Jewish students and began to hire Jewish faculty.[9] The end result was a growing number of Jewish dentists, physicians, academics, and lawyers. Protestant-dominated banks, investment companies, corporations, and law firms altered their hiring practices and began to admit Jews during the 1960s. A few Jews made fortunes as real estate promoters during the postwar boom years. Julius Tishman was said to be responsible for 13 percent of the city's new office buildings between 1945 and 1970.[10]

The mobility of New York Jews in the 1950s and 1960s was impressive, but it was part of an arduous process, as Richard Alba and Nancy Foner point out, that took hard work over many decades and still had its winners and losers.[11] A 1972 Federation of Jewish Philanthropies of New York study noted that the movement of Jews out of the working and lower middle classes since the 1950s was shadowed by the presence of impoverished Jews, usually elderly people, who had been bypassed by the postwar prosperity.[12]

Italians lagged behind Jews in mobility but achieved higher levels of education and better jobs than their parents, finding public sector employment in the post office, sanitation, and transportation.[13] Italians were influential in realms of culture and politics. In neighborhood shrines and festivals, Italian vernacular art blended the sacred and the secular. Italians were prominent in the vocal music of urban harmony, also known as doo-wop, and fluently mixed musical styles with African Americans. Two Italian Americans, Frank Sinatra, who grew up across the Hudson River from New York in Hoboken, New Jersey, and Tony Bennett, from Astoria, Queens, became two of the most acclaimed vocalists of the twentieth century. By the mid-1950s, New York had elected two Italian mayors—the incomparable La Guardia and the less memorable Vincent Impellitteri, a Democrat. In the House of Representatives, the left-leaning Vito Marcantonio succeeded La Guardia in representing East Harlem and was a strong presence until his defeat in 1950. Carmine DeSapio, the leader of Tammany Hall in the 1950s, was a national political presence.[14]

New York's Irish also found new economic opportunities in the city. After World War II, most abandoned working-class jobs, such as transit work. Prominent families including the McDonnells, the Murrays, and the Cuddihys made up the Irish elite. The Fifth Avenue apartment of James Francis McDonnell, the owner of a prosperous brokerage house, was at one time the largest in the city.[15]

Every Democratic county chairmanship was held by Irish Americans in 1945, even though La Guardia's mayoralty had diminished Tammany Hall and Irish political strength. Voters elected Irish-born Democrat William O'Dwyer as mayor in 1945 and reelected him in 1949. (His good name—won in part by prosecuting organized crime—was tarnished by allegations of corruption. He resigned from City Hall in 1950 to become the U.S. ambassador to Mexico.)[16]

The political strength of the Irish in the years immediately after World War II was a prelude to a gradual decline. As the Irish moved to the suburbs, their numbers and voting power in the city diminished. As the Irish entered the middle class, their embrace of politics as a profession gave way to employment in the corporate sector. Some Irish, in a move that would have shocked their grandparents, even became Republicans. By the 1960s, Tammany Democrats were losing power to a new generation of reform Democrats, whose numbers included many Jews. In 1963, Daniel Patrick Moynihan, discussing the New York Irish, wrote, "There were sixty or seventy years when the Irish were everywhere. They felt it was their town. It is no longer, and they know it. That is one of the things bothering them."[17]

Irish power in the Roman Catholic Church, however, remained strong. Francis Cardinal Spellman, archbishop of the Diocese of New York from 1939 until his death in 1967, downplayed his Irishness but not his politics or church building. Contributions from the increasingly prosperous New York Catholic community permitted him to build schools and hospitals and fund numerous charities. Spellman also cultivated politicians and business leaders. He stated his conservative views on morals, birth control, and church-state relations often and aggressively, and he vigorously endorsed Senator Joseph McCarthy's anticommunist campaign.[18]

As strong as the Irish were in the church, power struggles around City Hall suggested that changes were looming at the intersection of ethnicity and politics in postwar New York. In 1945, the Democrats, copying La Guardia, nominated an Italian American and a Jew for citywide offices. They ran many more after that. In 1953, the Democrat who won the mayoralty was a man with no distinct ethnic identity, a family link to the New Deal, and, in his first mayoral bid, the support of Tammany Hall: Robert F. Wagner Jr.[19]

Mayor Wagner, who served three terms (1954–1965), was a transitional figure between the city of the New Deal and the city of the politically tumultuous 1960s. Wagner was half-Irish and half-German. His father, an immigrant from Germany and a Tammany Democrat, was one of the foremost urban liberals of his generation. Elected to the U.S. Senate from New York in 1926, he sponsored some of the most important New Deal legislation on unions, Social Security, and public housing. Wagner was politically cautious (he often said, "when in doubt, don't") but capable of guile. After two terms, he repudiated the regulars and joined with the reform Democrats, who included many Jews and who had been gaining strength since the late 1950s. Wagner presided over an expansive coalition that included regular Democrats, liberal Jews, reformers, and African Americans—a base so broad that it was open to fracturing.[20]

Mayor Wagner's support for municipal unions and the effectiveness of municipal employees' organizations made public sector work attractive for working-class and modestly middle-class New Yorkers.[21] In 1958, he issued an executive order permitting city employees to organize and engage in collective bargaining.[22] Wagner's executive order, which ultimately received state backing, benefited unions such as District 37 of the American Federation of State,

County, and Municipal Employees (AFSCME). Teachers, social workers, and others also organized to win significant salary, health, and pension benefits from the city between 1958 and 1970. The mayor worked closely with labor leaders, who represented an important voting bloc. One scholar noted, "While Wagner could not always provide generous contracts to labor, he always took pains to give the union hierarchy a feeling of importance. No city initiative in labor policy was ever undertaken without first clearing it with organized labor."[23]

In midcentury New York, Jews and Italians entered municipal jobs in greater numbers as the public payroll expanded. There were roughly one hundred thousand city employees at the end of World War II, 200,706 in 1961, and 294,555 on the eve of the fiscal crisis in 1975. State and federal workers made the public sector workforce in the city even larger. After World War II, several Italians and Jews were appointed commissioners of city agencies. Jews were heavily represented among the city's public school teachers, amounting to about 60 percent of the instructional staff. Many other professionally trained Jews entered social work as the city expanded its social services. Italians had dominated the sanitation department for decades, and after 1945 they found other municipal employment opportunities as teachers, police officers, and clerks.[24] The Irish retained strongholds in the police and fire departments.

African Americans and Latinos struggled against discrimination to find employment. While salaries in the unionized construction trades were substantial during building booms, construction unions were mostly white. African American workers, who needed construction jobs if they were to find a good foothold in the city's economy, were generally barred from joining building trades unions and confined to less safe, less remunerative, and less available nonunion work.[25]

* * *

With rising incomes and growing tolerance that eased access to housing, white New Yorkers of immigrant stock enjoyed improved living conditions in new neighborhoods in the postwar years. Aided by state, city, and federal programs, the city experienced a building boom in private homes, rental apartments, and business offices after 1945. Much of the new housing went up in underdeveloped areas of the Bronx, Staten Island, and Queens.

The development of Canarsie in Brooklyn illustrates the growth of postwar communities. Located along Jamaica Bay, Canarsie was initially settled by a few thousand Dutch, Irish, Germans, and Scots. Italians and Jews began moving there in the 1920s. Although large parts of the area were marshland at the outset of World War II, by the 1950s developers gave the community a "new sleek look."[26] Two builders, Harry and Sidney Waxman, constructed private residences on more than two hundred acres of land. Canarsie's population rose from roughly three thousand in the 1920s to thirty thousand in 1950 and eighty thousand in 1970.[27] Many of the new residents—primarily Jewish and Italian homeowners—came from Brooklyn's Brownsville, fleeing the arrival there of African Americans. Brownsville's Jewish population declined from 175,000 in the 1930s to only five thousand, mostly elderly, in the 1960s.[28]

There were similar patterns in the Bronx and Queens. The Grand Concourse in the Bronx, developed in the 1920s, was a Jewish center with large apartment buildings, synagogues, and cultural institutions. But as African Americans and Latinos moved in during the 1960s, Jews moved northward to Riverdale and other neighborhoods on the periphery of the borough. The United Housing Foundation (UHF) built Co-op City in the northern Bronx to house eighty thousand persons, and Jews constituted its largest ethnic group for years. In South Jamaica, Queens, the UHF constructed Rochdale Village, the largest cooperative in the world at the time. In Rochdale's first decade, so many Jews and African Americans lived there that it was the largest integrated development in New York City.[29]

Italians demonstrated similar mobility in housing patterns. In the 1960s, they were still a presence in Lower Manhattan's Little Italy, just north of Chinatown, but many more lived in the Brooklyn neighborhoods of Canarsie, Red Hook, Bensonhurst, and Cobble Hill. Their numbers were augmented by postwar immigrants from Italy, whose arrival brought new vigor to aging neighborhoods. The future of Italian New York, however, lay in more middle-class neighborhoods. The Italian community in Staten Island boomed after 1964 with the construction of the Verrazano Bridge, which connected the island with Brooklyn. In the long run, changes in residence and work set off the movement of Italian American women into the middle class. In the 1980s in the old Italian neighborhood of Bensonhurst, Brooklyn, 10.2 percent of women were blue-collar workers. In South Richmond, a newer Italian neighborhood in southeastern Staten Island, the figure was 1.8 percent.[30]

White movement to new city neighborhoods was striking, but white migration to the suburbs was transforming. The rush to the suburbs in Greater New York was part of a national trend in postwar America. Commuter rails, highways, tunnels, and bridges enabled New Yorkers to live in Long Island, Westchester County, Rockland County, and New Jersey and commute to work in the city. The volume of car traffic greatly increased after 1945 and strained highway capacities. A second deck was added to the George Washington Bridge in 1962.[31] In addition to highway construction and automobile culture, the rush to the suburbs was driven by higher incomes from 1945 to the 1970s, governmental subsidies of mortgages, the constant search by Americans for greener pastures, and the desire to leave deteriorating neighborhoods, a combination of motives collectively termed "white flight."

The racial dimension of suburbanization was significant. Banks and other lending institutions refused to lend or sell to African Americans. Consequently, with few exceptions white families had access to the suburbs (thanks to federally funded highways) and could afford suburban homes (with federally sanctioned deductions for mortgages and maybe union wages). Levittown, Long Island, one of the foremost postwar suburbs, was racially segregated until the 1970s. African Americans and Latinos, who were unable to get mortgages and typically earning lower salaries, did not get their fair share of this bounty. While there were some African American and Latino communities to be found in the city's suburbs, by policy and practice most Latinos and African Americans were confined to the city's more troubled neighborhoods.[32]

In employment, housing, and eventually politics, the lives of Irish, German, Jewish, and Italian New Yorkers came to be shaped less by ethnicity (although this would be an enduring factor) and more by the fact that they were white. How and why this happened, its timing, and its gradations of significance are the subjects of enduring debates among scholars, but central to this complex development was suburbanization. Whites had access to suburban housing largely denied to Latinos and African Americans. By the 1960s, the division between an increasingly "black" city and its white suburbs was born. City neighborhoods acquired a newly racialized geography that hardened boundaries between people, between communities, and between New York City and its suburbs.[33]

The net outflow of whites from the city exceeded 400,000 in the 1940s, 1.2 million in the 1950s, and another 500,000 in the 1960s. Members of nearly every white ethnic group moved. A Federation of Jewish Philanthropies of New York study put the city's Jewish population at 2,114,000, in 1957, its highest total ever. By 1981, the estimate had fallen to just over one million, and the number decreased further until the early twenty-first century.[34]

The loss of so many middle-class taxpayers strained the city's finances, but perhaps more serious was the flight of jobs in the postwar decades. The Brooklyn Navy Yard, founded in 1801 when the frigate *Fulton* was built there, employed more than seventy thousand workers during World War II. Afterward, its economic and military importance rapidly declined; it closed in 1966.[35] In a parallel decline, the Brooklyn Army Terminal radically cut its staff. Businesses dependent upon the Army Terminal and the Navy Yard suffered. The borough's beer industry also fell upon hard times. In 1940, Brooklyn had 132 breweries, an all-time high. By the end of the 1950s, only four remained.[36]

Manufacturing plants, particularly those in the garment industry, began an exodus from the city that would accelerate after 1970. Containerized shipping—which relied on huge metal containers to hold goods and mechanical cranes to replace dockworkers—expanded in nearby New Jersey, shifting the heart of the port out of the city. In once-thriving waterfront neighborhoods on the west side of Manhattan and in Brooklyn, the employment of dockworkers declined. Other cities challenged New York's maritime supremacy.[37] The continued hemorrhaging of jobs and population would loom even larger after 1970.

Without white immigration from abroad and migration from other parts of the nation, the postwar decline of New York's white population, both in actual numbers and as a proportion of the total population, would have been greater. After World War II, more liberal immigration laws made possible a new influx of Europeans, chiefly from Southern and Eastern Europe; more than one million settled in New York between 1946 and 1970.[38] Modern New York was hospitable to its postwar newcomers and offered a number of government programs to help them settle.

Among the European immigrants were Jews, including the Hasidim from Central and Eastern Europe.[39] During the World War II years, Jewish refugees and survivors of the Holocaust entered the United States as "Displaced Persons." As the Cold War developed, they came as refugees. Although some early refugee programs called for the dispersal of refugees, many immigrants—especially Jews—wanted to remain in New York City. About one-quarter of the persons arriving under the Displaced Persons Acts of 1948 and 1950 stayed in the city, as did a similar number of other refugees entering in the 1950s.[40] Prominent among Jewish immigrants were the Hasidim, a movement of Orthodox Jews dating to Central Europe in the eighteenth century and distinguished by its piety, enthusiastic worship, rabbinic dynasties, and strong community life. In the long run, the postwar immigration of the Hasidim—who rejected the assimilation of earlier generations of immigrants—would alter the cultural profile of New York Jews.

As whites departed for the suburbs, African Americans and Puerto Ricans moved to the city.[41] African Americans from the South fled a Jim Crow social order, racial violence, economic hardship, and the postwar mechanization of agriculture, which threw black farmers off the land. At the same time, the lure of manufacturing jobs set many African Americans on the road north. New York's bus and train stations, which provided transportation links to Virginia, Georgia, Florida, and the Carolinas, became their Ellis Island. Puerto Rican migrants, driven by population growth and unemployment in their homeland, also migrated in growing numbers. Like the Irish and Germans of the mid–nineteenth century and the Jews and Italians of the early twentieth century, African Americans and Puerto Ricans would transform work, culture, and politics in New York.[42]

Between 1945 and the mid-1960s, thirty to fifty thousand Puerto Ricans migrated to New York City each year. As American citizens, they were not subject to immigration restrictions. They traveled largely by plane, inaugurating the first massive air migration in history. They went to New York because attempts in the 1950s to improve the Puerto Rican economy, such as Operation

7.1 Puerto Ricans headed for New York City at Newark Airport, 1947.

Source: Dick De Marsico, *New York World-Telegram and Sun* Newspaper Collection, Library of Congress.

Bootstrap, had only limited success.[43] East Harlem in Manhattan, where long-time Italian residents were moving to other sections of the city or to the suburbs, became the main area of Puerto Rican settlement. A second major neighborhood for Puerto Ricans emerged in the South Bronx; other enclaves arose in Brooklyn.

Many Puerto Ricans who entered were rural workers with low levels of education and limited English-language skills. They took jobs in the city's declining garment industry or in manual occupations. Both Puerto Rican men and women earned less money than most New Yorkers.[44] The Puerto Rican Department of Labor's Migration Division placed Puerto Ricans in jobs and helped others prepare for civil service examinations. The agency also helped Puerto Ricans adjust to life in New York and explained to school administrators the importance of teaching English to Puerto Rican children. Before the Migration Division disbanded in the 1970s, some staff went on to serve in federally funded urban projects and antipoverty agencies.[45] The Puerto Rican Forum, the Puerto Rican Family Institute (the only grassroots Puerto Rican family agency in the city), and the Puerto Rican Legal Defense and Education Fund sought to improve the lives of New York's Puerto Ricans. So did ASPIRA, an important organization founded in 1961 to promote higher education for Puerto Rican New Yorkers.[46]

The Roman Catholic Church also played a role in the Puerto Rican community. Most Puerto Ricans retained the Catholicism of their homeland after settling in New York, but the largely Irish-dominated church was slow to respond to their needs. Puerto Ricans were expected to become members of integrated English-speaking parishes, but many of the first migrants did not speak English well. In the 1950s, the church inaugurated new policies aimed at teaching clergy Spanish and Puerto Rican culture and encouraging them to hold services in Spanish.[47] Some priests worked to promote stability in Puerto Rican neighborhoods.

* * *

The migration of African Americans to New York was equally transformative. In 1940, the city's 450,000 black residents accounted for about 6 percent of the population. By 1970, they numbered 1,668,115 and constituted about 20 percent of the city's residents.[48] Natural population growth as well as immigration from the Caribbean contributed to this increase, but the most significant portion of the migration was from the South.[49]

All black New Yorkers, whether from the South or the Caribbean, faced the common problem of racism. Nowhere was the segregation of African Americans more noticeable at the close of World War II than in baseball, the so-called national pastime. Black baseball players had appeared in the New York Giants' Polo Grounds and in Yankee Stadium before 1945, but only with all-black teams that rented the stadiums for their games. In the 1940s, the Yankees earned more than $100,000 annually from renting their Bronx stadium and other fields in their farm system to black teams in the Negro Leagues. In 1946, the major league owners cited this added income as one reason not to desegregate.[50]

Organized efforts to integrate the national pastime, New York's legislative action against discrimination in employment, and more positive racial attitudes stemming from the war all increased the pressure to desegregate baseball. In 1947, Branch Rickey, the general manager of the Brooklyn Dodgers, hired Jackie Robinson to break the color line. In 1947, after a year in the Dodgers' farm club in Montreal, Robinson became the first African American to play in the big leagues. While blacks and most whites throughout the league cheered for Robinson, he was not warmly received by all the players. Dixie Walker, a popular Dodger, rallied other players to block Robinson from playing. The protest collapsed, however, and Walker requested a trade to another club. Rickey subsequently hired other black athletes, as did the New York Giants beginning in 1949. The Yankees dragged their feet and did not field black players until the end of the 1953 season, when they finally placed two African Americans on their roster.[51]

With struggle, African Americans also made gains in politics and municipal employment during the postwar decades. Although the growing number of African American New Yorkers suggested that they could become an influential voting bloc, gerrymandering slowed the growth of black electoral power. Before 1960, the highest municipal elective office achieved by a black New Yorker was Manhattan borough president. African Americans did best when they could draw support from black voters in specific districts, as did Harlem's Adam Clayton Powell Jr., the first African American in the city to serve in the House of Representatives. Successful black candidates for state and federal offices followed him as the number of African Americans in the city grew.[52]

Black politicians of West Indian descent were prominent in the city, giving rise to a belief—sometimes proudly asserted by West Indians, sometimes employed by whites to disparage native-born African Americans—that West Indians were more assertive and entrepreneurial than other blacks. By 1953, West Indian Democratic district leaders could be found in both Harlem and Brooklyn. J. Raymond Jones, "The Harlem Fox," was born in the Virgin Islands. Hulan Jack, elected Manhattan borough president in 1953, was born in British Guiana and raised on St. Lucia. In 1968, State Assemblywoman Shirley Chisholm—who was born in Brooklyn but spent much of her childhood in Barbados—won a seat in Congress.[53]

Not all African Americans agreed with strategies of working within regular political parties. Some urged blacks to build their own institutions within their communities instead of attempting to desegregate white ones. The Nation of Islam, the most important religious group urging separation, worked with black poor people, often dealing effectively with drug problems and employment issues. Although the group did not have an especially large following, it had an eloquent spokesman in Malcolm X. Although Malcolm X left the Nation of Islam one year before he was assassinated in 1965, he touched many black New Yorkers in enduring ways with his militancy, dignity, and ability to critique white racism.[54]

Racism and inequality took so many forms that African American demands for justice overflowed the channels of established politics to address unfairness in jobs, education, and housing. As early as the 1950s and continuing through the 1960s, African Americans in New York organized on behalf of civil rights. Directed by the National Association for the Advancement of Colored People (NAACP), the Congress of Racial Equality (CORE), and ad hoc groups, activists picketed construction sites and businesses, protesting against racial discrimination in hiring. African American ministers, including Adam Clayton Powell Jr. and the Rev. Milton Galamison of Brooklyn, were especially

TABLE 7.1 African American population of
New York City, 1900–1970

Year	Total
1900	60,666
1910	91,709
1920	152,467
1930	327,706
1940	458,444
1950	747,608
1960	1,087,931
1970	1,668,115

Source: Ira Rosenwaike, Population History of New York City
(Syracuse, NY: Syracuse University Press, 1972), 141.

important in the civil rights struggle.[55] These efforts won the support of some
politicians, who insisted that public building projects—including a number of
schools and the heavily picketed Downstate Medical Center in Brooklyn—
employ companies and unions with records of fair hiring practices.[56]

∗ ∗ ∗

African American difficulties on the job market were matched by problems in
the public school system. As far back as the La Guardia administration, black
New Yorkers had complained that poor facilities, weak teachers, and low expectations resulted in inferior education for their children. African American
parents and activists began to look ever more critically at the flaws of New York
City's public schools after 1954, when the Brown decision of the U.S. Supreme
Court ruled that segregated schools were unconstitutional. Kenneth Clark, the
psychologist and City College professor whose research had shaped the Supreme
Court's decision, turned his efforts to desegregating New York City's public
schools. City officials, well aware of opposition to integration among white parents, declined to make the changes in school zoning and teacher assignment
that might have altered the situation.[57]

As time passed, the increasing changes in the city's demographics made it harder to fashion school districts where black and white students could be brought together in neighborhood schools. In New York City, where neighborhoods were frequently defined by their ethnic character, opponents of integration who defended "neighborhood schools" were also implicitly defending white-majority neighborhoods.[58]

Because schools were the public institution that intersected most with the daily lives of families, women were prominent among both the supporters and opponents of integration. Traditional conceptions of women as homemakers gave them a platform for speaking in public on the subject of schools, families, and communities. Women were especially visible in Parents and Taxpayers (PAT), an organization with roots in western Queens and Brooklyn that opposed integration in the name of preserving neighborhood schools. The equally committed opponent of PAT was an organization called EQUAL, with a core principle of "quality education for *all* children *in integrated public schools.*" From 1964 to 1966, the most visible representative of EQUAL was Ellen Lurie, a fierce, committed, and deeply informed advocate for public education who lived in the Washington Heights section of Manhattan.[59]

If the city's job market and public schools put African Americans at a disadvantage, so too did its housing market. African Americans generally found housing available only in racially segregated areas or neighborhoods that were becoming all black from white flight. The black settlement of Brooklyn's Bedford-Stuyvesant, well on its way to becoming a racial ghetto by 1940, expanded rapidly to neighboring Crown Heights and Brownsville. "The speed of some of these neighborhood reversals could be blinding," writes the historian Harold Connolly. "In less than ten years much of East New York was transformed from a comfortable, predominately white, lower middle class community into an impoverished, overwhelmingly black and Puerto Rican area."[60] In the heavily Jewish Brownsville section of Brooklyn, as Wendell Pritchett observes, some neighborhood organizations faced with the arrival of African Americans "made flawed but sincere efforts to incorporate new residents." Coalitions of whites, blacks, and Latinos won battles over vital resources such as housing, but they could not thwart the neighborhood's decay in the 1960s or the effects of racism. Brownsville was beset by demographic and economic changes, ill-conceived public policies, and "the indifference of established citywide liberal institutions—labor unions, charitable organizations and advocacy groups." Similar tragedies befell other neighborhoods in other parts of the city.[61]

Constance Rosenblum's diagnosis of the decay of the Grand Concourse in the Bronx applied to other areas of the city as well: "The logarithm of neighborhood decay operated with a sickening predictability, underpinned by financial and governmental practices that, in retrospect, could only doom the community."[62] Beginning in the 1960s, thousands of buildings were simply abandoned by owners unable to pay their taxes. Once unoccupied, they were vandalized and fell victim to arson. City blocks in the South Bronx, Harlem, and Bedford-Stuyvesant looked as if they had been bombed in air raids.[63]

During the New Deal years, the federal government had embarked upon a modest public housing program. After World War II, building on these initiatives, the state and city, with federal backing, built housing for low-income as well as middle-class families. By 1990, the federal government had subsidized the construction of about 175,000 low-rent units, which housed approximately six hundred thousand New Yorkers. Of the nation's public housing projects, New York's had a reputation of being among the best, and there were long waiting lists for their apartments. Early in the postwar years, it was possible to find integrated housing projects where residents faced the future with optimism.[64]

However, urban renewal programs aimed at slum clearance sometimes reduced housing for the poor. In constructing highways, bridges, and projects like the Lincoln Center for the Performing Arts, builders tore down tenements and destroyed small businesses without always providing replacements for displaced tenants or business owners. Critics tagged urban renewal "Negro removal." In addition, corruption plagued slum clearance in New York City. Charges of scandal and of ignoring the poor became so frequent while Robert Moses ran New York City's urban renewal programs that he was removed as director of the Mayor's Slum Clearance Committee. After 1960, reformers and city officials encountered stiff opposition when they proposed scattering low-income housing in middle-class neighborhoods. To make ends meet, some poor families doubled up, which often led to severe crowding. In sum, adequate housing for the poor remained an elusive goal in the decades following World War II.[65]

Even middle-class black New Yorkers who found improved employment opportunities faced racial discrimination in renting and buying homes and apartments. In a few interracial middle-class neighborhoods, like the Laurelton section of Queens, community efforts maintained a mixed population for a number of years.[66] But these were the exceptions rather than the rule. Researchers found little change in housing segregation in the decades after World War II, despite city and federal efforts. Neither the city nor the federal government successfully halted discriminatory practices in the housing market.[67]

* * *

In the two decades after World War II, popular culture and the media in New York City charted a course from optimism to despair. When the 1949 film *On the Town* brought to the screen a wartime Broadway musical about sailors on leave in New York, it celebrated the city as a convivial place for young men and women. In the 1950s, young men—often Italian Americans, African Americans, and Puerto Ricans—on street corners voiced a new style of singing, doo-wop, grounded in African American vocal styles and gospel. Doo-wop emerged in neighborhoods with a strong consciousness of turf and gang fights, and it never entirely transcended its origins. (It took all of Dion DiMucci's street smarts to save the African American doo-wop superstar Frankie Lymon from a beating when Lymon visited DiMucci's home neighborhood of Belmont in the Bronx.) At its best, though, doo-wop was a hybrid musical form that expressed an inclusive and sharp New York vocal style.[68]

By the early 1960s, however, the city's ethnic transformation combined with the growth in crime to produce a menacing mood. Gang wars over turf, which had a strong ethnic dimension, signaled changes in the city's neighborhoods. They were also explored with a strong strain of sensationalism in the news media and popular culture. The 1961 film *West Side Story*, based on a Broadway musical produced in 1957, reprised the Romeo and Juliet story with a young Puerto Rican woman and a young Polish American man in a neighborhood of warring gangs—the Puerto Rico–born Sharks and the New York–born Jets. In 1949, when the play was first discussed, it was to involve a Jewish girl and a Catholic boy from the East Side. By 1961, that alignment of conflict simply seemed dated.[69]

In March 1964, New Yorkers were stunned to read newspaper reports that a young woman in the Kew Gardens section of Queens, Kitty Genovese, was stabbed to death despite her cries for help as her neighbors allegedly looked on passively. Coverage of the crime, especially in the *New York Times*, contributed to the belief that New York was a dangerous, uncaring, anonymous city. It would take decades for the full story to emerge, but by then its influence was cemented. As the historian Marcia M. Gallo has pointed out, almost everything in the early accounts of Genovese's death was wrong. Genovese—an Italian American, a lesbian, and a bar manager who drove a red Fiat—fought desperately to save her life and almost fended off her attacker. And she did not die while thirty-eight people looked on apathetically. One neighbor shouted to ward off her attacker, another called the police, and another went to Genovese's aid. In 1964, however, rising crime, changing racial demographics, and a reigning belief that cities promote apathy (which was contradicted by New York's long tradition of activism) left New Yorkers uneasy and willing to believe the worst about one another.[70]

* * *

By the early 1960s, New Deal New York was in trouble. The city was shaken by the decline of the old industrial/seaport economy and by changing demographics. As African Americans and their allies campaigned for school integration, Mayor Wagner responded cautiously. When confronted with evidence that some city schools were racially segregated, Wagner and the city's Board of Education fell back on the argument that the city's neighborhoods were racially and ethnically separated and that the school system could not fix that situation. The answer left African American parents angry and frustrated. At the same time, crime showed signs of rising, and black impatience with police brutality was growing.

All of these frustrations and conflicts converged in 1964. In February, the Reverend Milton Galamison, a leading integrationist from Brooklyn, and Bayard Rustin, fresh from organizing the March on Washington in 1963 where Martin Luther King Jr. delivered his iconic "I Have a Dream" speech, led a New York City public school boycott in support of school integration. Forty-five percent of the city's one million public school students stayed home (four times the usual number of absences). In response, an almost entirely white contingent of protesters opposed to school integration marched on City Hall and staged a boycott of their own. A second and smaller boycott by integrationists followed, then another march led by Rustin to commemorate the tenth anniversary of the Supreme Court's *Brown v. Board of Education*. Yet for all their energy and moral commitment, the integrationists were losing the battle for public opinion and political power. Divisions within the integrationist camp and the firm opposition of parents who opposed busing for school integration doomed the cause.[71]

Later in the summer of 1964, after a police officer confronted and killed a black teenager on Manhattan's Upper East Side, a riot erupted in Harlem.[72] New York was angry, fractious, and troubled. Mayor Wagner declined to run for a fourth term. The winner of the three-way race that followed was earnest, handsome John V. Lindsay—a liberal Republican who represented Manhattan's Upper East Side in Congress and supported the civil rights and the Great Society programs of President Lyndon Johnson, a Democrat.[73] With his opponents splitting the moderates and conservatives, Lindsay drew support from African Americans, reformers, and liberal Jews to win with 45 percent of the vote.[74]

Lindsay enjoyed enduring support from white reformers, many of them young people and Jews who were impatient with the pace of change in New York City. And, although some black leaders complained that Lindsay promised more than he was able to deliver, he won considerable praise from African Americans who appreciated his challenges to racist inequalities in housing and education and police brutality.[75]

Lindsay's programs also prompted a backlash that reshaped the city's ethnic politics. In 1966, with rising crime an issue and police conduct an ongoing concern in black neighborhoods, voters overwhelmingly rejected a plan to give civilians instead of police the majority of positions on a board that

7.2 When a police officer killed an African American youth in the summer of 1964, Harlem erupted. This assault took place at 133rd Street and Seventh Avenue.

Source: Dick De Marsico, *New York World-Telegram and Sun* Newspaper Collection, Library of Congress.

reviewed complaints about police conduct. The defeat was interpreted as a blow to New York liberalism and a rejection of civil rights activists. The vote also signaled a split between liberal Jewish professionals, who tended to support Lindsay's proposal, and more conservative working-class and lower-middle-class Jews and Roman Catholics, who opposed it.[76] Moving forward, as conservative elements rose among the city's Democrats and Republicans,

Jewish voters would be courted by both the Left and the Right—a distinct shift from the position of Jews in the city's electorate during the days of La Guardia and the New Deal.

＊＊＊

Lindsay's city included many black New Yorkers who had long looked to schooling as the road to a better future for their children. As the historian Jerald E. Podair noted, by the 1960s "New York effectively had a dual public school system. At a time when full participation in the economic life of the city was coming to depend ever more critically on educational achievement, New York public schools were essentially predetermining outcomes based on race."[77]

To ease the situation, the city experimented with elected district school boards in a limited number of districts to give parents more input into their children's education. In one district, Brooklyn's Ocean Hill–Brownsville, the firing of thirteen teachers and six supervisors set off a bitter dispute between the district leadership and the teachers' union, the United Federation of Teachers (UFT). The UFT, with a strongly Jewish membership, called district leaders anti-Semitic, community leaders accused the UFT of racism, and three citywide public school teacher strikes followed in 1968. One year later, New York adopted a citywide decentralization plan that gave neighborhoods their own elected school boards to run elementary and middle schools.[78]

In ethnic terms, the strikes were widely (if not always accurately) perceived as exposing and forcing a rift between teachers and parents and whites and blacks. The worst of these divisions tore at blacks and Jews. Much postwar New York liberalism had assumed, perhaps naively, a harmony of interests between blacks and Jews. The school strike of 1968—despite examples of blacks and Jews in different ways rejecting calls to follow racial loyalty narrowly—nonetheless was remembered as an episode when New York liberalism and black-Jewish relations began to come apart.

The "school wars" were only one conflict among many. African American and Puerto Rican activism, challenging structural inequalities and entrenched forms of bigotry, spanned everything from electoral politics to community activism to violent action. At their most radical, young African Americans and Latinos joined the Black Panther Party and the Young Lords. Both parties had a talent for attracting media attention and undertaking activities ranging from providing needed community services to offering critiques of American politics that likened minority communities to oppressed colonies. They also frightened police with their paramilitary appearance, a tendency that made the fraught relations between the New York City Police Department and people of color even more troubled. Bombings by Puerto Rican activists in the Fuerzas Armadas de Liberacion Nacional (FALN) and the assaults on police officers staged by a small number of African American radicals set the city on edge.

Such attacks, and the persistence of police corruption and brutality in African American and Latino neighborhoods, further polarized relations between the police and the communities they served.[79]

Puerto Rican and African American activists placed great faith in neighborhood institutions under community control, most prominently local school boards. Community school boards appeared to offer people a chance to exercise power from the bottom up as a first step to making city institutions more democratic and responsive to African American and Latino concerns. The boards also offered the prospect of integrating the newest New Yorkers into the political system the way Tammany had integrated previous generations of immigrants. Over time, however, many of the boards proved to be too weak institutionally to cope with the challenge of educating economically poor children living in difficult circumstances amid an indifferent bureaucracy. Some boards also became sources of corruption and patronage hiring.[80]

Higher education also felt the pressure of demands from African Americans and Puerto Ricans. For those who had earned a high school diploma and met admissions requirements, the city offered the chance of a free college education. Before the 1960s, however, few African Americans attended either private college or the tuition-free branches of the City University of New York (CUNY). In 1960, minority students accounted for only 5 percent of the matriculants in the city's municipal colleges, the same percentage as a decade earlier.[81]

Building on the momentum of the community-control movement, African American and Puerto Rican college students at CUNY schools protested in the spring of 1969, calling for open admission. They closed CUNY and pressured the Board of Higher Education to agree that beginning in fall 1970 all of New York City's high school graduates would be admitted to one of CUNY's branches.[82] The open-admissions policy offered real hope for the city's minority students, but it failed to address adequately the widely varying levels of quality in the city's public schools when it came to college preparation.

At CUNY, black student enrollment increased rapidly after an open-admissions policy was instituted in 1970. Within a decade, the number of African Americans attending college in New York rose from 30,061 to 114,172. By the 1980s, 37 percent of the students in CUNY's community colleges were African American, with a somewhat smaller percentage attending the four-year colleges. Puerto Rican enrollment increased as well.[83]

✳ ✳ ✳

The growing political clout of African Americans reaped dividends in municipal employment. Far underrepresented on the 1940 city payroll, blacks had reversed this by 1970. Political pressure, a growing commitment to equal opportunity in public employment, and affirmative-action programs after the 1960s opened up opportunities. As the sociologist Roger Waldinger has explained, "Government employment offers the one bright light in the generally dim jobs scene for blacks."[84] African Americans' employment patterns varied from agency to agency and rank to rank. They were prominent in agencies devoted to health and welfare but underrepresented in the police and fire departments and the top managerial positions of city agencies.[85]

Municipal government was the largest single employer in New York City, and in the 1970s city, state, and federal governments employed about one-third of working native-born blacks. Nonetheless, the private sector provided the vast majority of jobs for African Americans.[86] But for the African American working and middle classes, private-sector opportunities opened very slowly after World War II.[87]

Investigations in the 1940s and 1950s revealed that many New York hotels, manufacturers, and other businesses refused to hire blacks and that employment agencies continued to fill positions with whites only.[88] In the 1960s, the U.S. Equal Employment Commission reported either a total absence or token representation of blacks in banking, insurance, advertising, and communications (including publishing, radio, newspapers, and television). On the city's major newspapers, for example, African Americans accounted for less than 1 percent of white-collar employees. Employment opportunities were hardly better in the construction industry, where the Italian- and Irish-run unions restricted entry into their membership. Two reports by the City Commission on Human Rights in the 1960s revealed great ethnic imbalances in the building trades.[89] Progress in black employment in construction appeared in the 1970s, but building trade unions often resisted it through court actions.[90]

Other unions proved more accommodating to African Americans, including them as union members and even leaders. Membership in the American Federation of State, County, and Municipal Employees (AFSCME) was dominated by white males until the 1950s, when the union began major organizational drives among the city's low-paid employees (who were usually black women) in schools, hospitals, and government offices.[91] Among municipal transport workers, where as late as 1938 only a few African Americans were employed as porters and none as train operators, by the mid-1960s black workers held half of all nonsupervisory positions.[92] Most service employees in private hospitals were also recruited from people of color. Hospital Workers Union 1199, headed by older Jewish radicals, successfully organized most of these workers after New York State passed a law guaranteeing them the right to union representation in 1963. Black unionists also began to take over leadership in 1199 as older white leaders retired.[93]

Public sector employment was essential to the rise of the black middle class in New York City, and the presence of a substantial black middle class enabled New York City to remain a center of African American literary and artistic creativity. No other American city was as promising to black performers. Alvin Ailey arrived in New York during the 1950s, became a noted black dancer on Broadway, and formed the Alvin Ailey Dance Company in 1958. Ailey's inspired use of jazz and Afro-Caribbean dance along with other modern idioms and classical ballet soon won him international recognition.[94] Arthur Mitchell, an African American, joined the New York City Ballet in 1955, became a leading dancer within a few years, and then starred on Broadway. In 1969, he founded the acclaimed Dance Theater of Harlem. The Negro Ensemble Company, a theatrical group, received praise from mixed audiences. Lorraine Hansberry's play *A Raisin in the Sun* won acclaim on Broadway in the 1960s. The Schomburg Library in Harlem, a library and exhibition space with the nation's largest collection of materials on black history, attracted both scholars and the general public.

✳ ✳ ✳

Since the New Deal, New York City had been something of an urban social democracy. It was never perfect and never entirely transcended the racism of its time and place. African American and Latino New Yorkers had to fight their way into the city's institutions. Nevertheless, New York offered possibilities. The Rev. Calvin Butts III of Abyssinian Baptist Church, recalling the optimism of African American New Yorkers in the 1950s, paraphrased Langston Hughes: America never was America for him, but once New York City almost was.[95]

New York City's size and diversity generated huge needs and demands, and these were partially met by an impressive array of labor and civic organizations and institutions such as public hospitals and a public university. Federal subsidies played an important role in sustaining these endeavors. Washington politicians, however, began to question this state of affairs as early as the Lindsay administration. Many problems that beset the city—particularly rising crime and the decline of the city's seaport and manufacturing sectors—seemed beyond anyone's grasp.[96]

The city's expenditures grew rapidly in the late 1960s. As businesses left the city, taking jobs with them, rising expenses could not be covered by municipal tax revenues. With unemployment rising in the early 1970s and the city relying on short-term bonds to plug holes in its budget, New York's finances grew shaky. So did its political leadership.[97] Lindsay, whose political clout had waned by the end of his second term, was succeeded in 1974 by Abraham Beame, an immigrant, Democrat, and the city's first Jewish mayor. Whatever Beame had learned in a lifetime as a Democratic regular was sorely tested as the city entered a transformative fiscal crisis.[98] Mayor Beame tried budget cuts and layoffs, but the banks that New York City relied on were not impressed. The mayor turned to the federal government for help, but with a Republican in the White House and conservative politics ascendant throughout the country, help from Washington was not forthcoming. The response of President Gerald Ford was captured in an immortal *Daily News* headline: "Ford to City: Drop Dead."[99]

The fiscal crisis touched nearly all groups and was so severe that it took years for the city to recover. A combination of state politicians and bankers told the city what they demanded, and the city complied. Beame's mayoralty limped to a close. In the mayoral election of 1977, the first after the fiscal crisis, Beame was succeeded by Edward I. Koch, a onetime reformer from Greenwich Village who ran as a fiscal moderate. Under Beame and Koch, between 1975 and 1983 the city's budget shrank 22 percent. Tuition at the City University was imposed for the first time; some students were forced to drop out.[100] Teachers and many other municipal workers were laid off. Subway repairs were deferred, libraries cut their hours, potholes grew, and the city dropped many programs that aided both youth and senior citizens. The cuts were especially hard on poor and working-class New Yorkers, Latinos, and African Americans.[101] People of color were victims of a "last-hired, first-fired" policy. Arson and the abandonment of residential housing made the streets of the South Bronx and Brooklyn's Bushwick symbols of urban disaster. The closing of Sydenham Hospital in the heart of Harlem was a bitter blow. Though it had only 119 beds, Sydenham was the first hospital to desegregate its staff entirely and provide a

7.3 President Jimmy Carter and Mayor Abraham Beame in the South Bronx, 1977.

Source: Jimmy Carter Presidential Library and Museum.

professional home for African American doctors in the 1940s. Mayor Koch rejected repeated protests to keep it open, and Sydenham Hospital became another casualty of the fiscal crisis, one with a bitter racial edge.[102] In the end, over countless such episodes, New Deal New York was beaten to its knees.

✳ ✳ ✳

Looking beyond the budget cuts and the rubble in neighborhoods such as Harlem and the South Bronx, it was possible to glimpse activists at work on housing and community health. Equally important for New York's cultural life, the same streets that were written off as blighted produced new forms of poetry, music, dance, and visual art that transformed the sights and sounds of the city. As in previous generations, the new cultural forms were directly traceable to trends in migration and immigration.

New York's Latin music scene, well established by the 1920s and grounded in the Cuban *son* style, expanded with post–World War II migrations that brought more musicians and more styles of music and dance. Afro-Cuban jazz and the mambo flowered. Latin and African American styles of music and dance combined in fertile ways, among them the boogaloo. By the 1970s, performers and dancers in Cuban and Puerto Rican neighborhoods and in metropolitan venues were reveling in salsa, "an up-tempo performance of percussive Latin music and Afro-Caribbean-infused dance." Salsa was strongly identified with the culture and activism of the city's Puerto Ricans, but like most great cultural forms in polyglot New York, it was a hybrid and drew from both the city and the Spanish-speaking Caribbean. "The great salsero Eddie Palmieri," writes the historian Mark Naison,

> who grew up in Hunts Point with an Italian father and a Puerto Rican mother, and received his first musical training at Junior High School 52, staffed his first band, La Perfecta, with almost as many Black and White musicians as Puerto Ricans, one of whom, Barry Rodgers, was a Jewish kid from the South Bronx widely recognized as one of the greatest trombone players in the history of Latin music.[103]

The salsa scene was complemented by the Nuyorican Poets, whose writing recognized hardships, shouted affirmation, and claimed a unique cultural space in the lives of Puerto Rican New Yorkers. Miguel Piñero, one of the group's foremost poets, published bilingual plays and English-language poetry. His acclaimed "A Lower East Side Poem" pleads that when he dies, he does not want to be buried in Puerto Rico or in a Long Island cemetery but to have his ashes scattered "throughout the Lower East Side." His poem was a testament to the growth of the Puerto Rican community on the formerly Jewish Lower East Side.

The neighborhood, in the linguistic mix of Spanish and English known as Spanglish, became known as Loisaida. There, in 1973, Miguel Algarin—a poet and professor at Livingston College of Rutgers University—founded the Nuyorican Poets Café. The café, whose name proclaimed the hybrid identity of its founders, met first in Algarin's apartment and in 1975 moved to a facility on East Sixth Street. The Nuyorican Poets Café went on to become one of the foremost venues in the city for poetry, music, theater, and the visual arts.[104]

Far north of Loisaida, in the Bronx, where Jamaican immigrants and African Americans grappled with budget cuts that reduced music programs in the schools, people found new ways to make music. As DJs at dance parties worked two turntables at a time to create exciting mixes of music and rhythms, MCs spoke in rhymes that drew on Jamaican traditions of toasting and the verbal sparring that African Americans call "the dozens." The result was rap music—often traced to a party emceed by DJ Kool Herc (a Jamaican immigrant) at 1520 Sedgwick Avenue in 1973. By the 1970s, Morrisania, a community devastated by population loss, became the setting of a new music scene, grounded in rap, that was to become a central element in the larger culture of hip hop.[105]

Hip hop would take the world by storm and redefine popular culture on a global scale. But in the 1970s, it was impossible to see that far ahead in New York City. New Yorkers looked at the future and voted with their feet. From 1970 to 1980, the city's population fell from 7,894,862 to 7,071,639.[106]

* * *

Compared to the immigrants who preceded them in the early twentieth century, New York was a place of trial and turmoil for Puerto Ricans and African Americans. Puerto Ricans, like other people of color and women, were victims of a "last-hired, first-fired" policy of municipal layoffs during the 1975 budget crisis. While the educational achievements of second-generation Puerto Rican migrants exceeded those of the first, Puerto Ricans' dropout rate in the city's public schools remained alarmingly high. In the late 1980s, some studies placed it near 60 percent and declared that it had reached epidemic proportions. Under pressure from Puerto Rican organizations, the Board of Education established bilingual educational and other remedial and cultural programs in an attempt to cut the dropout rate. But the school system was beset by shortages of qualified teachers and funds, and many children eligible for bilingual education and remedial programs never received them.[107]

Poverty for blacks and Puerto Ricans after 1970 was a grim coda to the initial optimism of the postwar years. Poverty had declined for all New Yorkers, including blacks, after World War II, but then began to rise for blacks: in 1969, one-quarter of African Americans were below the federal poverty line.[108] By the 1980s, more than 40 percent of black families were headed by women, and two-thirds of these families were in poverty.[109]

* * *

Examining ethnicity, economics, and neighborhoods in this new city in the 1980s, the political scientist John Mollenkopf noticed a contradictory patchwork of changes. More New Yorkers were working, the average household was earning more, and in most neighborhoods housing stock was improving. But the prosperity was "unevenly distributed." Whites gained the most, blacks held steady, and Latinos lost prosperity relative to both groups.[110]

These changes could be plotted on a map. Neighborhoods of native-born African Americans, like Harlem and Bedford-Stuyvesant, and neighborhoods of Puerto Ricans, like East Harlem and the South Bronx, were places of declining or low gains in income. And in Central Harlem, which lost a third of its population in the 1960s and 1970s, African immigrants revived commercial life in the 1990s. Immigrant West Indians tended to avoid historically black neighborhoods, instead creating new enclaves of their own, like Flatbush in Brooklyn. Latino immigrants tended to steer away from Puerto Rican neighborhoods and formed their own communities in places like Dominican Washington Heights. Immigrant blacks and Latinos tended to participate in the labor force in higher numbers than native-born African Americans and Latinos. Overall, immigrant Latinos and blacks generally did better than native blacks and Latinos.[111]

In neighborhoods where African Americans and Puerto Ricans lived in poverty, crime rates were high, and heroin addiction was a plague even before the crack epidemic broke out in the mid-1980s. In the crack years, which were marked by bitter competition between drug dealers and a high number of murders, shootouts between dealers made many African American and Latino neighborhoods dangerous. The city spent millions of dollars to fight drugs, with limited success. Although violence in crime-ridden neighborhoods was perpetrated by a minority of residents, lurid headlines disparaged entire communities.[112] Eventually the crack epidemic subsided, but not before it shook a city already badly rattled. If drugs and crime were not enough, AIDS, which first emerged within the gay male community, appeared most threatening to IV drug users; by the late 1980s, AIDS afflicted a disproportionate number of black and poor New Yorkers.[113]

* * *

In only a little more than three decades since the end of World War II, New York City had fallen from what looked like an unassailable pinnacle of power.

The descendants of earlier waves of immigration—Irish, Germans, Jews, and Italians—could escape the city's troubles by moving to safer neighborhoods within New York or by leaving it altogether for the suburbs. Poverty and the segregated suburban housing market confined the newest arrivals, African Americans and Latinos, to battered city neighborhoods.[114]

During the 1980s and 1990s, the city's politics veered from the liberalism that had once been its hallmark. Decisive in this trend was Mayor Koch, a former member of Congress from Greenwich Village whose days as a reformer were well behind him when he won the mayoralty in 1977. The city's second Jewish mayor, Koch won votes from the more conservative Catholics and Jews who had disliked Lindsay. In his first mayoral bid, Koch supported the death penalty (which he had no authority over as mayor) and inveighed against "poverty pimps."[115] Koch began programs that rebuilt the battered streets of the South Bronx, but overall he presided over a conservative turn in the city's politics. He was needlessly polarizing in his dealings with African Americans and hostile to municipal unions. He also sought to revive the city's economy through the construction of upscale housing that would attract a more affluent population. Although the full impact of this would not become clear for years, it contributed to the long-term growth of inequality in the city. Koch, like most of his successors, pursued an economically conservative agenda that favored finance, business interests, and real estate.[116]

The city's spirit became smaller, tighter, and meaner under the pressures of economic decay, political shifts, and the fear of crime. On television in the 1970s, the image of working-class whites moved from *The Honeymooners'* loud-mouthed and soft-hearted Ralph Kramden in the 1950s to *All in the Family's* angry, sullen, and bigoted Archie Bunker in the 1970s. As Jim Sleeper observed, from the mid-1970s on there was "a decay in the city's white working-class idiom, from one that could express its grievances in tart humor, irony and flashing insight into one of sullen, evasive rationalization for attacks on blacks."[117]

Two ugly incidents in the 1980s exposed deep racial animosities. In 1986, in Howard Beach, a predominantly white and Italian American neighborhood in Queens, twelve white teenagers wielding baseball bats attacked three African American men after their car broke down in the neighborhood. One of the men fleeing the assault, Michael Griffith from Trinidad, was killed when he was hit by a car. His death was a reminder that many whites saw race, rather than national identity, when they confronted Caribbean immigrants. Protests followed, and Mayor Koch, whose relations with African Americans were often strained, said the incident was the equivalent of "a lynching" and called it "the most horrendous incident" of his mayoralty. Three of the teenagers were convicted of manslaughter and assault. Just three years later, Yusuf Hawkins—an African American teenager who went to Brooklyn's heavily Italian Bensonhurst section to buy a used car—was confronted by local white youths and shot to death. Protestors who marched in the neighborhood to condemn the crime were met with taunts and racial epithets. Eight young men were tried; three were convicted and sentenced to prison.[118]

Public discussions of these tragedies, conducted in an overheated media culture, tended to polarize ethnic differences. Killings of African Americans, as in the Howard Beach and Bensonhurst cases, evoked fierce protests led by black activists—Al Sharpton, Alton Maddox, Vernon Mason, Sonny Carson—who were often better at gaining media attention than they were at building institutional strength and winning elected office.[119]

Ultimately, political scandals, racial violence, and City Hall's deteriorating relations with African American and Latino communities weakened Koch during his third term. In 1989, Manhattan Borough President David Dinkins, a Harlem Democrat who combined a party regular's appreciation for political structure with liberal instincts on social issues, defeated Mayor Koch in the September 1989 Democratic primary, then narrowly beat Republican Rudolph Giuliani in the November general election to become the city's 106th and first African American mayor. Dinkins won with 90 percent of the city's black vote, 65 percent of its Hispanic vote, and only an estimated 27 percent of the white vote. Italians and Irish voted heavily for Giuliani. Dinkins did better among the traditionally Democratic Jewish electorate, but even there he received only about 40 percent of the ballots.[120]

Dinkins was by every instinct a bridge builder, but his uneven record as an executive and the city's continuing racial rancor undermined his administration.[121] Dinkins was booed and sprayed with beer when he took the side of lesbian, gay, bisexual, and transgender (LGBT) efforts to march in the St. Patrick's Day Parade.[122] Worse, in Crown Heights, Brooklyn, in the same year, tense relations between African Americans, Caribbean blacks, and Hasidic Jews exploded after a rabbi's motorcade accidentally struck and killed a black youth. A crowd retaliated by mortally wounding a Jewish man with no connection to the accident. Rioting and looting followed. A state report later criticized Dinkins for failing to act promptly and decisively in deploying the police to restore order.[123]

Crime began to drop during the Dinkins administration, but not early enough for the mayor to reap significant political benefits. The 1993 election witnessed another Dinkins-Giuliani confrontation. This time, Giuliani narrowly defeated Dinkins. Mayor Giuliani, a former federal prosecutor, embraced policing and the crime issue. When crime began to fall—because of more effective policing, younger New Yorkers turning away from crime and drugs, a more vigorous economy, and immigrants bringing new stability to neighborhoods—Giuliani reaped the rewards. The mayor was sufficiently liberal on social issues that he could win the votes of independents and Democrats along with more conservative white ethnic voters, but he had poor relations with African Americans throughout his mayoralty. Nevertheless, he was reelected in 1997.[124]

Giuliani and his critics, the historian Jerald Podair argues, disagreed over the meaning of equality. To African Americans and many liberal New Yorkers, equality was "an outcome and a result" that took into account racial inequalities. To Giuliani, equality was about race-neutral equality before the law. Giuliani showed little interest in courting black voters and reflexively sided with the police when they clashed with black men.[125] Yet Giuliani welcomed immigrants to his city, whatever their legal status, as a force for reviving the city. During his mayoralty, New York had the equivalent of a "don't ask, don't tell" policy for undocumented immigrants who sought schooling, social services, and health care.[126]

Through the 1990s, New York City's mayoral and ethnic politics followed patterns that had first emerged during the Koch era. The dominant chord in mayoral governance was social liberalism and fiscal conservatism, with Koch—and later Giuliani—building majorities grounded in blocs of white voters. When troubles emerged, both mayors suggested that any alternative to their rule would bring back the bad old days of Mayor Lindsay or Mayor Dinkins. Frustration among African American and Latino voters grew as power seemed to be beyond their grasp. Crime declined in the 1990s, dramatically reducing the death rate from murders in the city, but aggressive policing left many blacks and Latinos feeling that the crime drop was a "tainted victory," in the words of the sociologist Patrick Sharkey, that perpetuated aggressive styles of policing and coexisted with rising economic inequality that harm poor urban communities. One example of that came in 1999, when four undercover policemen seeking an armed rapist in the Bronx misinterpreted the gestures of Amadou Diallo, an unarmed African immigrant, and fired forty-one shots, killing him. Protests erupted, but the officers tried in the shooting were acquitted.[127]

* * *

Diallo's death was a tragedy, but it was not the only story to emerge from the Bronx. Looking back on her old neighborhood of Morrisania in the Bronx, Andrea Ramsey vividly recalls the camaraderie of the community where she grew up. "It wasn't a perfect world," she relates, "far from it, but it left me with a feeling that was good, and I think that's what a lot of people remember." In the 1960s, her neighborhood was afflicted by a wave of heroin addiction and street crime. Ramsey went to college, worked in the textile industry, married, went to graduate school, and then worked for many years in art therapy. She left Morrisania but stayed in the Bronx. When she returns to her old neighborhood, she can barely recognize it, but she knows that growing up in Morrisania left her, and others, with sustaining memories. "You can talk about all the bad things; you can talk about all of the horror stories," she says. "But when you go back in your memory, you try and remember good things. And there were enough of those things to realize that it was not just one person's fantasy. Those good things were real."[128]

Andrea Ramsey, like others from the South or Puerto Rico or the Caribbean, kept faith with the ideal of New York as a city where communities, schools, and cultural institutions nurture the best in human potential. Racism, segregation, economic decay, and crime destroyed such hopes for many. With good reason, Junot Diaz writes that New York, for many African Americans and Latinos, became a city of "A future that had been promised but never arrived."[129]

But even as the city struggled through the years of the urban crisis, by the 1980s there were signs that new people were coming to the city for the same reasons that migrants and immigrants had always come to New York: to find better jobs, to escape oppression, and to start life over again. The future of the city depended in large measure on how it responded to their dreams and their hard work.

CHAPTER 8

IMMIGRANTS IN A CITY REBORN:
1980–PRESENT

For Jumoke Rhodes, a Yoruba-speaking woman from Nigeria with two small children, life in New York City was perplexing. "I came to New York so that I could learn English," she told a *New York Times* reporter in 1982. "Here is an English-speaking country. What I got in my life is something else. I don't know where I am. Spain? China?"[1]

Her confusion was understandable: she lived in Elmhurst, Queens—a neighborhood in the midst of great changes wrought by immigration. Long home to Irish, German, and Italian New Yorkers, by 1982, the *New York Times* reporter Dena Kleiman observed, Elmhurst—with two hundred thousand immigrants from 110 countries, where students at the public schools spoke thirty-four languages—was the most diverse neighborhood in New York. Bengalis lived alongside Ecuadorians, the Dutch Reformed Church conducted services in Taiwanese, and a Greek immigrant who ran a pizzeria had trouble finding a common language to speak with his Indian customers.[2]

Kleiman's report was part of a series of articles entitled "A New Melting Pot: The City in the '80s" that explored a new surge in immigration, the largest since the early twentieth century. The touchstone for the articles was Elmhurst, a neighborhood of modest architecture beneath the number 7 elevated subway train. "This new surge is altering the city's ethnic texture," wrote Kleiman, "revitalizing many of its neighborhoods and reaffirming something that many have thought long lost—that despite the fiscal crisis, crime statistics and other drawbacks, the rags-to-riches promise of New York that attracted generations of immigrants is still very much alive."[3]

In the lives of Elmhurst's immigrants, Kleiman encountered something more complicated than stories of rags to riches. As with previous generations of new arrivals in the city, she found people holding down two or three jobs and working fourteen hours a day, seven days a week. She saw families sleeping five to a room and a couple who had, after much work and saving, put together $90,000 to buy a house. She met a Vietnamese family that had befriended an older Hungarian American couple and a young man from Colombia who worked as a busboy. He was far from attaining his dream of American riches and wondered whether he should swallow his pride and go home.[4]

Kleiman expressed some concern that the new immigrants would be poorly integrated into the city's civic fabric because of their diversity, the easing of old pressures to assimilate, and access to flights back to their countries of origin. Overall, however, she was cautiously optimistic about where the new immigration would lead. She quoted Frank Vardy, whose analysis of immigration for New York's Department of City Planning combined both statistical data and firsthand observations on city streets. "The word has leaked out," said Vardy. "You can make a living in this city, and you might even make it big."[5]

The new immigrants encountered a city whose economy was in the middle of a profound transformation. The wharves, warehouses, and factories that had made New York an economic powerhouse had been vanishing since the 1960s— and with them the jobs that paid decent if hard-earned wages to immigrants of earlier times. In their place, New York City saw a rise of low-paid service work and better-paid work in finances, real estate, and media. All of these changes would remake the city and challenge the energy and ingenuity of its newest peoples.

There were no assurances that the newest New Yorkers would fit well with either the city's older communities of European immigrant stock or its African American and Puerto Rican communities. Crime was high, the city's economy had only recently emerged from a protracted slump, and all of New York's previous waves of migration and immigration had been accompanied by periods of unrest and uncertainty.[6] In 1982, from the vantage point of a neighborhood of new immigrants like Elmhurst, both Kleiman's optimism and caution both seemed well-advised.

* * *

Immigration in the 1980s, as in earlier times, was powered by push-and-pull factors. Immigrants were pushed to the United States by political upheavals, humanitarian concerns, and economic factors. New York's economy staggered in the 1970s, but compared to difficult situations in other countries, it could seem attractive. Immigrants were also pulled to the United States by the possibilities for legal immigration opened up by a federal law that would confound

8.1 At the Statue of Liberty, President Lyndon B. Johnson praises immigration legislation that would transform the population of New York City and the United States (1965).

Source: Yoichi Okamato, LBJ Presidential Library.

both the expectations of both the legislators who drafted it and the president who signed it.

On a sunny October day in 1965, President Lyndon B. Johnson stood beneath the Statue of Liberty and signed a new immigration law that corrected, in his words, "a cruel and enduring wrong in the conduct of the American Nation": the system of national-origins quotas that dated to the 1920s. Johnson condemned the old system as a bulwark of "prejudice and privilege" that allowed just three countries to supply 70 percent of European immigrants to the United States. The new bill before him, Johnson said, would abolish the quota system. It would not be revolutionary, he said, but it would be consistent with the country's best traditions of fairness and pluralism: "This bill says simply that from this day forth those wishing to immigrate to America shall be admitted on the basis of their skills and their close relationship to those already here." "Now," he said, "under the monument which has welcomed so many to our shores, the American Nation returns to the finest of its traditions today."[7]

The poetry of Johnson's speech obscured its details. To appease legislators who feared a large influx of Mexicans and Central Americans, the new law established an unprecedented limit on the number of immigrants who would be admitted from the Western Hemisphere. At the same time, it eliminated the national-origins quota system for the Eastern Hemisphere that had governed American immigration since the 1920s, which favored Northern and Western Europeans, discriminated against Southern and Eastern Europeans, and virtually barred Asians. The 1965 law established instead a system that emphasized family unification and skills, with limits of twenty thousand on annual admissions from any one country, but set no limits on immigration of spouses, children, and parents of adult American citizens. The drafters of the bill expected that it would only slightly change the composition of the population of the United States. Instead, the law and subsequent legislation transformed the population of both the United States and New York City.[8]

As older European immigrants and their children continued to leave the city, new arrivals came from all over. Where earlier waves of European immigration were defined by two large groups—the Irish and Germans of the mid–nineteenth century and the Jews and Italians of the late nineteenth and early twentieth centuries—the newest New Yorkers came from many nations, among them the Dominican Republic, China, Mexico, Guyana, Ecuador, Jamaica, Trinidad and Tobago, and the former Soviet Union.[9]

The majority of immigrants came legally, but it was impossible to determine the precise number of undocumented immigrants in the city. A common strategy was to visit the city as a tourist and stay on after the visa expired, putting the individual in the population of the undocumented. In 2004, when the city's overall population was eight million, the Department of City Planning estimated that there were 583,000 undocumented immigrants.[10]

Immigrants settled in almost every part of the city. Even Staten Island, the borough with the lowest percentage of immigrants, still had sections—from Port Ivory to Mariner's Harbor in the northwest and from Stapleton down to South Beach in the southeast—that were 25 to 30 percent foreign-born. But certain areas had strikingly high concentrations of newcomers, above all the borough of Queens. The 7 train, rolling eastward from Midtown Manhattan, traversed a changing ethnic geography so dense and diverse that the line

TABLE 8.1 Foreign-born population of New York City, 1970 and 2011

Country of Birth	1970	Country of Birth	2011
Italy	212,160	Dominican Republic	380,160
Poland	119,604	China	350,231
USSR	117,363	Mexico	186,298
Germany	98,336	Jamaica	169,235
Ireland	68,778	Guyana	139,947
Cuba	63,043	Ecuador	137,791
Dominican Republic	51,231	Haiti	94,171
United Kingdom	48,798	Trinidad and Tobago	87,635
Austria	48,024	India	76,493
Jamaica	40,672	Russia	76,264

Source: "Foreign-Born Population by Area of Origin and Country of Birth, New York City, 1970–2011," in The Newest New Yorkers: Characteristics of the City's Foreign-Born Population (New York: Department of City Planning, 2013), 16.

became known as the "International Express." Consistent with the highly plural nature of the new immigration, neighborhoods were rarely homogeneous. Even where one group was numerically dominant, it rarely had the neighborhood entirely to itself. Flushing, Queens, through which the 7 runs, became the city's second major area of Chinese concentration, composed mainly of people of Taiwanese origin. Yet it also housed Koreans, Filipinos, and Indians. A tenth-grade Trinidadian student told an interviewer, "I have a neighbor that's Guyanese on one side and Spanish, Mexican on the other side. I have Indians around the corner."[11] Brooklyn, which closely followed Queens as the home of many immigrants, was the site of a new Chinatown in Sunset Park; Haitians, Jamaicans, and West Indians settled into Flatbush; and Jews from the Soviet Union moved into Brighton Beach.[12] In Manhattan, Washington Heights became a large Dominican community.

The past and the present met in striking juxtaposition. Sometimes, old houses of worship took on new layers of identity. In Jackson Heights, Queens, a building that was once a Lutheran church was reborn as a Buddhist community center and monastery for New York's Sherpas, the legendary Himalayan mountain guides who worked (more safely) in the city as taxi drivers.[13]

As immigration continued, old ethnic neighborhoods and institutions acquired new residents and new identities. Catholic churches, parishes, and schools battered by declining membership were still closing, but they would have been in even worse shape without the influx of Latino Catholics. Korean congregations brought to life many dying Protestant churches. Along with Orthodox Jews' high birthrates, the influx of Jewish immigrants halted the decline of Jews in the city and led to a modest increase in the Jewish population. In addition, growing numbers of Hindus, Buddhists, and Muslims brought religious diversity and energy to the city. In the formerly Italian streets of East Harlem, where after one hundred years the Festival of Our Lady of Mount Carmel Church was losing energy, Haitians who had worshipped the Madonna at Haiti's Ville de Bonheur learned of the festival, joined the celebration, and brought it back to life.[14]

For many years, the center of Arab settlement in New York City was on Brooklyn's Atlantic Avenue. Its shops, restaurants, and bakeries drew a population of Arab immigrants, dating to the early twentieth century, who were usually Christians. From the 1970s on, however, most Arab immigrants were Muslims, and their numbers fed the growth of Arab immigrant communities further afield in Brooklyn as well as in Queens.[15]

By 1993, the city held seventy old and newly established mosques. The annual holiday of Ramadan brought Arabs together with Muslims from Afghanistan, Egypt, Pakistan, and Bangladesh and included African American Muslims. Muslims also established schools in the city to provide religious and secular education for their children. In mosques, schools, and community centers, Muslims of different national backgrounds began to forge a common identity as New Yorkers. Equally important, like the Jewish immigrants before them who had adapted their faith to life in New York and the United States, Muslims inside and outside the city developed American versions of Islam.[16]

* * *

New York in the 1980s witnessed both an economic boom and growth in economic inequality. Employment rose in finance, corporate services, and public and nonprofit social services. More neighborhoods improved than decayed, and real household income grew citywide. The rise in inequality made for uneven prosperity, but the city nevertheless attracted immigrants, was strengthened by their arrival, and sustained their lives in the city.[17]

Sometimes, immigrants took jobs in well-established New York City institutions with pressing labor needs. With over 150 languages spoken in the city, the need for interpreters in schools, courts, and hospitals expanded as newcomers poured into the city. The city's universities and health care industry also attracted immigrants. Hospitals and medical schools in particular employed many physicians, nurses, medical technicians, and administrators as well as workers to clean rooms, prepare food, and care for patients. The working conditions and low pay of many of these jobs spurred the unionization of many hospitals.[18]

At other times, immigrant arrivals matching labor needs produced surprising niches. Many Koreans worked as medical professionals and played a crucial role in helping fill vacancies among interns and residents in municipal hospitals and providing care in neighborhoods inhabited by poor African Americans and Latinos. Koreans at one time operated 90 percent of the city's produce stores. Ecuadorans found jobs working beside Mexicans in mid-Manhattan garment shops owned by Koreans (half of whom had been professionals in Korea). Bangladeshi immigrants found jobs in construction, as cab drivers, delicatessen staff, and restaurant workers. A modest number of Israelis were conspicuous in the furniture-moving and livery-car industries. By 1992, Afghans, many of them refugees of the 1979 Soviet invasion of Afghanistan, owned over two hundred stores in New York; their restaurants included not only establishments that served Afghan food but fast-food chicken restaurants.[19]

The latest wave of immigration changed not only the face of New York but the cultural experience of immigration. Earlier generations of immigrants, especially Italians, had always gone back and forth between their home country and New York on ships. Air travel, which boomed in the post–World War II years, made such journeys faster and easier. John F. Kennedy International Airport replaced Ellis Island as the gateway to New York City. Equally important for the daily lives of immigrants in New York were changes in communication. The immigrants of the nineteenth century followed developments in their homelands through letters and newspapers, but satellite communications wove networks of international television, and changes in telephone technology made it possible to communicate in real time. Immigrants could live transnational lives in ways that would have amazed the immigrants of the early twentieth century. Dominicans, the most numerous of the new immigrants, said they lived "con un pie aquí y el otro allá": "one foot here and one foot there." Dominican Americans' dynamic and ongoing relationship with their home island was a defining feature of their lives in the United States, but in an era of fast flights and global communications it was hardly unique among immigrant groups. In Queens, Tulasi Ram Ghmirey told an interviewer that he wears two watches on his arm, a blue one set to the time in New York City and a green one set to the time in Nepal, so he can call his relatives there without waking them in the middle of the night.[20]

By the 1990s, the signs of New York City's new diversity were visible in everything from newspapers to cultural events. Eighty foreign-language and ethnic newspapers (including twenty-two dailies) were established between 1970 and 1990. By 1990, the city boasted Filipino, Korean, and Spanish newspapers and nine dailies alone in Chinese. The circulation of *Carib News*, founded by island immigrants in the 1980s, climbed to over sixty thousand within a few years. The Kapoor brothers, two Indian immigrants who emigrated from New Delhi in the mid-1970s, built a twenty-million-dollar-a-year empire of newsstands. Many were located in subway, bus, and railroad stations and staffed by South Asian immigrants.[21] Immigrant media wove connections between home countries and New York City and even within the city itself, cultivating complex identities grounded in both the city and larger diasporic communities.

The case of Chinese immigrants illuminates the continuities and changes wrought by the new immigration. The Chinese presence in New York City was old, but racist immigration laws in the nineteenth century, which were reformed to modest effect in World War II, kept the Chinese population in the city relatively low until the 1965 immigration law opened up new possibilities for Chinese immigration from Hong Kong, Taiwan, and eventually mainland China.[22]

In the 1980s, a Chinese settlement composed primarily of immigrants from Hong Kong emerged in the Sunset Park–Bay Ridge district of Brooklyn.

8.2 In downtown Flushing, Queens, almost 80 percent of immigrants are of Asian origin (2015).

Source: Yanping Nora Soong at English Wikipedia.

They occupied an area once known as Little Scandinavia, whose Norwegian residents had since moved to Staten Island or the suburbs.[23] As the twentieth century drew to a close, the arrival of new immigrants placed great pressure on housing in Chinatown. At the same time, Hong Kong investors, uneasy about the looming transfer of the city from British to Chinese control in 1997, purchased buildings in Chinatown, in Little Italy, and on the Lower East Side. Yet the ensuing expansion of Chinatown did not provide enough housing for immigrants. Prices soared, and many sought homes in the city's other boroughs.[24]

The work experiences of Chinese immigrants from the mainland were uneven. Even though Chinese immigration occurred during a period of decline in New York's garment industry, which had employed late-nineteenth- and early-twentieth-century European immigrants, the industry still offered opportunities for small enterprises that could adjust quickly to meet the demands of rapid changes in fashion. Immigrant capital provided startup funds for Chinatown's small garment shops, and Chinese women immigrants provided the largely low-cost labor. In Brooklyn, another Chinese garment center developed in Sunset Park.[25]

Anxious to help support their families and not yet fluent in English, these women had few good options, especially if they were here illegally. In violation of labor laws, they sometimes brought their preschool children to the shops during the working day and sometimes put their older children to work. Factory-safety laws were also regularly ignored, leading a state inspector to remark about one shop: "I've never seen a worse fire exit."[26] Occasionally friendship and kin networks produced a paternalistic relationship between boss and worker, but such ties were limited. Many garment factories recreated the conditions of the earlier immigrant sweatshops. In response to these conditions, the International Ladies' Garment Workers' Union managed to organize most of Chinatown's shops and more than twenty thousand women workers during the 1980s. For the women, unionization brought higher wages, safer conditions, and health insurance benefits.[27]

Some Chinese garment workers hoped to save enough money to open their own shops. A number of men succeeded in starting needle-trade factories, but by the late 1980s the rising costs of labor, spiraling prices for building space, and foreign competition made such enterprises risky. Indeed, by the early 1990s many Chinatown shops appeared to be in financial difficulty.[28]

Chinese restaurants endured, catering to residents and tourists in Lower Manhattan's Chinatown but also operating citywide. Chinese men riding bicycles through the crowded city streets delivered food to patrons. Abundant cheap, nonunion, Chinese male laborers, including immigrants who were smuggled into the United States without proper papers, kept the cost of running restaurants low. With limited English-language skills and few employment options, many sought jobs as cooks, waiters, and kitchen helpers. Some hoped to open their own restaurants. The few who realized this dream succeeded by running restaurants as family enterprises. Instead of paying wages to hired employees, they used the unpaid labor of family members and thereby reduced operating costs. The business of "Snakeheads," who brought undocumented Chinese immigrants to the United States for a price of several thousand dollars, appeared to decrease after 2000.[29]

Chinese immigrants included well-educated and higher-paid professionals. The economic success of the "Uptown" Chinese and the growing number of Chinese students in the city's elite high schools led some to call the Chinese a "model minority." Indeed, Chinese New Yorkers, along with other Asians, came to the fore in the 1980s as recipients of academic honors. Young Chinese students made up a disproportionate share of students in the city's academically selective high schools. These successes, however, obscured a more complex story. Younger and more recent settlers in Chinatown often lacked adequate English-language skills, and many struggled academically. Furthermore, the proportion of Chinese living at or below the national poverty line exceeded the city average. According to the 1980 census, 71 percent of the adults in Chinatown never finished high school, and over half could not speak English well. Many were products of the earlier bachelor societies who had been barred from decent jobs by racial discrimination; now, in their old age, they were living on meager funds. Ten years later, the census revealed that one-quarter of all families in Chinatown lived below the poverty line.[30]

Other Chinese immigrants lived outside ethnic enclaves, scattered throughout the city and in nearby suburbs. They constituted what Peter Kwong has called "the Uptown" Chinese—highly educated professionals employed by universities, corporations, and research and medical centers. "Uptown" Chinese professionals had often studied English in Taiwan and then came to America to complete their educations, especially in the sciences. From 1965 to 1985, some 150,000 Taiwanese students came to the United States; most remained by finding jobs after completing their studies. After 1990, students from China became a major group of foreign students in New York; many also stayed in the United States after finishing their studies. In contrast, Kwong points out, the immigrant residents of Chinatown tended to be working class, with lower levels of education and limited English-language skills.[31]

Compared to the Chinese, Dominicans were a relatively new immigrant group. They first ventured to the United States in significant numbers in the 1960s, fleeing economic difficulties and political repression. Many Dominicans were drawn to the garment industry, which was unfortunately contracting as they arrived in New York.[32]

Even as the garment industry declined, it provided some jobs for Dominican women, who also sought work in service industries. Though wages were low, these jobs gave Dominican women more independence than they had in their homeland. According to a municipal report issued in 2013, women headed

44 percent of Dominican households, and these households often lived below the poverty line.[33] However, many of their households had at least two workers, which pushed their family incomes above those of Puerto Ricans. Dominicans, like other Latinos, had lower-than-average educational-achievement levels and higher-than-average poverty rates. Nevertheless, they displayed a formidable work ethic.[34]

Dominican men sometimes accumulated enough capital to open garment factories, an enterprise dominated at the time by Chinese entrepreneurs. Other Dominican men could be found among the many Latinos who labored as construction workers, largely in the nonunion building-rehabilitation business. Dominicans also owned many of the city's eight thousand bodegas, small grocery stores catering to the growing Latin population.[35] By 1990, they controlled more than 70 percent of Hispanic-run businesses, even though they constituted less than 40 percent of the city's Latinos. In subsequent years, they expanded their presence in supermarkets and livery cabs.[36]

West Indians, in contrast, found jobs in the city's growing service economy. West Indian women, who outnumbered men in the migration process, worked as nurses, as nurse's aides, in childcare, and as domestics.[37] One city official noted in 1988 that New York City had six to eight thousand Caribbean businesses, with more in Brooklyn than any other borough. Brooklyn also had a strong Caribbean residential population; nearly half of the city's Caribbean blacks lived in Bedford-Stuyvesant, Flatbush, and Crown Heights. The more prosperous Caribbean peoples of African descent settled in Queens. Some West Indians rapidly found special niches of opportunity in the city's economy. For example, they operated many of New York City's car-service vehicles as well as the "dollar vans" that provided transport in sections of the city with poor mass-transit connections.[38]

West Indian family incomes, though less than those of whites, were higher than those of most Hispanics and native-born black New Yorkers, primarily because in many West Indian families both the husband and wife were in the workforce. In 1980, 74 percent of recent West Indian immigrant men and 66 percent of West Indian immigrant women were employed, rates higher than native-born blacks and many other immigrant groups. This pattern continued after 1980, with few West Indian families receiving public assistance and lower rates of poverty relative to other immigrant groups.[39]

Like English-speaking West Indians, Haitians, most of whom lived in Brooklyn, were unprepared for the racism they encountered in their search for housing and jobs. Because many were not native English speakers and lacked marketable skills, they labored in relatively low-paying service jobs. Those who were undocumented faced particularly difficult times in the job market.[40]

The annual West Indian American Day Carnival, held since 1969 along Brooklyn's Eastern Parkway, became one of the city's major ethnic events. Held on Labor Day weekend, it drew on Lenten-season rituals of the Caribbean and featured elaborate costumes, steel drums, loud and infectious music, and street vendors selling abundant quantities of Caribbean food, from codfish fritters to fresh coconuts to rum punch. Attracting people from across the Caribbean, even those without a Carnival tradition, the event became a significant expression of pan-Caribbean identity. The loud and energetic parade central to the event, which is open to all, drew an estimated eight hundred thousand spectators and participants by the late 1980s, and it has grown even larger since. Keeping order, especially during the festivities the night before, was sometimes a challenge. Nevertheless, the procession became a major and beloved civic event. Prominent sponsors supported the festivities, and politicians marched to greet the crowd. By 2010, it was common to read estimates of attendance that topped one million, surpassing other ethnic parades, including the venerable St. Patrick's Day Parade.[41]

The new immigration also brought to the city, in modest numbers, members of older ethnic communities—especially the Irish and Jews. When Irish economic growth in the 1960s collapsed during the oil crisis of the 1970s and the international recession of 1979–1980, a new generation of Irish men and women sought lives in New York. Unlike the Famine-era Irish of the nineteenth century, these "New Irish" were well educated and the children of a politically independent and culturally modern Ireland. They immigrated to America not to start a new life but to escape temporarily from economic failure in Ireland. Scattered surveys indicated that the "New Irish" immigrants were typically males who found work through the city's Irish community, primarily in construction. (In earlier generations, women were the majority of Irish immigrants.) In these jobs, they sometimes received wages off the books. "New Irish" women often worked in childcare in numbers comparable to West Indian women.[42]

The "New Irish" settled in older Irish American neighborhoods such as Woodside in Queens or Woodlawn in the Bronx, but to a degree they kept their distance from older, established Irish American organizations and were culturally distinct from the Irish Americans they encountered. In 2000, as the venerable St. Patrick's Day Parade on Fifth Avenue was marred by legal and political wrangling over the organizers' refusal to allow LGBT groups to march in the parade openly, a new procession appeared in Queens, organized by Brendan Fay, a gay Irish immigrant and activist. Named "Saint Pat's for All," the procession was founded "to celebrate Irish heritage and culture regardless of race, gender, creed or sexual orientation." Long before the disputes around the traditional Fifth Avenue parade were settled, "Saint Pat's for All" became an established and inclusive event on the city's annual calendar.[43]

Soviet Jews came to the city as refugees as early as the 1970s and then arrived in larger numbers after the 1989 Soviet liberalization. In Brighton Beach, Brooklyn, immigrants from the former Soviet Union created a "Little Odessa" complete with nightclubs and restaurants. "These clubs are a Russian's version of paradise," one émigré said. "Russians suffered from a lack of food for years and so the notion of dieting is alien to our culture. Every calorie is prized, even if it is all fat." Another settlement in Queens was populated by Jews from the Central Asian republics of the former Soviet Union.[44]

* * *

By 2000, New York's years of high crime were over, and the growth of the city suggested that the decades of urban crisis had passed. New York had reinvented its economy in ways that offered new immigrants real if constrained opportunities. Hundreds of thousands of native New Yorkers had left the city for the suburbs or other states, thus opening positions in the growing economy for immigrants. If employment in New York did not pay high wages, it did pay more than opportunities in countries such as Haiti, the Dominican Republic, Jamaica, and Bangladesh.

The wave of immigration gained widespread visibility in the early 1980s and transformed New York. It rivaled, in scale and significance, the prior waves of immigration that had remade the city. New York City, which lost population overall in the 1970s, gained about 800,000 immigrants during the 1980s and more than a million during the 1990s.[45] The new arrivals saved New York from the kind of severe population decline that had damaged other cities in the United States during this period. A municipal report noted that between 1970 and 2000 the city's immigrant population had doubled, bringing the number of foreign-born in the city to an all-time high of 2.87 million, or 36 percent of New York's population. The same report also credited immigrants with playing vital roles in reviving the city's workforce and housing stock. In 2000, a Quinnipiac University poll asked residents of New York City if the growth in immigration was good for the city. In response, 53 percent said yes; only 28 percent said no. Positive responses came from men, women, and all ethnic groups.[46]

A numerical comparison of the largest immigrant groups in the city before and after the new immigration speaks volumes. As late as 1970, the three largest immigrant groups in New York City were Italians (212,160), Poles (119,604), and immigrants from the Soviet Union (117,363). In 2011, the city's three largest immigrant groups were Dominicans (380,160), Chinese (350,231), and Mexicans (186,298).[47] The new arrivals complicated the ethnic profile of New York, transforming the definition of the people once called "minorities."

The number of Puerto Ricans in the city, for example, peaked in 1990. After that, they moved to Florida (where economic opportunities were better) or relocated within the New York metropolitan area to pursue opportunities in the suburbs or in small regional cities. As the number of Puerto Rican migrants

8.3 Williamsburg, Brooklyn, 2005.

Source: Seamus Murray, Wikimedia Commons.

declined and the number of Dominicans and then Mexican immigrants rose, the Latino profile of New York City changed. Where once the term "Hispanic" had been a synonym for Puerto Rican, the new term "Latino" embraced a multitude of Latin American nationalities, among them Puerto Ricans, Dominicans, Mexicans, Ecuadoreans, and more.[48]

A similar transformation occurred among black New Yorkers. In the early decades of the twentieth century, the city's black population grew though a combination of migration from the American South and, to a lesser extent, immigration from the Caribbean. By the 1960s, approximately a quarter of the city's black population was composed of immigrants. In subsequent decades, the percentage of immigrants in the city's black community grew. By 2000, immigrants from the Caribbean and Africa accounted for a third of black New Yorkers. Immigration changed what it meant to be black in New York City.[49]

As the sociologist Sherri-Ann P. Butterfield argues, "second-generation West Indians are expanding previous conceptions of 'blackness' to include multiple ethnic groups." Familiar categories like "Black" have come to include African Americans, English-speaking West Indians, French and Creole-speaking Haitians, black Latinos, and Africans. Similarly, "Asian" now includes not just the Chinese but also Indians, Bangladeshis, Koreans, Filipinos, and Pakistanis.[50]

By 2000, five of the ten New York City neighborhoods with the largest immigrant populations were in Queens (Flushing, Astoria, Elmhurst, Jackson Heights, and Corona); four were in Brooklyn (Bay Ridge–Bensonhurst, Gravesend-Homecrest, Flatlands-Canarsie, and Sunset Park–Industry City); and only one was in Manhattan (Washington Heights).[51]

✳ ✳ ✳

On the morning of September 11, 2001, voters went to the polls in a primary election to choose Democratic and Republican nominees for the office of mayor. The sun was bright and the sky a brilliant blue when jet liners commandeered by Islamist terrorists of the al-Qaeda organization crashed into the World Trade Center. In Lower Manhattan, 2,753 people died that day.[52] The death toll in the World Trade Center attacks reflected New York's status as both a city of immigrants and a city of global economic importance. The dead were not only from the United States but from countries including the United Kingdom, India, El Salvador, Canada, Israel, and the Dominican Republic.[53]

Businesses in Chinatown, a neighborhood close to the World Trade Center, were hit hard.[54] Some Chinese were able to move their shops to Brooklyn or relocate there by opening new shops; other small businesses relocated to Midtown Manhattan. Others never recovered.

With Lower Manhattan streets closed off, Union Square, long a meeting place for New Yorkers, became one of the city's largest memorial grounds. There, Roman Catholic mass cards rested alongside flags and Jewish *yahrzeit* candles. Staten Island, with its large percentage of uniformed city workers, was the setting of many funerals for police officers and firefighters. For months, the sound of bagpipes—reflecting the Irish presence in the city's police department and fire department—was a sound of mourning.[55]

The effect upon the city's Muslims was especially severe. In spite of their growing numbers and signs of acceptance—and a firmly interfaith response to the attacks in municipal ceremonies—Muslims came under suspicion after the destruction of the World Trade Center and faced increased harassment. Law-enforcement and immigration authorities placed Pakistani sections of Brooklyn under close scrutiny, and many Pakistani immigrants left New York entirely. At the same time, when the Associated Press disclosed a special secret unit in the New York City Police Department formed to spy on mosques, restaurants, and student organizations popular with Muslims, criticisms from civil libertarians were sharp. The department eventually disbanded the unit, but New York still struggles to balance individual rights, security, and cultural inclusion.[56]

The human and cultural aftershocks of 9/11 endured for years, along with the reverberations of the U.S. invasions of Afghanistan and Iraq that followed the attacks. They did not, however, alter New York's position as a city of immigrants and center of the global economy. Reports commissioned by the Russell Sage Foundation and published in 2005 concluded that the economic impact of the attack was short lived, and the long-range picture remained one of optimism.[57]

New York City's recovery from the attacks of September 11, 2001, was better than expected in part because the bitter ethnic politics of the Koch, Dinkins, and Giuliani years had declined. Many New Yorkers were exhausted with the rancor that surfaced during all three mayoralties, and the arrival of so many immigrants in the city softened some of the harder lines of ethnic conflict. Moreover, the high crime and fear that had scarred the city from the 1960s into the 1990s had ended. In the mayoral election of 2001, conducted only weeks after the attack on the World Trade Center, New Yorkers elected Republican candidate Michael Bloomberg—a wealthy businessman starting a second career in public office. Bloomberg narrowly defeated Mark Green, a Democrat long associated with the liberal, activist wing of his party. Green had alienated many Latinos and African Americans by beating Fernando Ferrer, the Puerto Rican borough president of the Bronx, in the Democratic mayoral primary. Bloomberg was Jewish, but he did not make much of this. More significant for the city's ethnic politics was the fact that his opponent Green, like Ruth Messinger in 1997, was a Jewish Democrat with deep roots in the party's liberal tradition. Bloomberg's victory over Green, like Giuliani's victory over Messinger, suggested that a strain of Jewish liberalism in the Democratic Party that dated to the New Deal was losing its edge.

At heart, Bloomberg was more a technocrat than a Republican. He hired able administrators to run city agencies and created a probusiness climate in city government. Unlike Giuliani, he kept in touch with African American leaders and did not always reflexively support the police after an officer shot someone. Bloomberg, a cosmopolitan international businessman, strove to make New York City an attractive place to visit, work, and live. "He steered the city in the direction cast by globalization, the technology revolution, and the rise of creative talent over muscle as the source of economic value," writes the historian Chris McNickle. Under Bloomberg, the city became a magnet for the global elite. He tried to expand the creation of middle-income jobs and promote affordable housing, but these efforts were no match for the larger forces of gentrification, which were accelerated by his goal of making the city a more attractive place for affluent urbanites. In 2012, the highest-paid 20 percent of all New Yorkers earned more than twenty-six times the poorest 20 percent. In Manhattan, the top 20 percent earned forty-two times the poorest 20 percent. A quip made the rounds that Manhattan was becoming another Monaco—an island for rich people and their servants.[58]

Unlike his predecessors, Bloomberg had no interest in ethnic politics. He did not spend his weekends conspicuously attending ethnic street fairs, and unlike Koch and Giuliani he did not politically exploit ethnic resentments. He lacked a common touch and was sometimes accused of being an elitist. But he presided over a city that was, despite the fears stoked by 9/11, more at peace with itself than it had been for decades. In the summer of 2005, when a white man beat a black man in a confrontation in Howard Beach—where a similar incident in 1986 had led to a fatality and an outpouring of anger—Bloomberg quickly condemned the assault and defused what might have become a crisis. When Bloomberg ran for a second term that same year, he easily defeated Democrat Fernando Ferrer, a Puerto Rican—winning approximately half of the black vote and a third of the Latino vote.[59]

The mayor won a third term in 2009, defeating Democrat William Thompson, the city comptroller and an African American, by a modest margin in a race marked by a low turnout. The mayor drew on his traditional areas of electoral strength, support, according to the *New York Times*: Staten Island, Queens, Jewish voters, white Roman Catholics, and voters who earned more than $200,000 a year—in effect, the more conservative and affluent elements in the city. Thompson ran strongest in the Bronx and drew even with Bloomberg among voters ages 18 to 29.[60]

Bloomberg's third term was uneven. The enduring problem of poor relations between the police department and African Americans persisted because the police department continued to use aggressive stop-and-frisk practices that disproportionately targeted black and Latino men, embittering relations between the police and people of color. The mayor nevertheless backed the practice. Bloomberg also could not settle the fears of terrorism and suspicion of Muslims that were part of the aftermath of 9/11. When a proposal surfaced to build a Muslim community center near the World Trade Center site to bring together people of all faiths, Republicans and some family members of 9/11 victims denounced the plan as an insult to the dead of September 11.[61]

In a speech Mayor Bloomberg delivered in August 2010, surrounded by religious leaders with the Statue of Liberty in the background, he passionately affirmed the constitutional right of Muslims to build a center in Lower Manhattan. Eventually, the proposal was approved. Then, in the complex and overheated real estate market of Lower Manhattan, the plan was delayed, and a new vision for the site emerged: a luxury condominium.[62]

By the end of the first decade in the twenty-first century, the wave of immigration that had become visible in the 1980s was so well established that the children of recent immigrants numbered 22 percent of the city's population. Another 11 percent of the population came from the "1.5 generation," people who arrived at a very early age, so, though immigrants, had essentially been educated and grown up in New York City. Together, they made up 33 percent of the city's residents. A major study of this cohort by Philip Kasinitz, John H. Mollenkopf, Mary C. Waters, and Jennifer Holdaway, focusing on the Chinese, South Americans (Colombian, Peruvian, and Ecuadoran), Dominicans, Russian Jews, and English-speaking West Indians, revealed some good news: among all groups, the second generation surpassed the educational level of their parents.[63]

The study also revealed that "most of the second generation seems likely to be strongly attached to the labor force overall and far less likely to work in distinctive ethnic niches than did their immigrant parents." Immigrant parents who worked long hours for low incomes in grocery stores or small businesses wanted their children to have better careers. Korean immigrants, for example, pushed their children to go to college and enter professions. Some Chinese and Russians did exceptionally well, but for most of the second generation, although success in the labor market meant surpassing their parents and even passing some native-born minorities, it stopped short of high-paying work.[64]

The study found that many second-generation New Yorkers were more interested in economic mobility than political activism. Nevertheless, researchers found that while retaining strong ethnic identification, they were at ease with becoming American and accepting of racial and cultural differences. In a city with a long history of conflict and exclusion, that was a sign of progress.

The study of the second generation also noted that neither Puerto Ricans nor native-born African Americans were faring as well as the children of recent immigrants. And the Community Service Society reported in 2010 that compared to other native-born Latino youth, Puerto Ricans were less likely to be enrolled in school, had lower levels of educational accomplishment, and had "alarmingly higher rates of disconnection and poverty."[65]

The political profile of Puerto Ricans was mixed. For years, the most prominent Puerto Rican politician in the city was Herman Badillo, who started his political life as a liberal Democrat but eventually became a Republican. Badillo served as borough president of the Bronx in the 1960s, in the U.S. House of Representatives in the 1970s, and as a deputy mayor in the Koch administration.[66] The idiosyncrasies of his political path, along with relatively low rates of voter registration and participation among Puerto Ricans (even though they were

U.S. citizens), diminished Puerto Rican electoral power. Over time, however, Puerto Rican activism and Puerto Ricans' institutional presence in politics, government, and community agencies translated into political strength. Even as New York City's Puerto Rican population declined, Puerto Ricans—and Latinos overall—won seats on the city council and became borough presidents. Nydia M. Velazquez won election to Congress from a newly created heavily Latino district in 1992,[67] and in 2014 Melissa Mark-Viverito, one of twenty-five Puerto Ricans elected to office throughout the city, became the first Puerto Rican to serve as speaker of the city council. Eleven out of fifty-one city council members were Latinos (all but one either Dominican or Puerto Rican). Nevertheless, the prize of the mayoralty eluded Latinos. Immigration meant that as the Latino community increased in numbers, it also grew more diverse. Puerto Ricans, once the prime group of Latinos in the city, were now one group among many.

African Americans, the group of New Yorkers with the longest history of struggling for justice in the city, also found themselves in circumstances marked by changes and continuities. African Americans, as in the past, lagged in being offered and obtaining more lucrative jobs in the business world. Nevertheless, blacks who sought work in the private sector did achieve some successes, and the city's major law firms and investment houses employed a limited number of African Americans in elite finance and banking positions.[68] As in previous generations, African Americans were more likely to find work in the public sector.

In 2012, African Americans made up only 22 percent of the city's population but were 32 percent of the municipal workforce. However, black New Yorkers were not employed so easily in the police and fire departments.[69] By 2015, a sustained effort to diversify the department and recruit black officers proved only a partial success. While the city was about 44 percent white, the police department was 50 percent white. African Americans, about 25 percent of the city's population, accounted for 15 percent of the force. In contrast, Hispanics were 27 percent of the force, close to their percentage of the city's population. Asians made up 6 percent of the force, about half of their presence in the city's population but a growing segment of the NYPD.[70]

The position of African Americans in the New York City Fire Department was even more problematic. Irish American domination of the fire department has been a longstanding tradition in New York City—nearly half of the firefighters killed on 9/11 were Irish American—and the department has long been slow to accept African Americans.[71] The first black firefighters faced difficulties in the hiring process and were harassed in the firehouses. Backed by court orders, the fire department gradually increased the number of African American firefighters. In 2014, 17 percent of new recruits to the FDNY were black, and 24 percent were Latino.[72]

African Americans' strength in public sector work did not, however, translate into a decisive political advantage for African Americans overall. In a diverse city where no single group commands an easily assembled majority, African Americans need allies to win public office. However, multiethnic alliances are difficult to build and hard to sustain—especially when conservative whites vote against black and Latino candidates. At the same time, immigration has increased the number of black identities to be found in New York, potentially expanding possibilities for political alliances but also making the formation of a citywide black vote more complex.[73]

During the almost twenty years since 9/11, New York City's rates of poverty and unemployment for blacks—along with Latinos and noncitizens—remained stubbornly high. In a global city, the gap between stagnant wages and high living expenses undermined the economic security of many New Yorkers.[74] Housing costs rose, especially in gentrifying neighborhoods, and home ownership became more difficult to attain. From 1990 to 2007, the cost of home ownership in New York City soared by 156 percent. Moreover, as the supply of affordable rental housing declined, New Yorkers with lower incomes confronted the challenge of spending an increasing portion of their household income on rent.[75]

8.4 New construction looms over the venerable Katz's Delicatessen on the Lower East Side (2018).

Source: Photograph by Robert W. Snyder.

The related problems of economic inequality, high housing costs, and gentrification appeared, with local variations, in neighborhoods such as Harlem, Washington Heights, and Williamsburg, Brooklyn. In gentrification's initial phase, new tenants or homeowners entered undervalued neighborhoods with an ethnic or historic character and affordable or vacant housing. The newcomers, who often sought more authentic urban experiences, were not necessarily rich but usually had higher incomes than the long-time residents. At first, the new arrivals injected vitality into old neighborhoods and improved aging housing stock. As neighborhoods revived, however, rents and real estate values rose. People of moderate income were forced to look ever further afield for affordable housing; one neighborhood's new gentrifier was often someone forced out of another community by rising rents. Early cases of gentrification could be found in the brownstone neighborhoods of Brooklyn Heights and Park Slope in the 1960s and 1970s, where the process of neighborhood change proceeded gradually. Later, when municipal zoning policies turned industrial areas into residential zones, changes accelerated, intensified, and took on a convulsive quality.[76]

New York was part of a global real estate market, but its elected officials lacked the legal and governmental power—or political will—to deal with the consequences. Developers often seemed one step ahead of city government. As the NYU Furman Center noted, rents rose everywhere in New York City in the 2000s, "most rapidly in the low-income neighborhoods surrounding central Manhattan."[77]

In the face of rising inequality, the city's immigrants and workers have shown impressive ingenuity in organizing movements on behalf of labor rights. Indeed, in public and private sector work, unions in New York City are stronger than they are in the rest of the country. Slightly more than one-quarter of wage and salary workers in the city were union members in 2015–2016. Immigrants organized new unions, like the New York Taxi Workers Alliance, a multiethnic union organized by South Asian immigrants, and new organizations, like Make the Road New York, which focuses on legal services, community organizing, and education within Latino and working-class communities. At the same time, immigrants, African Americans, and Puerto Ricans benefit from older organizations they inherited from earlier generations. For example, in South Jamaica, Queens, African Americans live in Rochdale Village, a limited-equity cooperative originally founded by the United Housing Foundation, a product of the Jewish immigrant-labor movement. The once vigorous Jewish community in Rochdale Village has departed, but the cooperative is a financially stable bastion of residential security for African Americans in an area with a high rate of real estate foreclosures.[78]

Immigrants have also made contributions to the city's economy on an impressive scale. In New York City, where more than one-third of the population consists of immigrants, immigrants represent 44 percent of the city's workforce and almost half of its small business owners.[79] Moreover, as the Fiscal Policy Institute points out, small businesses, where immigrants are especially innovative, have revitalized many neighborhoods.[80] In short, immigrants have been crucial in rebuilding the city's economy and in making it function today. "Immigration," as David Dyssegaard Kallick notes, "has been centrally important to the economy of New York City in recent decades. Immigrants—driving overall population growth—have often been an important part of neighborhood revitalization and have helped the city as a whole rebound from the days of underinvestment, abandoned buildings, and the fiscal crisis of the 1970s."[81] New York, as Joe Salvo and Peter Arun Lobo note, has become "A City Dependent on Immigration."[82]

* * *

As in previous waves of immigration, newcomers brought new forms of music to the city but also created new musical hybrids that resounded around the world. Certain forms of music might remain part of an ethnic identity—Dominicans in Washington Heights danced to meringue and Trinidadians enjoyed calypso— but in multiethnic New York, with so many immigrants from the Caribbean, making music was often an invitation to cultural exchange. Haitian musicians adopted Latin and African American styles, bands eager for broad appeal within the Latino community learned to play both salsa and meringue, and Jamaican reggae became the soundtrack of a pan–West Indian identity at Brooklyn's annual West Indian Carnival. Their music also circulated in the Caribbean and eventually reached listeners in Europe, Africa, and Latin America. New York, where musical forms mix within and among immigrant communities at an international crossroads, became a global city for music.[83]

The importance of a new generation of immigrants in the city—and the challenges they faced building a home there—gained memorable theatrical form in 2008, when the musical *In the Heights* opened on Broadway. The play was the product of Lin-Manuel Miranda, a Puerto Rican New Yorker who conceived the musical, wrote its lyrics and music, and played a lead role. Miranda was at once an insider and outsider in New York: he grew up in largely Dominican Inwood, at the uppermost end of Manhattan, just north of Washington Heights. His father, however, was a member of the Koch administration and had a deep love of Broadway musicals. Educated at the one of the city's academically rigorous public schools, Hunter College High School, and at Wesleyan University, Miranda infused his musical with the music, rhythms, and dance styles of Latino and African American New York.[84]

Like earlier generations of immigrants, the characters of *In the Heights* wrestle with what it means to make a home, the contradictory calls of ambition and community, and the place of gender in immigration. It is women who turn the world upside down as they rebel against traditions, confinements, and expectations. Unlike the musical *West Side Story*, which in 1957 depicted Puerto Ricans as newly arrived outsiders, *In the Heights* features Latinos as full inheritors of New York City's immigrant past. The city and its songs are theirs, but what will become of them is not clear. Some of the play's characters are marked for upward mobility, some aren't, and some are leaving the neighborhood to find cheaper rents.[85]

In 2015, Miranda followed *In the Heights* with the musical *Hamilton*, an even bigger hit. *Hamilton* used rap and the new sounds and rhythms of the city to tell the story of Alexander Hamilton, an immigrant to New York from the British West Indies who attended King's College (which became Columbia University), soldiered with George Washington in the American Revolution, pressed for a constitution with a strong central government, and served as the first secretary of the Treasury. In Miranda's telling, Hamilton was the prototypical scrappy immigrant, eager to work his way to the top.[86]

Yet even as *Hamilton* attempted to illuminate the past in new ways, it was very much a musical of its own time and place—a New York City, during Barack Obama's presidency, that had gained a new layer of identity with the arrival of recent immigrants. The musical's majority African American and Latino cast played the Founders with a pronounced sense of their flaws, limitations, and hypocrisies. *Hamilton*'s focus on a Founder from the British West Indies affirmed New York's past and present links to the Caribbean, the original home of so many post-1965 immigrants. In one number in the show, Hamilton and the French Marquis de Lafayette talk about the coming battle of Yorktown. Their exchange is punctuated by a line that draws strong applause: "Immigrants: we get the job done."[87]

✳ ✳ ✳

Throughout history, observers have looked to certain New York neighborhoods to understand the impact of immigration on the city. In the middle of the nineteenth century, Charles Dickens and other European tourists gazed at the Five Points in Lower Manhattan, home of Irish and German immigrants and African Americans. In the late nineteenth century, Jacob Riis looked at the Lower East Side to fathom where Jewish, Italian, and Chinese immigrants were taking the city. By the 1920s, tourists and social critics looked uptown to African Americans in Harlem. At the turn of the twenty-first century, observers with questions about the evolving significance of immigration in New York City looked eastward to Queens. If Queens lacked the narrow streets that made the Lower East Side picturesque and the boulevards that made Harlem dynamic, it had a variety of people that was extraordinary. Indeed, as early as 1992, the census declared Queens the most diverse county in the entire country.[88]

Roger Sanjek, an anthropologist at Queens College of the City University of New York, looked closely at the Elmhurst-Corona section of Queens—an area the *New York Times* recognized in 1982 as a site of increased immigration. In 1960, the neighborhood was 98 percent white; by 1990, it was only 18 percent white. "Established residents of German, Irish, Polish, Italian, Jewish and other European ancestries," Sanjek wrote, "now lived among African, African American, Chinese, Colombian, Cuban, Dominican, Ecuadorian, Filipino, Haitian, Indian, Korean, Mexican, Puerto Rican and other new neighbors."

Frederick Wiseman, the documentary filmmaker famed for his searching examinations of communities and institutions, produced *In Jackson Heights*, a three-hour documentary on that Queens neighborhood. Wiseman captured the minutiae of everyday life in a neighborhood where 167 languages are spoken by people from Afghanistan, Bangladesh, China, India, Mexico, Pakistan, and every country in South America. Taking his camera into streets, stores, and community meetings, Wiseman depicts people wrestling with work, change, and activism. The film warmly depicts the neighborhood's LGBT community and its annual parade.[89]

For all their differences, the two projects shared one conclusion: in Queens, the latest surge of immigration to New York City had worked out reasonably amicably. Wiseman, who showed how the threat of economic displacement loomed over Jackson Heights, nevertheless affirmed the neighborhood's commitment to democracy and pluralism by closing his film with a shot of the number 7 train heading toward Manhattan as fireworks burst overhead.[90]

Sanjek had a similar appreciation for the hard-won pluralism of Queens but also acknowledged its limits. Like other New York City neighborhoods, Elmhurst-Corona has its own segregated housing patterns, but they did not always conform to a ghetto paradigm. By the late 1970s, in the black enclave of Lefrak City, African Americans were amassing political power and earning more than many of their white neighbors. Sanjek also found local whites who were more comfortable with immigrants than African Americans and immigrants who felt little in common with African Americans. Viewing all of this with cautious optimism, Sanjek pointed out that the kind of racial and ethnic transformation that had occurred in Elmhurst-Corona is taking place across the United States. For better and for worse, but mostly for the better, Queens is indeed "the future of us all."[91]

AFTERWORD

On Manhattan's Lower East Side, where Jacob Riis once pondered how the other half lives, the streets are marked with the contradictory consequences of immigration, reform projects, and the ceaseless engine of New York's economy. Sometimes, change eases the lives of city dwellers. The alley that Riis and his team of photographers depicted as "Bandits' Roost" is long gone, razed in 1897 along with the rest of Mulberry Bend (thanks in part to Riis's crusading journalism) and replaced with Columbus Park. Instead of toughs in derby hats there are children on swings, basketball players, soccer players, and elderly Chinese on park benches holding sing-alongs. Walk north and east to Ludlow Street, where Riis found whirling activity in the sweatshops of the Jewish quarter, and at Ludlow and Broome streets in 2017 a new condominium apartment building looms overhead. At 242 Broome Street, eleven of the fifty-five apartments are designated as affordable, reflecting the city's efforts to increase the supply of moderately priced housing. An affordable one-bedroom apartment sells for $224,861; a three-bedroom apartment costs $331,703. The remaining forty-four units are market rate, ranging from $1.6 million for a one-bedroom apartment to $6.25 million for a penthouse. The website marketing 242 Broome Street offers "a legacy of new beginnings" on the Lower East Side in a neighborhood that is "a mentality, an attitude and a philosophy."[1]

The arrival of "condominium residences" with "contemporary luxury and style" heralds a new era in the history of Broome Street, but the questions Riis asked in the same neighborhood about immigration, poverty, inequality, and city life endure because they are grounded in historical patterns that define New

York City's past and present.[2] Waves of migration and immigration repeatedly bring new peoples to the city. Global economic patterns bring booms and busts that sharpen both ambitions and inequalities. Generations of radicals and reformers, often spearheaded by immigrants and women, have addressed many of the city's most grinding injustices, but it is difficult for one city to overcome international sources of inequality and the stubborn persistence of racism in America politics and culture.

In 2013 Bill de Blasio, the city's public advocate and former Brooklyn city council member, won the mayoral election running as a proud liberal Democrat. Charging that New York had become "a tale of two cities," he promised to reduce economic inequality, create affordable housing, improve early childhood education, and reform the stop-and-frisk policing practices that had poisoned relations between the city's police department and African American residents. The presence of his African American wife and biracial children in advertisements and campaign events broadened his appeal while sharpening his criticisms of the racial implications of the Bloomberg administration's policing policies.[3]

In his inaugural address, de Blasio invoked a long line of New Yorkers, including Mayor Fiorello La Guardia, First Lady Eleanor Roosevelt, and the singer and activist Harry Belafonte, who "stood up to say that social and economic justice will start here and will start now." The election was notable not only for its rejection of the moderate to conservative policies that had dominated city politics (with the exception of the Dinkins administration) since the Koch years but for what it revealed about the new ethnic alignments of the city's electorate.[4]

The votes of non-Hispanic whites were important to the mayoral victories of Koch, Giuliani, and Bloomberg, but such voters are a diminishing presence in the electorate. Between 1990 and 2013, the urban policy analyst Joseph P. Viteritti reports, "the proportion of the voters who were non-Hispanic whites dropped from 54 to 42 percent." In the same time period, the percentage of black voters declined to 24 percent, the percentage of Hispanic voters grew to 23 percent, and the percentage of Asian voters grew to 10 percent. At the same time, the percentage of whites in the municipal workforce was declining, enabling de Blasio to assemble a more ethnically diverse base of support than his liberal predecessors.[5]

Translating his victory into a full realization of his progressive agenda proved a challenge. The new mayor had to confront not only the police department, which had vexed liberal mayors during the Lindsay and Dinkins administrations, but also divisions within his own coalition—especially on the issue of school integration. Liberal whites, especially new arrivals in historically black neighborhoods, were wary of sending their children to local schools with high rates of poverty and uneven levels of performance. African Americans saw the white newcomers as harbingers of higher rents and the displacement of black residents. In meeting his promise to create affordable housing, de Blasio faced a real estate industry keen to make profits, people with low to moderate incomes who desperately need places to live, and neighborhood residents who feared that new construction would destroy the familiar scale and character of their communities. The worst possibility that confronted de Blasio was that his housing efforts would be too small to create real change but large enough to anger residents who wanted to preserve their neighborhoods. Overall, in his first term de Blasio fulfilled many of his promises. He ordered the city's lawyers to stop fighting a ruling issued by a federal judge during the Bloomberg years that found the city's use of stop and frisk unconstitutional. The city modified police practices, and, contrary to some predictions, crime remained low. De Blasio also established universal prekindergarten education and created or preserved some affordable housing.[6]

Three years into de Blasio's first term, the problem of uneven support for the city from state government was dramatically compounded at the federal level when Donald J. Trump, running as a Republican, won the 2016 presidential election. Trump, born in Queens, campaigned with a mixture of nativism, racism, misogyny, and promises to "make America great again." He was deeply unpopular in his home town, however, and voters' rejection of his nativism was a reminder that New York values its immigrant heritage.[7]

One year later, de Blasio won reelection, defeating his Republican opponent with 66 percent of the vote. Although his majority was impressive and his campaign spoke the old language of liberal New York, the city's uneven relations with state government and the hostility of the Trump administration meant it would be difficult to translate de Blasio's victory into enduring achievements.

Contemporary calls for racial and ethnic inclusion and for economic justice bring to mind the words of the Nuyorican poet Miguel Piñero: "No hay nada nuevo en Nueva York," "There is nothing new in New York."[8] Indeed, in this fast-paced and ever-changing city, it is easy to lose sight of how twenty-first-century questions are debated on terrain shaped by the weight of history. While it can be misleading to think of New York as an utterly unique city, it is possible to identify its defining traits: a dynamic economy, visible extremes of wealth and poverty, neighborhoods that are either ethnically defined (Manhattan's Chinatown) or extraordinarily heterogeneous (Elmhurst, Queens), turf-based political activism, a contentious political culture grounded in ethnic mobilizations and coalition building, Democratic Party dominance in local politics, a broad acceptance of ethnic diversity that is contradicted by an enduring strain of racism toward people of African descent, and a fertile popular culture defined by ethnic hybrids. All of these are shaped by New York City's history of immigration and migration.[9]

A.1 New Americans: a naturalization ceremony at the New-York Historical Society, 2016.

Source: Don Pollard, New-York Historical Society.

From the city's beginnings, the historian Thomas Bender points out, the dominant understanding of politics and society in New York "embraced difference, diversity, and conflict—as well as the dollar." The city became home to a multiethnic population when the Dutch West India Company—eager to make money but short of ready hands—actively encouraged non-Dutch settlers, grudgingly accepted Jews, and imported enslaved Africans. For those with the freedom to take up the opportunity, the Dutch policy of tolerating foreigners was a way to escape poverty and persecution and begin life anew. For all the changes in the city once known as New Amsterdam, it is still true that immigration and migration are the products of needs and desires, of push and pull. Since its earliest days, New York has drawn migrants and immigrants because it is a city of refuge and a place of opportunity. Famine in Ireland, pogroms in Russia, lynchings in the American South, and hard times in the Dominican Republic have all sent people packing for New York. The city that drew people across the generations did not have to be perfect; it just had to be better than the place they left behind. In this equation, New York has benefited from hard times in other places. It has also challenged the hopes and aspirations of new arrivals.[10]

New York became a "city of the world," but its peoples have much in common: the newest arrivals typically have to wrestle a living from an unforgiving labor market. They came to find better opportunities, they frequently faced hostility, and they made wrenching adjustments to life in a new city. To get by, almost all sought out their compatriots and created institutions to help them cope with the city. Starting at the bottom of the economic pile, each first generation inevitably found life exceedingly hard.[11]

Within this broad pattern, however, there have been marked differences in group experiences. European Protestants generally have had an easier time adjusting, especially those who arrived with some combination of knowledge of the English language, formal education, and profitably applied vocational skills. Thus Walloons, Irish Protestants, Scandinavians, French Huguenots, English, Welsh, and Dutch were able to acculturate quickly and eventually assimilate. Even Germans, considered somewhat clannish, found it possible to join the mainstream of New York society after a generation or two. If anything, the anti-German sentiment of World War I accelerated both the decline of New York's German culture and the movement of German Americans into the city's mainstream.

For Catholics and Jews, the situation was somewhat different. Irish Catholics were welcomed for their labor but despised and ill-treated for their poverty and religion. Over time, however, Irish Americans improved their economic condition, gained political power, and eventually won acceptance.[12] Jews encountered anti-Semitism from the time they first set foot in Dutch New Amsterdam, yet they too prospered. Anti-Semitism remains a concern, but it does not shape Jewish choices about jobs, education, or residence as it did in previous generations. The city's Italians, often scorned for their poverty and Catholicism, were slower to prosper but nonetheless have experienced nearly full acceptance in New York's institutional life.

Acculturation—participation in the life of the larger city—does not necessarily require total assimilation. Most descendants of European immigrants have chosen a path somewhere between those two extremes and by the second or third generation in the city achieve everything from modest comfort to extraordinary prosperity. The choices and opportunities of immigrants and migrants of African, Asian, and Latino descent—who are sometimes set apart from people of European descent by appearance and skin color—have not been nearly so generous.[13]

African Americans came first as slaves and, when slavery ended, endured generations of racial discrimination in nearly all phases of city life. The earliest Asian immigrants, the Chinese, found their lives restricted by bigotry for decades. Racism has declined since the 1940s but not nearly to the extent that intolerance toward national and religious minorities has. If New York's ability to absorb generations of immigrants reflects the best possibilities of the United States, the enduring existence of racism in the city illuminates New York's inability to overcome America's national sin. "Whereas whiteness is an asset for newcomers of European ancestry," the sociologist Nancy Foner observes, "dark skin brings disadvantages."[14]

During the last fifty years, a new generation of immigrants—many from nations barely represented in the city before World War II—has established whole new neighborhoods. Once again, the drama of immigration is being played out on the streets of New York. Whether these new ethnic groups will evolve the way past groups have remains to be seen. If the city's history of pluralism gives grounds for cautious optimism, the economic history of New York is more sobering.

Since its founding, New York has been an economically dynamic city, its prosperity shaped by global patterns of trade, investment, and manufacturing. As a consequence, the city has long been shaped by economic currents beyond its control. Equally important, the inequality of income and wealth has been an old theme in the city's history. In colonial New York, the rise of the merchant class grew side by side with the enslavement of Africans. In the nineteenth century, slavery was central to New York's economic growth. The city's businesses made a considerable part of their income by shipping cotton and providing credit and goods to slave-owning Southern planters. The richest New Yorkers held a large share of the city's wealth from the Gilded Age into the years before the Great Depression of the 1930s. From the Great Depression through the 1970s, their share declined. Working- and middle-class people gained. Since the 1980s, however, the rich in New York City have gotten significantly richer. The growth of highly paid financial industries, the increasing attractiveness of life in New York City, and the soaring value of New York real estate have all made the city a magnet for the global elite as a residence, place to work, or object of investment or speculation.[15]

Given the enduring importance of immigration in New York's economy and political life, immigrants and people with immigrant roots can be found among both the city's plutocrats and proletarians. Yet the city that is often described as the capital of capitalism has also birthed movements and institutions that have sought to overturn, or at least ease, inequality. Indeed, since the nineteenth century, some of the most significant responses to inequality and to the challenge of governing a diverse city have emerged from immigrant communities. Tammany Hall was storied for its corruption, but in a time when many New Yorkers knew gnawing poverty it won votes with ethnic loyalties, patronage jobs, and small acts of charity delivered without condescension. The immigrant radicals, labor unionists, and reformers of the late nineteenth and early twentieth centuries played important roles in building the reforms that distinguished both the Progressive Era and the New Deal. In the postwar years, in the face of economic decline and the weakening of public and governmental institutions, African Americans and Latinos tried to make New York live up to its higher ideals. Since the 1970s and the fiscal crisis, however, along with a conservative turn nationwide, the city's egalitarian visions and programs have generally weakened. New York needs outside financial assistance if it is to enact robust progressive policies, but this is unlikely after the election of President Trump in 2016.[16]

With or without Washington, New York will continue to evolve in ways that sometimes reflect the past and sometimes depart from it. The continuities are strong in popular culture, where the city's dense mix of peoples creates new hybrids of music and dance—as they have since the nineteenth century, when Irish and African American dancers met in the saloons of Lower Manhattan and swapped steps in a process that ultimately produced tap dancing. In the twentieth century, African American and Jewish musicians exchanged riffs and improvisations in ways that defined both jazz and Broadway musicals. In the 1950s, white, black, and Latino singers produced the urban harmonies of doo-wop. Hip hop is the product African American, Latino, and Afro-Caribbean musicians and dancers. To be sure, the long history of African American artists' creativity and inspiration has not been matched by fair economic rewards and the full benefits of citizenship. Overall, however, the long history of popular culture in New York City is an enduring testament to the genius of hybrids and the creative powers of outsiders trying to become insiders.[17]

The press of change is strongest in the city's neighborhoods. New York's ethnic enclaves are sometimes romanticized as places that preserve old and authentic ways, but they are better understood as places of ceaseless change where the old gives way to the new. The Irish are long gone from the Five Points and all but gone from places like Inwood in northern Manhattan. When the suburban descendants of immigrants visit New York City today, they absorb immigrant history through walking tours and visits to institutions like the Tenement Museum on the Lower East Side or the Museum of Chinese in America. To grasp the newest dimensions of immigrant life in New York, it is useful to visit Jackson Heights, Queens—one of the most diverse communities in the United States and the kind of polyethnic neighborhood that has emerged from the most recent surge in immigration. In Jackson Heights, a walk northward from the station of the elevated number 7 subway immediately puts a pedestrian in a Little India, where bhangra music blares and shop windows display saris. A few blocks to the east, however, signs of South Asia give way to Mexican taco stands; Colombian, Peruvian, and Ecuadoran restaurants; and the sounds of Latin music. Half of the neighborhood's residents speak Spanish; others speak Chinese, Urdu, Hindi, Russian, Portuguese, Greek, or Korean. Altogether, Jackson Heights is said to be the home of 167 languages.[18]

Turf is central to ideas of politics and identity in New York City, but in an era of globalization—when international movements of people and capital can overwhelm urban communities—the meaning of ethnic turf is changing. Noted ethnic enclaves—the Irish Five Points, the Jewish Lower East Side,

Black Harlem—were never quite as monolithic as their names implied, but they gave the majority of their inhabitants a sense of belonging in a city that could be less than welcoming. They also served as strongholds in electoral politics. For African Americans and Latinos, in particular, such neighborhoods were both culturally important and the presumed staging grounds for eventual campaigns for political power. The economic crisis of the 1970s, followed by the conservative turn in the city's politics, disrupted these visions. So did the growth of a more plural population (thanks to immigration), which made the important task of building ethnic political alliances more intricate and difficult. The latest layer of complications in the politics of turf is the growing diversity of historically African American neighborhoods.

As the political science and sociology professor John Mollenkopf points out, from the 1920s to the 1960s Harlem was the focal point of the New York's African American population and its cultural heart. Nevertheless, Harlem lost population, especially when its middle class—faced with crime, economic decay and social problems and eager for better housing—left for better conditions in neighborhoods such as Bedford-Stuyvesant in Brooklyn. In recent years, however, the populations of Harlem and Bedford-Stuyvesant have both grown. White gentrifiers are an important part of this change, but they have significant company: both neighborhoods have seen growth in their number of foreign-born blacks, native and foreign-born Hispanics, and native and foreign-born Asians. "Harlem," Mollenkopf concludes, "is one small, if important part of a larger picture. Across the city, immigration, the aging and out-migration of the native-born minority populations, the labor-market shift to the services (and growing polarization of wealth), the paring-back of the welfare state, and technological changes have been reshaping black neighborhoods." In this context, single parents with low levels of education and little work experience—who are disproportionately represented in Harlem—are in a difficult position. "Given the persistent poverty among native-born minorities," he concludes, "increased overall inequality, and the upward mobility of many new immigrant groups, one might be tempted to say that the glass remains no more than half full."[19]

New Yorkers take pride in living in a city built by immigrants. Mayors have praised immigrants, and the city maintains an office devoted to immigrant affairs. In 2018, a municipal report extolled New York's "long and proud history as the quintessential city of immigrants."[20]

What future lies ahead for the residents of an increasingly pluralistic New York City? For native-born white citizens and many immigrants, the nation's business, financial, and cultural capital continues to hold out promises of success. Even so, in a city and country with a long history of racism, in an era when a significant percentage of immigrants are people of color, it would be dangerous to assume that all will automatically work out well. As the sociologist Mary C. Waters observes:

Whether the tolerance and acceptance immigrants and their children experience in New York City will spread to the rest of the country, or the intolerance and exclusion that characterizes other parts of the country will spread to New York, is an open question. Meanwhile, the race to fix ongoing racial inequality is even more pressing, as immigration increases the numbers of people facing ongoing racial inequality.[21]

New York, thanks to its dynamic economy and polyglot peoples, is forever a work in progress. It nourishes hopes and shatters them, fulfills and frustrates idealism, and then—just once in while—proves that it is possible to be tough without being mean and generous without being a sucker. Above all, despite its frictions and inequalities, it rebukes nativists and proves that it is indeed possible for all the nations under heaven to live together in one great city.

ACKNOWLEDGMENTS

*A*ll *the Nations Under Heaven: Immigrants, Migrants, and the Making of New York*, is the second edition of a book that reflects decades of research, writing, conversations, and friendship.

The first edition, by David M. Reimers and the late Frederick M. Binder, was supported with sabbaticals from the College of Staten Island and New York University. Librarians at New York University, branches of the City University of New York, Columbia University, Fordham University, and the New York Public Library provided indispensible assistance. Thomas Kessner and Carl Prince read portions of the manuscript and offered useful advice, as did Leonard Dinnerstein, George Lankevich, and Phil Hosay when they read entire drafts. At Columbia University Press, Kate Wittenberg and Leslie Bialler were a pleasure to work with.

The second edition reunites a partnership that dates to the fall of 1979, when Robert W. Snyder, then a new doctoral student in American history at New York University, worked as a teaching assistant in Professor David M. Reimers's course in immigration history. The book also draws on Snyder's work at *Newsday* in the 1980s exploring immigration and New York City with the late Bernie Bookbinder, a superb journalist. This new edition of *All the Nations Under Heaven* has benefited from the advice of anonymous readers at Columbia University Press and the editorial guidance of Philip Leventhal, Michael Haskell, Rob Fellman, and Miriam Grossman. Librarians at Rutgers University–Newark, the New York Public Library, and the New York Society Library helped us countless times. Kat Morgan and Michaela Correa assisted with proofreading and research. Peter Eisenstadt and Clara Hemphill provided invaluable advice on historical and editorial matters. Any responsibility for errors is our own.

David M. Reimers

Robert W. Snyder

NOTES

1. A Seaport in the Atlantic World: 1624–1820

1. Anthony Stevens-Acevedo, Tom Weterings, and Leonor Alvarez Francés, *Juan Rodriguez and the Beginnings of New York City* (New York: Dominican Studies Institute, 2013), 2–8. The story of Juan (or Jan) Rodriguez appears with variations in, among other books, Edwin G. Burrows and Mike Wallace, *Gotham: A History of New York City to 1898* (New York: Oxford University Press, 1999), 19; and Graham Russell Hodges, *Root and Branch: African Americans in New York and East Jersey, 1613–1863* (Chapel Hill: University of North Carolina Press, 1999), 6.
2. On the importance of seeing New York's origins in a global perspective, see Thomas Bender, *A Nation Among Nations: America's Place in World History* (New York: Hill and Wang, 2006), 39–40, 44.
3. George J. Lankevich, *American Metropolis: A History of New York City* (New York: NYU Press, 1998), 3–4.
4. Alice P. Kenney, *Stubborn for Liberty: The Dutch in New York* (Syracuse, NY: Syracuse University Press, 1975), 19.
5. Burrows and Wallace, *Gotham*, 20; and David Steven Cohen, "How Dutch Were the Dutch of New Netherland?," *New York History* 62 (1981): 54–55.
6. Oliver Rink, "The People of New Netherland," *New York History* 62 (1981): 28, 10; Burrows and Wallace, *Gotham*, 24–26.
7. Oliver Rink, "The People of New Netherland," 13.
8. Burrows and Wallace, *Gotham*, 5–6; Anne-Marie Cantwell and Diana diZerega Wall, *Unearthing Gotham: The Archaeology of New York City* (New Haven, CT: Yale University Press, 2001), 143–45, Robert Grumet quote on 145; Evan Haefill, *New Netherland and the Dutch Origins of American Religious Liberty* (Philadelphia: University of Pennsylvania Press, 2012), 91.

9. Thomas Archdeacon, *New York City, 1664–1710: Conquest and Change* (Ithaca, NY: Cornell University Press, 1976), 32; Cohen, "How Dutch Were the Dutch of New Netherland?," 43, 51, 57.

10. Russell Shorto, *The Island in the Center of the World: The Epic Story of Dutch Manhattan and the Forgotten Colony That Shaped America* (New York: Doubleday, 2004), 121–28; Alan Taylor, *American Colonies* (New York: Viking, 2002), 252–55; Donna Merwick, *The Shame and the Sorrow: Dutch-Amerindian Encounters in New Netherland* (Philadelphia: University of Pennsylvania Press, 2006), 205–6, 266–67; Burrows and Wallace, *Gotham*, 12–13, 35–40; Kenney, *Stubborn for Liberty*, 27–28; Cantwell and Wall, *Unearthing Gotham*, 145.

11. Quoted in Kenney, *Stubborn for Liberty*, 2.

12. Tyler Anbinder, *City of Dreams: The Four-Hundred-Year Epic History of Immigrant New York* (New York: Houghton Mifflin Harcourt, 2016), 26–29.

13. Cohen, "How Dutch Were the Dutch of New Netherland?," 43, 51, 55, 57; Oliver Rink, *Holland on the Hudson: An Economic and Social History of Dutch New York* (Ithaca, NY: Cornell University Press,1986), 231–33.

14. Rink, *Holland on the Hudson*, 231–33.

15. Rink, *Holland on the Hudson*, 228–33; Haefill, *New Netherland*, 169–76.

16. Julie Scelfo, *The Women Who Made New York* (Berkeley, CA: Seal, 2016), 13.

17. Burrows and Wallace, *Gotham*, 61.

18. Howard Rock, *Haven of Liberty: New York Jews in the New World, 1624–1865* (New York: NYU Press, 2012), 7–9.

19. Rock, *Haven of Liberty*, 11.

20. Jacob Marcus, *Early American Jewry: The Jews of New York, New England, and Canada, 1649–17* (Philadelphia: Jewish Publication Society of America, 1951), 21–22.

21. Quoted in Morris U. Schappes, *A Documentary History of the Jews in the United States, 1654–1875* (New York: Schocken, 1971), 2–4.

22. Quoted in Schappes, *A Documentary History of the Jews in the United States*, 4–5.

23. Deborah Dash Moore, Jeffrey S. Gurock, Annie Polland, Howard B. Rock, and Daniel Soyer, with a visual essay by Diana L. Linden, *Jewish New York: The Remarkable Story of a City and a People* (New York: NYU Press, 2015), 14–17.

24. Rock, *Haven of Liberty*, 22.

25. Joyce Diane Goodfriend, *Before the Melting Pot: Society and Culture in Colonial New York City, 1664–1730* (Princeton, NJ: Princeton University Press, 1992), 10; Leslie M. Harris, *In the Shadow of Slavery: African Americans in New York City, 1626–1863* (Chicago: University of Chicago Press, 2003), 15.

26. Graham Hodges, *Root and Branch*, 8–12, 142; Goodfriend, *Before the Melting Pot*, 52.

27. Harris, *In the Shadow of Slavery*, 23–26; Shorto, *The Island in the Center of the World*, 273–74; and Hodges, *Root and Branch*, 12–14.

28. Hodges, *Root and Branch*, 7–13.

29. Hodges, *Root and Branch*, 7–13; Harris, *In the Shadow of Slavery*, 23–26; Christopher Moore, "A World of Possibilities," in *Slavery in New York*, ed. Ira Berlin and Leslie M. Harris (New York: New Press, 2005), 42.

30. Hodges, *Root and Branch*, 13. Sometimes an enslaved person had to make a payment to their owner. See also Harris, *In the Shadow of Slavery*, 23–26.

31. Hodges, *Root and Branch*, 9–18.

32. Goodfriend, *Before the Melting Pot*, 16. Goodfriend's analysis of population figures indicates that as many as 76 percent of the white population of New Amsterdam by 1664 may have been Dutch.

33. Norval White, *New York: A Physical History* (New York: Athenaeum, 1987), 20. The Heere Gracht, or Gentlemen's Canal, was filled in 1676 to form Broad Street. Also see Morton Wagman, "Liberty in New Amsterdam: A Sailor's Life in Early New York," *New York History* 64 (April 1983): 109. On New Amsterdam and the "Dutch Atlantic," see Susanah Shaw Romney, *New Netherland Connections: Intimate Networks and Atlantic Ties in Seventeenth-Century America* (Chapel Hill: University of North Carolina Press, 2014), 17–19, 70–71, 86–86, 95–102, 145–50.

34. Burrows and Wallace, *Gotham*, 72–74; and Bender, *A Nation Among Nations*, 40.

35. Archdeacon, *New York City, 1664–1710*, 97–98.

36. Goodfriend, *Before the Melting Pot*, 24.

37. Burrows and Wallace, *Gotham*, 82–83.

38. Archdeacon, *New York City, 1664–1710*, 97–98.

39. Thomas Archdeacon, "Anglo-Dutch New York, 1676" in *New York: The Centennial Years, 1676–1976*, ed. Milton Klein (Port Washington, NY, 1976), 100–4; Goodfriend, *Before the Melting Pot*, 56–57.

40. The Huguenots' experience is covered in Jon Butler, *The Huguenots in America: A Refugee People in a New World Society* (Cambridge, MA: Harvard University Press, 1983).

41. Archdeacon, *New York City, 1664–1710*, 53–54.

42. Joseph Dudley served as governor for only seven months before being replaced by Sir Edmund Andros in December 1686.

43. Archdeacon, *New York City, 1664–1710*, 104, 114, 115.

44. Burrows and Wallace, *Gotham*, 97–102.

45. Goodfriend, *Before the Melting Pot*, 85.

46. Archdeacon, *New York City, 1664–1710*, 142.

47. On exogamous marriages, see Kenney, *Stubborn for Liberty*, 125.

48. Bruce M. Wilkenfeld, "New York City Neighborhoods, 1730," *New York History* 57 (April 1976): 177, 180.

49. Archdeacon, "Anglo-Dutch New York," 31.

50. Quoted in Bayrd Still, *Mirror for Gotham: New York as Seen by Contemporaries from Dutch Days to the Present* (Westport, CT: Greenwood, 1956), 21.

51. Quoted in Archdeacon, *New York City, 1664–1710*, 33.

52. Butler, *The Huguenots in America*, 7, 57–58, 146–47. On the wards of colonial Manhattan and their ethnic geography, see Eric Homberger, *The Historical Atlas of New York City: A Visual Celebration of Four Hundred Years of New York City's History* (New York: Henry Holt, 1994, 2005), 40–43.

53. Butler, *The Huguenots in America*, 156–57.

54. Butler, *The Huguenots in America*, 147–53; Goodfriend, *Before the Melting Pot*, 77–78. Popular election of municipal officers was provided for in the municipal charter of 1686, the Dongan Charter.

55. Butler, *The Huguenots in America*, 158–61, 169–73, 187–98.

56. Archdeacon, *New York City, 1664–1710*, 45–46. The estimated Jewish population of the city stood at 100 in 1695, 300 in 1750, and 350 in 1794, according to Hyman B. Grinstein, *The Rise of the Jewish Community of New York, 1654–1860* (Philadelphia: Jewish Publication Society, 1945), 469. Rock gives a figure of 250 at the time of the American Revolution in *Haven of Liberty*, 71, 46.

57. Dash Moore et al., *Jewish New York*, 14–17.

58. Marcus, *Early American Jewry*, 35–42; Schappes, *A Documentary History of the Jews*, 18–19, 26–30.

59. Quoted in Still, *Mirror for Gotham*, 22.
60. Quoted in Archdeacon, "Anglo-Dutch New York, 1776," 29.
61. Marcus, *Early American Jewry*, 48, 55, 57; Grinstein, *The Rise of the Jewish Community in New York, 1654–1860*, 31.
62. Jill Lepore, *New York Burning: Liberty, Slavery, and Conspiracy in Eighteenth-Century Manhattan* (New York: Knopf, 2005), 182–83.
63. Burrows and Wallace, *Gotham*, 89.
64. Eric Foner, *Gateway to Freedom: The Hidden History of the Underground Railroad* (New York: Norton, 2015), 28–29. On English slavery, see Jill Lepore, "The Tightening Vise," in *Slavery in New York*, ed. Ira Berlin and Leslie M. Harris (New York: New Press, 2005), 60–61; on Pinkster, see Shane White, "'It Was a Proud Day': African Americans, Festivals, and Parades in the North, 1741–1834," *Journal of American History* 81 (June 1994): 18–21, 23–24, 30–31.
65. Lepore, *New York Burning*, 24; Lepore, "The Tightening Vise," 60–62.
66. Craig Steven Wilder, *A Covenant with Color: Race and Social Power in Brooklyn* (New York: Columbia University Press, 2000), 23–26; Richard Kluger, *Indelible Ink: The Trials of John Peter Zenger and the Birth of America's Free Press* (New York: Norton, 2016), 106.
67. Edgar McManus, *A History of Slavery in New York* (Syracuse, NY: Syracuse University Press, 1966), 45–47; Foner, *Gateway to Freedom*, 30–33.
68. Hodges, *Root and Branch*, 77–81, 152–55, 174–76; McManus, *A History of Negro Slavery*, 70–75.
69. McManus, *A History of Negro Slavery*, 101–8.
70. An account of the 1712 rebellion is Kenneth Scott, "The Slave Insurrection in New York in 1712," *New York Historical Quarterly* 45 (January 1961): 43–74.
71. McManus, *A History of Negro Slavery*, 124–25. For an excellent study of the 1741 revolt, see Lepore, *New York Burning*.
72. Burrows and Wallace, *Gotham*, 169–70; Steven Jaffe, *New York at War: Four Centuries of Combat, Fear, and Intrigue in Gotham* (New York: Basic Books, 2012), 67–71.
73. Mike Rapport, *The Unruly City: Paris, London, and New York in the Age of Revolution* (New York: Basic Books, 2017), xxxi.
74. Alan Taylor, *American Colonies*, 308; Ruma Chopra, *Unnatural Rebellion: Loyalists in New York City During the Revolution* (Charlottesville: University of Virginia Press, 2011), 20; Bruce Martin Wilkenfeld, "Revolutionary New York, 1776," in *New York: The Centennial Years, 1676–1976*, ed. Thomas Archdeacon and Milton Klein (Port Washington, NY: Kennitat, 1976), 43–47, 52, 55–56, 68.
75. Richard M. Ketchum, *Divided Loyalties: How the American Revolution Came to New York* (New York: Henry Holt, 2002), 13.
76. Chopra, *Unnatural Rebellion*, 14–15; Raymond Mohl, "Poverty in Early America. A Reappraisal: The Case of New York City," *New York History* 50 (January 1969): 4–27; Christine Stansell, *City of Women: Sex and Class in New York, 1789–1860* (New York: Knopf, 1986), 6.
77. Archdeacon, *New York City, 1664–1710*, 144–45; Patricia U. Bonomi, *A Factious People: Politics and Society in Colonial New York* (New York: Columbia University Press, 1971), 25–26.
78. Wilkenfeld, "Revolutionary New York, 1776," 61–62, 67; Still, *Mirror for Gotham*, 21–22; and quote from Samuel Shaw, *The Journals of Major Samuel Shaw, the First American Consul at Canton* (Boston: Wm. Crosby and H. P. Nichols, 1847), 11.
79. Jaffe, *New York at War*, 102–3.

80. Jaffe, *New York at War*, 102–3; Graham Russell Hodges, "Liberty and Constraint," in *Slavery in New York*, ed. Ira Berlin and Leslie M. Harris (New York: New Press, 2005), 103.

81. Hodges, "Liberty and Constraint," 104–7; Jaffe, *New York at War*, 108–9.

82. Wilkenfeld, "Revolutionary New York, 1776," 62; Jay Dolan, *The Immigrant Church: New York's Irish and German Catholics, 1815–1865* (Baltimore, MD: Johns Hopkins University Press, 1982), 11; Burrows and Wallace, *Gotham*, 265–70, 281–87; Maya Jasanoff, *Liberty's Exiles: American Loyalists in the Revolutionary World* (New York: Knopf, 2011), 317–19.

83. Burrows and Wallace, *Gotham*, 265.

84. Ira Rosenwaike, *Population History of New York City* (Syracuse, NY: Syracuse University Press, 1972), 16–21; Sidney Pomerantz, *New York, an American City, 1783–1803: A Study of Urban Life* (Port Washington NY: I. J. Friedman, 1938), 203–5.

85. Pomerantz, *New York, an American City*, 204–205; Frances Childs, *French Refugee Life in the United States, 1790–1800* (Baltimore, MD: Johns Hopkins University Press, 1940), 195–99; Dolan, *The Immigrant Church*, 9.

86. Pomerantz, *New York, an American City*, 205–6.

87. Quoted in *New York, an American City*, 206.

88. Quoted in *New York, an American City*, 203. See also James Morton Smith, *Freedom's Fetters: The Alien and Sedition Laws and American Civil Liberties* (Ithaca, NY: Cornell University Press, 1956), 162.

89. Rosenwaike, *Population History*, 16; and Robert Albion, *The Rise of New York Port, 1815–1860* (repr., Boston, 1984; originally Hamden, CT: Archon, 1939), 8. The city's political prominence as the seat of state and national governments, however, had been lost to Albany (1797) and Philadelphia (1790).

90. Pomerantz, *New York, an American City*, 204, 206, 208.

91. Anne Boylan, "Women in Groups: Analysis of Women's Benevolent Organizations in New York and Boston, 1797–1840," *Journal of American History* 71 (December 1984), 499–501.

92. Hodges, *Root and Branch*, 163–65.

93. Edgar McManus, "Anti-Slavery Legislation in New York," *Journal of Negro History* 46 (October 1961): 208–10; Arthur Zilversmit, *The First Emancipation: The Abolition of Slavery in the North* (Chicago: University of Chicago Press, 1967), 146–49.

94. Foner, *Gateway to Freedom*, 39–43; Hodges, *Root and Branch*, 177–78.

95. See Shane White, *Somewhat More Independent: The End of Slavery in New York City, 1790–1810* (Athens: University of Georgia University Press, 1991); Leo Hirsch, "The Negro and New York, 1783 to 1865," *Journal of Negro History* 16, no. 4 (October 1931): 391; Foner, *Gateway to Freedom*, 44–45.

96. See Phyllis Field, *Politics of Race in New York: The Struggle for Black Suffrage in the Civil War Era* (Ithaca, NY: Cornell University Press, 1982), for the struggle to gain the ballot for black men.

97. Hodges, *Root and Branch*, 239–43.

98. Hodges, *Root and Branch*, 197–98, 206–10.

99. W. Jeffrey Bolster, *Black Jacks: African American Seamen in the Age of Sail* (Cambridge, MA: Harvard University Press, 1997), 160–61, 176, 183, 185, 191, 218–20, 222–30, 235–36, 238.

100. Kyle Bulthus, *Steeples Over the City Streets: Religion and Society in New York's Early Republic Congregations* (New York: NYU Press, 2014), chap. 5; Foner, *Gateway to Freedom*, 67–73; Hodges, *Root and Branch*, 199–200, 238–39, 243–44, 247–51.

101. See Bernie Bookbinder, with research by Robert W. Snyder and photography by Harvey Weber, *City of the World: New York and Its People* (New York: Abrams, 1989), 93–94; and Robert G. Albion, *The Rise of New York Port: 1815–1860* (New York: Charles Scribner's Sons, 1970), 12.

102. Albion, *The Rise of New York Port*, 38–43; "The Port of Liverpool," information sheet 34, National Museums Liverpool, http://www.liverpoolmuseums.org.uk/maritime/archive/sheet/34.

103. Albion, *The Rise of New York Port*, 95–97, 99–101, 118, 120–21.

104. Edward Robb Ellis, *The Epic of New York City: A Narrative History* (New York, 1990), 216–17; Albion, *The Rise of New York Port*, 13, 14, 85–94; Robert Ernst, *Immigrant Life in New York City, 1825–1863* (repr., New York: Coward-McCann, 1979; original printing, New York, 1949), 14.

105. Edward Spann, *The New Metropolis, New York City, 1840–1857* (New York: Columbia University Press, 1981), 405; Bookbinder, *City of the World*, 103–4, and Ernst, *Immigrant Life in New York*, 17–18.

106. Quote in Spann, *The New Metropolis*, 3–4.

107. New York City's population, which stood at 96,373 in 1810, rose to 813,669 by 1860. The neighboring city of Brooklyn by that latter date had attained a population of 266,661. See Rosenwaike, *Population History*, 16, 36, 51.

108. Albion, *The Rise of New York Port*, 235, 241–42, quote, 242; Spann, *New Metropolis*, 7.

2. Becoming a City of the World: 1820–1860

1. The drawing of the *Kossuth*, reproduced in Terry Coleman's masterful *Going to America* (New York: Pantheon, 1972), first appeared in *Gleason's Pictorian Drawing Room Companion* 1, no. 6 (August 9, 1851): 85. Immigration records verify that a ship called the *Kossuth* carried immigrants from Liverpool to New York in 1851. See the list of passengers in "Ship Kossuth, Liverpool to New York: CMSIED 9808251," http://www.dippam.ac.uk/ied/records/33973.

2. Edwin G. Burrows and Mike Wallace, *Gotham: A History of New York City to 1898* (New York: Oxford University Press, 1999), 649–66. On cotton in the world economy and shipping, see Sven Beckert, *Empire of Cotton: A Global History* (New York: Knopf, 2014), 200–7, 217–18.

3. Robert G. Albion, *The Rise of New York Port: 1815–1860* (New York: Charles Scribner's Sons, 1970), 337, 418.

4. In 1860, Brooklyn's foreign-born population was 39 percent of its total of 256,661 residents. On this statistic and more, see Ira Rosenwaike, *Population History of New York* (Syracuse, NY: Syracuse University Press, 1972), 36, 39, 63.

5. On immigration in these years, see Juliana F. Gilheany, "Subjects of History: English, Scottish, and Welsh Immigrants in New York City, 1820–1860," PhD diss., New York University, 1989, 32. For examples of the varying but devastating statistics regarding the Great Famine, see "Great Famine" in *The Oxford Companion to Irish History*, 2nd ed., ed. S. J. Connoly (Oxford: University of Oxford Press, 2012), 239–40; and R. F. Foster, *Modern Ireland* (New York: Penguin, 1988), 323–24.

6. Richard Stott, *Workers in the Metropolis: Class, Ethnicity, and Youth in Antebellum New York City* (Ithaca, NY: Cornell University Press, 1990), 80.

7. Stott, *Workers in the Metropolis*, 77–82.

8. Dorothee Schneider, *Crossing Borders: Migration and Citizenship in the Twentieth-Century United States* (Cambridge, MA: Harvard University Press, 2011), 14–15.

9. Gilheany, "Subjects of History," 50–58. Detailed descriptions of the numerous hazards of the voyage are found in Albion, *The Rise of New York Port*, 341–49; and Schneider, *Crossing Borders*, 11–18.

10. Robert Ernst, *Immigrant Life in New York City, 1825–1863* (New York: Octagon, 1979), 25–29; Albion, *The Rise of New York Port*, 348–49.

11. Albion, *The Rise of New York Port*, 350–52; Ernst, *Immigrant Life*, 29–32.

12. George Templeton Strong, July 7, 1857, cited in William V. Shannon, *The American Irish: A Political and Social Portrait* (Amherst: University of Massachusetts Press, 1989), 3.

13. Hasia Diner, "The Most Irish City in the Union: The Era of the Great Migration," in *The New York Irish*, ed. Ronald H. Bayor and Timothy J. Meagher (Baltimore, MD: Johns Hopkins University Press, 1996), 94.

14. Quoted in Jay P. Dolan, *The Immigrant Church: New York's Irish and German Catholics, 1815–1865* (Baltimore, MD: Johns Hopkins University Press, 1975), 33. See also Kerby A. Miller, *Emigrants and Exiles: Ireland and the Irish Exodus to North America* (New York: Oxford University Press, 1985).

15. Maureen Fitzgerald, *Habits of Compassion: Irish Catholic Nuns and the Origins of New York's Welfare System, 1830–1920* (Urbana: University of Illinois Press, 2006), 65.

16. The 1855 census of Irish male workers in the Sixth Ward reveals that almost 53 percent were unskilled laborers, 34 percent were skilled artisans and members of the building trades, and fewer than 145 were in other occupations, ranging from clerical workers, shopkeepers, and salesmen to professionals and factory owners. See Carol Pernicone, "The 'Bloody Ould Sixth,' a Social Analysis of a New York City Working-Class Community in the Mid–Nineteenth Century," PhD diss., University of Rochester, 1973, 71–72, 100–1, 163.

17. Fitzgerald, *Habits of Compassion*, 65.

18. James R. Barrett, *The Irish Way: Becoming American in the Multiethnic City* (New York: Penguin, 2012), 77.

19. Christine Stansell, *City of Women: Sex and Class in New York, 1789–1860* (New York: Knopf, 1986), 156; David Katzman, *Seven Days a Week: Women and Domestic Service in Industrializing America* (New York: Oxford University Press, 1978), 66–67.

20. Faye E. Dudden, *Serving Women: Household Service in Nineteenth-Century America* (Middletown, CT: Wesleyan University Press, 1983), 61.

21. Stansell, *City of Women*, 156–65; Tyler Anbinder, "Moving Beyond 'Rags to Riches': New York's Irish Famine Immigrants and Their Surprising Savings Accounts," *Journal of American History* 99, no. 3 (December 2012): 741–70; Margaret Lynch-Brennan, *Irish Immigrant Women in Domestic Service in America, 1840–1930* (Syracuse, NY: Syracuse University Press, 2009), 60–121.

22. Stansell, *City of Women*, 178; Fitzgerald, *Habits of Compassion*, 56.

23. Dolan, *The Immigrant Church*, 32; Shannon, *The American Irish*, 40.

24. Shannon, *The American Irish*, 40.

25. Edward Robb Ellis, *The Epic of New York City: A Narrative History* (New York: Basic Books, 1990), 231, 233; Barrett, *The Irish Way*, 16–29, 37–50; Tyler Anbinder, *Five Points: The Nineteenth-Century New York City Neighborhood That Invented Tap Dancing, Stole Elections, and Became the World's Most Notorious Slum* (New York: Free Press, 2001), 27–32.

26. Iver Bernstein, *The New York City Draft Riots: Their Significance for American Society and Politics in the Age of the Civil War* (New York: Oxford University Press, 1990), 5, 119–20; Ernst, *Immigrant Life in New York City*, 107; Barrett, *The Irish Way*, 18–20, 27; Anbinder, *Five Points*, 274–92; Elliot J. Gorn, "'Good-Bye Boys, I Die a True American': Homicide, Nativism, and Working-Class Culture in Antebellum New York," *Journal of American History* 74, no. 2 (September 1987): 388–410.

27. George J. Lankevich, *American Metropolis: A History of New York City* (New York: NYU Press, 1998), 74.

28. Burrows and Wallace, *Gotham*, 761–66; also Peter G. Buckley, "To the Opera House: Culture and Society in New York City, 1820–1869," PhD diss., State University of New York at Stony Brook, 1984.

29. Dolan, *The Immigrant Church*, 6.

30. Ellis, *New York City*, 268, 361; Dolan, *The Immigrant Church*, 165. For a biography of Archbishop Hughes, see Richard Shaw, *Dagger John: The Unquiet Life and Times of Archbishop John Hughes* (New York: Paulist, 1977).

31. Edward Spann, *The New Metropolis: New York City, 1840–1857* (New York: Columbia University Press, 1981), 29.

32. Ellis, *The Epic of New York City*, 268, 361.

33. Dolan, *The Immigrant Church*, 56. Dolan claims "that not more than 60 percent and closer to 40 percent of the people attended Sunday services in the 1860s" (56).

34. Frederick M. Binder, *The Age of the Common School, 1830–1865* (New York: John Wiley and Sons, 1974), 64.

35. The school controversy is covered in John Pratt, "Governor Seward and the New York City School Controversy, 1840–1842," *New York History* 42 (1961): 351–65.

36. Quoted in Pratt, "Governor Seward and the New York City School Controversy," 362.

37. Dolan, *The Immigrant Church*, 104–5.

38. Dolan, *The Immigrant Church*, 108.

39. Dolan, *The Immigrant Church*, 109; Joseph McCadden, "Governor Seward's Friendship with Bishop Hughes," *New York History* 57 (1966): 179.

40. Quoted in Robert Ernst, "Economic Nativism in New York City During the 1840s," *New York History* 29 (April 1948): 173.

41. Douglas T. Miller, "Immigration and Social Stratification in Pre–Civil War New York," *New York History* 49 (April 1968): 159, 167.

42. Miller, "Immigration and Social Stratification," 162.

43. Spann, *The New Metropolis*, 41.

44. Quoted in Leonard R. Riforgiato, "Bishop John Timon, Archbishop John Hughes, and Irish Colonization: A Clash of Episcopal Views on the Future of the Irish and the Catholic Church in America," in *Immigration to New York*, ed. William Pencak, Selma Berrol, and Randall M. Miller (Philadelphia: Balch Institute for Ethnic Studies, 1991), 33.

45. Riforgiato, "Bishop John Timon," 43.

46. McCadden, "Governor Seward's Friendship with Bishop Hughes," 177–78; Leo Hershkowitz, "The Native American Democratic Association in New York City," *New York Historical Quarterly* 46 (January 1962): 50. The Know Nothings in 1854 advocated barring all Catholics from public office: Spann, *The New Metropolis*, 338.

47. Leo Hershkowitz, "The Native American Democratic Association in New York City," 41; Ira M. Leonard, "The Rise and Fall of the American Republican Party in New York City, 1843–1845," *New York Historical Quarterly* 50 (April 1966): 151; Spann, *The New Metropolis*, 338; Miller, *Emigrants and Exiles*, 329.

48. Hidaka Hirota, *Expelling the Poor: Atlantic Seaboard States and the Nineteenth-Century Origins of American Immigration Policy* (New York: Oxford University Press, 2017), 4–8, 56, 83, 97, 107–11, 157, 165–79, 207–11, and appendix E, "Persons Assisted or Excluded from New York by the Commissioners of Emigration and the State Board of Charities, 1850–1890," 219–20.

49. Fitzgerald, *Habits of Compassion*, 70–71.

50. Carroll Smith-Rosenberg, *Religion and the Rise of the American City: The New York City Mission Movement, 1812–1870* (Ithaca, NY: Cornell University Press, 1971), 94.

51. Smith-Rosenberg, *Religion and the Rise of the American City*, 98.

52. James Sigurd Lapham, "The German Americans of New York City, 1860–1890," PhD diss., St. John's University, 1977, 17; Dolan, *The Immigrant Church*, 10; Dorothee Schneider, *Trade Unions and Community: The German Working Class in New York City, 1870–1900* (Urbana: University of Illinois, 1994), 1–22.

53. Dolan, *The Immigrant Church*, 35.

54. Stanley Nadel, "From the Barricades of Paris to the Sidewalks of New York: German Artisans and the European Roots of American Labor Radicalism," in *Immigration to New York*, ed. William Pencak, Selma Berrol, and Randall M. Miller (Philadelphia: Balch Institute for Ethnic Studies, 1991), 33.

55. Schneider, *Trade Unions and Community*, 22–24.

56. Stanley Nadel, *Little Germany: Ethnicity, Religion, and Class in New York City* (Urbana: University of Illinois Press, 1990), 63, 75–79.

57. Edward T. O'Donnell, *Ship Ablaze: The Tragedy of the Steamboat* General Slocum (New York: Broadway, 2003), 29.

58. Lapham, "The German-Americans," 19, 44; Nadel, *Little Germany*, 88.

59. Spann, *The New Metropolis*, 25–26; Nadel, "From the Barricades," 71.

60. Rebecca Fried, "No Irish Need Deny: Evidence for the Historicity of NINA Restrictions in Advertisements and Signs," *Journal of Social History* 49 (Summer 2016): 829–52; Richard Jensen "No Irish Need Apply?," http://historynewsnetwork.org/article /160234.ol.

61. Nadel, *Little Germany*, 1, 29–32.

62. Otto Lohr, "Das New York Deutschtum der Vergangenheit," in *Das Deutsche Element der Stadt New York*, ed. Otto Spengler (New York, 1913), 12; quoted in Nadel, *Little Germany*, 36. See also Schneider, *Trade Unions and Community*, 15–16.

63. O'Donnell, *Ship Ablaze*, 29.

64. Dolan, *The Immigrant Church*, 70.

65. Nadel, *Little Germany*, 49, 37–39.

66. Quoted in Nadel, *Little Germany*, 93.

67. Nadel, *Little Germany*, 92–93; Dolan, *The Immigrant Church*, 72–73.

68. Nadel, *Little Germany*, 90–91. Nadel also discusses the divisive issue of the hierarchy's strong pro-temperance position, which found little support in the German community, on 128–29.

69. Nadel, *Little Germany*, 92; Lapham, "German-Americans," 55. By 1890, Manhattan housed 12 German parishes; in 1891, Brooklyn numbered 23 German parishes. See Lapham, "German-Americans," 49–50.

70. Lapham, "German-Americans," 54–59.

71. Dolan, *The Immigrant Church*, 73, 80–81; Nadel, *Little Germany*, 92–95.

72. Nadel, *Little Germany*, 120–28; Ernst, *Immigrant Life*, 139.

73. Ernst, *Immigrant Life*, 85, 112, 114.

74. Ernst, *Immigrant Life*, 109; Nadel, *Little Germany*, 97.

75. Deborah Dash Moore, Jeffrey S. Gurock, Annie Polland, Howard B. Rock, and Daniel Soyer, with a visual essay by Diana L. Linden, *Jewish New York: The Remarkable Story of a City and a People* (New York: NYU Press, 2017), 53–59.

76. Dash Moore et al., *Jewish New York*, 43–50; Burrows and Wallace, *Gotham*, 748–49. On the importance of Temple Emanu-El, see Jenna Weisman Joselit, "Temple Emanu-El," in *The Encyclopedia of New York City*, 2nd ed., ed. Kenneth T. Jackson (New Haven, CT: Yale University Press, 2010), 1289.

77. Amie Klempnauer, "Ethical Culture Society of New York," in *The Encyclopedia of New York City*, 2nd ed., ed. Kenneth T. Jackson (New Haven, CT: Yale University Press, 2010), 422; Ernst, *Immigrant Life*, 139.

78. Ernst, *Immigrant Life*,153–55; Lapham, "German-Americans," 25–27.

79. Ernst, *Immigrant Life*, 153–55; Nadel, *Little Germany*, 154.

80. Lapham, "German-Americans," 69–71.

81. Stott, *Workers in the Metropolis*, 219, 228, 221; Nadel, *Little Germany*, 104–6; Lapham, "German-Americans," 27.

82. Ernst, *Immigrant Life*, 130–31; Nadel, *Little Germany*, 120–21.

83. Nadel, *Little Germany*, 107, 108; Ernst, *Immigrant Life*, 131. The description of the Turnverein festival of 1856 is quoted in Bernie Bookbinder, with research by Robert W. Snyder and photography by Harvey Weber, *City of the World: New York and Its People* (New York: Abrams, 1989), 25.

84. Annie Polland and Daniel Soyer, *Emerging Metropolis: New York Jews in the Age of Immigration, 1840–1920* (New York: NYU Press, 2012), 39–43.

85. Ernst, *Immigrant Life*, 108–11. For German union activity, see Schneider, *Trade Unions and Community*, 58–88, 119–208.

86. Ernst, *Immigrant Life*, 115–17; Lapham, "German-Americans," 37–38; Nadel, *Little Germany*, 124–25.

87. Ernst, *Immigrant Life*,118–21; Lapham, "German-Americans," 38–42; Nadel, *Little Germany*, 128–30, 137.

88. Christiane Harzig, "The Role of German Women in the German American Working-Class Movement in Late Nineteenth-Century New York," *Journal of American History* 9 (1989): 95, 98.

89. Gilheany, "Subjects of History," 111–15, 123–24, 137–40.

90. Gilheany, "Subjects of History," 137–45.

91. Michael A. Gordon, *The Orange Riots: Irish Political Violence in New York City, 1870 and 1871* (Ithaca, NY: Cornell University Press, 1993), 22–23.

92. Gordon, *The Orange Riots*, 22.

93. Ernst, *Immigrant Life*, 42–45.

94. Michael Contopoulos, "The Greek Community of New York City: Early Years to 1910," PhD diss., New York University, 1972, chaps. 1–2; Sister Adele Dabrowski, "A History and Survey of the Polish Community in Brooklyn," MA thesis, Fordham University, 1946, 78–79, 152; Kate Claghorn, "The Foreign Immigrant in New York City," *Industrial Commission* 15 (Washington, 1908): 472; Josephine Hendin, "Italian Neighbors," in *Greenwich Village: Culture and Counterculture*, ed. Richard Beard and Leslie Berlowitz (New Brunswick, NJ: Rutgers University Press, 1993), 142–44; Scott D. Seligman, *Tong Wars: The Untold Story of Vice, Money, and Murder in New York's Chinatown* (New York: Viking, 2016), 1–5.

95. Dolan, *The Immigrant Church*, 13–15; Pernicone, "The 'Bloody Ould Sixth,'" 33.

96. Pernicone, "The 'Bloody Ould Sixth,'" 36; Ernst, *Immigrant Life*, 193. For a map of the Sixth Ward in 1840, see "Map of the Sixth Ward in the City of New York" (1860),

collections of the Museum of the City of New York, http://collections.mcny.org/Col
lection/Map-of-the-Sixth-Ward-in-the-City-of-New-York-2F3XC5U9NCRK.html.

97. The wards cited had the highest percentage of Irish and German immigrants in 1855. Ernst, *Immigrant Life*, 193; Stott, *Workers in the Metropolis*, 204–5.

98. Pernicone, "The 'Bloody Ould Sixth,'" 33–34.

99. Quoted in Dolan, *The Immigrant Church*, 34.

100. Quoted in Dolan, *The Immigrant Church*, 34

101. Stott, *Workers in the Metropolis*, 169.

102. Gilheany, "Subjects of History," 153.

103. Gilheany, "Subjects of History," 172.

104. Lankevich, *American Metropolis*, 71–75.

105. In her study of the Sixth Ward, Carol Pernicone found that young Irish immigrants were an exception to the rule, generally preferring to board with Irish families rather than in boardinghouses. Pernicone, "The 'Bloody Ould Sixth,'" 62, 63.

106. Based on the account in Thomas B. Gunn, *The Physiology of New York Boarding-Houses* (New York: Mason Brothers, 1857), 111–12; cited in Pernicone, "The 'Bloody Ould Sixth,'" 63.

107. Stott, *Workers in the Metropolis*, 214–16.

108. Pernicone, "The 'Bloody Ould Sixth,'" 63.

109. Catherine McNeur, *Taming Manhattan: Environmental Battles in the Antebellum City* (Cambridge, MA: Harvard University Press, 2014), 160–70.

110. Ernst, *Immigrant Life*, 54; David Oshinsky, *Bellevue: Three Centuries of Medicine and Mayhem at America's Most Storied Hospital* (New York: Doubleday, 2016), 40–43.

111. Oshinsky, *Bellevue*, 40–41.

112. Quoted in Burrows and Wallace, *Gotham*, 593.

113. Burrows and Wallace, *Gotham*, 135.

114. Anbinder, *Five Points*, 347–49, 353; McNeur, *Taming Manhattan*, 29, 60, 65–66, 197.

115. Anbinder, *Five Points*, 86.

116. Quoted in Roy Lubove, *The Progressives and the Slum: Tenement House Reform in New York City* (Pittsburgh, PA: University of Pittsburgh Press 1962), 7; Dolan, *The Immigrant Church*, 34; Bayard Still, *Mirror for Gotham: New York as Seen by Contemporaries from Dutch Days to the Present* (New York: NYU Press, 1956), 243.

117. Eric Foner, *Gateway to Freedom: The Hidden History of the Underground Railroad* (New York: Norton, 2015), 47; Rhoda Freeman, "The Free Negro, in New York City in the Era Before the Civil War," PhD diss., Columbia University, 1966, 219–22.

118. Ellis, *New York City*, 231–32.

119. Quoted in Still, *Mirror for Gotham*, 123. An excellent study of the Five Points is Anbinder, *Five Points*.

120. Freeman, "The Free Negro," 229–31; Walker, "The Afro American," 13–16; Graham Hodges, *Root and Branch, African Americans in New York and East New Jersey, 1613–1863* (Chapel Hill: University of North Carolina Press, 1999), 210, 235; Leslie M. Harris, "From Abolitionist Amalgamators to 'Rulers of the Five Points': The Discourse of Interracial Sex and Reform in Antebellum New York City," in *Sex, Love, Race: Crossing Boundaries in North American History*, ed. Martha Hodes (New York: NYU Press, 1999), 192, 197, 200–7.

121. Quoted in Shane White, "Black Life in Freedom: Creating a Popular Culture," in *Slavery in New York*, ed. Ira Berlin and Leslie M. Harris (New York: New Press, 2005), 171.

122. Eric Lott, *Love and Theft: Blackface Minstrelsy and the American Working Class* (New York: Oxford University Press, 1993); Alexander Saxton, "Blackface Minstrelsy and

Jacksonian Ideology," *American Quarterly* 27, no 1. (March 1975): 3–28; W. T. Lhamon Jr., *Raising Cain: Blackface Performance from Jim Crow to Hip Hop* (Cambridge, MA: Harvard University Press, 2000); W. T. Lhamon Jr., *Jump Jim Crow: Lost Plays, Lyrics, and Street Prose of the First Atlantic Popular Culture* (Cambridge, MA: Harvard University Press, 2003).

123. Shannon, *The American Irish*, 49–50; Anthony Gronowicz, "Labor's Decline Within New York City's Democratic Party from 1844 to 1884," in *Immigration to New York*, ed. William Pencak, Selma Berrol, and Randall M. Miller (Philadelphia: Balch Institute for Ethnic Studies, 1991), 9.

124. Stott, *Workers in the Metropolis*, 236.

125. Ernst, *Immigrant Life*, 165; Shannon, *The American Irish*, 15, 52.

126. Burrows and Wallace, *Gotham*, 825.

127. Stott, *Workers in the Metropolis*, 236; Shannon, *The American Irish*, 52–54.

128. Hirsch, "The Negro and New York," 436–37; Albon P. Man Jr., "Labor Competition and the New York Draft Riots of 1863," *Journal of Negro History* 36 (October 1951): 376–77. Rhoda Freemen ("The Free Negro," 289–90) does not believe the Irish and blacks were in direct competition.

129. Man, "Labor Competition," 393–94; Leon Litwack, *North of Slavery: The Negro in the Free States, 1790–1860* (Chicago: University of Chicago Press, 1961), 160.

130. Man, "Labor Competition," 389–90.

131. Jane Dabel, *A Respectable Woman* (New York: NYU Press, 2008), 63–67.

132. Leslie M. Alexander, *African or American? Black Identity and Political Activism in New York City, 1784–1861* (Urbana: University of Illinois Press, 2012), 126–30.

133. Quoted in Hirsch, "The Negro and New York," 424–25.

134. Freeman, "The Free Negro," 320–46, 356–72.

135. Robert Swan Jr., "Did Brooklyn (N.Y.) Blacks Have Unusual Control Over Their Schools: Period I: 1815–45?," *Afro Americans in New York Life and History* 7 (July 1983): 25–46.

136. Quoted in Gilbert Osofsky, "The Enduring Ghetto," *Journal of American History* 40 (September 1968): 246, 253.

137. Manisha Sinha, *The Slave's Cause: A History of Abolition* (New Haven, CT: Yale University Press, 2016), 142; Walker, "The Afro American," 140–45; Dabel, *A Respectable Woman*, 141–46.

138. Shane White, "Black Life in Freedom," in *Slavery in New York*, ed. Ira Berlin and Leslie M. Harris (New York: New Press, 2005), 179–80.

139. Foner, *Gateway to Freedom*, 1–4.

140. For the role of New York City in the underground railroad, see Foner, *Gateway to Freedom*, 165–172. For the important role of David Ruggles, consult Graham Hodges, *David Ruggles: A Radical Black Abolitionist and the Underground Railroad in New York City* (Chapel Hill: North Carolina University Press, 2010).

141. Alexander, *African or American?*, 122.

142. John Strausbaugh, *City of Sedition: The History of New York City During the Civil War* (New York: Twelve Hachette Book Group, 2016), 21.

143. On Republican nativism, see James M. McPherson, *Ordeal by Fire: The Civil War and Reconstruction* (New York: Knopf, 1982), 89–91. On the New York elite accommodating the South, see Sven Beckert, *The Monied Metropolis: New York City and the Consolidation of the American Bourgeoisie, 1850–1896* (New York: Cambridge University Press, 2001), 85–97. Also see Burrows and Wallace, *Gotham*, 866.

144. Nadel, *Little Germany*, 135; Ernst, *Immigrant Life*, 167.
145. Anthony Gronowicz, *Race and Class Politics in New York City Before the Civil War* (Boston: Northeastern University Press, 1998), 157.
146. Burrows and Wallace, *Gotham*, 844–45, 849–51; Anbinder, *City of Dreams*, 202–3.
147. Anbinder, *City of Dreams*, 120–26; Beckert, *The Monied Metropolis*, 85–90.
148. James McPherson, *Ordeal by Fire*, 127; Burrows and Wallace, *Gotham*, 867–68.
149. McPherson, *Ordeal by Fire*, 142–45. For the quote, see "Bombardment of Fort Sumter," *New York Herald*, April 13, 1861.

3. Progress and Poverty: 1861–1900

1. Edwin G. Burrows and Mike Wallace, *Gotham: A History of New York City to 1898* (New York: Oxford University Press, 1999), 868–70. The Union Square rally is covered in "New-York to the Rescue!" *New York Times*, April 21, 1861. See Emile Dupré, letter of April 26, 1861, in Walter D. Kamphoefner and Wolfgang Helbich, eds., *Germans in the Civil War: The Letters They Wrote Home* (Chapel Hill: University of North Carolina Press, 2006), 44.
2. Kamphoefner and Helbich, *Germans in the Civil War*, 39, 48, 52–59, quote from 58.
3. Burrows and Wallace, *Gotham*, 870.
4. Burrows and Wallace, *Gotham*, 870–71.
5. Burrows and Wallace, *Gotham*, 872.
6. Kenneth T. Jackson, "The Civil War," in *The Encyclopedia of New York City*, 2nd ed., ed. Kenneth Jackson (New Haven, CT: Yale University Press, 2010), 264.
7. Sven Beckert, *The Monied Metropolis: New York City and the Consolidation of the American Bourgeoisie, 1850–1896* (New York: Cambridge University Press, 2001), 117–18.
8. Burrows and Wallace, *Gotham*, 873–75.
9. Burrows and Wallace, *Gotham*, 875.
10. Burrows and Wallace, *Gotham*, 877–79.
11. Burrows and Wallace, *Gotham*, 883–84; Ernst McKay, *The Civil War and New York City* (Syracuse, NY: Syracuse University Press, 1990), 216.
12. Terry L. Jones, "The Fighting Irish Brigade," *New York Times*, December 11, 2012.
13. James M. McPherson, *Ordeal by Fire: The Civil War and Reconstruction* (New York: Knopf, 1982), 297–98.
14. McPherson, *Ordeal by Fire*, 355–57.
15. Quoted in McKay, *The Civil War*, 196, 150; quoted in Jay Dolan, *The Immigrant Church: German and Irish Catholics in New York City* (Baltimore, MD: Johns Hopkins University Press, 1975), 24–25.
16. Adrian Cook, *The Armies of the Streets: The New York City Draft Riots of 1863* (Lexington: University of Kentucky Press, 1974), 55–58, 62–63, 72–73, 88–91, 117, 129; Burrows and Wallace, *Gotham*, 893; Howard Rock, *Haven of Liberty: New York Jews in the New World, 1624–1865* (New York: NYU Press, 2012), 245, 249.
17. Cook, *Armies of the Streets*, 77–84, 98–100, 132–36, 140–44, 158, 203.
18. Cook, *Armies of the Streets*, 77, 83, 159, 133.
19. Cook, *Armies of the Streets*, 72, 101, 118–19, 196, 106; Wallace and Burrows, *Gotham*, 890, 894.

20. Cook, *Armies of the Streets*, 163–64, 175–77; Burrows and Wallace, *Gotham*, 895.

21. Burrows and Wallace, *Gotham*, 896.

22. Cook, *Armies of the Streets*, 174–75; Burrows and Wallace, *Gotham*, 897, 904–5; David Quigley, *Second Founding: New York City, Reconstruction, and the Making of American Democracy* (New York: Hill and Wang, 2004), 24.

23. Jackson, "The Civil War," 264.

24. Quigley, *Second Founding*, 39–44, 59, 64.

25. See Thomas Nast, "This Is a White Man's Government," *Harper's Weekly* 12 (September 5, 1868): 568.

26. Quigley, *Second Founding*, 71–72, 81–89.

27. William Shannon, *The American Irish* (Amherst: University of Massachusetts Press, 1989), 68.

28. On the plasterer Peter Garvey, see Bernie Bookbinder, with research by Robert W. Snyder and photography by Harvey Weber, *City of the World: New York and Its People* (New York: Abrams, 1989), 63. One the general operations of the Tweed Ring, see Thomas Kessner, *Capital City: New York City and the Men Behind America's Rise to Economic Dominance, 1860–1900* (New York: Simon and Schuster, 2003), 136–49.

29. On the outcome of the war and the Irish, see McKay, *The Civil War and New York City*, 75–76. On the Orange riot, see Iver Bernstein, *The New York City Draft Riots: Their Significance for American Society and Politics in the Age of the Civil War* (New York: Oxford University Press, 1991), 228–33. For a detailed description of the riot as well as one the previous year, see Stephen J. Sullivan, "The Orange and Green Riots (New York City: July 1870 & 1871)," *New York Irish History* 6 (1991–1992): 4–12, 46–59; and Michael Gordon, *The Orange Riots: Irish Political Violence in New York City, 1870 and 1871* (Ithaca, NY: Cornell University Press, 1993).

30. Bookbinder, *City of the World*, 21–22.

31. Burrows and Wallace, *Gotham*, 1008.

32. Bookbinder, *City of the World*, 63–65.

33. Burrows and Wallace, *Gotham*, 1009; Edward T. O'Donnell, *Henry George and the Crisis of Inequality: Progress and Poverty in the Gilded Age* (New York: Columbia University Press, 2015), 85.

34. Ira M. Leonard, "The Rise and Fall of the American Republican Party in New York City, 1843–1845," *New York Historical Quarterly* 50 (April 1966): 155, 192; Joseph J. McCadden, "Governor Seward's Friendship with Bishop Hughes," *New York History* 47 (April 1966): 179; Shannon, *The American Irish*, 71; Stanley Nadel, *Little Germany: Ethnicity, Religion, and Class in New York City, 1845–1880* (Urbana: University of Illinois Press, 1990), 152; James Lapham, "The German-Americans of New York City, 1860–1890," PhD diss., St. Johns University, 1977, 227–29; Burrows and Wallace, *Gotham*, 1010–11.

35. Nadel, *Little Germany*, 15; Quigley, *Second Founding*, 145–48, 157, 161; Sven Beckert, "Democracy in the Age of Capital: Contesting Suffrage Rights in Gilded Age New York," in *The Democratic Experiment: New Directions in American History*, ed. Meg Jacobs, William Novak, and Julian E. Zelizer (Princeton, NJ: Princeton University Press, 2009), 147–52, 158–60, 164–67.

36. Lawrence H. Fuchs, *The American Kaleidoscope: Race, Ethnicity, and the Civic Culture* (Hanover, NH: University Press of New England, 1990), 22.

37. Lapham, "The German-Americans," 167–73.

38. Lapham, "The German-Americans," 12; Nadel, *Little Germany*, 155, 159.

39. On Germans and anarchism, see Tom Goyens, *Beer and Revolution: The German Anarchist Movement in New York City, 1880–1914* (Champaign: University of Illinois Press, 2007).

40. Goyens, *Beer and Revolution*, 183–87.

41. Kessner, *Capital City*, 155–56, 165–79, 183–205; O'Donnell, *Henry George and the Crisis of Inequality*, 35. Gompers quoted in Nadel, *Little Germany*, 153.

42. Lapham, "The German-Americans," 185, 189; Nadel, *Little Germany*, 153–54.

43. On the cultural dimensions of Kleindeutschland, see Nadel, *Little Germany*, 104–18. McCabe is quoted in Robert W. Snyder, *The Voice of the City: Vaudeville and Popular Culture in New York* (New York: Oxford University Press, 1989), 11. For an insightful analysis of New York popular culture with attention to Germans, see Sabine Haenni, *The Immigrant Scene: Ethnic Amusements in New York, 1880–1920* (Minneapolis: University of Minnesota Press, 2008). Also see "Bottles from 19th Century German Beer Garden Found at Bowery Hotel Site," *dna.info*, May 1, 2014, https://www.dnainfo.com/new-york/20140501/chinatown/bottles-from-19th-century-german-beer-garden-found-at-bowery-hotel-site.

44. Fuchs, *The American Kaleidoscope*, 45.

45. Bookbinder, *City of the World*, 65.

46. Bookbinder, *City of the World*, 65. Also see Steven P. Erie, *Rainbow's End: Irish Americans and the Dilemmas of Urban Machine Politics, 1840–1985* (Berkeley: University of California Press, 1988), 39–40, 47–57, 65–66.

47. See James C. Nicholson, *The Notorious John Morrissey: How a Bare-Knuckle Brawler Became a Congressman and Founded Saratoga Race Course* (Lexington: University of Kentucky Press, 2016), 5–10, 12–14, 24–27, 29–37, 66–73, 85–90, 94–96.

48. Nicholson, *The Notorious John Morrissey*, 100–1, 127–29, 130–35, 138–46. On the endurance of Morrissey in song, see Dan Milner and Paul Kaplan, *A Bonnie Bunch of Roses: Songs of England, Ireland, and Scotland* (New York: Oak, 1983), 80–82.

49. Shannon, *The American Irish*, 72–73. Also see O'Donnell, *Henry George and the Crisis of Inequality*, 86.

50. Anthony Gronowicz, "Labor's Decline Within New York City's Democratic Party from 1844 to 1884," in *Immigration to New York*, ed. William Pencak, Selma Berrol, and Randall Miller (Philadelphia: Balch Institute Press, 1991), 16.

51. Dolan, *The Immigrant Church*, 12–15, 22–23.

52. Maureen Fitzgerald, *Habits of Compassion: Irish Catholic Nuns and the Origins of New York's Welfare System, 1830–1920* (Baltimore, MD: Johns Hopkins University Press, 2006), 58–59.

53. Fitzgerald, *Habits of Compassion*, 136.

54. George J. Marlin and Brad Miner, *Sons of Saint Patrick: A History of the Archbishops of New York from Dagger John to Timmytown* (San Francisco: Ignatius, 2017), 107.

55. Bernadette McCauley, *Roman Catholic Sisters and the Development of Catholic Hospitals in New York City* (Baltimore, MD: Johns Hopkins University Press, 2005), 62–65.

56. McCauley, *Roman Catholic Sisters*, 1–2.

57. McCauley, *Roman Catholic Sisters*, 94.

58. McCauley, *Roman Catholic Sisters*, 127–133.

59. Beckert, *The Monied Metropolis*, 257–68.

60. David Hammack, *Power and Society: Greater New York at the Turn of the Century* (New York: Russell Sage, 1982), 69.

61. Beckert, *Monied Metropolis*, 265; Annie Polland and Daniel Soyer, *Emerging Metropolis: New York Jews in the Age of Immigration, 1840–1920* (New York: NYU Press, 2012), 141.

62. Polland and Soyer, *Emerging Metropolis*, 42, 76–79.

63. See Clifton Hood, *In Pursuit of Privilege: The Making of New York City's Upper Class and the Making of a Metropolis* (New York: Columbia University Press, 2017), 204, 211; Edith Wharton, *The House of Mirth* (New York: Charles Scribner's Sons, 1905), 21, 23–25, 195; Hermione Lee, *Edith Wharton* (New York: Knopf, 2007), 612–13, 748; Irene C. Goldman, "The 'Perfect Jew' and *The House of Mirth*: A Study in Point of View," *Modern Language Studies* 23, no. 2 (Spring 1993): 25–34.

64. Greg King, *A Season of Splendor: The Court of Mrs. Astor in Gilded Age New York* (Hoboken, NJ: John Wiley & Sons, 2009), 348.

65. Beckert, *Monied Metropolis*, 267; Beckert, "Democracy in the Age of Capital," 163–67.

66. Chris Nickel, *To Be Mayor of New York* (New York: Columbia University Press, 1993), 9.

67. Snyder, *The Voice of the City*, 113–14.

68. Mick Moloney, liner notes to the CD *McNally's Row of Flats: Irish American Songs of Old New York*, by Harrigan and Braham, prod. Mick Moloney and John Doyle (2005); also James H. Dormon, "Ethnic Cultures of the Mind: The Harrigan-Hart Mosaic," *American Studies* 3, no. 2 (Fall 1992): 21–22; and James R. Barrett, *The Irish Way: Becoming American in the Multiethnic American City* (New York: Penguin, 2012), 161.

69. "McNally's Row of Flats," words by Ed Harrigan, music by David Braham (Wm. A. Pond and Co., 1882).

70. Barrett, *The Irish Way*, 164.

71. On the relational dimension of Irish culture in American cities, see Barrett, *The Irish Way*, 282–85; for lyrics, see "Muldoon the Solid Man," written and sung by Ed Harrigan (New York: E. H. Harding, 1874). The song is discussed in Don Meade, "The Life and Times of Muldoon, The Solid Man," http://blarneystar.com/Muldoon6.4.11.pdf.

72. O'Donnell, *Henry George and the Crisis of Inequality*, 74–80.

73. O'Donnell, *Henry George and the Crisis of Inequality*, 36–41.

74. O'Donnell, *Henry George and the Crisis of Inequality*, xxii–xxiii, 43–60, 63–66.

75. O'Donnell, *Henry George and the Crisis of Inequality*, 98–117, 119–21; 208; *Der Socialist* quoted on 220.

76. O'Donnell, *Henry George and the Crisis of Inequality*, 212–13.

77. O'Donnell, *Henry George and the Crisis of Inequality*, 211–33.

78. O'Donnell, *Henry George and the Crisis of Inequality*, 234–38.

79. O'Donnell, *Henry George and the Crisis of Inequality*, 252–68.

80. Daniel Czitrom, *New York Exposed: The Gilded Age Police Scandal That Launched the Progressive Era* (New York: Oxford University Press, 2016), 1–6, 10–16.

81. Timothy J. Gilfoyle, *City of Eros: New York, Prostitution, and the Commercialization of Sex, 1790–1920* (New York, 1992), 253.

82. See Czitrom, *New York Exposed*, 135–36, 238–44, 248–55, 261.

83. Czitrom, *New York Exposed*, 294.

84. O'Donnell, *Henry George and the Crisis of Inequality*, 256–76.

85. Mary Ovington, *Half a Man: The New Negro in New York City* (New York: Longman, 1911); Gilbert Osofsky, *Harlem: The Making of a Ghetto* (New York: Harper and Row, 1968); Seth Scheiner, *Negro Mecca: The Negro in New York City, 1865–1915* (New York: NYU Press, 1965); for Brooklyn, Harold Connolly, *A Ghetto Grows in Brooklyn* (New York: NYU Press, 1977).

86. Marilynn Johnson, *Street Justice: A History of Police Violence in New York City* (Boston: Beacon, 2003), 57. *Street Justice* provides an excellent account of the riot.

87. Osofsky, *Harlem*, 46.

88. Osofsky, *Harlem*, 50–52.

89. Johnson, *Street Justice*, 61–69; Czitrom, *New York Exposed*, 294–95.
90. Johnson, *Street Justice*, 63. Moss gathered 83 affidavits about police abuse. His collection was eventually published in Frank Moss, *The Story of the Riot* (New York: Arno, 1969).

4. Slums, Sweatshops, and Reform: 1880–1917

1. Sadie Frowne, "The Story of a Sweatshop Girl," *Independent* 54 (September 25, 1902): 2279–2282. Frowne dictated her story to the *Independent*.
2. Frowne, "The Story of a Sweatshop Girl."
3. For conditions in Europe, see Philip Taylor, *The Distant Magnet: European Emigration to USA* (London: Eyre and Spottiswoode, 1971), chaps. 2–3; and John Bodnar, *The Transplanted* (Bloomington: University of Indiana Press, 1985).
4. Quoted in Howard Sachar, *A History of the Jews in America* (New York: Knopf, 1992), 119.
5. See Nancy Foner, *From Ellis Island to JFK: New York's Two Great Waves of Immigration* (New Haven, CT: Yale University Press, 2000), 9–35. Also see Dorothee Schneider, *Crossing Borders: Migration and Citizenship in the Twentieth-Century United States* (Cambridge, MA: Harvard University Press, 2011).
6. Quoted in Sachar, *A History of the Jews in America*, 127.
7. For a view of the Ellis Island process, see Ronald Bayor, *Encountering Ellis Island* (Baltimore, MD: Johns Hopkins University Press, 2014).
8. See Fifty-Seventh Congress, Chap. 102, Pub. L. no. 162, "An Act to regulate the immigration of aliens into the United States," March 3, 1903.
9. David Hammack, *Power and Society: Greater New York at the Turn of the Century* (New York: Russell Sage, 1982), 31–39.
10. Irving Howe, *The World of Our Fathers* (New York: Simon and Schuster, 1976), 80–84.
11. Sister Adele Dabrowski, "A History and Survey of the Polish Brooklyn Community," MA thesis, Fordham University, 1946, 78–79, 152; Louis Winnick, *New People in Old Neighborhoods: The Role of New Immigrants in Rejuvenating New York's Communities* (New York: Russell Sage, 1990), 95; Gregory Orfalea, *Before the Flames: A Quest for the History of Arab Americans* (Austin: University of Texas Press, 1989), 75–78; Philip Kayal and Joseph Kayal, *The Syrian-Lebanese in America: A Study in Religion and Assimilation* (Boston: Twayne, 1975), 87–88.
12. The 1882 ban was temporary, but it was extended in subsequent years and finally repealed in 1943. Then China was granted a small immigration quota. Certain classes of Chinese could still come to America, and ways were found to get around the ban to permit "paper sons" (supposed sons of Chinese American citizens) to immigrate to America. But in general the limits imposed severe restrictions on Chinese immigration. See Ronald Takaki, *Strangers from a Different Shore: A History of Asian Americans* (Boston: Little Brown, 1989), 416–18.
13. Takaki, *Strangers from a Different Shore*, 251–52.
14. Madison Grant is quoted in Annie Polland and Daniel Soyer, *Emerging Metropolis: New York's Jews in the Age of Immigration, 1840–1920* (New York: NYU Press, 2012), 246–47.
15. Sachar, *A History of the Jews in America*, 141; Gerald Sorin, *A Time for Building: The Third Migration, 1880–1920* (Baltimore, MD: Johns Hopkins University Press, 1992),

42, 63; Moses Rischin, *The Promised City: New York's Jews, 1870–1914* (Cambridge, MA: Harvard University Press, 1962), 243; Stephen F. Brumberg, *Going to America, Going to School: The Jewish Immigrant Public School Encounter in Turn-of-the-Century New York City* (New York: Praeger, 1986), 55.

16. Gerald Sorin, *A Time for Building*, 23, 33; Ronald Sanders, *Shores of Refuge: A Hundred Years of Jewish Emigration* (New York: Holt, 1988), chaps. 1–2. A strong account of an influential pogrom is Stephen J. Zipperstein, *Pogrom: Kishinev and the Tilt of History* (New York: Liveright, 2018).

17. "Nearly 67 percent of gainfully employed Jewish immigrants who arrived between 1899 and 1914 possessed industrial skills—a much higher proportion than any other national group." Sorin, *A Time for Building*, 75.

18. Howe, *World of Our Fathers*, 59. Thomas Kessner provides occupational data on Jewish immigrants arriving in the United States between 1895 and 1910. Among the most numerous of the 395,823 reported skilled workers were 145,272 tailors, 36,138 carpenters and joiners, 23,519 shoemakers, and 23,179 seamstresses. Thomas Kessner, *The Golden Door: Italian and Jewish Immigrant Mobility in New York City, 1880–1915* (New York: Oxford University Press, 1977), 33.

19. Sorin, *A Time for Building*, 38, 39, 249–50; also Howe, *World of Our Fathers*, 58.

20. Rischin, *The Promised City*, 76, 78.

21. Rischin, *The Promised City*, 92–94; Sorin, *A Time for Building*, 70–71; Howe, *World of Our Fathers*, 69, 149; Sachar, *A History of the Jews*, 141.

22. Howe, *World of Our Fathers*, 98.

23. Sachar, *A History of the Jews*, 164.

24. Sachar, *A History of the Jews*, 170; Howe, *World of Our Fathers*, 133; Sorin, *A Time for Building*, 84.

25. Howe, *World of Our Fathers*, 133–33; Sachar, *A History of the Jews*, 193–96; Sorin, *A Time for Building*, 214–18. For a thorough and scholarly account of the Kehillah, see Arthur A. Goren, *The Kehillah Experiment, 1908–1922* (New York: Columbia University Press, 1970).

26. For a general view of German Jewish immigrants, see Deborah Dash Moore, Jeffrey S. Gurock, Annie Polland, Howard B. Rock, and Daniel Soyer, with a visual essay by Diana L. Linden, *Jewish New York: The Remarkable Story of a City and a People* (New York: NYU Press, 2017), 77–93.

27. Dash Moore et al., *Jewish New York*, 77–93.

28. Rischin, *The Promised City*, 101–103; Howe, *World of Our Fathers*, 230–35.

29. Howe, *World of Our Fathers*, 230–35; Leonard Dinnerstein, "Education and the Advancement of American Jews," in *American Education and the European Immigrant, 1840–1940*, ed. Bernard J. Weiss (Urbana: University of Illinois Press, 1982), 44–60.

30. Rischin, *The Promised City*, 103–104.

31. The best overview of the *landsmanshaftn* is Daniel Soyer, *Jewish Immigrant Associations and American Identity* (Cambridge, MA: Harvard University Press, 2012).

32. Howe, *World of Our Fathers*, 185.

33. Sachar, *A History of the Jews*, 197–98; Soyer, *Jewish Immigrant Associations*, 51–59.

34. Rischin, *The Promised City*, 105.

35. Sachar, *A History of the Jews*, 133, 198.

36. Dash Moore et al., *Jewish New York*, 91–96, 143; Rischin, *The Promised City*, 56–58.

37. Rischin, *The Promised City*, 56–58; Sorin, *A Time for Building*, 77, 118, 192; Selma Berrol, "In Their Image: German Jews and the Americanization of the Ost Juden," *New York History* 63 (October 1982): 421–22.

38. Kessner, *The Golden Door*, 9–10; Polland and Soyer, *Emerging Metropolis*, 39–40, 119; Sorin, *A Time for Building*, 74.

39. Sachar, *A History of the Jews*, 145; Rischin, *The Promised City*, 245; Sorin, *A Time for Building*, 114.

40. Rischin, *The Promised City*, 178.

41. Sorin, *A Time for Building*, 114–15; Sachar, *A History of the Jews*, 182.

42. Kessner, *The Golden Door*, 57; Moore et al., *Jewish New York*, 94–96.

43. Sachar, *A History of the Jews*, 176–83; Tony Michels, *A Fire in Their Hearts: Yiddish Socialists in New York* (Cambridge, MA: Harvard University Press, 2005), 1, 4–5, 15, 41–50.

44. See "Bund" in *Jewish Virtual Library*, http://www.jewishvirtuallibrary.org/bund; and in the *YIVO Encyclopedia of Jews in Eastern Europe*, http://www.yivoencyclopedia.org/article.aspx/Bund; Howe, *World of Our Fathers*, 292; Sorin, *A Time for Building*, 115, 118, 119; Polland and Soyer, *Emerging Metropolis*, 184; Michels, *A Fire in Their Hearts*, 26–28, 61, 64–68, 70, 251; Christine Stansell, *American Moderns: Bohemian New York and the Creation of a New Century* (New York: Metropolitan, 2000), 367–37, 120–26, 226, 270–71, Emma Goldman quoted on 36.

45. Sorin, *A Time for Building*, 118, 192.

46. In 1913, the Tammany loyalist Aaron Jefferson Levy became the majority leader of the State Assembly. See Rischin, *The Promised City*, 230.

47. Rischin, *The Promised City*; 228–33; Sachar, *A History of the Jews*, 176.

48. Sachar, *A History of the Jews*, 76–78; Rischin, *The Promised City*, 166, 133.

49. Hasia Diner, *The Jews of the United State, 1654 to 2000* (Berkeley: University of California Press, 2000), 160–61.

50. On the significance of socialism in the Jewish immigrant community and on London's popularity, see Polland and Soyer, *Emerging Metropolis*, chap. 6. On socialism and immigrant Jews, see Michels, *A Fire in Their Hearts*, 1–25, 75–79, 113–24.

51. Rischin, *The Promised City*, 35.

52. Quoted in Sorin, *A Time for Building*, 175.

53. Galician and Hungarian Jews appointed their own chief rabbi in 1892, Joshua Segal. The following year, Rabbi Hayim Vidrowitz, recently arrived from Moscow, declared himself "Chief Rabbi of America." Howe, *World of Our Fathers*, 195. Also see Rischin, *The Promised City*, 148.

54. Brumberg, *Going to America, Going to School*, 70. A survey of Orthodox synagogues in 1917 revealed that only 23 percent employed rabbis and only 13 percent provided religious schools. See Sachar, *A History of the Jews*, 190–91.

55. Polland and Soyer, *Emerging Metropolis*, 100–101.

56. Gurock, "Americanized Synagogue," 7.

57. Sorin, *A Time for Building*, 184–87; Howe, *World of Our Fathers*, 197–200.

58. Sydney Stahl Weinberg, "Longing to Learn: The Education of Jewish Immigrant Women in New York City, 1900–1933," *Journal of American Ethnic History* 8 (Spring 1989): 108–9.

59. Howe, *World of Our Fathers*, 281; Dinnerstein, "Education and the Advancement of American Jews," 50. Jewish students represented approximately 20 percent of all-female Hunter College's enrollment during this period.

60. Up to 1903, compulsory-attendance laws permitted students to leave school at age twelve or upon completion of the fifth grade. That year, the age was raised to fourteen and the grade to six; in 1913, the age/grade requirement was upped to sixteen and eight. However, the laws were not vigorously enforced. Many children left school at age nine or ten. Of all children entering public schools in 1913, only one-third reached the eighth

grade. Berrol, "Public Schools and Immigrants," in Weiss, *American Education,* 36–38; Weinberg, "Longing to Learn," 115–19.

61. Quoted in Brumberg, *Going to America, Going to School,* 13.

62. Selma Berrol, "Public Schools and Immigrants," 32. See also Selma Berrol, *Immigrants at School: New York City, 1898–1914* (New York: Arno, 1978).

63. Quoted in Sydney Stahl Weinberg, "The Education of Jewish Immigrant Women in New York City," 119.

64. Berrol, "Public Schools and Immigrants," 36–37. See also Alan Kraut, *Silent Travelers: Germs, Genes, and the "Immigrant Menace"* (New York: Basic Books, 1994), 228–32.

65. Quoted in Weinberg, "Longing to Learn," 119.

66. Sorin, *A Time for Building,* 106; Berrol, "Public Schools and Immigrants," 39.

67. Dinnerstein, "Education and the Advancement of American Jews," 49.

68. Weinberg, "Longing to Learn," 113, 121; Howe, *World of Our Fathers,* 238.

69. Quoted in Dinnerstein, "Education and Advancement of American Jews," 49–50.

70. Howe, *World of Our Fathers,* 520, 523; Sachar, *A History of the Jews,* 202–3.

71. Quoted in Sorin, *A Time for Building,* 120.

72. Dinnerstein, "Education and the Advancement of American Jews," 47; Weinberg, "Longing to Learn," 114.

73. Quoted in Sorin, *A Time for Building,* 103; Sachar, *A History of the Jews,* 204.

74. Every letter, whether printed in the paper or not, received a reply from either Cahan or the column editor, S. Kornbluth. Sachar, *A History of the Jews,* 204–5.

75. There were between 250 and 300 coffee shops on the Lower East Side by 1905. Rischin, *The Promised City,* 142; Sachar, *A History of the Jews,* 200.

76. Howe, *World of Our Fathers,* 417–28; Sachar, *A History of the Jews,* 205–8. For Morris Rosenfeld's "My Resting Place," see https://yiddishkayt.org/view/morris-rosenfeld/.

77. Sachar, *A History of the Jews,* 210.

78. Quoted in Sachar, *A History of the Jews,* 213.

79. Mike Wallace, *Greater Gotham: A History of New York City from 1898 to 1919* (New York: Oxford University Press, 2017), 473–74. Also see Kathy Peiss, *Cheap Amusements: Working Women and Leisure in Turn-of-the-Century New York* (Philadelphia: Temple University Press, 1986).

80. See Robert W. Snyder, *The Voice of the City: Vaudeville and Popular Culture in New York* (New York: Oxford University Press, 1989; pbk. with new preface by author and Chicago: Ivan R. Dee, 2000), 104–29.

81. Sorin, *A Time for Building,* 99.

82. Howe, *World of Our Fathers,* 460–64.

83. Quoted in Sachar, *A History of the Jews,* 211.

84. Sachar, *A History of the Jews,* 211–12; Howe, *World of Our Fathers,* 480.

85. Thomas J. Ferraro, *Feeling Italian: The Art of Ethnicity in America* (New York: NYU Press, 2005), 9.

86. George Pozzetta, "The Italians of New York City, 1890–1914," PhD diss., University of North Carolina, 1971, 78, 94, 104–7; Caroline Ware, *Greenwich Village, 1920–1930* (1935; repr. New York: Octagon, 1977), 152–57.

87. Wallace, *Greater Gotham,* 231; Clifton Hood, *722 Miles: The Building of the Subways and How They Transformed New York* (New York: Simon and Schuster, 1993), 85; Pozzetta, "The Italians of New York City," 94; Donna Gabaccia, "Little Italy's Decline: Immigrant Renters and Investors in a Changing City," in *The Landscape of Modernity: Essays on New York City, 1900–1940,* ed. David Ward and Olivier Zunz (New York: Russell Sage, 1992), 247.

88. Robert Orsi, *The Madonna of 115th Street: Faith and Community in Italian Harlem, 1880–1950* (New Haven, CT: Yale University Press, 1985), 14–17; Anthony L. LaRuffa, *Monte Carmelo: An Italian-American Community in the Bronx* (New York: Breach and Science, 1988), 17–18.

89. Pozzetta, "The Italians of New York City," 332–38.

90. Pozzetta, "The Italians of New York City," 85.

91. Donna Gabaccia, *From Sicily to Elizabeth Street: Housing and Social Change Among Italian Immigrants, 1880–1930* (Albany: SUNY Press, 1984), 54; *Report of the U.S. Immigration Commission, Immigrants in Cities* (Washington, DC, 1911), 26:16.

92. Kate Claghorn, "The Foreign Immigrant in New York City," in *Industrial Commission* (Washington, DC: 1908), 15:474.

93. Claghorn, "The Foreign Immigrant in New York City," 472.

94. Orsi, *The Madonna of 115th Street*, 29.

95. Jacob Riis, *How the Other Half Lives: Studies Among the Tenements of New York* (1890; New York, 1971), 56.

96. Stephan Talty, *The Black Hand: The Epic War Between a Brilliant Detective and the Deadliest Secret Society in American History* (New York: Houghton Mifflin Harcourt, 2017), 44.

97. Talty, *The Black Hand*, 204–16.

98. Claghorn, "The Foreign Immigrant in New York City," 474.

99. Talty, *The Black Hand*, 10.

100. Kessner, *The Golden Door*, 51–52, 55.

101. Kessner, *The Golden Door*, 57.

102. Pozzetta, "The Italians of New York City," 339–41.

103. Pozzetta, "The Italians of New York City," 60–64.

104. Miriam Cohen, *From Workshop to Office: Two Generations of Italian Women in New York City* (Ithaca, NY: Cornell University Press, 1993), 21.

105. Sister Mary Fabian Matthews, "The Role of the Public School in the Americanization of the Italian Immigrant Child in New York City, 1900–1914," PhD diss., Fordham University, 1966, 97–98; Cohen, *From Workshop to Office*, 121.

106. *Report of the U.S. Immigration Commission, Immigrants in Cities*, 200.

107. Cohen, *From Workshop to Office*, 41–44.

108. Cohen, *From Workshop to Office*, 118–20.

109. For a critique of Americanization, see Alex Nowrasteh, "The Failure of the Americanization Movement," *Cato at Liberty*, December 18, 2014, https://www.cato.org/blog/failure-americanization-movement. For a defense of it, see John Press, "Frances Kellor and the Quest for Participatory Democracy," PhD diss., New York University, 2010.

110. Pozzetta, "The Italians of New York City," 351–54, 356–63.

111. Quoted in David Katzman and William M. Tuttle Jr., eds., *Plain Folk* (Urbana: University of Illinois Press, 1982), 12.

112. Thomas Kessner, *Fiorello H. La Guardia and the Making of Modern New York* (New York: McGraw Hill, 1989), 30–40.

113. Jennifer Guglielmo, *Living the Revolution: Italian Women's Resistance and Radicalism in New York City, 1880–1945* (Chapel Hill: University of North Carolina Press, 2010), 141–43.

114. Donna Gabaccia, *Militants and Migrants: Rural Sicilians Become American Workers* (New Brunswick, NJ: Rutgers University Press, 1988), 127–45, 237–38.

115. Pozzetta, "The Italians of New York City," 252–66, 243–428.

116. Pozzetta, "The Italians of New York City," 231–32.

117. Pozzetta, "The Italians of New York City," 267.
118. Pozzetta, "The Italians of New York City," 267.
119. Mary Brown, "Italian Immigrants and the Catholic Church in the Archdiocese of New York, 1880–1950," PhD diss., Columbia University, 1987, 49.
120. Denise DeCarlo, "The History of the Italian *Festa* in New York City, 1880s to the Present," PhD diss., New York University, 1990, 47.
121. Quoted in Ana Maria Diaz-Stevens, *Oxcart Catholicism on Fifth Avenue* (Notre Dame, IN: University of Notre Dame Press, 1993), 75.
122. Joseph Sciorra, *Built with Faith: Italian American Immigration and Catholic Material Culture in New York City* (Knoxville: University of Tennessee Press, 2015), 9–14, 33, 53, 98–100, 198, quote on 10.
123. Pozzetta, "The Italians of New York City," 269–79.
124. Richard Gambino, *Blood of My Blood* (Garden City, NY: Doubleday, 1975), 212.
125. Brown, "Italian Immigrants," 221–26; Pozzetta, "The Italians of New York City," 295–303.
126. Pozzetta, "The Italians of New York City," 277–89; Brown, "Italian Immigrants," 225–26, 320–37.
127. Allen F. Davis, *Spearheads for Reform: The Social Settlements and the Progressive Movement, 1890–1914* (New York: Oxford University Press, 1967), 34–35; Elizabeth I. Perry, "Men Are from the Gilded Age, Women Are from the Progressive Era," *Journal of the Gilded Age and Progressive Era* 1, no. 1 (January 2002): 25–35.
128. Davis, *Spearheads for Reform*, 99–101.
129. Doris Daniels, "Building a Winning Coalition: The Suffrage Fight in New York State," *New York History* 60 (January 1979): 66.
130. Wallace, *Greater Gotham*, 505–582.
131. Marjorie N. Feld, *Lillian Wald: A Biography* (Chapel Hill: University of North Carolina Press, 2008), 27, 36–38, 86–87; Blanche Weisen Cook, "Female Support Networks and Political Activism: Lillian Wald, Crystal Eastman, Emma Goldman," in *A Heritage of Her Own: Toward A New Social History of American Women*, ed. Nancy F. Cott and Elizabeth F. Pleck (New York: Simon and Schuster, 1979), 412–44.
132. For union activity, see Wallace, *Greater Gotham*, 649–80.
133. Guglielmo, *Living the Revolution*, 179–85.
134. Quoted in Howe, *World of Our Fathers*, 298.
135. Tyler Anbinder, *City of Dreams: The Four-Hundred-Year Epic History of Immigrant New York* (New York: Houghton Mifflin Harcourt, 2016), 434.
136. This account relies on the excellent book by Richard Greenwald, *The Triangle Fire, the Protocols of Peace, and Industrial Democracy in Progressive Era New York* (Philadelphia: Temple University Press, 2005), 129–38.
137. Schneiderman is quoted in Dash Moore et al., *Jewish New York*, 172–73.
138. Greenwald, *The Triangle Fire*, 189–98.
139. Perry, "Men Are from the Gilded Age, Women Are from the Progressive Era," 35–37. Lemlich is quoted in Moore et al., *Jewish New York*, 176.
140. Frances Bzowski, "Spectacular Suffrage: Or, How Women Came Out of the Home and Into the Streets and Theaters of New York City To Win the Vote," *New York History* 76 (January 1995): 63.
141. An excellent summary of the movement is Miriam Cohen, "Women and the Progressive Movement," Guilder Lehrman Institute of American History, *History Now* (2012).
142. Bzowski, "Spectacular Suffrage," 64–65.

143. See Elinor Lerner, "Jewish Involvement in the New York City Woman Suffrage Movement," *American Jewish History* 70 (June 1981): 442–61; Eleanor Flexner, *Century of Struggle: The Women's Rights Movement in the United States* (Cambridge, MA: Harvard University Press, 1959), 290; Moore et al., *Jewish New York*, 176.

5. New Times and New Neighborhoods: 1917–1928

1. In Jeff Kisseloff, *You Must Remember This: An Oral History of Manhattan from the 1890s to World War II* (New York: Harcourt Brace Jovanovich, 1989), 118.
2. Timothy J. Hatton and Jeffrey G. Williamson, *Global Migration and the World Economy: Two Centuries of Policy and Performance* (Cambridge, MA: Harvard University Press, 2005), 181.
3. Quoted in Steven H. Jaffe, *New York at War: Four Centuries of Combat, Fear, and Intrigue in Gotham* (New York: Basic Books, 2012), 184.
4. Carl Wittke, *German Americans and the World War* (Columbus: Ohio State Archaeological and Historical Society, 1936), 130, 136.
5. See Lena Prummer, "German American and Socialist 'Imagined Communities': Journalism in the *New Yorker Staats-Zeitung* and the *New Yorker Volkszeitung* During World War I," unpublished essay in possession of Robert W. Snyder.
6. Jaffe, *New York at War*, 303.
7. Jaffe, *New York at War*, 288. Despite such criticism, Hillquit received 28 percent of the votes. For his account, see Morris Hillquit, *Loose Leaves from a Busy Life* (New York: Rand School Press, 1934), 180–210.
8. Quoted in Susan Canedy, *America's Nazis* (Menlo Park, NJ: Markgraf, 1990), 12.
9. Frederick Luebke, *Bonds of Loyalty: German Americans and World War I* (Dekalb: Northern Illinois University Press, 1974), 231, 249; Works Progress Administration Files, New York City Archives, "The Germans of New York City"; Anita Rapone, *The Guardian Life Insurance Company, 1860–1920: A History of a German-American Enterprise* (New York: NYU Press, 1987), 143–55. See also Erik Kirschbaum, *Burning Beethoven: The Eradication of German Culture in the United States During World War I* (Madison: University of Wisconsin Press, 2015).
10. Quoted in Alter F. Landesman, *Brownsville: The Birth, Development, and Passing of Jewish Community in New York* (New York: Bloch, 1969), 287–88.
11. On the war and Progressives, see Eric Foner, *The Story of American Freedom* (New York: Norton, 1998), 168–69; Christopher Capozzola, *Uncle Sam Wants You: World War I and the Making of the Modern American Citizen* (New York: Oxford University Press, 2008), 12–13; Jackson Lears, *Rebirth of a Nation: The Making of Modern America* (New York: HarperCollins, 2009), 337–42. For the case of anarchists opposed to the American invasion of Russia, see Richard Polenberg, *Fighting Faiths: The Abrams Case, the Supreme Court, and Free Speech* (New York: Viking, 1987). The Socialist Party's response to the war and wartime repression are addressed in Ernest Freeberg, *Democracy's Prisoner: Eugene V. Debs, The Great War, and the Right to Dissent* (Cambridge, MA: Harvard University Press, 2008), 40–45, 60–61, 105–9, 130–31, 145–47, 323–24; and David M. Kennedy, *Over Here: The First World War and American Society* (New York: Oxford University Press, 1980), 26–27.
12. Kevin Kenny, "American-Irish Nationalism," in *Making the Irish American: History and Heritage of the Irish in the United States*, ed. J. J. Lee and Marion R. Casey (New

York: NYU Press, 2006), 289–95; Donald Nevin, *James Connolly: "A Full Life"* (Dublin: Gill and Macmillan, 2006), chap. 14, "Industrial Workers of the World."

13. John Patrick Buckley, *The New York Irish: Their View of American Foreign Policy, 1914–1921* (New York: Arno, 1976), esp. chaps. 2–3.

14. Jaffe, *New York at War*, 202, 212.

15. Jeffrey T. Sammons and John H. Morrow Jr., *Harlem's Rattlers and the Great War: The Undaunted 369th Regiment and the African American Quest for Equality* (Lawrence: University Press of Kansas, 2014), 189–242, 303–56.

16. The stories of the Harlem Hellfighters and the 308th Infantry are both told in Richard Slotkin, *Lost Battalions: The Great War and the Crisis of American Nationality* (New York: Henry Holt, 2005), 305–63, 369–73.

17. Tony Michels, *A Fire in Their Hearts: Yiddish Socialists in New York* (Cambridge, MA: Harvard University Press, 2005), 221–28; New York State Archives, *The Lusk Committee: A Guide to the Records of the Joint Legislative Committee to Investigate Seditious Activities: A Guide to the Records Held in the New York State Archives* (1992); Beverly Gage, *The Day Wall Street Exploded: A Story of America in Its First Age of Terror* (New York: Oxford University Press, 2009), 1.

18. For a thorough treatment of the immigration restrictions of the 1920s, see Mae Ngai, *Impossible Subjects: Illegal Aliens and the Making of Modern America* (Princeton, NJ: Princeton University Press, 2004), 21–55. It should be noted that other Western Hemisphere nations also resorted to immigration restriction.

19. Chin Jou, "Contesting Nativism: The New York Congressional Delegation's Case Against the Immigration Act of 1924," *Federal History* (2011): 70; Tyler Anbinder, *City of Dreams: The Four-Hundred-Year Epic History of Immigrant New York* (New York: Houghton Mifflin, 2016), 463–69.

20. US Department of Homeland Security, *Legal Permanent Residents, 2011* (Washington, DC, 2011), 8.

21. Clifton Hood, *722 Miles: The Building of the Subways and How They Transformed New York* (New York: Simon and Schuster, 1993), 214–19; Richard Plunz, *A History of Housing in New York City: Dwelling Type and Social Change in the American Metropolis* (New York: Columbia University Press, 1990), 122–24.

22. Plunz, *A History of Housing in New York City*, 42.

23. Quoted in Jill Jonnes, *We're Still Here: The Rise, Fall, and Resurrection of the South Bronx* (New York: Fordham University Press, 1986), 51–56.

24. Ira Rosenwaike, *Population History of New York City* (Syracuse, NY: Syracuse University Press, 1972), 133.

25. Rosenwaike, *Population History of New York City*, 93; Lloyd Ultan and Gary Hermalyn, *The Bronx in the Innocent Years, 1890–1925* (New York: Harper and Row, 1985), xiii; Marion R. Casey, "Twentieth-Century Irish Immigration to New York City: The Historical Perspective," *New York Irish History* 3 (1988): 25–26.

26. Marion Casey, "Bronx Irish: An Example of Internal Migration in New York City, 1900–1950," seminar paper, New York University, May 1989; Evelyn Gonzalez, *The Bronx* (New York: Columbia University Press, 2004), 94–95; Peter J. Donaldson, "A Life in the City," *America* 147 (October 16, 1982): 205–6.

27. William O'Dwyer, *Beyond the Golden Door* (New York: St. Johns University, 1987), 90–91.

28. Casey, "The Bronx Irish," 16.

29. Deborah Dash Moore, *At Home in America: Second-Generation New York Jews* (New York: Columbia University Press, 1981), 19–20.

30. Constance Rosenblum, *Boulevard of Dreams: Heady Times, Heartbreak, and Hope Along the Grand Concourse in the Bronx* (New York: NYU Press, 2009), 5.

31. Landesman, *Brownsville*, 95.

32. Quoted in Egon Mayer, *From Suburb to Shtetl: The Jews of Boro Park* (Philadelphia: Temple University Press, 1979), 21–23.

33. Mayer, *From Suburb to Shtetl*, 24.

34. Moore, *At Home in America*, 37–38, 42; Selma C. Berrol, "Manhattan's Jewish West Side," *New York Affairs* 10 (Winter 1987): 13–31; Jeffrey S. Gurock, *When Harlem Was Jewish, 1870–1930* (New York: Columbia University Press, 1979), 164; Jeffrey S. Gurock, *Jews in Gotham: New York Jews in a Changing City, 1920–2010* (New York: NYU Press, 2012), 21.

35. Jenna Weissman Joselit, *New York's Jewish Jews: The Orthodox Community in the Interwar Years* (Bloomington: Indiana University Press, 1990), 2.

36. Joselit, *New York's Jewish Jews*, 119–21.

37. Joselit, *New York's Jewish Jews*, chaps. 4–5.

38. Moore, *At Home in America*, 77.

39. Moore, *At Home in America,*, 123–47.

40. Robert Orsi, *The Madonna of 115th Street: Faith and Community in Italian Harlem* (New Haven, CT: Yale University Press, 1985), 14–19, 42; David Ment and Mary Donovan, *The People of Brooklyn* (New York: Brooklyn Educational and Cultural Alliance, 1980), 69–71; Ralph Foster Weld, *Brooklyn Is America* (1950; New York: AMS Press, 1967), 137–40; Rosenwaike, *Population History of New York*, 167.

41. Joseph Sciorra, *Built with Faith: Italian American Immigration and Catholic Material Culture in New York City* (Knoxville: University of Tennessee Press, 2015), xxiii–xxiv, 33, 110.

42. See Orsi's excellent book *The Madonna of 115th Street*, 1–12.

43. Mary Brown, "Italian Immigrants and the Catholic Church in the Archdiocese of New York, 1880–1950," PhD diss., Columbia University, 1987, 334–57.

44. Ronald Bayor, *Neighbors in Conflict: The Irish, Germans, Jews, and Italians of New York City, 1929–1941*, 2nd ed. (Urbana: University of Illinois Press, 1988), 22–23; Moore, *At Home in America*, 95–96.

45. Joshua B. Freeman, *In Transit: The Transport Workers Union in New York City, 1933–1966* (New York: Oxford University Press, 1989), 26–28; Bayor, *Neighbors in Conflict*, 23.

46. Freeman, *In Transit*, 26–29.

47. Quoted in Ruth Jacknow Markowitz, *My Daughter, the Teacher: Jewish Teachers in the New York City Schools* (New Brunswick, NJ: Rutgers University Press, 1993), 15.

48. See Casey, "The Bronx Irish."

49. For vaudeville and ethnic culture in New York, see Robert W. Snyder, *The Voice of the City: Vaudeville and Popular Culture in New York* (New York: Oxford University Press, 1989), 45–63.

50. Quoted in Peter Levine, *Ellis Island to Ebbets Field: Sport and the American Jewish Experience* (New York: Oxford University Press, 1992), 89.

51. Howe's comment can be found Irving Howe, *A Margin of Hope: An Intellectual Biography* (New York: Simon and Schuster, 1981), 1–2.

52. Levine, *From Ellis Island to Ebbets Field*, 131–37.

53. Levine, *From Ellis Island to Ebbets Field*, 78–86, 254–57.

54. Bernie Bookbinder, with research by Robert W. Snyder and photography by Harvey Weber, *City of the World: New York and Its People* (New York: Abrams, 1990), 172; Levine, *From Ellis Island to Ebbets Field*, 132–136.

55. Jeffrey Sammons, *Beyond the Ring: The Role of Boxing in American Society* (Urbana: University of Illinois Press, 1988), 92.
56. Moore, *At Home in America*, 95–97; Deborah Dash Moore, Jeffrey Gurock, Annie Polland, Howard Rock, and Daniel Soyer, *Jewish New York: The Remarkable Story of a City and a People* (New York: NYU Press, 2017), 224.
57. Gurock, *Jews in Gotham*, 46–48.
58. Henry Feingold, *A Time for Searching: Entering the Mainstream, 1920–1945* (Baltimore, MD: Johns Hopkins University Press, 1992), 126–27.
59. Quoted in Miriam Cohen, *From Workshop to Office: Two Generations of Italian Women in New York City, 1900–1950* (Ithaca, NY: Cornell University Press, 1993), 145.
60. Cohen, *From Workshop to Office*.
61. *Journal of Retailing* 8 (October 1932): 92–93.
62. Howe, *A Margin of Hope*, 1–2.
63. Bayor, *Neighbors in Conflict*, 17–18.
64. Cohen, *From Workshop to Office*, 145.
65. Cohen, *From Workshop to Office*, chap. 5.
66. Gerald Meyer, *Vito Marcantonio: Radical Politician* (Albany: SUNY Press, 1989), 10–11.
67. Paul Moses, *An Unlikely Union: The Love-Hate Story of New York's Irish and Italians* (New York: NYU Press, 2015), 181.
68. Lizette van Hecke, "The NYC Department of Sanitation Association," *NYC Garbage Project*, https://newyorkgarbage.wordpress.com/the-nyc-department-of-sanitation/.
69. Federal Writers' Project, *The Italians of New York* (New York: Random House, 1938), 161–67, 171, 174–76.
70. Simone Cinotto, *The Italian American Table: Food, Family, and Community in New York City* (Urbana: University of Illinois Press, 2013), 166.
71. Hasia Diner, *Hungering for America: Italian, Irish, and Jewish Foodways in the Age of Migration* (Cambridge, MA: Harvard University Press, 2001), 22–33, 48–51, 57, 62, 66–67, 76–77.
72. Lisa McGirr, *The War on Alcohol: Prohibition and the Rise of the American State* (New York: Norton, 2015), 33–34, 108.
73. Quoted in Thomas Kessner, *Fiorello H. La Guardia and the Making of Modern New York* (New York: McGraw Hill, 1989), 358.
74. Jenna Weissman Joselit, *Our Gang: Jewish Crime and the New York Jewish Community, 1900–1940* (Bloomington: University of Indiana Press, 1983), 106–17.
75. Joselit, *Our Gang*, 140–56.
76. Quoted in Joselit, *Our Gang*, 146.
77. Joselit, *Our Gang*, 140–47; "Arnold Rothstein," http://www.jewishvirtuallibrary.org/arnold-rothstein.
78. Mark Haller, "Bootleggers and American Gambling, 1920–1950," in Commission on the Review of the National Policy Towards Gambling, *Gambling in America* (Washington, DC, 1976), appendix 1, 109; Alan Block, *East Side–West Side: Organizing Crime in New York, 1930–1950* (New Brunswick, NJ: Rutgers University Press, 1983), 183–89, 225–27, 246–49; Humbert Nelli, *The Business of Crime: Italians and Syndicate Crime in the United States* (New York: Oxford University Press, 1976), 109, 193–95.
79. Ronald Takaki, *Strangers from a Different Shore: A History of Asian Americans* (Boston: Little Brown, 1989), 242–45, 250–51.
80. Scott D. Seligman, *Tong Wars: The Untold Story of Vice, Money, and Murder in New York's Chinatown* (New York: Viking, 2016), 3–18, 66–81.

81. The history of the hand laundry and the union it spawned is covered in Renqiu Yu, *"To Save China, To Save Ourselves": The Chinese Hand Laundry Alliance of New York* (Philadelphia: Temple University Press, 1992), 31–49.

82. Mitziko Sawada, *Tokyo Life, New York Dreams: Urban Japanese Visions, 1890–1924* (Berkeley: University of California Press, 1996), 13–40.

83. WPA Files, "The Koreans in New York"; Joan Jensen, *Passage from India: Asian Indian Immigrants to North America* (New Haven, CT: Yale University Press, 1988), 19, 168; New York State Advisory Committee to the U.S. Commission on Civil Rights, *The Forgotten Minority: Asian Americans in New York City* (1977), 14; WPA Files, "The Indonesians in New York."

84. For the Bengali Muslims, see Vivek Bald, *Bengali Harlem and the Lost Histories of South Asian America* (Cambridge, MA: Harvard University Press, 2013), 189–91.

85. Norwegians are covered in David Mauk, *The Colony That Rose from the Sea: Norwegian Maritime Migration and Community in Brooklyn, 1850–1910* (Urbana: University of Illinois Press, 1997), 51–66.

86. Ment and Donovan, *The People of Brooklyn*, 66–69.

87. Ment and Donovan, *The People of Brooklyn*, 107–9.

88. Ment and Donovan, *The People of Brooklyn*, 109–15.

89. Warren Moscow, *What Have You Done for Me Lately? The Ins and Outs of New York City Politics* (Englewood Cliffs, NJ: Prentice Hall, 1967), 119–20.

90. Jeffrey Gerson, "Building the Brooklyn Machine: Irish, Jewish, and Black Political Succession in Central Brooklyn, 1919–1964," PhD diss., City University of New York, 1990.

91. Charles Green and Basil Wilson, *The Struggle for Black Empowerment in New York City* (New York: Praeger, 1989), 7.

92. George Furniss, "The Political Assimilation of Negroes in New York City, 1870–1965," PhD diss., Columbia University, 1969, 195–97; Michael Goldstein, "Race Politics in New York City, 1890–1930," PhD diss., Columbia University, 1973, 213–14.

93. See also Marsha Hunt Hiller, "Race Politics in New York City, 1890–1930," PhD diss., Columbia University, 1972, 231–53, 324–71.

94. Goldstein, "Race Politics," 214–27, 303; David Goldberg, *Black Firefighters and the FDNY: The Struggle for Jobs, Justice, and Equity in New York City* (Chapel Hill: University of North Carolina Press, 2017), 72. On New York City's firemen and police, see Ginger Otis, *Firefight: The Century-Long Battle to Integrate New York's Bravest* (New York: Palgrave, 2015); and Arthur Browne, *One Righteous Man: Samuel Battle and the Shattering of the Color Line in New York* (Boston: Beacon, 2015).

95. Goldstein, "Race and Politics," 315–23, 328–30.

96. Goldstein, "Race and Politics," 315–23, 328–30; Cheryl Greenberg, *Or Does It Explode? Black Harlem in the Great Depression* (New York: Oxford University Press, 1991), 95.

97. See Hiller, "Race Politics," 33–50, 57–80, for a discussion of Brooklyn politics.

98. Craig Steven Wider, *A Covenant with Color: Race and Social Power in Brooklyn* (New York: Columbia University Press, 2000), 140; Harold Connolly, *A Ghetto Grows in Brooklyn* (New York: NYU Press, 1977), 99–100, 102–10.

99. Virginia Sanchez Korrol, *From Colonia to Community: The History of Puerto Ricans in New York City, 1917–1948* (Westport, CT: Greenwood, 1983), 13; Joseph Fitzpatrick, *Puerto Rican Americans: The Meaning of Migration to the Mainland*, 2nd ed. (Englewood Cliffs, NJ: Prentice Hall, 1987), 38–40; Meyer, *Vito Marcantonio*, 145–47; Jonathan Gill, *Harlem: The Four-Hundred-Year History from Dutch Village to Capital of Black America* (New York: Grove, 2011), 244–45.

100. Seth Scheiner, *Negro Mecca: A History of the Negro in New York City, 1865–1915* (New York: NYU Press, 1965), 221.
101. Scheiner, *Negro Mecca*, 221.
102. Gilbert Osofsky, *Harlem: The Making of a Ghetto* (New York: Harper and Row, 1966), 77–80.
103. Osofsky, *Harlem*, 82–86.
104. Osofsky, *Harlem*, 92–104.
105. Quoted in Osofsky, *Harlem*, 106–7.
106. Osofsky, *Harlem*, 105–6, 109–10, 113–18.
107. On neighborhood conditions, see Claude McKay, *Home to Harlem* (New York: Pocket, 1940), 23–28; James Weldon Johnson, *Black Manhattan* (New York: Knopf, 1938), 3. For the Harlem renaissance generally, see Nathan Huggins, *Harlem Renaissance* (New York: Oxford University Press, 1971); David Levering Lewis, *When Harlem Was in Vogue* (New York: Knopf, 1981); Cheryl A. Wall, *Women of the Harlem Renaissance* (Bloomington: Indiana University Press, 1995); Cheryl A. Wall, *The Harlem Renaissance: A Very Short Introduction* (New York: Oxford University Press, 2016), 1–2; Gill, *Harlem*, 239.
108. Gill, *Harlem*, 261–62.
109. For the Garvey movement, see Judith Stein, *The World of Marcus Garvey: Race and Class in Modern Society* (Baton Rouge: Louisiana University Press, 1986), 38–60, 273–80.
110. Irma Watkins-Owens, *Blood Relations: Caribbean Immigrants and the Harlem Community, 1900–1930* (Bloomington: Indiana University Press, 1996), 4.
111. Watkins-Owens, *Blood Relations*, 93–105.
112. Watkins-Owens, *Blood Relations*, 93.
113. Watkins-Owens, *Blood Relations*, 94.
114. Osofsky, *Harlem*, 136–41.
115. Frank Byrd interview, New York City, 1938, http://www.loc.gov/resource/wpalh2.21011010.
116. Greenberg, *Or Does It Explode?*, 14–29.
117. Greenberg, *Or Does It Explode?*, 28.
118. On Cantor, see Snyder, *The Voice of the City*, 49–52, 157. On the broader theme of Jewish contributions in popular culture in these years, see Dash Moore et al., *Jewish New York*, 253–54.
119. Gill, *Harlem*, 264–72.
120. Ferraro, *Feeling Italian*, 28–48, Stella quote on 46.
121. Mario Puzo, *The Fortunate Pilgrim* (New York: Ballantine, 1997), 20, 26–29. For a discussion of the novel, see Thomas J. Ferraro, *Feeling Italian: The Art of Ethnicity in America* (New York: NYU Press, 2005), 72–89.
122. Puzo, *The Fortunate Pilgrim*, 26.
123. Puzo, *The Fortunate Pilgrim*, 27–28.

6. Times of Trial: 1929–1945

1. Lillian D. Wald, *Windows on Henry Street* (Boston: Little, Brown, 1934), 227.
2. Mason B. Williams, *FDR, La Guardia, and the Making of Modern New York* (New York: Norton, 2013), 90–96; Thomas Kessner, *Fiorello H. La Guardia and the Making of Modern New York* (New York: McGraw-Hill, 1989), 165–70.

3. Quoted in Kessner, *Fiorello H. La Guardia*, 170.
4. Barbara Blumberg, *The New Deal and the Unemployed: The View from New York City* (Lewisburg, PA: Bucknell University Press, 1979), 17.
5. David Schneider and Albert Deutsch, *The History of Public Welfare in New York State, 1867–1940* (Montclair, NJ: Patterson and Smith, 1969), 296.
6. From Mary Agnes Hamilton, *In America Today* (1932), quoted in Bayrd Still, *Mirror for Gotham* (New York: NYU Press, 1956), 318.
7. Miriam Cohen, *From Workshop to Office: Two Generations of Italian Women in New York City, 1900–1950* (Ithaca, NY: Cornell University Press, 1993), 97; Robert Orsi, *The Madonna of 115th Street: Faith and Community in Italian Harlem, 1880–1950* (New Haven, CT: Yale University Press, 1985), 43; Simone Cinotto, *The Italian American: Food, Family, and Community in New York City* (Urbana: University of Illinois Press, 2013), 22.
8. Quoted in Howard Sachar, *A History of the Jews in America* (New York: Knopf, 1992), 429.
9. Alfred Kazin, *A Walker in the City* (London: Gollancz, 1952), 38–39.
10. Quoted in Jonathan Gill, *Harlem: The Four-Hundred-Year History from Dutch Village to Capital of Black America* (New York: Grove, 2011), 282.
11. New York State Temporary Commission on the Condition of the Colored Urban Population, *Second Report* (Albany, NY, 1939), 32–37.
12. Larry Greene, "Harlem in the Great Depression, 1928–1934," PhD diss., Columbia University, 1979, 98–146, 431–46; Cheryl Greenberg, *"Or Does It Explode?": Black Harlem in the Great Depression* (New York: Oxford University Press, 1991), 121–22.
13. New York State Temporary Commission, *Second Report*, 37.
14. Greenberg, *Or Does It Explode?*, 79.
15. For the relief situation, see Greene, "Harlem in the Great Depression," chap. 8; Greenberg, *Or Does It Explode?*, chap. 6.
16. Greenberg, *Or Does It Explode?*, 181–86; Harold X. Connolly, *A Ghetto Grows in Brooklyn* (New York: NYU Press, 1977), 117–23. See also the conditions described in Mayor La Guardia's Commission on the Harlem Riot of March, 1935, *Complete Report* (New York, 1969).
17. Scott D. Seligman, *Tong Wars: The Untold Story of Vice, Money, and Murder in New York's Chinatown* (New York: Viking, 2016), 243.
18. Seligman, *Tong Wars*, 243.
19. Ronald Bayor, *Neighbors in Conflict: The Irish, Germans, Jews, and Italians of New York City, 1929–1941* (Urbana: University of Illinois Press, 1988), 10–14; worker quoted in Blumberg, *The New Deal and the Unemployed*, 17–18; Beth Wenger, *New York Jews and the Great Depression: Uncertain Promise* (New Haven, CT: Yale University Press, 1996), 16–17; Cohen, *Workshop to Office*, 162–65.
20. Wenger, *New York Jews and the Great Depression*, 55–56.
21. Wenger, *New York Jews and the Great Depression*, 63.
22. Cohen, *Workshop to Office*, chap. 1.
23. For the plight of Jewish New Yorkers during the Great Depression, see Wenger, *New York Jews in the Great Depression*.
24. For the impact of the Depression, see Mary Brown, "Italian Immigrants and the Catholic Church in the Archdiocese of New York, 1880–1950," PhD diss., Columbia University, 1987.
25. William Welty, "Black Shepherds: A Study of Leading Negro Clergymen in New York City, 1900–1940," PhD diss., New York University, 1969.

26. Greenberg, *Or Does It Explode?*, 58–61.

27. Greenberg, *Or Does It Explode?*, 105.

28. Greenberg, *Or Does It Explode?*, 107.

29. Greenberg, *Or Does It Explode?*, 55–58.

30. See Greg Robinson, "Powell, Adam Clayton, Jr.," in *The Encyclopedia of New York City*, 2nd ed., ed. Kenneth Jackson (New Haven, CT: Yale University Press, 2010), 1031–32; Charles V. Hamilton, *Adam Clayton Powell: The Political Biography of an American Dilemma* (New York: Atheneum, 1992).

31. Wenger, *New York Jews and the Great Depression*, 152. See also Schneider and Deutsch, *The History of Public Welfare in New York*, chaps. 16–17.

32. Kessner, *Fiorello H. La Guardia*, 155.

33. Herbert Mitgang, *Once Upon a Time in New York: Jimmy Walker, Franklin Roosevelt, and the Last Great Battle of the Jazz Age* (New York: Free Press, 2000), 53.

34. George J. Lankevich, *American Metropolis: A Brief History of New York City* (New York: NYU Press, 1998), 162–163.

35. Quoted in Greenberg, *Or Does It Explode?*, 42–43.

36. Roger Waldinger, "The Ethnic Politics of Municipal Jobs" (Institute of Industrial Relations, UCLA, April 1993), 16.

37. Mitgang, *Once Upon a Time*, 196–198; Kessner, *Fiorello La Guardia*, 155–65, 219, 233–36.

38. Kessner, *Fiorello La Guardia*, 237–53.

39. Thomas Kessner, "La Guardia, Fiorello," in *The Encyclopedia of New York City*, 2nd ed., ed. Kenneth Jackson (New Haven, CT: Yale University Press, 2010), 717–718.

40. Arthur Mann, *La Guardia: A Fighter Against His Times, 1882–1933* (Philadelphia: Lippincott, 1959), 156–57.

41. See Howard Zinn, *La Guardia in Congress* (Ithaca, NY: Cornell University Press, 1958), esp. chaps. 6, 7, 8 and 11.

42. Chris McNickle, *To Be Mayor of New York* (New York: Columbia University Press, 1993), 32–40; Arthur Mann, *La Guardia Comes to Power 1933* (Philadelphia: Lippincott, 1956), chaps. 5–6; Charles Green and Basis Wilson, *The Struggle for Black Empowerment in New York City* (New York: Praeger, 1989), 7. The percent of civil service jobs obtained by competitive examination went from 55 to 75 percent between 1935 and 1939.

43. Kessner, *Fiorello La Guardia*, 287–90.

44. Kessner, *Fiorello La Guardia*, 194–96, 575; Paul Moses, *An Unlikely Union: The Love-Hate Story of New York's Irish and Italians* (New York: NYU Press, 2015), 239.

45. George Furniss, "The Political Assimilation of Negroes in New York City, 1870–1965," PhD diss., Columbia University, 1969, 291–329; Thomas M. Henderson, "Harlem Confronts the Machine: The Struggle for Local Autonomy and Black District Leadership," *Afro-Americans in New York Life and History* 3 (July 1979): 51–68.

46. Greene, "Harlem in the Great Depression," 116.

47. Greenberg, *Or Does It Explode?*, 114–19.

48. Greenberg, *Or Does It Explode?*, 136.

49. Greene, "Harlem in the Great Depression," 323–50.

50. Williams, *City of Ambition*, 148–54.

51. Kessner, *Fiorello La Guardia*, 299–304; Robert Caro, *The Power Broker* (New York: Vintage, 1975), chaps. 23–24.

52. Williams, *City of Ambition*, 152–159; *Times* quote on 155.

53. Caro, *The Power Broker*, 489–94, 510–14, 557–60; for a less critical view of Moses, see Joel Schwartz, "Robert Moses and the Modern City: The Transformation of

New York," in *The Encyclopedia of New York City*, 2nd ed., ed. Kenneth Jackson (New Haven, CT: Yale University Press, 2010), 856. For a careful of examination of public pools and integration in Moses's New York, see Marta Gutman, "Race, Place, and Play: Robert Moses and the WPA Swimming Pools in New York City," *Journal of the Society of Architectural Historians* 67, no. 4 (December 2008): 532–61. On discrimination in New Deal projects, including employment, see Greenberg, *Or Does It Explode?*, 153–63.

54. Caro, *The Power Broker*, 432–44.

55. Caro, *The Power Broker*, 199.

56. Kessner, *Fiorello La Guardia*, 320–42; Caro, *The Power Broker*, 610–13.

57. Richard Plunz, *A History of Housing in New York City: Dwelling Type and Social Change in the American Metropolis* (New York: Columbia University Press, 1990), 227.

58. Williams, *City of Ambition*, 243.

59. David Kennedy, *Freedom from Fear: The American People in Depression and War, 1929–1945* (New York: Oxford University Press, 1989), 254.

60. See Sharon Ann Musher, *Democratic Art: The New Deal's Influences on American Culture* (Chicago: University of Chicago Press, 2015), 112–19.

61. Federal Writers' Project, *New York City Guide* (New York: Random House, 1939), 49–52. Also see the related volume *New York Panorama* (New York, 1938).

62. On Ellison, see Musher, *Democratic Art*, 3; and Sara Rutkowski, *Literary Legacies of the Federal Writers Project: Voices of the Depression in the Postwar Era* (New York: Palgrave Macmillan, 2017), 37. On Shahn, see Diana L. Linden, *Ben Shahn's New Deal Murals: Jewish Identity in the American Scene* (Detroit, MI: Wayne State University Press, 2015), 1, 65–67, 71–73, 86–91.

63. Greenberg, *Or Does It Explode?*, 165; Gill, *Harlem*, 311–12; "One-Way Ticket: Jacob Lawrence's Migration Series and Other Visions of the Great Movement North," https://www.moma.org/calendar/exhibitions/1495.

64. Williams, *City of Ambition*, 201–4.

65. Robert P. Ingalls, *Herbert H. Lehman and New York's Little New Deal* (New York: NYU Press, 1975), 131.

66. Irving Bernstein, *Turbulent Years: A History of the American Workers, 1933–1941* (Boston: Houghton Mifflin, 1969), 84.

67. Bernstein, *Turbulent Years*, 89.

68. For the teachers, see Marjorie Murphy, *Blackboard Unions: The AFT and the NEA, 1900–1980* (Ithaca, NY: Cornell University Press, 1990), 135; and Diane Ravitch, *The Great School Wars, New York City, 1805–1973* (New York: Basic Books, 1974), 236–39. The drop in immigration enabled the city to ease crowding in the schools and reduce class size.

69. Joshua B. Freeman, "Catholics, Communists, and Republicans," in *Working-Class America: Essays on Labor, Community, and Society*, ed. Daniel J. Walkowitz and Michael H. Frisch (Urbana: University of Illinois Press, 1983), 256–75.

70. On the TWU, see Joshua B. Freeman, *In Transit: The Transport Workers in New York City, 1933–1966* (New York: Oxford University Press, 1989), esp. chaps. 9 and 11.

71. Freeman, *In Transit*, esp. chap. 6; Kessner, *Fiorello La Guardia*, 460–61.

72. Renqui Yu, *"To Save China, To Save Ourselves": The Chinese Hand Laundry Alliance of New York* (Philadelphia Temple University Press, 1992), chap. 2.

73. Jeffrey Gurock, *Jews in Gotham: New York Jews in a Changing City, 1920–2010* (New York: NYU Press, 2012), 53.

74. Gurock, *Jews in Gotham*.

75. Nathan Glazer, *The Social Basis of American Communism* (New York: Harcourt, Brace, 1961), 116–17, 138–40. The few thousand communists in New York represented one-third to one-half of the party's national membership.

76. Gill, *Harlem*, 297.

77. Mark Naison, *Communists in Harlem During the Depression* (New York: Grove, 1983), 39, 297.

78. Naison, *Communists in Harlem During the Depression*, 110, 136, 271–72, 288, 312–13.

79. Kessner, *Fiorello La Guardia*, 408–19; McNickle, *To Be Mayor of New York*, 37.

80. Kennedy, *Freedom from Fear*, 315, 398.

81. Bayor, *Neighbors in Conflict*, 29.

82. Frank Kingdom, "Discrimination in Medical Colleges," *American Mercury* 56 (October 1945): 394; Walter R. Hart, "Anti-Semitism in NY Medical Schools," *American Mercury* 65 (July 1947): 56.

83. Ruth Jacknow Markowitz, *My Daughter, the Teacher: Jewish Teachers in the New York City Schools* (New Brunswick, NJ: Rutgers University Press, 1993), 15, 18–30.

84. Bayor, *Neighbors in Conflict*, 26–27, 33–40; McNickle, *To be Mayor of New York*, 32–40.

85. Bayor, *Neighbors in Conflict*, 28.

86. Gill, *Harlem*, 303; Mayor La Guardia's Commission, *Complete Report*, 7–9.

87. *Complete Report*, 18.

88. *Complete Report*, 11; Naison, *Communists in Harlem During the Great Depression*, 141–48.

89. Peter M. Rutkoff and William Scott, *New School: A History of the New School for Social Research* (New York: Free Press, 1998), chap. 5.

90. On German Jews in Washington Heights, see Robert W. Snyder, *Crossing Broadway: Washington Heights and the Promise of New York* (Ithaca, NY: Cornell University Press, 2015), 27–33; and Steven M. Lowenstein, *Frankfurt on the Hudson: The German-Jewish Community of Washington Heights, 1933–1938* (Detroit, MI: Wayne State University Press, 1989).

91. Walter Isaacson, *Kissinger: A Biography* (New York: Simon and Schuster, 1992), 34–35; Tyler Anbinder, *City of Dreams: The Four-Hundred-Year Epic History of Immigrant New York* (New York: Houghton Mifflin Harcourt, 2016), 498–99, 501–2.

92. Bayor, *Neighbors in Conflict*, 59–63.

93. Kessner, *Fiorello La Guardia*, 521.

94. Nancy Carnevale, *A New Language, A New World* (Urbana: University of Illinois Press, 2009), 140.

95. John Diggins, *Mussolini and Fascism: The View from America* (Princeton, NJ: Princeton University Press, 1972), 134–37, 303–4, 346–48. Anarchists like Carlo Tresca had always been vehemently antifascist and foes of Mussolini. Kessner says that Pope's views continued into the war years: Kessner, *Fiorello H. La Guardia*, 518–19. On Tresca, see Dorothy Gallagher, *All the Right Enemies: The Life and Murder of Carlo Tresca* (New Brunswick, NJ: Rutgers University Press, 1988).

96. Bayor, *Neighbors in Conflict*, 78–86. For a summary of the history of Italy, Nazi Germany, anti-Semitism, and the Holocaust, see "Italy," in *Holocaust Encyclopedia*, https://www.ushmm.org/wlc/en/article.php?ModuleId=10005455.

97. William Scott, *The Sons of Sheba's Race: African-Americans and the Italo-Ethiopian War, 1935–1941* (Bloomington: University of Indiana Press, 1993), chap. 9.

98. Scott, *The Sons of Sheba's Race*, chap. 11; Naison, *Communists in Harlem*, 157, 262–63, 195–96.

99. Bayor, *Neighbors in Conflict*, 97–107.

100. Evelyn Gonzalez, *The Bronx* (New York: Columbia University Press, 2004), 105.
101. For a wide-ranging collection of essays on New York and the Spanish Civil War, see Peter N. Carroll and James D. Fernandez, eds., *Facing Fascism: New York and the Spanish Civil War* (New York: Museum of the City of New York and NYU Press, 2007).
102. Patrick J. McNamara, "Pro-Franco Sentiment and Activity in New York City," in *Facing Fascism*, ed. Carroll and Fernandez, 95–101; Bayor, *Neighbors in Conflict*, 87–97; Kennedy, *Freedom From Fear*, 398–400. An excellent account of Americans and the war in Spain is Adam Hochschild, *Spain in Our Hearts: Americans in the Spanish Civil War, 1936–1939* (New York: Houghton Mifflin Harcourt, 2016).
103. Bayor, *Neighbors in Conflict*, 65.
104. The Federal Writers' Project, *WPA Guide to New York City* (New York: Random House, 1939), 251–52.
105. See Jaffe, *New York at War*, 232–33; Yu, *To Save China, To Save Ourselves*, 77–99.
106. Joseph A. Wytrawal, *Poles in American History and Tradition* (Detroit, MI: Wayne State University Press, 1969), 386–87.
107. The Pulaski Day parade of 1943, for example, featured signs and banners urging support for the Polish American division of the National War Fund. See "25,000 Poles March in Aid of War Fund," *New York Times*, October 11, 1943.
108. Richard Lingeman, *Don't You Know There Is a War On? The American Home Front, 1941–1945* (New York: Putnam, 1970), 331.
109. For the response to the Holocaust, see David Wyman, *The Abandonment of the Jews: America and the Holocaust, 1941–1945* (New York: Pantheon, 1984).
110. "Italians in City Back U.S. in War: Populations of 'Little Italys' Stunned but Stress Their Allegiance to America," *New York Times*, December 12, 1941.
111. "Loyalty of Italian-Americans Lauded at Columbus Day Rally: 25,000 Jamming Circle at Annual Tribute to Discover Hear Pleas for Tolerance for Minority Groups in US," *New York Times*, October 13, 1942.
112. "Yorkville Hushed as U.S. Enters War," *New York Times*, December 12, 1941.
113. "Effigies of Hitler Hung in Yorkville," *New York Times*, October 16, 1942.
114. Jaffe, *New York at War*, 237–38, 255–57.
115. Jaffe, *New York at War*, 260–61. On Japanese Americans in wartime New York, see Greg Robinson, "Resettlement in New York," in *Densho Encyclopedia*, https://encyclopedia.densho.org/Resettlement%20in%20New%20York/.
116. Greenberg, *Or Does It Explode?*, 198–200; Blumberg, *The New Deal and the Unemployed*, 268–69. On women in the Brooklyn Navy Yard, see Arnold Sparr, "Looking for Rosie: Women Defense Workers in the Brooklyn Navy Yard, 1942–1946," *New York History* 8, no. 3 (July 2000): 320–25, 328–30, 333–35, 340.
117. Greenberg, *Or Does It Explode?*, 202–7.
118. Gordon Bloom, F. Marion Fletcher, and Charles Perry, *Negro Employment in Retail Trade* (Philadelphia: University of Pennsylvania, 1972), 40.
119. Bloom, Fletcher, and Perry, *Negro Employment in Retail Trade*, 42.
120. Jaffe, *New York at War*, 251–54.
121. Richard Goldstein, *Helluva Town! The Story of New York City During World War II* (New York: Free Press, 2010), 175–80, quote from 178.
122. Gerald Meyer, "Frank Sinatra: The Popular Front and an American Icon," *Science and Society* 66, no. 3 (Fall 2002): 318–20; Frank Ross and Mervyn LeRoy, prod., and Albert Maltz, writer, *The House I Live In* (RKO Radio Pictures, 1945); Lewis Allen, also known as Abel Meeropol (words) and Earl Robinson (music), "The House I Live In" (New York: Chappell and Co., 1942).

123. For the riot, see Dominic Capeci Jr., *The Harlem Riot of 1943* (Philadelphia: Temple University Press, 1977).

124. Blumberg, *The New Deal and the Unemployed*, 268–69; Greenberg, *Or Does It Explode?*, 199.

125. Greenberg, *Or Does It Explode?*, 223.

126. Greenberg, *Or Does It Explode?*, 136–41.

127. Dominic J. Capeci Jr., "Fiorello H. La Guardia and the Stuyvesant Town Controversy of 1943," *New-York Historical Society Quarterly* 62 (October 1978): 292.

128. Samuel Zipp, *Manhattan Projects: The Rise and Fall of Urban Renewal in Cold War New York* (New York: Oxford University Press, 2010), 76–78.

129. Capeci, "Fiorello H. La Guardia and the Stuyvesant Town Controversy of 1943," 295.

130. Zipp, *Manhattan Projects*, 118–23, 209; Arthur Simon, *Stuyvesant Town, USA: Pattern for Two Americas* (New York: NYU Press, 1970).

131. See Deborah Dash Moore, *GI Jews: How World War II Changed a Generation* (Cambridge, MA: Harvard University Press, 2004), 249–64; Salvatore J. Lagumina, *The Humble and the Heroic: Wartime Italian Americans* (Amherst, NY: Cambria, 2006).

7. City of Hope, City of Fear: 1945–1997

1. This section is based on Andrea Ramsey's interview in Mark Naison and Bob Gumbs, *Before the Fires: An Oral History of African American Life in the Bronx from the 1930s to the 1960s* (New York: Fordham University Press, 2016), xi–xiv, 127–30, 173–74, 166.

2. Naison and Gumbs, *Before the Fires*, xi–xiv.

3. Naison and Gumbs, *Before the Fires*, 126–33, quote on 133.

4. Naison and Gumbs, *Before the Fires*, xii.

5. On population, see Ira Rosenwaike, *Population History of New York City* (Syracuse, NY: Syracuse University Press, 1972), 109, 141, 192–93; and Campbell Gibson and Kay Jung, *Historical Census Statistics on Population Totals by Race*, Population Division, Working Paper 76 (Washington, DC: U.S. Census Bureau, 2005), "Table 33. New York—Race and Hispanic Origin for Selected Large Cities and Other Places: Earliest Census to 1990."

6. See Robert J. Gordon, *The Rise and Fall of American Growth and the U.S. Standard of Living Since the Civil War* (Princeton, NJ: Princeton University Press, 2016), 535–65.

7. For the struggle against discrimination, see Herman D. Bloch, *The Circle of Discrimination: An Economic and Social Study of the Black Man in New York* (New York: NYU Press, 1969); and Milton R. Konvitz, *A Century of Civil Rights* (New York: Columbia University Press, 1961).

8. For the New York City Commission on Human Rights, see Gerald Benjamin, *Race Relations and the New York City Commission on Human Rights* (Ithaca, NY: Cornell University Press, 1974).

9. Konvitz, *A Century of Civil Rights*, 197–201, 225–28; Leonard Dinnerstein, *Anti-Semitism in America* (New York: Oxford University Press, 1994), 158–59, 238–39.

10. US Equal Employment Opportunity Commission, Discrimination in White Collar Employment, *Hearings*, New York City, January 1968, 667–79; Howard Sachar, *A History of the Jews in America* (New York: Knopf, 1992), 649–50.

11. Richard Alba and Nancy Foner, "The Second Generation from the Last Great Wave of Immigration: Setting the Record Straight," *Migration Information Source* (October 1, 2006): 2.

12. The New School for Social Research, *New York's Jewish Poor and the Jewish Working Class* (New York: Federation of Jewish Philanthropies, 1972), 13–18, 26–28.

13. Roger Waldinger, *Still the Promised City: African Americans and New Immigrants in Post Industrial New York* (Cambridge, MA: Harvard University Press, 1996), 102–6.

14. On Italians and American popular culture, see Thomas J. Ferraro, *Feeling Italian: The Art of Ethnicity in America* (New York: NYU Press, 2005), 90–106, 175–77; and Maria Laurino, *The Italian Americans: A History* (New York: Norton, 2015), chaps. 15, 17. On Italian vernacular art, see Joseph Sciorra, *Built with Faith: Italian American Imagination and Catholic Material Culture in New York City* (Knoxville: University of Tennessee Press, 2015).

15. Dennis Clark, "The Irish in the American Economy," in *The Irish in America: Emigration, Assimilation, and Impact*, ed. P. J. Drudy (Cambridge: Cambridge University Press, 1985), 241–44; John Cooney, *An American Pope: The Life and Times of Francis Cardinal Spellman* (New York: Times Books, 1984), 101–2.

16. Chris McNickle, "Flynn, Edward J." and "O'Dwyer, William," both in *The Encyclopedia of New York City*, 2nd ed., ed. Kenneth T. Jackson (New Haven, CT: Yale University Press, 2010), 461, 952–53.

17. Daniel Patrick Moynihan, "The Irish" (1963), reprinted in *Making the Irish American: History and Heritage of the Irish in the United States*, ed. J. J. Lee and Marion R. Casey (New York: NYU Press, 2006), 475–76, 481, 503–12, quote on 475. On DeSapio, see Chris McNickle, "DeSapio, Carmine (Gerard)," in *The Encyclopedia of New York City*, 2nd ed., ed. Kenneth T. Jackson (New Haven, CT: Yale University Press, 2010), 362.

18. For an overall view of Spellman's power, see George J. Marlin and Brad Miner, *Sons of Saint Patrick: A History of Archbishops from New York from Dagger John to Timmytown* (San Francisco: Ignatius, 2017), 212–50.

19. For a defense of Impellitteri's mayoralty, see Salvatore J. La Gumina, *New York at Mid-Century: The Impellitteri Years* (Westport, CT: Greenwood, 1992).

20. Chris McNickle, *To Be Mayor of New York* (New York: Columbia University Press, 1993), 169; Robert W. Snyder, *Crossing Broadway: Washington Heights and the Promise of New York* (Ithaca, NY: Cornell University Press, 2015), 55.

21. Joshua Freeman, *Working-Class New York: Life and Labor Since World War II* (New York: New Press, 2000), 201–14.

22. Freeman, *Working-Class New York*, 202.

23. Martin Shefter, *Political Crisis/Fiscal Crisis: The Collapse and Revival of New York City* (New York: Columbia University Press, 1992), 115–19; David R. Eichenthal, "Changing Styles and Strategies of the Mayor," in *Urban Politics*, ed. Jewel Bullush and Dick Netzer (Armonk, NY: M. E. Sharpe, 1990), 70.

24. Theodore Lowi, *At the Pleasure of the Mayor: Patronage and Power in New York City, 1898–1958* (New York: Free Press of Glencoe, 1964), fig. 8.2; Shefter, *Political Crisis/Fiscal Crisis*, 115–17; Joan Weitzman, *City Workers and Fiscal Crisis: Cutbacks, Givebacks, and Survival: A Study of the New York Experience* (New Brunswick, NJ: Rutgers University Press, 1979), 1–2, 10.

25. See John Mollenkopf, "The Postindustrial Transformation of the Political Order in New York City," in *Power, Culture, and Place: Essays on New York City*, ed. John Mollenkopf (New York: Russell Sage, 1988), 230–41.

26. Jonathan Reider, *Canarsie: The Jews and Italians of Brooklyn Against Liberalism* (Cambridge, MA: Harvard University Press, 1985), 15.

27. Reider, *Canarsie*, 15–19.

28. Melanie Leftkowitz, "Diverse Housing, Parks and Challenges in Canarsie, Brooklyn," *Wall Street Journal*, August 22, 2014.

29. On the Grand Concourse, see Constance Rosenblum, *Boulevard of Dreams: Heady Times, Heartbreak, and Hope Along the Grand Concourse in the Bronx* (New York: NYU Press, 2009). On Rochdale Village, see Peter Eisenstadt, *Rochdale Village: Robert Moses, 6,000 Families, and New York City's Great Experiment in Integrated Housing* (Ithaca, NY: Cornell University Press, 2010), 3–20, 131–53, 245–51.

30. On postwar Italian immigration, see Sciorra, *Built with Faith*, xxxii–xxiv. For Staten Island, see Nadia H. Youssef, *Population Dynamics on Staten Island: From Ethnic Homogeneity to Diversity* (New York: Center for Migration Studies, 1991). On Italian American women, see William Egelman, "Traditional Roles and Modern Work Patterns: Italian-American Women in New York City," in *American Women, Italian Style: Italian Americana's Best Writings on Women*, ed. Carol Bonomo Albright and Christine Palamidessi Moore (New York: Fordham University Press, 2011), 81–83.

31. For a critical assessment of the influence of Moses, see Robert Caro, *The Power Broker: Robert Moses and the Fall of New York* (New York: Vintage, 1975), 7–21.

32. On the movement to the suburbs nationally, consult Kenneth T. Jackson, *Crabgrass Frontier: The Suburbanization of the United States* (New York: Oxford University Press, 1985), 241–45; and Craig Steven Wilder, *A Covenant with Color: Race and Social Power in Brooklyn* (New York: Columbia University Press, 2000), 201–17. Also see Barbara M. Kelly, "Levittown," in *Encyclopedia of New York State*, ed. Peter Eisenstadt (Syracuse, NY: Syracuse University Press, 2005), 886–87.

33. On ethnicity in postwar New York, see Joshua M. Zeitz, *White Ethnic New York: Jews, Catholics, and the Shaping of Postwar Politics* (Chapel Hill, NC: University of North Carolina Press, 2007), 11–38. The literature on whiteness is vast. Among the valuable entries in the debates that surround it are David Roediger, *The Wages of Whiteness: Race and the Making of the American Working Class* (London: Verso, 1999); Matthew Frye Jacobson, *Whiteness of a Different Color: European Immigrants and the Alchemy of Race* (Cambridge, MA: Harvard University Press, 1999); and Eric L. Goldstein, *The Price of Whiteness: Jews, Race, and American Identity* (Princeton, NJ: Princeton University Press, 2008).

34. Paul Ritterbrand and Steven M. Cohen, "The Social Characteristics of the New York Area Jewish Community, 1981," *American Jewish Year Book* (1984): 128–29.

35. Joseph Palisi, "The Brooklyn Navy Yard," in *Brooklyn USA: The Fourth Largest City in America*, ed. Rita Miller (New York: Columbia University Press), 19–24.

36. A good example is Sunset Park in Brooklyn; see Tarry Hum, *Making a Global Neighborhood: Brooklyn's Sunset Park* (Philadelphia: Temple University Press, 2014), 43–71. See also K. Austin Kerr, "Brewing and Distilling," in *The Encyclopedia of New York City*, 2nd ed., ed. Kenneth T. Jackson (New Haven, CT: Yale University Press, 2010), 153–54.

37. On containerization, see Marc Levinson, *The Box: How the Shipping Container Made the World Smaller and the World Economy Bigger* (Princeton, NJ: Princeton University Press, 2006), 96–100, 235–38, 271–73; also Louis Winnick, "Letter from Sunset Park, NY," *City Journal* 1 (Winter 1991): 79.

38. New York City Department of City Planning, *The Newest New Yorkers* (New York: Department of City Planning, 1992), 27.

39. Jeffrey S. Gurock, *Jews in Gotham: New York Jews in a Changing City, 1920–2010* (New York: NYU Press, 2012), 124–25.

40. US Commission on Displaced Persons, *The DP Story: The Final Report of the United States Commission on Displaced Persons* (Washington, DC, 1952), 244; Lyman White,

300,000 New Americans: The Epic of a Modern Immigrant-Aid Society (New York: Harper, 1957), 316–19; Leonard Dinnerstein, *America and the Survivors of the Holocaust* (New York: Columbia University Press, 1982), 288; Administrator of the Refugee Relief Act of 1953, *Final Report* (Washington, 1953).

41. Joe Salvo and Arun Peter Lobo, "Population," in *The Encyclopedia of New York City*, 2nd ed., ed. Kenneth T. Jackson (New Haven, CT: Yale University Press, 2010), 1019–1020; Rosenwaike, *Population History of New York City*, 132–43.

42. Virginia Sanchez Korrol, "Puerto Ricans," in *The Encyclopedia of New York City*, 2nd ed., ed. Kenneth T. Jackson (New Haven, CT: Yale University Press, 2010), 1059.

43. Joseph Fitzpatrick, *Puerto Rican Americans* (Englewood Cliffs, NJ: Prentice Hall, 1987), 14–27; Nathan Glazer and Patrick Moynihan, *Beyond the Melting Pot* (Cambridge, MA: MIT Press, 1961), 91–98.

44. Department of City Planning, *Puerto Rican New Yorkers in 1990* (New York: Department of City Planning, 1994), iv, 53–55. Also see U.S. Commission on Civil Rights, *Puerto Ricans in the Continental United States: An Uncertain Future* (Washington, 1976); and Lloyd Rogler and Rosemary Santana Cooney, *Puerto Rican Families in New York City: An Inter-generational Process* (Maplewood, NJ: Waterfront, 1984).

45. A discussion of the division can be found in Michael Lapp, "The Migration Division of Puerto Rico and Puerto Ricans in New York City, 1948–1969," in *Immigration to New York*, ed. William Pencak, Selma Berrol, and Randall Miller (Philadelphia: Balche Institute, 1991), 198–214.

46. Fitzpatrick, *Puerto Rican Americans*, 52–58.

47. Fitzpatrick, *Puerto Rican Americans*, 117–35.

48. Rosenwaike, *Population History*, 139–42.

49. Rosenwaike, *Population History*, 139–42.

50. Jules Tygiel, *Baseball's Great Experiment: Jackie Robinson and His Legacy* (New York: Oxford University Press, 1983), 84–85, 287–88, 294–95.

51. Tygiel, *Baseball's Great Experiment*, 224–26, 244–45, 295–99.

52. On black politics in New York City, see Charles Green and Basil Wilson, *The Struggle for Black Empowerment in New York City* (New York: Praeger, 1989), 85–113; Edwin Lewinson, *Black Politics in New York City* (New York: Astra, 1974), 88–89, 144–59; and John C. Walter, *The Harlem Fox: J. Raymond Jones and Tammany, 1920–1970* (Albany: SUNY Press, 1989).

53. On West Indian politicians in New York, see Philip Kasinitz, *Caribbean New York: Black Immigrants and the Politics of Race* (Ithaca, NY: Cornell University Press, 1992), 9–10, 207–23, 251–55. On Shirley Chisholm, see http://history.house.gov/People/List ing/C/CHISHOLM,-Shirley-Anita-(C000371)/.

54. On Malcolm X, see Manning Marable, *Malcolm X: A Life of Reinvention* (New York: Viking, 2011).

55. On the role of the churches, see Green and Wilson, *The Struggle for Black Empowerment*, 59–83.

56. Benjamin, *Race Relations*, 173–77; *Amsterdam News*, August 25, 1962, July 20, 1963, July 27, 1963, October 12, 1963, November 23, 1963; and Wilder, *A Covenant with Color*, 212–25.

57. Snyder, *Crossing Broadway*, 74–76.

58. Snyder, *Crossing Broadway*, 78–81.

59. Snyder, *Crossing Broadway*, 80–87.

60. Harold Connolly, *A Ghetto Grows in Brooklyn* (New York: NYU Press, 1977), 133–34.

61. Wendell Pritchett, *Brownsville, Brooklyn: Blacks, Jews, and the Changing Face of the Ghetto* (Chicago: University of Chicago Press, 2002), 5–7, 101–3, 142–45.

62. Rosenblum, *Boulevard of Dreams*, 177–81.

63. Flora Davidson, "City Policy and Housing Abandonment: A Case Study of New York City, 1965–1973," PhD. diss., Columbia University, 1979, 20–23.

64. Nicholas Dagen Bloom, *Public Housing That Worked: New York in the Twentieth Century* (Philadelphia: University of Pennsylvania Press, 2008), 1–10.

65. Forty years after he published his book, Caro still held to his harsh view of Moses. See Robert Caro, "The Power Broker, 40 Years Later," *New York Times*, December 10, 2014. For a favorable view of Moses, see the essays in Hillary Ballon and Kenneth Jackson, eds., *Robert Moses and the Modern City: The Transformation of New York* (New York: Norton, 2007). On the conflict over scatter-site public housing in Forest Hills, Queens, see Jonathan Soffer, *Ed Koch and the Rebuilding of New York City* (New York: Columbia University Press, 2010), 108–11. On the challenges of creating affordable housing in the postwar years, see Estelle Gilson, "What Hope for the Homeless People?" *Columbia* 14 (March 1989): 15. See also Michael A. Stegman, "Housing," in *Setting Municipal Priorities, 1987*, ed. Charles Brecher and Raymond Horton (New York: NYU Press, 1986), 197–219.

66. City Commission on Human Rights (CCHR), *Arson, Vandalism, and Other Racially Inspired Violence in New York City* (December 8, 1972), 6.

67. Benjamin, *Race Relations*, 100–4, 230–35; Brian Purnell, *Fighting Jim Crow in the County of Kings: The Congress of Racial Equality in Brooklyn* (Lexington: University of Kentucky Press, 2013), 60–89; Mireya Navarro, "Segregation Issue Complicates de Blasio's Housing Push," *New York Times*, April 14, 2016.

68. Simone Cinotto, "Italian Doo-Wop: Sense of Place, Politics of Style, and Racial Crossovers in Postwar New York City," in *Making Italian America: Consumer Culture and the Production of Ethnic Identifies*, ed. Simone Cinotto (New York: Fordham University Press, 2014), 164–67, 174–77.

69. Ernesto R. Acevedo-Munoz, *West Side Story as Cinema: The Making and Impact of an American Masterpiece* (Lawrence: University Press of Kansas, 2013), 1–2. On gangs, see Eric C. Schneider, *Vampires, Dragons, and Egyptian Kings: Youth Gangs in Postwar New York* (Princeton, NJ: Princeton University Press, 2001).

70. Marcia M. Gallo, *"No One Helped": Kitty Genovese, New York City, and the Myth of Urban Apathy* (Ithaca, NY: Cornell University Press, 2015), xiii–xxiii.

71. Clarence Taylor, *Knocking at Our Own Door: Milton A. Galamison and the Struggle to Integrate New York City Schools* (New York: Columbia University Press, 1997), 137–45, 147–51, 155–59, 161–64, 167–69, 171–75; Snyder, *Crossing Broadway*, 82–84.

72. The riot is covered in Michael W. Flamm, *In the Heat of the Summer: The New York Riots of 1964 and the War on Crime* (Philadelphia: University of Pennsylvania Press, 2016), 79–104.

73. See Vincent Cannato, "Lindsay, John V.," in *The Encyclopedia of New York City*, 2nd ed., ed. Kenneth T. Jackson (New Haven, CT: Yale University Press, 2010), 750–51.

74. Snyder, *Crossing Broadway*, 86–88.

75. Lindsay's efforts are covered in Vincent J. Cannato, *The Ungovernable City: John Lindsay and His Struggle to Save New York* (New York: Basic Books, 2001). On Lindsay, reformers and black New Yorkers, see the essays in *America's Mayor: John V. Lindsay and the Reinvention of New York*, ed. Sam Roberts (New York: Museum of the City of New York and Columbia University Press, 2010), especially Charlayne Hunter-Gault, "Black and White," 42–57; and John Mollenkopf, "The Politics of Change," 102–17.

76. Marilynn S. Johnson, *Street Justice: A History of Police Violence in New York City* (Boston: Beacon, 2003), 239–51.

77. See The Mayor's Commission on Black New Yorkers, *Report* (1988), 130–32, 148–59; Taylor, *Knocking at Our Own Door*, 116–17; and Jerald E. Podair, *The Strike That Changed New York: Blacks, Whites, and Ocean Hill–Brownsville* (New Haven, CT: Yale University Press, 2002), 17.

78. Mayor's Advisory Panel on Decentralization of the New York City Schools, *Reconstruction for Learning* (New York, 1967), 1–2, 4–5, 73–75; Gurock, *Jews in Gotham*, 37–38; Podair, *The Strike That Changed New York*, 123–51, 207–9; and Deborah Dash Moore, Jeffrey S. Gurock, Annie Polland, Howard B. Rock, and Daniel Soyer, with a visual essay by Diana L. Linden, *Jewish New York: The Remarkable Story of a City and a People* (New York: NYU Press, 2017), 295–304.

79. See Rohit T. Aggarwala and Kenneth T. Jackson, "Terrorism," in *The Encyclopedia of New York City*, 2nd ed., ed. Kenneth T. Jackson (New Haven, CT: Yale University Press, 2010), 1292–93; Fritz Umbach, *The Last Neighborhood Cops: The Rise and Fall of Community Policing in New York Public Housing* (New Brunswick, NJ: Rutgers University Press, 2011), 95–96; Johnson, *Street Justice*, 266–76; and Peniel E. Joseph, *Waiting 'til the Midnight Hour: A Narrative History of Black Power in America* (New York: Henry Holt, 2006), 262–69.

80. On community institutions and struggles for power, see Thomas J. Sugrue, *New York: Sweet Land of Liberty: The Forgotten Struggle for Civil Rights in the North* (New York: Random House, 2008), 475–78; and Ira Katznelson, *City Trenches: Urban Politics and the Patterning of Class in the United States* (Chicago: University of Chicago Press, 1981), 115–124, 135–189. On Evelina Antonetty, see Sonia Song-Ha Lee, *Building a Latino Civil Rights Movement: Puerto Ricans, African Americans, and the Pursuit of Racial Justice in New York City* (Chapel Hill: University of North Carolina Press, 2014), 1, 152–54, 176, 223–24; and Adina Back and Evelina Lopez Antonetty, "'Parent Power': The United Bronx Parents and the War on Poverty," in *The War on Poverty: A New Grassroots History, 1964–1980*, ed. Annelise Orleck and Lisa Harirjian (Athens: University of Georgia Press, 2011), 184–208.

81. David Lavin, Richard Alba, and Richard Silberstein, *Right Versus Privilege: The Open-Admissions Experiment at the City University of New York* (New York: Free Press, 1981), 1–5, 9–20.

82. Lavin, Alba, and Silberstein, *Right Versus Privilege*, 1–5, 9–20.

83. Lavin, Alba, and Silberstein, *Right Versus Privilege*, chap. 5; Mayor's Commission on Black New Yorkers, *Report*, 12–14, 193.

84. Waldinger, *Still the Promised City*, 206.

85. Mayor's Commission on Black New Yorkers, *Report*, 93. A number of mayors, dating to the 1950s, had issued orders about nondiscrimination in municipal hiring.

86. Mayor's Commission on Black New Yorkers, *Report*, 208–12.

87. Bloch, *The Circle of Discrimination*, 49–78.

88. Bloch, *The Circle of Discrimination*, 49–56.

89. US Equal Employment Opportunity Commission, *Discrimination in White Collar Employment*, Hearings, New York City (January 1968), 557–664; CCHR, *Bias in the Building Industry: An Updated Report, 1963–1967* (1967). See also Bloch, *Circle of Discrimination*, 125–50; Report of the New York Advisory Committee, "Discrimination in the Building Trades: The New York City Case," in *Contemporary Labor Issues*, ed. Walter Fogel and Archie Klingartner (Belmont, CA: Wadsworth, 1966), 288–95.

90. Mayor's Commission on Black Yorkers, *Report*, 54, 91. The commission based its conclusions on a 1982 study by the Community Service Society of New York City.

91. Bernard Bellush and Jewel Bellush, *Union Power in New York: Victor Gotbaum and District Council 37* (New York: Praeger, 1984), 233–36.

92. Freeman, *In Transit*, 28, 152.

93. For 1199, see Leon Fink and Brian Greenberg, *Upheaval in the Quiet Zone: A History of the Hospital Workers Union 1199* (Urbana: University of Illinois Press, 1989), 210–233.

94. *New York Times*, December 2, 1989.

95. Snyder, *Crossing Broadway*, 125. For New York as something of an urban social democracy, see Freeman, *Working-Class New York*, 99.

96. Sam Roberts, "City in Crisis I," in *America's Mayor: John V. Lindsay and the Reinvention of New York*, ed. Sam Roberts (New York: Museum of the City of New York and Columbia University Press, 2010), 11–25.

97. Kim Phillips-Fein, *Fear City: New York's Fiscal Crisis and the Rise of Austerity Politics* (New York: Metropolitan, 2017), 28–38, 41–44.

98. Phillips-Fein, *Fear City*, 44–45; Chris McNickle, "Abraham D. Beame," in *The Encyclopedia of New York City*, 2nd ed., ed. Kenneth T. Jackson (New Haven, CT: Yale University Press, 2010), 106.

99. Freeman, *Working- Class New York,* 256–57, 270–71; Phillips-Fein, *Fear City*, 177–84.

100. Rodriguez-Fraticelli, "Higher Education Task Force," 25; Mayor's Commission on Black New Yorkers, *Report*, 80.

101. Freeman, *Working-Class New York*, 270–72; Phillips-Fein, *Fear City*, 206–10, 212–18, 220–26.

102. Phillips-Fein, *Fear City*, 296–302.

103. Juan Flores, *Salsa Rising: New York Latin Music of the Sixties Generation* (New York: Oxford University Press, 2016), 1–27, 32, 106–19, 233–35; Caesar Miguel Rondon, *The Book of Salsa: A Chronicle of Urban Music from the Caribbean to New York City* (Chapel Hill: University of North Carolina Press, 2008), 11–27; Mark Naison, "Migration and Musical Creativity in Bronx Neighborhoods," *Migracoes* 7 (October 2010): 206; "Rhythm and Power: Salsa in New York," Museum of the City of New York, http://www.mcny.org/exhibition/rhythm-power.

104. Miguel Piñero, *Outlaw: The Collected Works of Miguel Piñero* (Houston: Arte Public Press, 2010); Roland Regiardi-Laura, "Nuyorican Poets Café," in *The Encyclopedia of New York City*, 2nd ed., ed. Kenneth T. Jackson (New Haven, CT: Yale University Press, 2010), 949.

105. Mark Naison, "Morrisania: The Birthplace of Hip Hop," https://explorepartsunknown.com/the-bronx/morrisania-the-birthplace-of-hip-hop/; Naison, "Migration and Musical Creativity in Bronx Neighborhoods," 208–12; Jeff Chang, *Can't Stop Won't Stop: A History of the Hip-Hop Generation* (New York: St. Martin's, 2005), 67–82, 90–97, 129–36.

106. Salvo and Lobo, "Population," in *The Encyclopedia of New York City*, 2nd ed., ed. Kenneth T. Jackson (New Haven, CT: Yale University Press, 2010), 1020.

107. Equal Employment Opportunity Committee of New York, *Equal Employment Opportunity in New York City Government, 1977–1987* (October 1988); Samuel Weiss, "New York's Dropouts-to-Be: A Grim Class Portrait," *New York Times*, April 11, 1989; Neil A. Lewis, "Dropout Rate Unchanged, Despite More Spending," *New York Times*, April 13, 1989; Clara Rodriguez, *Puerto Ricans Born in the USA* (Boston: Unwin Hyman, 1989), 121–24; Rosa M. Torruellas, "The Failure of the New York Public Educational

System to Retrain Hispanic and Other Minority Students," *Centro Newsletter* (June 1986), 3–6; Jane Perlez, "Hundreds of Bilingual School Jobs Go Begging: Search for Bilingual Teachers Goes Poorly for City Schools," *New York Times*, August 21, 1986; Thomas J. Lueck, "Immigrant Enrollment Rises in New York City Schools," *New York Times*, April 16, 1993; Sam Dolnick, "Report Shows Plight of Puerto Rican Youth," *New York Times*, October 28, 2010.

108. Tobier, *The Changing Face of Poverty*, 38; Richard Levine, "New York City's Economic Growth Fails to Curb Rise of 'New Poverty': As Some People Escape Poverty, Others Enter It," *New York Times*, February 28, 1989; Thomas J. Lueck, "Study Says Poverty Rose to 25% in New York City," *New York Times*, June 10, 1992.

109. Tobier, *The Changing Face of Poverty*.

110. John Mollenkopf, *New York City in the 1980s:A Social, Economic, and Political Atlas* (New York: Simon and Schuster, 1993), 41.

111. Mollenkopf, *New York City in the 1980s*, 41–49. On Harlem, see Jonathan Gill, *Harlem: The Four-Hundred-Year History from Dutch Village to Capital of Black America* (New York: Grove, 2011), 409–11, 428–34; and Zain Abdulah, *Black Mecca: The African Muslims of Harlem* (New York: Oxford University Press, 2010).

112. Michel Marriott, "Treatment for Addicts Is as Elusive As Ever," *New York Times*, July 9, 1989; Michel Marriot, "Potent Crack Blend on the Streets Lures a New Generation to Heroin," *New York Times*, July 13, 1989; Snyder, *Crossing Broadway*, 162–66; Patrick Sharkey, *Uneasy Peace: The Great Crime Decline, the Renewal of City Life, and the Next War on Violence* (New York: Norton, 2018), xi–xxii, 99–102.

113. Michael Javen Fortner, *Black Silent Majority: The Rockefeller Drug Laws and the Politics of Punishment* (Cambridge, MA: Harvard University Press, 2015), esp. introduction, chap. 1; Linda Villarosa, "America's Hidden HIV Epidemic," *New York Times*, June 6, 2017.

114. Douglas Massey and Nancy A. Denton, *American Apartheid: Segregation and the Making of the Underclass* (Cambridge, MA: Harvard University Press, 1998), 64, 68, 70–72, 76, 83–88, 98–109, 114, 121.

115. On the election, see Jonathan Soffer, *Ed Koch and the Rebuilding of New York City* (New York: Columbia University Press, 2010), 142. For an insightful discussion of the Koch coalition, see John Mollenkopf, *A Phoenix in the Ashes: The Rise and Fall of the Koch Coalition in New York City Politics* (Princeton, NJ: Princeton University Press, 1994), 6–7, 103–5.

116. On Koch's base of support and his political thinking, see Jonathan Soffer, *Ed Koch and the Rebuilding of New York* (New York: Columbia University Press, 2010), 92, 108, 142, 226–227, 252–254, 398–403; and Robert W. Snyder, "Forget the Contrarians: Ed Koch Was a True Liberal," *History News Network*, February 5, 2013, http://historynewsnetwork.org/article/150482. On the Koch coalition, see Mollenkopf, *A Phoenix in the Ashes*, 3–10, 13, 17, 100–28, 184–5. Also see Kim Moody, *From Welfare State to Real Estate: Regime Change in New York City* (New York: Norton, 2007).

117. Jim Sleeper, "Boodling, Bigotry, and Cosmopolitanism: The Transformation of a Civic Culture," *Dissent* (Fall 1987): 416.

118. On the Howard Beach incident, see Claudia Gryvatz Copquin, *The Neighborhoods of Queens*, with an introduction by Kenneth T. Jackson (New Haven: Yale University Press, 2007), 92–93; and Sam Roberts, "A Racial Attack That, Years Later, Is Still Being Felt," *New York Times*, December 18, 2011, https://cityroom.blogs.nytimes.com/2011/12/18/a-racial-attack-that-years-later-is-still-being-felt. On race and Howard Beach, see Nancy Foner, *From Ellis Island to JFK: New York's Two Great Waves of Immigration*

(New Haven, CT: Yale University Press, 2000), 150. On the Koch reaction, see Joyce Purnick, "A Break with the Past: Koch and Racial Attack," *New York Times*, January 6, 1987. On Bensonhurst, see Sewell Chan, "The Death of Yusuf Hawkins, 20 Years Later," *New York Times*, August 21, 2009, https://cityroom.blogs.nytimes.com/2009/08/21/the -death-of-yusuf-hawkins-20-years-later/.

119. On the general tenor of debate in these years, see Freeman, *Working-Class New York*, 303–4.

120. Charles Green and Basil Wilson, *The Black Struggle for Empowerment* (New York: Praeger, 1989), 98–101; Michael Oreskes, "Blacks in New York: The Anguish of Political Failure: Blacks and New York City Politics: Struggles for Power Brings Frustration," *New York Times*, March 31, 1987; E. J. Dionne Jr., "Nomination in View," *New York Times*, April 20, 1988; Sam Roberts, "Almost Lost at the Wire: Dinkins Weathered a Last-Minute Surge of White Democrats Defecting to Giuliani," *New York Times*, November 9, 1989. For politics after 1970, see Mollenkopf, *A Phoenix in the Ashes*; and McNickle, *To Be Mayor of New York*. There are excellent accounts of the Dinkins election and recent politics in New York in Asher Arian et al., *Changing New York City Politics* (New York: Routledge, 1991).

121. On Dinkins as a bridge builder, see J. Phillip Thompson III, *Double Trouble: Black Mayors, Black Communities, and the Call for a Deep Democracy* (New York: Oxford University Press, 2006), 199.

122. On the parade, see James Barron, "Beer Showers and Boos for Dinkins at Irish Parade," *New York Times*, March 17, 1991. On the history of the St. Patrick's Day Parade, see Jane Gladden Kelton, "New York City St. Patrick's Day Parade: Invention of Contention and Consensus," *Drama Review: TDR* 29, no. 3, Processional Performance (Autumn 1985): 93–105.

123. On Crown Heights, see Edward Shapiro, *Crown Heights: Blacks, Jews, and the 1991 Brooklyn Riot* (Lebanon, NH: Brandeis University Press, 2006); and a revealing collection of interviews, "The Crown Heights Riots, 25 Years Later" in *Gothamist*, August 18, 2016, http://gothamist.com/2016/08/18/crown_heights_riots_dinkins.php. On the ethnic and racial alignments in Crown Heights, see Foner, *From Ellis Island to JFK*, 150–51.

124. Sam Roberts, "Many Tiny Ripples Create a Sea Change," *New York Times*, November 4, 1993. For a biography of Giuliani, see Wayne Barrett, *Rudy!: An Investigative Biography of Rudy Giuliani* (New York: Basic, 2000).

125. On Giuliani and differing ideas about equality, see Jerald Podair, "'One City, One Standard': The Struggle for Equality in Rudolph Giuliani's New York," in *Civil Rights in New York City: From World War II to the Giuliani Era*, ed. Clarence Taylor (New York: Fordham University Press, 2011), 204–5, 217–18.

126. Deborah Sontag, "New York Officials Welcome Immigrants, Legal or Illegal," *New York Times*, June 10, 1994; Fred Siegel, *The Prince of the City: Giuliani, New York, and the Genius of American Life* (San Francisco: Encounter, 2005), 340; Kavitha Rajagopalan, *Muslims of Metropolis: The Stories of Three Immigrant Families* (New Brunswick, NJ: Rutgers University Press, 2008), 167–69; Foner, *From Ellis Island to JFK*, 52.

127. Joanne Reitano, *The Restless City: A Short History of New York from the Colonial Times to the Present* (New York: Routledge, 2006), 210–13; Sharkey, *Uneasy Peace*, xix–xxii.

128. Ramsey interview and biography in Naison and Gumbs, *Before the Fires*, 130–33, 186.

129. Junot Díaz, "New York: Science Fiction," in *Empire City: New York Through the Centuries*, ed. Kenneth T. Jackson and David S. Dunbar (New York: Columbia University Press, 2002), 963.

8. Immigrants in a City Reborn: 1980–present

1. Dena Kleiman, "A Surge of Immigrants Alters New York's Face," *New York Times*, September 27, 1982.
2. Kleiman, "A Surge of Immigrants Alters New York's Face"; William E. Leuchtenberg, "Queens," in *American Places: Encounters with History*, ed. William E. Leuchtenberg (New York: Oxford University Press, 2002), 243, 245.
3. Kleiman, "A Surge of Immigrants Alters New York's Face."
4. Kleiman, "A Surge of Immigrants Alters New York's Face"; Dena Kleiman, "Immigrants Encountering Choice Between Friendship and Isolation," *New York Times*, December 24, 1982; Dena Kleiman, "Children of Immigrants Feel a Real Pride in Their Origins," *New York Times*, October 28, 1982; Dena Kleiman, "For Some, a New Country Has Meant a Hard Life," *New York Times*, October 14, 1982.
5. Frank Vardy, quoted in Kleiman, "A Surge of Immigrants Alters New York's Face."
6. For general trends, see Matthew Drennan, "Economy," in *The Encyclopedia of New York City*, 2nd ed., ed. Kenneth T. Jackson (New Haven, CT: Yale University Press, 2010), 394–400; for recent employment, see Fiscal Policy Institute Report, "New York City's Recovery Finally Starts Generating Wage Gains" (2015); and for the plight of the bottom third of the economy, see Community Service Society, *Getting Ahead: An Upward Mobility Agenda for New Yorkers in 2016* (New York, 2015).
7. "LBJ on Immigration: President Lyndon B. Johnson's Remarks at the Signing of the Immigration Bill, October 3, 1965," http://www.lbjlibrary.org/lyndon-baines-johnson/timeline/lbj-on-immigration. For a recording of Johnson's address at the signing of the law, curated by the LBJ Presidential Library, see http:// www.youtube.com/watch?v=oQNP5XKMNls.
8. For black immigrants from the Anglophone islands of the Caribbean (which before 1965 had a small quota as former British colonies), the 1965 law was the beginning of a long process that put them on the same legal footing as other nations in the Western Hemisphere and later the rest of the world, opening the possibility for more immigration than had been the case before 1965. David M. Reimers, "The Impact of Immigration Legislation: 1875 to the Present," in *The Oxford Handbook of American Immigration and Ethnicity*, ed. Ronald H. Bayor (New York: Oxford University Press, 2016), 18–21; Aristide R. Zolberg, "Immigration Control Policy: Law and Implementation," in *The New Americans: A Guide to Immigration Since 1965*, ed. Mary C. Waters and Reed Ueda, with Helen B. Marrow (Cambridge, MA: Harvard University Press, 2007), 30–31. See also "LBJ on Immigration."
9. On the range and scale of the new immigration, see DCP, *The Newest New Yorkers* (2013), 2, 13; *The Newest New Yorkers* (2000), xi.
10. On the undocumented, see Nancy Foner, "Introduction: New Immigrants in a New New York," in *New Immigrants in New York*, ed. Nancy Foner (New York: Columbia University Press, 1987); and Arun Peter Lobo and Joseph Salvo, "A Portrait of New York's Immigrant Mélange," in *One Out of Three: Immigrant New York in the Twenty-First Century*, ed. Nancy Foner (New York: Columbia University Press, 2013), 51–52. For the city's total population in 1990 and 2000, see DCP, *The Newest New Yorkers* (2013), 10. On the growth of the city's population to 8,500,000 in 2015, see U.S. Census Bureau, "Quick Facts," July 2015. For the Pew report, see Jeffrey Passel and D'Vera Cohn, "Twenty Metro Areas Are Home to Six in Ten Unauthorized Immigrants in the US" (Pew Foundation, 2017).

11. DCP, *The Newest New Yorkers* (2000), xii; quote from Natasha Warikoo, "Cosmopolitan Ethnicity: Second-Generation Indo-Caribbean Identities," in *Becoming New Yorkers: Ethnographies of the New Second Generation*, ed. Phil Kasinitz, John Mollenkopf, and Mary Waters (New York: Russell Sage, 2004), 380. A survey based on the 1970 census revealed a wide distribution of Filipinos in New York City. *Filipino Reporter*, October 15, 1974; Joseph Berger, "From Philippines, with Scrubs: How One Ethnic Group Came to Dominate the Nursing Field," *New York Times*, November 24, 2003. Many Asian medical professionals lived near the hospitals that employed them. In 2003, 30 percent of Filipinas were nurses or some other kind of health professional in the New York City area.

12. John Mollenkopf, *New York City in the 1980s: A Social, Economic, and Political Atlas* (New York: Simon and Schuster, 1993), 20; Claudia Gryvatz Copquin, *The Neighborhoods of Queens* (New Haven, CT: Yale University Press, 2007); and Stéphane Tonnelat and William Kornblum, *International Express: New Yorkers on the 7 Train* (New York: Columbia University Press, 2017).

13. Corey Kilgannon, "After Mt. Everest, The Bronx," *New York Times*, January 22, 2012; Sarah Maslin Nir, "A Rare Buddhist Ceremony in Queens, Paid for with a Life's Savings," *New York Times*, July 17, 2012; John Leland, "Sherpas of Elmhurst," *New York Times*, July 14, 2014.

14. Samuel G. Freedman, "Flock Returns Anew to East Harlem Madonna," *New York Times*, July 17, 1986; Robert Orsi, "The Religious Boundaries of an Inbetween People: Street Feste and the Problem of the Dark-Skinned Other in Italian Harlem, 1920–1990," *American Quarterly* 44, no. 3 (September 1992): 322–35.

15. For figures on Arab immigration and church affiliation, see Gregory Orfalea, *Before the Flames* (Austin: University of Texas Press, 1988), 314–18. For a detailed look at young Yemeni men working in Brooklyn restaurants, see Shalom Staub, *Yemenis in New York City: The Folklore of Ethnicity* (London: Association Universities Press, 1989).

16. On Muslims in New York, see Kavitha Rajagopalan, *Muslims of Metropolis: The Stories of Three Immigrant Families* (New Brunswick, NJ: Rutgers University Press, 2008). For more recent attitudes among Muslims, see Jeff Diamant, "American Muslims Are Concerned, but Also Satisfied with Their Lives," Pew Research Center, July 26, 2017, http://www.pewresearch.org/fact-tank/2017/07/26/american-muslims-are-concerned-but-also-satisfied-with-their-lives/. Our thanks to Jeff Diamant, historian of American religion, for his insights on the Americanization of Islam.

17. Mollenkopf, *New York City in the 1980s*, 5–6.

18. David Dyssegaard Kallick, "Immigration and Economic Growth in New York City," in *One of Three: Immigrant New York in the Twenty-First Century*, ed. Nancy Foner (New York: Columbia University Press, 2013).

19. Illsoo Kim, *New Urban Immigrants: The Korean Community of New York City* (Princeton, NJ: Princeton University Press, 1981), chap. 5; Pyong Gap Min, "Koreans: Changes in New York in the Twenty-First Century," in *One Out of Three: Immigrant New York in the Twenty-First Century*, ed. Nancy Foner (New York: Columbia University Press, 2013), 160–65; Margaret Chin, *Sewing Women: Immigrants and the New York Garment Industry* (New York: NYU Press, 2005), 58–60; Donatella Lorch, "Bangladeshis Divided by Two Worlds: A Law Student and Mother Says Independence is Hard to Attain," *New York Times*, October 10, 1991; Elizabeth Bogen, *Immigrants in New York* (New York: Praeger, 1987), 38; DCP, *The Newest New Yorkers* (1980s), 46; Moshe Shokeid, *Children of Circumstances: Israeli Emigrants in New York* (Ithaca, NY: Cornell University Press, 1988); Donatella Lorch, "An Ethnic Road to Riches: The Immigrant Job Specialty," *New York Times*, January 12, 1992.

20. My thanks to Led Black for help with this translation. Tulasi Ram Ghimrey tells his story in Warren Lehrer and Judith Sloan, *Crossing the Boulevard: Strangers, Neighbors, and Aliens in a New America* (New York: Norton, 2003), 89.

21. Marvine Howe, "New York's Foreign-Language Press May Lack a Giant but Not Diversity," *New York Times*, September 15, 1985; Albert Scardino, "A Renaissance for Ethnic Papers: Ethnic Newspapers Thrive Under a Rain of Immigrants," *New York Times*, August 22, 1988; Linda Basch, "The Vincentians and Grenadians: The Role of Voluntary Associations in Immigrant Adaptation to New York City," in *New Immigrants in New York*, ed. Nancy Foner (New York: Columbia University Press, 1987), 159–94; "New York's New World," *Daily News*, December 10, 1990.

22. See Xiao-huang Yin, "China: People's Republic of China"; and Jennifer Holdaway, "China: Outside the People's Republic of China," both in *The New Americans: A Guide to Immigration Since 1965*, ed. Mary C. Waters and Reed Ueda, with Helen B. Marrow (Cambridge, MA: Harvard University Press, 2007), 340–46, 355–58.

23. Marvine Howe, "City's Third Chinatown Is Emerging in Brooklyn," *New York Times*, September 13, 1987.

24. Claudia H. Deutsch, "Beneath the Bustle, a Malaise Emerges: Restaurants Ail and Space to Let Signs Are Evident," *New York Times*, December 6, 1992.

25. This discussion of the garment industry is based on Roger Waldinger, *Through the Eye of the Needle: Immigrants and Enterprise in New York's Garment Trade* (New York: NYU Press, 1986), chaps. 6 and 7; and Chin, *Sewing Women*.

26. Constance L. Hays, "Immigrants Strain Chinatown's Resources," *New York Times*, May 30, 1990.

27. For unionization among the women, see Xiaolon Bao, *"Holding up More Than Half the Sky": Chinese Women Garment Workers in New York City, 1948–92* (Urbana: Illinois University Press, 2001).

28. Waldinger, *Through the Eye of the Needle*, chap. 9.

29. For a discussion of Chinese (Taiwanese) business generally, see Hsian-Shui Chen, *Chinatown No More: Taiwan Immigrants in Contemporary New York* (Ithaca, NY: Cornell University Press, 1992). On the smuggling of immigrants, see Patrick Keefe, *The Snakehead: An Epic Tale of the Chinatown Underworld and the American Dream* (New York: Doubleday, 2009).

30. Samuel G. Freedman, *Small Victories: The Real World of a Teacher, Her Students, and Their High School* (New York: Harper and Row, 1990), 26–28; Fox Butterfield, "Year of Snake Marks Decade of Change in Chinatown," *New York Times*, February 7, 1989; Kathleen Teltsch, "House Calls to Help New York's Elderly Chinese: Changes in Family Structure Have Left More in Need," *New York Times*, February 26, 1989; DCP, *Manhattan Bridge Area Study: Chinatown* (New York: Department of City Planning, 1979), 31–32; Ashley Dunn, "Southeast Asians Highly Dependent on Welfare in US: 30% of Families Get Aid," *New York Times*, May 19, 1994.

31. Peter Kwong, *The New Chinatown*, 2nd ed. (New York: Hill and Wang, 1996), 60–67.

32. Peggy Levitt, "Dominican Republic," in *The New Americans: A Guide to Immigration Since 1965*, ed. Mary C. Waters and Reed Ueda, with Helen B. Marrow (Cambridge, MA: Harvard University Press, 2007), 399–401.

33. *The Newest New Yorkers* (2013), 98, 105.

34. Sherri Grasmuck and Patricia Pessar, *Between Two Islands: Dominican International Migration* (Berkeley: University of California Press, 1991), chap. 7; Silvio Torres-Saillant and Ramona Hernandez, "Dominicans," in *One Out of Three: Immigrant New York in the Twenty-First Century*, ed. Nancy Foner (New York: Columbia University Press, 2013), 224–226. For the working-class nature of Dominican Washington Heights

in Manhattan, see Robert W. Snyder, *Crossing Broadway: Washington Heights and the Promise of New York* (Ithaca, NY: Cornell University Press, 2015), 140, 152–53, 201–4.

35. Waldinger, *Through the Eye of the Needle*, 146–47; Diana Balmori: *Hispanics in the Construction Industry in New York City, 1960–1982* (New York: NYU Press, 1983); Marvine Howe, "Bodegas Find Prosperity Amid Change," *New York Times*, November 19, 1986.

36. Linda Chavez, *Out of the Barrio: Toward a New Politics of Hispanic Assimilation* (New York: Basic Books, 1991), 150–51; Ramona Hernandez and Silvio Torres-Saillant, "Perspectives on Dominicans in New York City," in *Latinos in New York: Communities in Transition*, ed. Sherrie Baver, Angelo Falcon, and Gabriel Haslip-Viera (South Bend, IN: University of Notre Dame Press, 2017), 162; and, on Dominicans in the livery cab industry and more, see Christian Krohn-Hansen, *Making New York Dominican: Small Business, Politics, and Everyday Life* (Philadelphia: University of Pennsylvania Press, 2013).

37. Data on West Indian employment is drawn from Philip Kasinitz, *Caribbean New York: Black Immigrants and the Politics of Race* (Ithaca, NY: Cornell University Press, 1992), chap. 3; and DCP, Office of Immigrant Affairs, *Caribbeans in New York City* (New York: DCP, 1985), 4.

38. DCP, *Caribbeans in New York City*, 4; Kasinitz, *Caribbean New York*, 54–67, 105–6; Alison Mitchell, "Vans Vie Illegally for New York Bus Riders: The Transit Agency Has to Contend with Issues of Race and Service," *New York Times*, January 24, 1992. On dollar vans, see "New York's Shadow Transit," http://projects.newyorker.com/story/nyc-dollar-vans/.

39. Kasinitz, *Caribbean New York*, 104, 176–78. Data on more recent family incomes can be found in DCP, *Newest New Yorkers* (2013), 104.

40. Michel Laguerre, *American Odyssey: Haitians in New York City* (Ithaca, NY: Cornell University Press, 1984), 93–95, 105–6.

41. Kasinitz, *Caribbean New York*, 133–34, 140–59; Matthew Purdy, "Parade Shows off West Indian Political Clout," *New York Times*, September 6, 1994. The parade and celebrations surrounding it were on occasion marred by isolated but deadly crimes. Andrew Elliott and Jonathan P. Hicks, "A Joyous West Indian Parade Ends with Violence," *New York Times*, September 2, 2003; Nikita Stewart and Michael Schwartz, "2 Killed at Brooklyn Festivities Despite Heightened Security," *New York Times*, September 6, 2016; "West Indian Carnival," https://www.bklynlibrary.org/ourbrooklyn/carnival/.

42. Linda Dowling Almeida, *Irish Immigrants in New York City, 1945–1995* (Bloomington: Indiana University Press, 2001), 61–82.

43. On the LGBT community in Jackson Heights, see Fernanda Santos, "Gay Community Center in Queens Is at a Crossroads," *New York Times*, July 14, 2010; and E. E. Lippincott, "An Anti-Gay Attack Rekindles Ever-Present Fears," *New York Times*, September 2, 2001. On the parade dispute, see Margaret Hartmann, "The Gay Rights Battle Over New York's Saint Patrick's Day Parade: A History," *New York*, March 16, 2014, http://nymag.com/daily/intelligencer/2014/03/gay-rights-st-patricks-day-parade.html; Joseph P. Fried, "New Accents and Old Brogue Quietly Reshape Woodside," *New York Times*, August 13, 1990. On "Saint Pat's for All," see http://www.stpatsforall.org/aboutus.

44. A comprehensive account of immigrant Soviet Jews is Fran Markowitz, *A Community in Spite of Itself: Soviet Jewish Émigrés in New York* (Washington, DC: Smithsonian Institution, 1993). Also see Jennifer Barber, "The Soviet Jews of Washington Heights," *New York Affairs* 10 (Winter 1987): 34–43; Annelise Orleck, "Soviet Jews," in

One Out of Three: Immigrant New York in the Twenty-First Century, ed. Nancy Foner (New York: Columbia University Press, 2013), 100–14; Marvine Howe, "Émigrés Deluge New York Agencies," *New York Times*, March 21, 1989; Douglas Martin, "Brighton Beach: Views of Gorbachev," *New York Times*, February 21, 1987; Maria Newman, "Émigrés Who Want to Assimilate Pick Co-Op City," *New York Times*, February 9, 1992; and Chris Hedges, "Where Soviet Émigrés Finally Let Loose: On Their Own Turf in Brooklyn," *New York Times*, August 11, 1990.

45. DCP, *The Newest New Yorkers: Characteristics of the City's Foreign-Born Population* (New York: DCP, 2013), 2, 10, 163–75.

46. DCP, *Newest New Yorkers* (2000), xiv; Kallick, "Immigration and Economic Growth in New York City," 86. For the poll, see question 48 at https://www.qu.edu/news-and-events/quinnipiac-university-poll/new-york-city/release-detail?ReleaseID=635.

47. See Lobo and Salvo, "A Portrait of New York's Immigrant Mélange," 38.

48. National Institute for Latino Policy, *Report* (October 12, 2017), 2.

49. Sam Roberts, "New York City Losing Blacks, Census Shows," *New York Times*, April 3, 2006.

50. Sherri-Ann P. Butterfield, " 'We're Just Black': The Racial and Ethnic Identities of Second-Generation West Indians in New York," in *Becoming New Yorkers: Ethnographies of the New Second Generation*, ed. Phil Kasinitz, John Mollenkopf, and Mary Waters (New York: Russell Sage, 2004), 289.

51. DCP, *The Newest New Yorkers* (2000), xii.

52. Roberta Newman, Anthony Robins, and Robert W. Snyder, "September 11, 2001," in *The Encyclopedia of New York State*, ed. Peter Eisenstadt (Syracuse, NY: Syracuse University Press, 2005), 1395–1401; https://www.911memorial.org/faq-about-911.

53. On the origins of the dead, see "Morbidity and Mortality Weekly Report," CDC, http://www.cdc.gov/mmwr/preview/mmwrhtml/mm51spa6.htm.

54. Margaret Chin, "Moving On: Chinese Garment Workers After 9/11," in *The Social Impact of 9/11*, ed. Nancy Foner (New York: Russell Sage, 2005), 195.

55. Newman, Robins, and Snyder, "September 11, 2001," 1399.

56. Matt Apuzzo and Adam Goldman, *Enemies Within: Inside the NYPD's Secret Spying Unit and Bin Laden's Final Plot Against America* (New York: Simon and Schuster, 2013); Jennifer Gonnerman, "Fighting for the Immigrants of Little Pakistan," *New Yorker*, June 26, 2017.

57. Howard Chernick, "Introduction," in *Resilient City: The Economic Impact of 9/11*, ed. Howard Chernick (New York: Russell Sage, 2005), 3; Bruce W. Dearstyne, *The Spirit of New York: Defining Events in the Empire State's History* (Albany: SUNY Press, 2015), 306–22.

58. Chris McNickle, *Bloomberg: A Billionaire's Ambition* (New York: Skyhorse, 2017), 231, 301–8.

59. On the Howard Beach incident in 2005, see Patrick Healy and Sam Roberts, "Like Sharpton Himself, City and Its Fears Have Calmed Since '86," *New York Times*, July 2, 2005; Corey Kilgannon, "Attacker Guilty of Hate Crimes in Howard Beach," *New York Times*, June 10, 2006. On the 2005 mayoral election, see Sam Roberts, "Mayor Crossed Ethnic Barriers for Big Victory," *New York Times*, November 10, 2005.

60. David W. Chen and Michael Barbaro, "Bloomberg Wins Third Term as Mayor in Unexpectedly Close Race," *New York Times*, November 3, 2009; Juan González, *Reclaiming Gotham: Bill de Blasio and the Movement to End America's Tale of Two Cities* (New York: New Press, 2017), 151–55.

61. On Bloomberg, policing, his third term, and Muslims, see McNickle, *Bloomberg*, 87–95, 274–98. Also see "The Strip Clubs Near the 'Hallowed Ground' That Is

Ground Zero," *Forward*, August 17, 2010, http://forward.com/sisterhood/130110/the
-strip-clubs-near-the-hallowed-ground-that-is-g/.

62. On the mayor's response to opponents of the center, see Michael Barbaro and Javier C.
Hernandez, "Mosque Plan Clears Hurdle in New York, Bloomberg Pleads for Religious
Tolerance," *New York Times*, August 4, 2010. On the evolution of the site's use, see
"Luxury Condos at 'Ground Zero Mosque' Site Aim High on Pricing," http://www
.bloomberg.com/news/articles/2015-09-25/45-park-place-pricing-ground-zero-mosque
-condos-aim-above-market-rate. Also see Rosemary R. Corbett, *Making Moderate
Islam: Sufism, Service, and the "Ground Zero Mosque" Controversy* (Stanford, CA:
Stanford University Press, 2017), 1–5, 183–202.

63. Our analysis here is indebted to Philip Kasinitz, John H. Mollenkopf, Mary C. Waters,
and Jennifer Holdaway, *Inheriting the City: The Children of Immigrants Come of Age*
(New York: Russell Sage, 2008); and to an essay derived from the same study by Philip
Kasinitz, John H. Mollenkopf, and Mary C. Waters, "The Next Generation Emerges,"
in *One Out of Three: Immigrant New York in the Twenty-First Century*, ed. Nancy Foner
(New York: Columbia University Press, 2013), 267–82.

64. Kasinitz et al., *Inheriting the City*, 342–69.

65. Sam Roberts, "Poverty Rate Is Up in New York City and Income Gap Is Wide, Census
Data Show," *New York Times*, September 19, 2013; quoted in Angelo Falcon, "The Vanishing Puerto Rican Student at the City University of New York," National Institute
for Latino Policy, August 14, 2012; Lazar Treschan, "Latino Youth in New York City"
(Community Service Society, 2010).

66. See Virginia Sanchez Korrol, "Badillo, Herman," in *The Encyclopedia of New York City*,
2nd ed., ed. Kenneth T. Jackson (New Haven, CT: Yale University Press, 2010), 80; and
the essays in James Jennings and Monte Rivera, eds., *Puerto Rican Politics in Urban
America* (Westport, CT: Greenwood, 1984).

67. Kasinitz et al., *Inheriting the City*, 279; Maria Newman, "From Puerto Rico to Congress, a Determined Path," *New York Times*, September 27, 1992. In September 1994,
Puerto Rican Roberto Ramirez was elected chairman of the Democratic Party in the
Bronx, the first Hispanic to hold that position in any of the state's counties. However,
the power of the Bronx Democratic machine is a shadow of what it was in the days of
bosses Ed Flynn and Charles Buckley. Just a year earlier, it failed to carry the borough
for Ramirez in his unsuccessful bid for the citywide post of public advocate. See Matthew Purdy, "Hispanic Chairman for Bronx Democrats Symbolizes Changing Face
of the Party," *New York Times*, October 1, 1994.

68. John Mollenkopf, *A Phoenix in the Ashes: The Rise and Fall of the Koch Coalition in
New York City Politics* (Princeton, NJ: Princeton University Press, 1994), 66; "Blacks
Still Find Wall Street Foreign Territory," *CNBC News*, August 28, 2013.

69. See Arthur Browne, *One Righteous Man: Samuel Battle and the Shattering of the Color
Line in New York* (Boston: Beacon, 2015).

70. William J. Bratton, *Crime and Enforcement Activity in New York City, January 1–December 31, 2015*, C1; David Goodman, "More Diversity in New York City's
Police Dept., but Blacks Lag," *New York Times*, December 16, 2013; Quick Facts,
United States Census Bureau, http://www.census.gov/quickfacts/table/PST045215
/3651000.

71. Michael Schwirtz, "For Fire Dept., Diversity Amid Tension: Minorities Account for
62% of New Recruits," *New York Times*, December 4, 2013.

72. Ginger Adams Otis, *Firefight: The Century-Long Battle to Integrate New York's Bravest* (New York: Palgrave, 2015); David Goldberg, *Black Firefighters and the FDNY: The*

Struggle for Jobs, Justice, and Equity in New York City (Chapel Hill: University of North Carolinas Press, 2017), 319.

73. For a good analysis of race and ethnicity in recent New York City politics, framed as a comparison with Los Angeles, see John Mollenkopf and Raphael J. Sonenshein, "New York City and Los Angeles: Government and Political Influence," in *New York and Los Angeles: The Uncertain Future*, ed. David Halle and Andrew A. Beveridge (New York: Oxford University Press, 2013), 137–43.

74. See John Krampner, Jihyun Shin, Danny Silitonga, and Vicky Virgin, *Center for Economic Opportunity Poverty Measure 2005–2014: An Annual Report from the Office of the Mayor* (CEO: New York City, 2016), 14. Measuring poverty is a complex effort. The CEO Poverty Measure Report is calculated to produce a more accurate measure of poverty than calculations that use older methods (22, 36, 56–58).

75. NYU Furman Center, *State of New York City's Housing and Neighborhoods in 2016*, 36–37; *State of New York City's Housing and Neighborhoods in 2008*, 9–19; Michael Greenberg, "Tenants Under Siege: Inside New York City's Housing Crisis," *NYRB*, August 17, 2017; Fiscal Policy Institute, "Grow Together or Pull Further Apart?" 16.

76. Two excellent books on gentrification are Suleiman Osman, *The Invention of Brownstone Brooklyn: Gentrification and the Search for Authenticity in Postwar New York* (New York: Oxford University Press, 2011); and Lance Freeman, *There Goes the Hood: Views of Gentrification from the Ground Up* (Philadelphia: Temple University Press, 2006).

77. On real estate costs, see NYU Furman Center, *State of New York City's Housing and Neighborhoods in 2015* (New York: NYU School of Law and Wagner School of Public Service, 2016), 4–5, 51. On the imbalance between city and state powers in the face of powerful changes, see Gerald E. Frug and David J. Barron, *City Bound: How States Stifle Urban Innovation* (Ithaca, NY: Cornell University Press, 2008).

78. On unions, see Ruth Milkman and Stephanie Luce, *The State of the Unions 2016: A Profile of Organized Labor in New York City, New York State, and the United States* (New York: Murphy Institute, CUNY, 2016), 1, 6. On LGBT activism in unions, see Miriam Frank, *Out in the Union: A Labor History of Queer America* (Philadelphia: Temple University Press, 2014), 43–45, 102–5, 120–23. On foreclosures in South Jamaica, see Ewa Kern-Jedrychowska, "Foreclosure Crisis Still Plagues Jamaica as Families Struggle to Keep Homes," *dnainfo*, September 6, 2016, https://www.dnainfo .com/new-york/20160906/jamaica/foreclosure-crisis-still-plagues-jamaica-as -families-struggle-keep-homes. Also see Peter Eisenstadt, *Rochdale Village: Robert Moses, 6,000 Families, and New York City's Great Experiment in Integrated Housing* (Ithaca, NY: Cornell University Press, 2010), 247–48. On taxis, immigration, and New York's economy, see Graham Russell Gao Hodges, *Taxi: A Cultural History of the New York City Cabdriver* (Baltimore, MD: Johns Hopkins University Press, 2007); and Biju Mathew, *Taxi: Cabs and Capitalism in New York City* (Ithaca, NY: Cornell University Press, 2008).

79. On immigrants and small businesses, see David Dyssegaard Kallick, *Immigrant Small Businesses in New York City* (New York: Fiscal Policy Institute, 2011); and Thomas D. Napoli, "The New York City Economy," *Report 8–2014*, November 2013, 1.

80. Fiscal Policy Institute, "Main Street Business Owners Playing an Outsized Role," January 14, 2015; State Comptroller, "The Role of Immigrants in the New York City Economy," Report 8-12014, November 2013, https://osc.state.ny.us/osdc/rpt7-2016.pdf.

81. Kallick, "Immigration and Economic Growth in New York City," 86.

82. Lobo and Salvo, "A Portrait of New York's Immigrant Mélange," 52.

83. Ray Allen and Lois Wilcken, eds., *Island Sounds in the Global City: Caribbean Popular Music and Identity in New York* (Chicago: University of Illinois Press, 2001), 1–5.
84. Snyder, *Crossing Broadway*, 219–22.
85. Snyder, *Crossing Broadway*, 221–22.
86. Robert W. Snyder, "*Hamilton*: Musical Theater, History with a Twist," *The Record*, August 11, 2015.
87. Snyder, "*Hamilton*"; Roisin O'Connor, "'Immigrants (We Get The Job Done)': Lin Manuel Miranda Unveils Powerful Video," *Independent*, June 29, 2017.
88. Copquin, *The Neighborhoods of Queens*, xiii
89. Frederick Wiseman, dir., *In Jackson Heights* (2015).
90. Lehrer and Sloan, *Crossing the Boulevard*, preface.
91. Roger Sanjek, *The Future of Us All: Race and Neighborhood Politics in New York City* (Ithaca, NY: Cornell University Press, 1998), 53–60, 348–60, 366, 388–93.

Afterword

1. On the sites that Riis photographed, see Bonnie Yochelson, *Jacob A. Riis: Revealing New York's Other Half: A Complete Catalogue of His Photographs* (New Haven, CT: Yale University Press, 2015), 38–39; Carol Groneman, "Mulberry Bend," in *The Encyclopedia of New York City*, 2nd ed., ed. Kenneth Jackson (New Haven, CT: Yale University Press, 2010), 862; and Verlyn Klinkenborg, "The Conscience of Place: Where the Other Half Lived," *Mother Jones*, July/August 2001. Information on 242 Broome Street is from https://242broomenyc.com/lower-east-side/, a photograph of a poster at the construction site for 242 Broome outlining the costs of affordable housing there in the possession of Robert W. Snyder, and a telephone interview conducted by Robert W. Snyder with staff at the sales office for 242 Street Broome on December 7, 2017. On 242 Broome Street and the larger Essex Crossing project that it is part of, and their formula for additional affordable housing, see Charles V. Bagli, "City Plans Redevelopment of a Lower Manhattan Site," *New York Times*, September 18, 2013.
2. 242 Broome Street, https://242broomenyc.com/.
3. On de Blasio's mayoral victory in 2013, see Juan González, *Reclaiming Gotham: Bill de Blasio and the Movement to End America's Tale of Two Cities* (New York: New Press, 2017), 161–71; Joseph P. Viteritti, *The Pragmatist: Bill de Blasio's Quest to Save the Soul of New York* (New York: Oxford University Press, 2017), 151–63; and maps and statistics at "Election 2013," *New York Times*, November 6, 2013, http://www.nytimes.com/projects/elections/2013/general/nyc-mayor/map.html.
4. Viteritti, *The Pragmatist*, 161; "Text of Bill de Blasio's Inauguration Speech," *New York Times*, January 1, 2014, https://nyti.ms/1eVQxUy.
5. Viteritti, *The Pragmatist*, 161–62.
6. Viteritti, *The Pragmatist*, 175–94, 203–14, 224–28. On Bloomberg, de Blasio, and stop and frisk, see Chris McNickle, *Bloomberg: A Billionaire's Ambition* (New York: Skyhorse, 2017), 87–95.
7. On Trump and New York, see Peter Eisenstadt and Robert W. Snyder, "P. T. Barnum with Malevolence," *History News Network*, March 8, 2016, http://historynewsnetwork.org/article/162211. On the Justice Department investigation of Trump for racial discrimination in housing, which ended without an admission on his part of

wrongdoing, see Michael Kranish and Robert O'Harrow Jr., "Inside the Government's Racial Bias Case Against Donald Trump's Company, and How He Fought It," *Washington Post*, January 23, 2016. On Trump and the case of the Central Park Five, in which Trump pressed for the death penalty for defendants who were eventually exonerated, see Sarah Burns, "Why Trump Doubled Down on the Central Park Five," *New York Times*, October 17, 2016.

8. Miguel Piñero, "No Hay Nada Nuevo en Nueva York," in *Nuyorican Poetry: An Anthology of Puerto Rican Words and Feelings*, ed. Miguel Algarín and Miguel Piñero (New York: William Morrow, 1975), 67.

9. Nancy Foner, *From Ellis Island to JFK: New York's Two Great Waves of Immigration* (New Haven, CT: Yale University Press, 2000), 6–11; Nancy Foner, "Introduction: Immigrants in New York City in the New Millennium," in *One Out of Three: Immigrant New York in the Twenty-First Century*, ed. Nancy Foner (New York: Columbia University Press, 2013), 1–27; Nancy Foner, "Immigration History and the Remaking of New York," in *New York and Amsterdam: Immigration in the New Urban Landscape*, ed. Nancy Foner, Jan Rath, Jan Willem Duyvendak, and Rogier van Reekum (New York: NYU Press, 2014), 29–47; John Mollenkopf and Raphael J. Sonenshein, "New York and Los Angeles: Government and Political Influence," in *New York and Los Angeles: The Uncertain Future*, ed. David Halle and Andrew A. Beveridge (New York: Oxford University Press, 2013), 137, 139–42, 146–50; Viteritti, *The Pragmatist*, 71–73, 77, 78, 81, 88, 91, 93, 95–96, 122, 216–20; McNickle, *Bloomberg*, 299–300; Thomas Bender, *The Unfinished City: New York and the Metropolitan Idea* (New York: New Press, 2002), 185–86, 190–93, 195–97.

10. Bender, *The Unfinished City*, 192.

11. The phrase "city of the world" is from Walt Whitman, "City of Ships," in *Leaves of Grass* (1867 ed.), http://whitmanarchive.org/published/LG/1867/poems/176.

12. Sam Roberts, "In Search of Irish, or, The Greening of the Suburbs," *New York Times*, March 17, 1988.

13. For an examination of resurgent ethnicity, see Mary C. Waters, *Ethnic Options: Choosing Identities in America* (Berkeley: University of California Press, 1990).

14. Nancy Foner, introduction to *One Out of Three*, 14.

15. Richard Florida, *The New Urban Crisis: How Our Cities Are Increasing Inequality, Deepening Segregation, and Failing the Middle Class—and What We Can Do About It* (New York: Basic Books, 2017), 35–38, 40–46, 69–72, 79–90, 186–87; McNickle, *Bloomberg*, 226–27, 231–32; Viteritti, *The Pragmatist*, 124–30.

16. On the gulf between de Blasio and Trump, see Viteritti, *The Pragmatist*, 232–33.

17. Philip Kasinitz, "Immigrants, the Arts, and the 'Second-Generation' Advantage in New York," in *New York and Amsterdam: Immigration in the New Urban Landscape*, ed. Nancy Foner, Jan Rath, Jan Willem Duyvendak, and Rogier van Reekum (New York: NYU Press, 2014), 265–74, 277–82. For an acute guide to the city's culturally fertile places, see Marci Reaven and Steve Zeitlin, *Hidden New York: A Guide to Places That Matter* (New Brunswick, NJ: Rutgers University Press, 2006).

18. Jewish Lower Manhattan is usefully analyzed in Hasia R. Diner, *Lower East Side Memories: The Jewish Place in America* (Princeton, NJ: Princeton University Press, 2000); and *Remembering the Lower East Side*, ed. Hasia R. Diner, Jeffrey Shandler, and Beth S. Wenger (Bloomington: Indiana University Press, 2000). On the new "polyethnic neighborhoods," see Foner, *One Out of Three*, 17. On Jackson Heights, see Robert Snyder, "In a New York City Neighborhood, the Challenges—and Potential—for

America's Urban Future," *The Conversation*, February 8, 2016, http://theconversation
.com/in-a-new-york-city-neighborhood-the-challenges-and-potential-for-americas
-urban-future-52421.

19. John Mollenkopf, "The Evolution of New York City's Black Neighborhoods," *Mét-
ropolitiques*, May 9, 2017, http://www.metropolitiques.eu/The-Evolution-of-New-York
-City-s.html.

20. Mayor's Office of Immigrant Affairs, *State of Our Immigrant City* (New York,
March 2018), 8.

21. Mary C. Waters, "Nativism, Racism, and Immigration in New York City," in *New York
and Amsterdam: Immigration in the New Urban Landscape*, ed. Nancy Foner, Jan Rath,
Jan Willem Duyvendak, and Rogier van Reekum (New York: NYU Press, 2014), 165.

INDEX